Read What People Are Saying About This Book:

"An excellent collection of the lessons learned so far in massively multiplayer game development and operation. Following the advice here could save companies millions of dollars."

Gordon Walton

VP, Executive Producer, *The Sims Online*, Maxis

"Jess and Bridgett were there from the beginning. What they have delivered is a keen, comprehensive, realistic, and highly articulate work that anyone involved in the online gaming medium should put on the top of their list of must-read books."

Jonathan Baron

Executive Producer, Xbox Online, Microsoft Corporation

"This book is professional and detailed, and is so much better than all the ad-hoc information available online. A must-read if you're in this industry."

Matthew Manuel

Rune Stone Inc.

"Developing Online Games: An Insider's Guide is the best book ever published on what may be the most complex creative endeavor in media today: building, launching, and maintaining a persistent online world. The authors have been through the fire, and they offer a wealth of historical and practical advice that anyone contemplating entering this market would be foolish not to read."

Jason Bell

Sr. Vice President Creative Development, Infogrames, Inc.

"Whether you're thinking about making your first online game or you're already making your tenth, you can't miss the invaluable insights offered in this book."

Scott Hartsman

Technical Director, *EverQuest*, Sony Online Entertainment

"Any game developer who embarks on an MMG project without reading this book is making a huge mistake."

Greg Co... ...s Section Editor, Forum Nokia;

Chief Cre... ...

Consultant and Advisor, The Themis Group

Developing Online Games:
An Insider's Guide

Contents at a Glance

Developing Online Games:
An Insider's Guide

Jessica Mulligan and Bridgette Patrovsky

New Riders

201 West 103rd Street, Indianapolis, Indiana 46290
An Imprint of Pearson Education
Boston • Indianapolis • London • Munich • New York • San Francisco

Developing Online Games: An Insider's Guide

International Standard Book Number: 1-5927-3000-0

Library of Congress Catalog Card Number: 2002117135

Printed in the United States of America

First edition: March 2003

07 06 05 04 03   7 6 5 4 3 2 1

Interpretation of the printing code: The rightmost double-digit number is the year of the book's printing; the rightmost single-digit number is the number of the book's printing. For example, the printing code 03-1 shows that the first printing of the book occurred in 2002.

Trademarks

All terms mentioned in this book that are known to be trademarks or service marks have been appropriately capitalized. New Riders Publishing cannot attest to the accuracy of this information. Use of a term in this book should not be regarded as affecting the validity of any trademark or service mark.

Warning and Disclaimer

Every effort has been made to make this book as complete and as accurate as possible, but no warranty of fitness is implied. The information is provided on an as-is basis. The authors and New Riders Publishing shall have neither liability nor responsibility to any person or entity with respect to any loss or damages arising from the information contained in this book or from the use of the CD or programs that may accompany it.

Publisher
David Dwyer

Associate Publisher
Stephanie Wall

Production Manager
Gina Kanouse

Senior Product Marketing Manager
Tammy Detrich

Publicity Manager
Susan Nixon

Development Editor
Chris Zahn

Project Editor
Jake McFarland

Indexer
Larry Sweazy

Proofreader
Karen Gill

Composition
Gloria Schurick

Manufacturing Coordinator
Dan Uhrig

Interior Designer
Kim Scott

Cover Designer
Aren Howell

Table of Contents

Part III   Launching and Managing a Game

About the Authors

In her 16 years in the online gaming industry, **Jessica Mulligan** has been involved in the design, development, and/or post-launch management of more than 50 online games, including *ADD: NeverWinter Nights* on AOL, *Descent Online*, *Anarchy Online*, and *Ultima Online*. She is the co-author of *Joint Strike Fighter Strategy Guide* (Prima) and the author of the long-running industry column "Biting the Hand," now in its sixth year and found on Skotos.net. Jessica was the co-founder of The Themis Group in 2001 and remains on the Board of Directors. She is currently a consultant in online game design, development, and management, living in Southern California.

Bridgette Patrovsky, a respected executive in the online services industry since 1988, was the founder and CEO of Access 24, the first attempt at melding the Internet with online services. She began her career in high technology in the mid-1980s, working with the executives and engineering staff at Everex Computers on the design of the world's first multiprocessor, fault-tolerant PCs. Bridgette was a founder of Interplay Online Services in 1994 (later Engage Games Online), she served as the CEO of online service pioneer GEnie in 1998, and she was a third-party producer for Sony Online's *EverQuest* during launch in 1999. Her consulting clients have included some of the biggest names in the industry, including Sierra Online, Paramount Studios, IDT, Origin Systems, Sony Online Entertainment, and Electronic Arts.

About the Technical Reviewers

These reviewers contributed their considerable hands-on expertise to the entire development process for *Developing Online Games*. As the book was being written, these dedicated professionals reviewed all the material for technical content, organization, and flow. Their feedback was critical to ensuring that *Developing Online Games* fits our readers' need for the highest-quality technical information.

Richard Allan Bartle co-wrote the first virtual world, MUD (Multi-User Dungeon), in 1978, thus being at the forefront of the online games industry from its inception. A former university lecturer in artificial intelligence, he is an influential writer on all aspects of virtual world design and development. As an independent consultant, Richard has worked with almost every major online games company in the UK and the US to exist over the past 20 years. In addition to virtual worlds, he also maintains an interest in mobile phone games. His designs to date have elicited over a million SMS messages a month in the UK alone.

Richard lives with his wife, Gail, and their two children, Jennifer and Madeleine, in a village just outside Colchester, Essex, England. He works in virtual worlds.

Scott Hartsman joined the *EverQuest* team as Technical Director in late 2001, just in time for *Shadows of Luclin*. His roles have included support, design, programming, management, and he has been involved with 20 titles spanning 6 online services over the past 15 years. Scott got his start in the industry writing content for a small commercial MUD called *Scepter*, moved on to *GemStone II* and *GemStone III* from there, and somewhere along the line realized that he could quite contentedly spend the rest of his career building online worlds.

Gordon Walton has been authoring games and managing game development since 1977. He has a bachelor of science degree from Texas A&M in computer science. He has personally developed more than two dozen games and managed the development of hundreds more.

Gordon has spoken at every Game Developers Conference since it began, on topics ranging from game design to programming to business. He has had his own development company (twice), been development manager for Three-Sixty Pacific and Konami America, vice president of development for GameTek, senior vice president and general manager of Kesmai Studios, vice president of online services for Origin Systems managing *Ultima Online*, and is currently vice president and executive producer of *The Sims Online* at Maxis. Gordon is personally committed to building the medium of MMP games to surpass the reach and impact of standalone computer games.

Acknowledgments

This book would not have been possible or as comprehensive without the kind cooperation of the following groups and individuals:

Richard Bartle, Scott Hartsman, and Gordon Walton, for agreeing to do the technical review of the book and catch our thumb-fingered mistakes before we embarrassed ourselves in public. Any mistakes or errors left in the manuscript belong to the authors, not to our reviewers.

Jessica's employer, The Themis Group (www.themis-group.com), and CEO Alex Macris for allowing us to use portions of their consulting materials, including the "short" version of the company's unique and innovative Player Satisfaction Matrix found in Chapter 8, "Getting into the Design."

All the people who agreed to be interviewed for the book; your comments on the theory and practice of online game design were revealing, to say the least.

To Vincent DiDonato, stepfather extraordinaire: What good is it having a "dad" with an English degree from Columbia University if you can't impose? Thanks, Vince.

Also, a special thanks to the guys, Bob, Mark, Dave, and Aki, at the Iguana Café, Key West, Florida, for the cheese sandwiches, the café con leches, and for keeping it real at 4 a.m. You guys are the best!

Tell Us What You Think

As the reader of this book, you are the most important critic and commentator. We value your opinion and want to know what we're doing right, what we could do better, what areas you'd like to see us publish in, and any other words of wisdom you're willing to pass our way.

As the Associate Publisher for New Riders Publishing, I welcome your comments. You can fax, email, or write me directly to let me know what you did or didn't like about this book—as well as what we can do to make our books stronger. When you write, please be sure to include this book's title, ISBN, and author, as well as your name and phone or fax number. I will carefully review your comments and share them with the author and editors who worked on the book.

Please note that I cannot help you with technical problems related to the topic of this book, and that due to the high volume of email I receive, I might not be able to reply to every message.

Fax: 317-581-4663

Email: stephanie.wall@newriders.com

Mail: Stephanie Wall
        Associate Publisher
        New Riders Publishing
        201 West 103rd Street
        Indianapolis, IN 46290 USA

Foreword

by **Raph Koster**

You might wonder why I'm the one writing a foreword to this book. After all, this book doesn't have very kind things to say about game designers. I think they merit maybe half a page, with a grudging admission that they are useful and even valuable—and many pages worth of "don't trust 'em" admonitions that are enough to make you think that they probably burgle your house at night and make off with your family heirlooms and your grandmother's jewelry.

If you ask me (one such crazy designer), online game design is actually the tough nut to crack. After all, things like how to run a service business, how to manage a large team, how to budget time correctly for large-scale beta testing, how to manage a gaming community the size of Cincinnati—those things are theoretically well-understood, right? Right? The issues that are coming down the pike, like the legality of commerce in virtual assets, untangling the mess of statutes governing online communications (Free speech? Publication? Telephone conversation?), empowering player-entered content without further harming the already-wounded concept of intellectual property—those are to my mind the real challenges.

You won't find those topics in this book. That's because those pie-in-the-sky topics are completely useless unless you understand the basics.

No, this book isn't really about online game design. It's about the nitty-gritty details of what it takes to actually make and launch an online game. And as such, it's long overdue. After all, we've been making online games commercially now for nigh on two decades, and we keep seeing the same mistakes being made: people forgetting that online games are a service industry, not a packaged goods industry; people forgetting to budget enough time for quality assurance; the fact that you only get one launch, so you had better make it damn impressive.

Other than the fact that this book neglects designers to such a shameful degree, it's basically indispensable. If you follow all the advice in it, you're much more likely to successfully create and launch an online game. What most reassures those of us already in the industry, which we find plenty competitive enough already, thank you, is that you're liable to ignore the advice.

Why do I say that? Well, because the authors, Jessica and Bridgette, have been proclaiming this particular gospel from the mountaintops for much of those two decades. They have many accumulated years worth of hands-on knowledge of the genre. If people haven't listened to them by now, they're probably not going to. Which leaves more room in the market for the smart people—those who listened.

The fact of the matter is that the history of online game development is littered with very expensive carcasses. Companies that failed to appreciate basic lessons from the carcasses of companies previous. Teams that were convinced that they, and only they, had the magic key to unlock all the wonders (and infinite money, perhaps?) of the mainstream online game. In a word, arrogance, and its close cousin hubris.

I'll let you in on a secret—the smartest people in game development or indeed any walk of life are those who never stop learning. Who aren't afraid of good ideas and information regardless of their source. Who aren't afraid to learn from their mistakes, however painful those mistakes may have been.

And that, perhaps, may be the most valuable thing about this book—it's a compendium of the mistakes made, and the lessons learned from them. Don't tell anyone, but there's even one particularly embarrassing anecdote featuring yours truly, which the authors kindly left my name off of. Look at it this way—I made the mistake, and now Jess and Bridgette tell you about it so that *you* don't have to make it yourself.

We're facing an interesting time period in online game development. The budgets are rising rapidly, and the team sizes are climbing commensurately. The minimum feature set required for a competitive persistent world as I write this has nearly doubled in length over the course of the last five years—and the time allotted to the development cycle isn't expanding to match. It's an exciting time, but also an increasingly competitive time. It will not be long until really serious money starts chasing the dream of cyberspace that has been articulated by so many science fiction authors over the years. We're already seeing budgets north of $20 million dollars for a triple-A massively multiplayer role-playing game. This is not territory that most developers are used to playing in, nor is it forgiving of ignorance.

There's a paucity of material to refer to out there in the world. But in this book, you will find a sizable chunk of the accumulated wisdom of many veterans, taken directly from their experiences in the trenches. Some of them are even game designers (but don't discount their words merely because of that one damning fact). You'll read about the stories of failed launches, and what went right with the ones that worked. You'll learn why it is that getting the "casual online game player" to pay a monthly subscription fee is akin to a mythical quest for the end of the rainbow. You'll grow to appreciate the fact that 90% of the hard work in online gaming comes after you finish building the game—precisely at the moment when a single-player game shop says "phew!" and has a ship party followed by a vacation.

As far as the value to designers, well, I was actually teasing. Check out Chapter 2, "Planning and Budgeting," if you want to know what the *real* obstacle to tackling the fun design problems is: a failure to organize and manage the design process effectively. Most massively multiplayer RPG projects start out with grand visions and don't even get halfway there simply because they underestimate the difficulty of getting just the basics in place. And for that as well, this book offers a roadmap.

Perhaps the best material in the book, however, is at the very end: the appendices with case studies, lessons learned, and practical advice taken directly from those who have been there—and I don't mean been there in the distant past when everything was done differently from today or people who've made a MUD or two and think they know all there is to know about persistent world gaming—no, I mean people who are working actively right now in the field, learning and making fresh mistakes right on the cutting edge.

Online worlds are *hard*. I've been doing them for only seven years or so, and hardly a day goes by when I don't get a sinking feeling in my stomach, realizing that some whole new area of knowledge is missing from my library. Thankfully, this volume goes a long way toward filling some of the shameful gap on the bookshelves. Read it—memorize it even. Don't get too caught up in the figures and numbers—those are bound to change, may even be outdated by the time this sees print. Focus on the core lessons, because those are unchanging.

Then maybe we can see about cracking those tough design issues and opening the doors to cyberspace with projects built on solid fundamentals. As Bridgette puts it, indulge in a little more of the "esoteric, dream-state BS" precisely because we know we've gotten the basics right. And maybe by then designers won't have such a bad rap, because we'll know better.

Raph Koster
Dec. 15th, 2002

Introduction

This book is for all experience levels. At times, we will focus on low-level issues. This may come across as pedantic or patronizing to those with years of experience in our industry. However, it seems to be the peculiar fate of online gaming that people who understand it the least have had—and continue to have—the most control over it.

In other, more mature industries, this might not be such a problem. Decades of tradition, policy, and procedure, passed from person to person with changes in the employee roster, have tended to act as a sanity check and keep newcomers with initiative from reinventing the wheel every couple of years. Even completely incompetent executives who have risen to positions of power due to politics and contacts instead of through merit can fall back on such traditions and get by without ruining the company.

In an industry as young as online gaming, however, having people in command positions who don't understand the industry or its customer base can be—and has been—disastrous. Back in the day, online games charged at hourly rates were significant profit centers for the old online services such as GEnie, America Online (AOL), and CompuServe. When the dominant service AOL turned to a flat-rate model in December 1996, everyone else had to follow suit or certainly perish. That opened the gates for the popularity of flat rates in online gaming, first with 3DO's *Meridian 59* (*M59*) in late 1996, and then with Electronic Arts' *Ultima Online* (*UO*) in late 1997. *UO* set the pricing trend until 2001 with the $9.95-per-month model.

This was a pretty huge mistake, as even Richard Garriott, creator of the *Ultima* series and now a principal at NCSoft in Austin, Texas, admits; the flat rate should have been much higher, at least in the $20-per-month range.

As these talented amateurs struggle in power dominance meta-games to control revenue from online gaming, the collateral damage has been extensive and nearly fatal. When the definitive history of online gaming is written years from now, the analysts will look back and note that the executives in charge of online gaming nearly killed it with their greed and incompetence.

We're at a point where hundreds of millions of dollars have been wasted since 1997. Some major publishers, such as THQ, won't touch a massively multiplayer game with a 10-foot pole right now. The incredibly bad launches of much-hyped products such as *Anarchy Online* and *World War II Online* have bruised the industry's reputation even more. That reputation was somewhat repaired with Mythic Entertainment's successful launch of *Dark Age of Camelot* in the Fall of 2001 and the stable launch of Microsoft and Turbine's *Asheron's Call 2* in November 2002, but quite a few executives and people with money are just hanging back and biding their time. Depending on what happens with the launches of two highly anticipated games scheduled for late 2002 and early 2003, Sony Online's *Star Wars: Galaxies* and Electronic Arts' *The Sims Online*, we're likely to see one of two outcomes: either a renewed interest in the development of online gaming as a whole, with even more games being planned, or a retreat back into the wait-and-see period the industry went through from 1991–1997.

So once again, we're at a nexus in online gaming. A once-profitable niche of the proprietary online services industry is currently saddled with the reputation of being a money pit; whatever gets tossed in never seems to come back out. Hundreds of millions have been tossed away, yet you can't turn around without having one more press release shoved in your face, announcing another entry into the market. Annually, reports from the likes of Jupiter Communications, Forrester Research, and Dataquest trumpet that this will be a multi-billion-dollar industry "real soon now." The average estimate was $1.6 billion by 2001. If you go back and re-read the revenue estimates in those reports, you'll see we aren't even *close*. Why? Simply because the three most important facts about online gaming have been ignored or misconstrued by most game publishers and developers:

➤ Most online games are mistakenly designed for the launch, not for the post-launch.

➤ Ninety percent of the work comes *after* the online game is launched.

➤ If you don't manage the expectations of the players, the players will have unreasonable expectations.

And therein lies the reason for this book. Although online games and especially persistent worlds are complex and expensive undertakings, they are not brain surgery or rocket science. The reason for so many high-profile failures (and I count underperforming financially in that description) has been a failure to learn from the history of online games development. Check the online game timeline in Appendix E, "Online World Timeline"; our history goes back to at least 1969. You would assume that in that time there would have been plenty of mistakes made and lessons learned, and you would be correct in that assumption.

The thing is, these new guys and gals who run today's online games business never bothered to learn from those mistakes, so they keep making them over and over again. They think that it's all about the *game*, and that is so wrong that it continually boggles those of us who have been making and running these games for decades. The game is only a small part of it—the hook to bring the customer to the table and sample your wares. Without understanding that 90% of the work begins after the launch, what that work is, and what it means to manage the expectations of the players, any online game is doomed before the first word of the design treatment is laid to paper. That work speaks to the game community and the service aspect of the product being provided.

In this book, we will attempt to explain what all of this means. This book is not meant to be a perfect design, development, and management roadmap from A to Z, with all the waypoints noted in detail; if we tried to do that, you'd have to hire a couple of husky guys to carry the book out of the store for you, and they'd probably want additional hernia insurance before making the attempt. Rather, we will try to point out where others have made mistakes, where the hidden traps are that have snared so many in this industry, and how you can find and avoid them. We assume that you and your people know what it means to program, draw, and model in three dimensions and that you have only a hazy idea of the problems involved with building an online game. We will not assume, however, that you've ever built an online game before.

Throughout the book, the "voice" in which Bridgette and I speak is aimed at leaders, such as team leads, producers, and senior management. That doesn't mean everyone involved or interested in the entire process won't find something that applies to them; it is a convenience used because many of the issues discussed start with leadership and maintaining just enough control of the process to keep things moving smoothly without stifling creativity or innovation. In that sense, this book is just as much about practical application as it is about theory; the two go hand in hand, with practical application springing from theory that has worked in the field.

For me personally, this book is the culmination of 16 years of designing, developing, and managing online games, most of which was spent laboring in obscurity for barely more than food money out of pure love of the genre. In that, I was not alone; the people who did the real heavy lifting to build this industry—the MUSEs, Mythics, Kangaroo Koncepts, Beyond Softwares, Kesmais, Simutronics, and ICIs—at times could barely sustain themselves and keep the games up and running. It wasn't until quite recently in our history that the market was big enough for these independent, or "indie," developers to actually make a decent profit. The sad part is that their contributions to making this industry what it is, and could be, are often ignored or unknown.

In large part, it is to those pioneers who spent years dodging arrows for the pure love of it all that this book is dedicated. Without them, there would be no reason to write it.

So, sincerely: Thanks, guys.

Jessica Mulligan
Southern California
December 2002

Part I

Executive Considerations

Chapter 1

The Market

KEY TOPICS

- Do We Enter the Market?
- Basic Considerations
- How and Which Niche?
- Market Analysis: Who Are These People, Anyway?

"Stop rushing products out the door!"

Richard Garriott, executive at NCSoft and creator of the *Ultima* series

You will notice a common theme throughout this book: Classic and retail hybrid online games are relatively easy, but persistent worlds (PWs) are very hard. Almost all publishers have classics and retail hybrids on the market. These have become a natural extension of classic board and card games, real-time strategy games, and first-person shooters. Adding Internet playability into an otherwise solo-play home game is an easy decision for executives to make, because most games these days are designed with that inherent capability. The tools, design issues, and other considerations to take into account when deciding to give a thumbs-up or thumbs-down to a classic or hybrid project are pretty well known throughout the industry.

When it comes to PWs, however, the situation changes dramatically. Let us repeat: PWs are *hard*.

➤ Hard to design

➤ Hard to build

➤ Hard to test

➤ Hard to support

PWs are also brutally expensive. Publishers eyeing the success of *EverQuest* (*EQ*), *Ultima Online* (*UO*), and *Dark Age of Camelot* are trying to determine whether they, too, can profit from the PW market. Some of these publishers will inevitably make poor decisions based on a lack of awareness of mistakes made by publishers of earlier games. We love these games and this business. We want to help minimize the number of poor decisions made along the inevitable way toward bigger, better PWs. Because of this, we've focused most of the text on the problems and considerations of creating PWs.

There are some other assumptions we've made that may seem somewhat patronizing: We've assumed that most people reading this book don't really have an understanding of what an online game is, who the audience is for each niche, or the considerations they should take into account when deciding whether or not to make one. We've made that assumption based on our personal experience over the past 16 years. Most folks in the development community, from the executive level on down, have never been involved in the hands-on development of an online game of any type.

Most development teams creating online games right now have worked on, at best, a retail hybrid game. Remember: The differences between the levels of complexity of classic, hybrid, and PW games are extreme. Failure to appreciate the differences allows enthusiastic and sincerely motivated development teams to earnestly sell executives on the benefits of developing games the executives wouldn't touch if they understood the differences. This happens a lot more often than you might think. Hundreds of millions of dollars since 1997 didn't get wasted by making Internet versions of *Chutes and Ladders*.

This first chapter is intended to give some basic information and advice, based on real-world experience, to those who are in positions either to propose the development of new online games or to decide whether or not to commit money toward developing them. What questions should be answered by or asked of an online game proposal? Where is relevant information found (and how is it presented) that will allow financial gatekeepers to make well-founded decisions on whether or not to actually spend the time and money on developing one?

Much of what you'll read in this chapter is going to look like Business 101. In truth, it is. It has been our experience that many companies entering this field do not do even the most basic research. If they did, they would realize that they are entering a market unlike any other. The most common mistake made at the executive level is not making an effort to fully understand the market, the players, and all the moving parts of both development and post-launch management. When executives take the time to do this basic research, an enthusiastic and well-meaning development team proposing an expensive online game gets asked a certain set of follow-up questions. Executives who do not learn the basics of this market run the risk of being swept up in the enthusiasm of sincere programmers; in attempting to make their mark on the industry, some have committed Sagan-esque amounts of money to projects that might have succeeded if they had been subjected to more judicious and informed scrutiny. The *Late Show with David Letterman* has a recurring shtick in which various objects are dropped from a gravitationally significant height above an alley in New York. They plummet at high velocities and make their resulting marks on the pavement. Executives who do not learn the fundamentals of this market risk making their marks in analogous ways and learning the hard way that "rise" is only one of a number of words commonly associated with "meteoric."

This, more than any other reason, was the cause of all the high-profile failures in 2001. When you look closely at the one major success of 2001, *Dark Age of Camelot*, you will find a development group and management team with more than a decade of experience in online games who applied all the hard lessons they had learned about programming, customer service (CS), and player relations over that time.

Do We Enter the Market?

For all the excitement surrounding PW games and the semi-mystical properties they supposedly have for creating revenue, not everyone should necessarily get involved in all the market channels, or even in the overall market. These games take more commitment in money, people, and CS than the standard "fire and forget" retail unit; if you aren't prepared to make that commitment, why risk making a meteoric fall?

If you're still interested, then you need to understand the basic differences between the markets, which are covered in more detail later. Here's the big difference, however:

A PW isn't just a game; it is also a service.

Grind that idea into your head right now. It is another of the recurring themes of this book. If you don't understand what this statement means by the time you've finished reading the book, do not, under *any* circumstances, attempt to enter the PW market. You need to do more research first, until you understand what that one sentence really means.

Basic Considerations

The questions that most executives have been asking about PW proposals and projects are generally the same ones they have used with success in evaluating the viability and progress of standard retail games:

➤ What are we selling?

➤ To whom are we selling?

➤ What will the game cost to develop?

➤ How long will the game take to develop?

➤ What will it cost to get the game on the shelf?

➤ How much money is the game likely to bring in?

As more than a few publishers and developers found out the hard way in 2001, those questions are not nearly comprehensive enough to gauge the viability of a PW proposal. The questions list should look more like this:

➤ What are we selling on the gameplay side?

➤ What are we selling on the in-game community side?

➤ What are we selling on the out-of-game community side?

➤ Which of the three main player profiles are we primarily selling to?

➤ Are my developers experienced in PW games?

➤ What will it cost to develop the game?

➤ What will it cost to perform scaled testing of the game?

➤ What will it cost to deploy the network operators, hardware, and bandwidth at launch?

➤ What will it cost to ramp up and deploy CS and community relations personnel?

➤ How long will all this take?

➤ What will it cost to get the disc on the shelf?

➤ When do I amortize the service costs?

➤ How many months of service before I see a return on the investment?

➤ Which expensive consultants should I hire to tell me if the answers I get to these questions really are the right answers?

These are only the basic considerations. The more you know about PWs (also known as massively multiplayer online games or MMOGs), the better and deeper the questions you can ask. If there are good answers to your deeper questions, they will tend to be more complex and inter-related than answers to the simpler questions about simpler games. Yet, you have to do this digging, especially if you're considering plunking down several million dollars. There is a difference between leaving your footprint on the Sands of Time and leaving a splatter pattern on the pavement outside David Letterman's studio.

How and Which Niche?

No one seriously doubts that PW/MMOG-type online gaming is going to grow as a market. Analysts and industry experts differ on when and how fast, but the evidence is clear—the next big market sector expansion is going to come in this area. For that reason, nearly every game publisher except Nintendo has short- and medium-range plans to get into the PW/MMOG market sector. For its part, Nintendo's representatives have stated publicly that they just don't see the need right now, with the console online market just getting started. However, they reversed course in April 2002 and announced that the GameCube would, indeed, have Internet access capability by the end of the year and that Sega would be porting online games *Phantasy Star I & II* to work with the GameCube.[1]

The "traditional" online gaming market is actually three separate and distinct market segments with only a little bit of crossover among them. The following definitions will help you to make good decisions on what to develop and how much to spend.

---

1. See "Nintendo to Link GameCube to the Web," Bloomberg/Tokyo, *Taipei Times*, April 4, 2002.

The Classic Games Market

Represented in this market are games familiar to just about everyone, such as chess, poker, hangman, spades, Hasbro's *Risk*, *Scrabble*, backgammon, and hearts. We might not be experts in these games, but most of us know at least the basic mechanics of play.

These games have become commodities, offered for free play on aggregator and portal sites such as Yahoo!, Internet Gaming Zone, and the like.

It is hard to make any money from this market segment. Current game sites and portals are using these games as loss leaders in attempting to attract enough people to charge decent advertising rates for page views.

The Retail Hybrid Market

These are games exemplified by *Quake II*, *Unreal Tournament* (*UT*), and *Age of Empires*. These games not only feature solo or standalone home play, but they also connect to the Internet for multiplayer action in player blocks that range from 2–64 players per game session. The average number of players allowed per session is somewhere between 8 and 16, depending on the game's design. Real-time strategy games and first-person three-dimensional (3D) shooters dominate this category.

The retail hybrid concept has also become a commodity. While the player does have to buy the retail unit, the games can then be played in multiuser mode online for free.

The PW Market

This sector is exemplified by games such as *EQ*, *UO*, and *Dark Age of Camelot*. The key differentiators of this category are as follows:

> ➤ The games feature a PW, in that the player creates a character, persona, or handle that identifies him/her in the game and which can be grown and altered over a period of time. In *UO*, this is represented by a character whose skills and possessions grow with playing time. In *Air Warrior*, it is represented by a character's kill/death ratio.

➤ Another differentiator is that PWs are currently the one measurable working business model in online gaming due to the monthly subscription model. Players who subscribe to these games tend to stay in them—and pay for them—for months or years. Basic subscription fees range from $9.89 to $12.95 per month, and are trending upward.

Market Analysis: Who Are These People, Anyway?

If you've been in the video/computer game market for a number of years, you probably feel you know the market pretty well, you have a good handle on who the consumer is, and you understand what consumers want and what their buying patterns are. If you bring this hard-won market information to bear on the online game sector, however, you will be somewhere between significantly and utterly, horribly wrong.

Online players buy computer and video games, of course, but the online gaming market must be treated separately from the standard video/computer market. This is especially true for the PW sector, though a little less so for hybrids such as *Half-Life*, *StarCraft*, and *Quake Arena*. The key here is the differing objectives: Home players are looking for a good solo experience, while online players are looking for opportunities to have a good time competing and/or cooperating with other humans, as well as socializing. (We'll revisit socializing later—it is hugely important to your success and it doesn't mean what you probably think it means.)

Based on current Internet access statistics and game buying patterns researched by the IDSA and research analysts at groups such as Forrester, DFC Intelligence, and Dataquest, there are at least 100 million people in the US who play some form of video or computer game occasionally. On the broader world market, that may extend to as many as 300 million. Of these, maybe as many as 100 million actually play some form of online game regularly.

The Three Markets

Based on our experience in the online services industry going to back to 1986, the online game market is divided into three broad consumer segments: hard-core, moderate, and mass-market. As of January 2002, virtually all gameplay takes place on a personal computer (PC), with a very small number playing Dreamcast console games online. There are no major PW clients for the Apple/Mac at this time. (The client is the software installed on the player's computer. It is required to access and play the game.)

The Hard-Core Market

Hard-core PC gamers may be relatively small in number, but do they ever spend a lot of time and money on their hobby! Reliable estimates put the number of these players at between at least 4 million and possibly as many as 6.5 to 7 million in the US alone, of which at least half play either PWs or retail hybrids regularly online. The total worldwide may be as high as 15 million.

It may be helpful to think of these players as typical technology "early adopters." They'll play anything, anytime, but they prefer the more complicated, challenging games. They tend to try each new market offering, at least in open, free Beta tests, and are much more forgiving of technical instability and bugs than the moderate or mass-market consumer. The hard-core player plays a lot—it is not at all unusual for them to play 20 or more hours per week. They are a relatively small percentage of the consumer base, but they have wide open pockets for a game they want to try or (in the case of subscription-based PW games) a game they want to keep on enjoying. It is the hard-core PC game players who have been behind the success of products like *EQ*, *Diablo II*, *UO*, and *CounterStrike*.

The Moderate Market

Moderate gamers are the great untapped market segment of online game players. These consumers tend to spend substantial amounts of time and money on games, but are often slow to adopt new technologies/products. Their population is more difficult to estimate than that of the hard-core segment. We believe there are probably 15–20 million people in the US that fit into this category and perhaps double that worldwide, of which maybe half actually play or have played an online game of some kind.

At first glance, moderate consumers look much like hard-core players: They spend quite a bit of money on video and computer games and tend to play quite a bit on a weekly basis. The difference is that many of them are actually afraid of getting as involved as their hard-core counterparts; they know what a time and money drain hard-core online gaming can be. Some are constrained by the financial aspects, afraid of spending more money than they think they should. Some are similarly concerned about spending more time than they (or their parents, spouses, or others) think is psychologically healthy and/or generally prudent on a game. They are often sensitive to monthly subscription price pressure and thus are less likely to stay with an online game unless it works extremely well at launch.

The Mass-Market Segment: The Horde

Mass-market consumers tend to prefer playing games that are easy to learn and short in duration. They grew up on familiar card, casino, and word games, such as poker, bridge, and various forms of trivia, and also on social board games, such as *Scrabble*, *Monopoly*, and *Risk*. It seems likely there are at least 70 million of these consumers in the U.S., and from 140–200 million worldwide. The current mass-market online game niche is probably around 35 million in the US and 60–100 million worldwide.

The three player markets are best expressed as a pyramid, as shown in Figure 1.1, with the high-paying hard-core players resting at the apex. From a marketing perspective, the most important point is that there is little movement between these online gaming population groups. Think of the overall game-playing population as a pyramid, with the mass-market gamer at the base and the hard-core gamer at the top. As a general rule, about 70% of the game-playing population sits at the base in the mass-market gamer category. Somewhere between 15–20% rests in the moderate gamer middle area, and the rest are the hard-core gamers. For ease and conservatism, we've rounded off the hard-core players to 10% and moderates to 20% of the overall market.

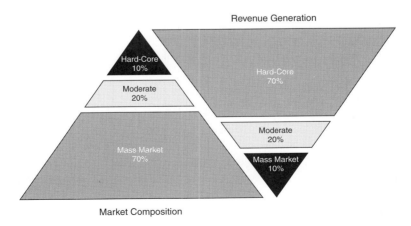

Figure 1.1   The Pyramid today.

Historically, there has only been about 10–12% movement between the groups, meaning, for example, that only about 10% of the moderate group has been willing to step up to the hard-core group, either temporarily or permanently, or that only about 10% of the mass-market group has been willing to take the plunge into the moderate group. What is more likely to happen is that a mass-market or moderate gamer will stick a toe in the water to test the next higher niche, but remain in his/her market group. Much of this is due to the fact that most online games are developed by hard-core gamers for other hard-core players.

On the obverse of that, play movement down the pyramid is inclusive, meaning that hard-core gamers will play products suited to the entire pyramid while remaining hard-core gamers, and moderate gamers will certainly partake of mass-market games while remaining in the moderate group.

It is that low upward movement on the pyramid that typifies revenue generation for both second- and third-generation online games. Traditionally, the hard-core group at the top of the pyramid has represented 70–80% of the available revenue. The hard-core gamer will spend whatever it takes in time, money, and dedication to enjoy an online game, especially a PW game. These people are fanatics; if multiplayer tic-tac-toe is all that is available, this group will try to power-game it. For the past 16 years, they have provided the income that has supported the development of new online games.[2]

That approximate 70–80/10 revenue rule still applies today. However, advances in technology and the continually dropping expense of a game-capable PCs are broadening the opportunities for publishers, offering the potential to move those percentages to 80/20—in effect, a potential doubling or tripling of the revenue generated.

How? First, the game player niche market percentages may remain the same, but the total overall size of the market will continue to grow. Currently, only about 8% of the world population, or about 514 million people,[3] are connected to the Internet. Given

---

2. As a case in point, note that the original *AD&D: NeverWinter Nights* PW game on AOL brought in between $5 million and $7 million annually from 1992 to 1997. This happened even though the technology was based on SSI's Gold Box *AD&D* series, which featured EGA graphics and basic SoundBlaster driver support from even earlier games at a time when SVGA graphic cards and SoundBlaster 16 bit or 32 bit with AWE were the standards. The facts that the game had good depth and breadth and that the world and characters were persistent were its key success factors.

3. Source: NUA Internet Surveys. See www.nua.com/surveys/how_many_online/index.html for a continual survey of worldwide Internet access by region.

current growth rates of about 30–40 million new users per year and the potential of new and less costly Internet-capable game consoles and interactive TV set-top boxes to expand the market, that percentage seems certain to rise to at least 10%, or 600 million users, by the end of 2005, with a reasonable chance of rising to one billion Internet users, or about 15% of the world population, in that time. Effectively, we could see a doubling of the available market in five years.

Additionally, with the moderate niche being double the size of the hard-core group, as well as being willing to spend quite a bit more money on gaming than the mass-market group, this group is becoming a key target for online game publishers. Publishers are beginning to plan their game designs and technology requirements around retaining the hard-core group while making a broader appeal to the moderates. The idea is to be more inclusive and encourage more moderate gamers to at least test-drive the upper-range products.

Important note: It won't matter how large the total market grows if you base your games on Western mythology and deliver them in English only. Will it matter to you how many millions of Chinese have access to the Internet in five years? They won't be playing your game unless you plan and design for it.

Player Lifecycles

The key to extending the life of an online game to encompass years is to understand the four phases of the unique player lifecycle and how to attack the weaknesses of each phase. Figure 1.2 is a representation of the four-phase PW player lifecycle.

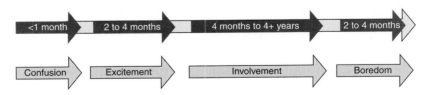

Figure 1.2 The ideal PW game player lifecycle.

Each of the phases requires some explanation:

> ➤ **Confusion**—Historically, this is where the most churn develops, after the initial rush of early adopters, during the two- to three-month "honeymoon" period after a game's launch. New players often don't read documentation or do online research on how to get the most out of a game, so when they enter the game for the first time, there is an element of confusion about how the interface works and what actions to perform to advance their character's skills, weaponry, money, and so forth.
>
> If the subscriber does not receive enough guidance and human contact during this period, he or she will most often quit, as fully 90% of the industry's churn occurs during this phase. New players who receive effective help within the first hour of play have a 90% chance of staying for two to three months. If the new player receives human guidance quickly, chances are very good that he/she will become "hooked" and move on to the next phase.

> ➤ **Excitement**—The player is primarily there for the game, as he/she now understands how it works and how to advance within it. At this time, he/she is also making more personal, societal contacts and learning more about the background story of the game. This phase lasts between two and four months. If the player makes sufficient community contacts (joins a guild or team, or has a regular group of in-game friends he/she plays with), he/she will generally move on to the next phase.

> ➤ **Involvement**—This is the longest subscription period of the player lifecycle and is hinged on community involvement. If the player becomes attached to an in-game micro-community (guild, team, what have you), that micro-community generally becomes involved in the meta-functions of the game, such as an ongoing story plot, holding team events, and so forth. Players who move into the involvement phase normally subscribe to the game for a period of years. For example, about 25,000 of *UO*'s original 100,000 players, who started their involvement in 1997, were still subscribed to the game in late 2000.

> ➤ **Boredom**—At some point, all players will become bored with a game, regardless of the strength of the community. If they cannot be recaptured through new content or features, they generally churn out within two to four months of boredom setting in. In some cases, they may hang out for quite a while longer with their friends in the game, if the teaming and chat features are sufficiently strong.

So, with PWs, it isn't just a case of matching up a new game idea with an identifiable market demographic and pushing forward; before you even make a decision, you have to be thinking about what is going to happen months and years after the game is launched.

The Four Keys to Success

The four keys to success in this industry are preparation, execution, testing, and follow-through, which probably seems like unnecessary Business 101 to most of you. The plain fact of the matter is, however, that online game developers violate this common-sense four-step process regularly.

Developers are generally creative people who got into the industry to create games; they are also young and inexperienced as a whole. While you may understand that phase one, preparation, is the key to success throughout the whole process, your team is anxious to get to phase two, execution. As discussed elsewhere in this book, almost every online game team gives a passing nod to completing preparation (the design), but generally moves into development (execution) as fast as they can get there. They want to see how some of their ideas actually work, and fast. "Making" is fun; "complete planning" is not.

While passion and enthusiasm are necessary to any endeavor, starting the coding process (execution) without a complete thought down on paper is just asking for trouble, and trouble usually obliges. (The word "architecture" is often used in conjunction with the word "software." Game software is sometimes designed by teams of people who have not made the neural connection between the facts that: [a] few, if any, buildings designed by Fuller, Wright, Pei, etc. [or even Gaudi] have fallen down, even though [b] those creative people went through the tedious exercise of actually drawing the buildings in detail, on paper, before breaking ground.)

Of these four principles, follow-through is observed mostly in the breach and the other three are incompletely followed.

Preparing Means Completing the Design Before Coding Begins

Online games are an organizational nightmare. Even something as relatively simple as a retail hybrid can become significantly complicated in the multiplayer design phase because of tradeoffs between making the interface and inter-player communications simple enough to use to attract players yet "full featured" enough to be competitive in the market.

Unique to the game industry, everything done in an online game has a ripple effect that can reach out and bite players long after the game is launched. Like dropping a pebble in a pond and watching the waves ripple out to the other side, one wrong decision (that might take only seconds to make) made during the design phase of a project can create months of unanticipated work down the line. Early in an online game project, wrong decisions are generally related to not truly completing the design documents before beginning the coding. Almost every online game has finished the design *after* execution has begun, resulting in increased development and testing periods. In general, when more attention is given to thorough design, less time (and consequently, less money) is required to code and test that design. Keep in mind that the execution, testing, and follow-through stages will be built on this design document and will involve every department from marketing and testing to CS.

As far as we know, every major and most of the several minor online games launched since 1997 finished the design of the follow-through tools and procedures after testing had begun. In many cases, products were launched without final code for support features. They weren't adequately prepared to serve the customer, and you can imagine the results: lost customers, bad word of mouth, and millions of dollars left on the table.

Design for the *Real* Market   Every online game has been designed for one niche: the developers. You can't just design a game developers want to play; they are a niche market with easily readable preferences. A well-designed game allows for new players *and* features that attract several types of players (see Part II, "Design and Development Considerations").

Design the Change Control Process Before You Begin Coding   Without a change control process (CCP), there is no way to avoid cowboy coding, nerfing, the neat stuff syndrome, and other problems you'll read about later. Immature procedures and the absence of a process for change control are two of the top problems in the online game industry today. It would not be exaggerating to say that they are among the major contributors to subscriber churn in PW games.

Executing Means Developing

And developing means sticking to the design. The design is a roadmap with a route clearly marked. This is the route to be followed, not the optional exercise some development teams make it. Inexperienced programmers overlook the fact that every change has a ripple effect.

Following the design doesn't mean you can't be flexible when the need arises. Occasional changes to the design may be required, especially when technology standards change. Use the CCP to modify the design when necessary.

If something must be scaled back, never put the follow-through tools or service technology on the cutting-room floor. Every PW that has done so has paid a heavy price.

Testing: It Isn't Design!

What the testing phase is not: This phase is *not* for adding neat new features and systems that weren't included in the design. Other online games were forced to do this due to the lack of a finished design. This resulted in an imbalance between systems and overall system instability.

What the testing phase is: Testing is for checking the design implementation, increasing system stability, testing simultaneous player load limits, locating (and fixing) bugs, and game balancing.

Follow-through: The Software Is a Service

Part III, "Launching and Managing a Game," will deal with this concept at length. Here are three good guidelines to keep in mind as you decide whether or not to press forward with your project:

➤ **Customer service**—Players want you to deal with them honestly and with integrity. They want you to have two-way communication in-game, by telephone, and on the web.

➤ **System stability**—Players want a reliable system that is up and available for play as much as humanly possible.

➤ **Retention**—Honest, prompt CS and good technical stability that maximizes game up-time are the two best retention factors.

Chapter 2

Planning and Budgeting

KEY TOPICS

- Cost of Entry
- Budgeting and Return on Investment (ROI) Factors
- Talent Pool: Management and Hiring Issues
- Differentiation Between Product and Service
- Budgeting the Development and Launch

The game industry historically has not been very good at estimating or controlling costs. The online game portion of the industry has not done any better. Still, the opportunity is there if developers understand what they need to do up front. This chapter provides developers with what they need to know and think through before they jump in over their heads.

Cost of Entry

Everyone sees the dollar signs associated with online games, but few people truly understand the costs.

Classic games are cheap and easy for anyone to do. It is hard to provide any kind of meaningful differentiation from the hundreds of competing products on sites around the world. Development costs range from a few thousand to $60,000, trending toward the low end. However, unless you own a gaming portal or plan to repurpose a game as a retail solo-play home unit, it doesn't make a lot of financial sense to get into this arena.

Hybrids are fairly easy to get into as well; such a project adds only one or two people to the development team, and the code and processes for adding Internet connectivity to a game should be well-known. Because publishers and developers normally don't support hybrid gameplay with a host site, but merely fix bugs, optimize network code over time, and sometimes add new multiplayer maps and play styles, hybrids are very cost effective as a means of entry into the field. These are "fire and almost forget" projects; post-launch costs are minimal. There is some change developing in this area as publishers begin to offer minimal "play areas" for their games on their sites, but these are not yet "the" places to play.

In general, persistent worlds (PWs) are hideously expensive, but even a medium hit can bring in millions of dollars per year for 5–10 years. The absolute minimum development cost we've heard is around $2.5–$3 million, but that was for a project that reused client and server code from a previous PW and didn't add any new bells and whistles. In other words, this will produce a product that doesn't have the production values of a top-of-the-line hybrid, which most large publishers would find unacceptable, given the added financial outlay required to launch and support a PW.

The average PW development cost today runs well over $7 million, and $10–$12 million projects are more typical than unusual. The launch costs of a PW are decidedly non-trivial, too, and are currently at between $3 and $5 million and rising. This figure includes all the hardware and bandwidth to host the players, plus the customer service (CS), player relations, technical support and billing, and account management staff needed at launch to support the game.

Budgeting and Return on Investment (ROI) Factors

"No one thinks of everything needed in the beginning, or they probably wouldn't start these games in the first place. They are really big, have a lot of unknowns, and can present serious surprises during development. I'm not clear anyone has ever done one to the budget initially planned. As overall massively multiplayer (MMP) industry knowledge improves, I expect this will change."

Gordon Walton, executive producer for *The Sims Online*

During our interviews for this book, what Gordon expressed was a common theme for those who had been through the design, development, and launch processes of a PW at least once.

Business Models

"The business model for the game should be well-developed before you commence development. Make sure that everyone in your team and organization understands the business plan, as this one is fundamental for everything you will do the next couple of years."

Thomas Howalt, project manager for Funcom AS' *Anarchy Online*

Interestingly, most teams start design and development without a clear idea of their exact business model. This can lead to major confusion, with the pricing model changing several times during development, thus resulting in confusion among the team of just what they are supposed to be building and for whom.

When you come right down to it, there are just two business models for online games: either the players pay or someone else does. Up to now, the three main models used for revenue generation have been advertising, promotions, and sponsorships; retail hybrids; and subscription fees.

Advertising, Promotions, and Sponsorships

During the dot-com boom, which resembled a land rush with everyone trying to snare all the eyeballs possible in hopes of being able to find a way to monetize them later, the highly touted model was advertising. This was always a spurious model; well over 50% of all supposed "ad buys" on the Internet from the period of 1995–2000 were simply ad exchanges between major sites, a sort of "I'll put up $10 million in value of your ads on my site, and you return the favor on yours." Each site then recorded a $10 million ad buy and $10 million in ad revenue. Naturally, someone forgot to tell the press, so the growth of Internet advertising looked quite nice in news stories.

Internet users are notorious for not clicking through on ads. For a few years, before ad buyers woke up and realized they were being swindled, sites were paid solely by how many people viewed an ad. Now, ad buyers want to see evidence of click-through rates because that's a figure that means something to the advertiser. More and more, we're seeing payment based on click-through rather than the elusive and easily manipulated site visitors number, paid by CPM, or cost per thousand viewers.

The ad-based model was never going to work for more than a few big sites anyway, and then only as relatively low incremental income. That doesn't mean you shouldn't do it; just don't think it will fully pay for development and management—the chances are overwhelmingly against it.

Promotions and sponsorships (in which an advertiser gets his/her logo plastered all over a web site or product for a certain period of time) are ancillary revenue generators that are seeing a small resurgence lately. This isn't creating much revenue for many sites; you're lucky to get $5,000 for a month of sponsorship or a promotion program. However, advertisers seem to see some value in it and it is on the rise again.

These are all incremental revenue sources, however, and the amount of income you generate from them is never going to match expenditures; for that matter, online games sites are fortunate to have them make up 10% of costs.

Retail Hybrids

Some publishers see hybrids as a good balancing point among the Golden Fleece-like rewards of intense player loyalty, visible Internet presence, a built-in market for follow-up products associated with a successful, actual online-only game, and the Scylla and Charybdis–like dangers known to be involved in actually developing, launching, and supporting one. The theory here is that Internet connectivity and multiplayer options in an otherwise solo-play home game boost sales. No publisher has yet provided proof of what those additional sales might be like, although common wisdom projects 10–15% additional sales.

To get a significant boost from adding Internet playability, however, you have to invest time and money into more than just adding to the retail game's code, as Blizzard did by setting up the no-charge battle.net host servers for their games. There is more than a casual connection between the fact that battle.net hosts hundreds of thousands of game sessions per week and the fact that Blizzard's *Diablo II* shipped two *million* units to retail establishments in the first publishing run and did a second run a couple weeks later of a reputed one million additional units. Compare this to the baseline of performance in the retail game industry, where an average number for first printings is less than 50,000 and first runs of even 250,000 are only seen for much-anticipated products from established developers and publishers.

It is unknown what Blizzard pays in host hardware, bandwidth, and network operations costs, but the play obviously paid off for them. At the industry average calculation figure of $15 revenue per retail unit, Blizzard grossed at least $30 million in the first print run and something approaching $15 million in the second. It seems unlikely that *Diablo II's* development costs and the total operations costs of battle.net since day one added up to even 30% of that $45 million.

The moral of this story: You'll get better results if you host the gamers yourself and host them well. Blizzard had a good game and good CS to offer. Just shipping with Internet capability might garner *some* extra sales; differentiating yourself by providing the whole experience will almost certainly have that effect.

It is interesting to note that the casual evidence shows that the closer you get to the PW model, the better your chances for bringing in more revenue.

Subscription Fees

When it comes to making serious amounts of money with gaming online, the keys are PWs and subscription fees. This is where the money is currently being made. In 2001 alone, the world's top five subscription fee games had an estimated 2.8 million subscribers and brought in an estimated $207 million. With *The Sims Online* scheduled to launch in late 2002 and *Star Wars Galaxies* in early 2003, those figures are certain to escalate.

Note the revenue figures in Table 2.1. While these revenue figures are small compared to the whole PC game market, compare them to the revenue figures a mere five years ago, in 1997, which were estimated at less than $40 million. That's a huge leap in only five years. If you add the myriad other smaller niche for-pay games into the total, 2001 was probably closer to $230 million. The industry is almost certain to top $300 million in gross revenue in 2002, and the figures here are conservative estimates.

In other words, the potential of subscription-based games is enormous—as are the up-front costs to make them, but the returns can be incredible.

Table 2.1   Subscription Game Estimated Revenues, 2001–2002

Game	Number of Subscriptions	2001	2002
EverQuest	424,000	$60,000,000	$65,000,000
Ultima Online	235,000	$30,000,000	$35,000,000
Lineage (Korean)	2,000,000	$96,000,000	$96,000,000
Asheron's Call	100,000	$15,000,000	$15,000,000
Dark Age of Camelot	100,000	$6,000,000	$30,000,000
Star Wars Galaxies	500,000	$ -	$20,000,000
The Sims Online	500,000	$ -	$20,000,000
Totals	**3,885,000**	**$207,002,001**	**$281,002,002**

All figures are estimates, based on public statements by the publishers or developers or experienced estimates by the authors. Note that *Lineage*'s revenues are heavily based on cyber café fees from Korea, where most of the gameplay and subscription charges occurred in 2001. *Lineage* claims 4,000,000 registered accounts, but it is unknown how many of those are truly active, so a more conservative figure of 2,000,000 was used. Also note that for *Dark Age of Camelot*, launched in fall of 2001, the 2001 revenues are based on retail sales plus three months' estimated gross revenues, and 2002 revenues assume *Dark Age of Camelot* hit the 200,000-subscriber mark fairly early in the year.

Launch Costs

"I think the most common, biggest mistake that can happen is not budgeting enough money for server/online costs. In addition to the cost of the server boxes, there are also bandwidth charges, maintenance costs, and other items that are commonly overlooked but that also have to be taken into consideration."

Scott Hawkins, executive producer for Sega, co-founder and VP of Production at Sneaky Rabbit Studios

When trying to calculate the ROI potential of subscription-based games, you have to understand that the costs are much different from those of standard games. There is a huge disconnect in executives' understanding of the margins. The standalone packaged goods side of the industry sees margins of 60–80%, while margins of 30–40% for service industries are considered golden. Again, that seems obvious to the most casual observer, but it is also often overlooked. The industry gossip about why Take-Two dropped WolfPack's PW game *Shadowbane* from their development roster in early 2001 was they finally realized just how much it was going to cost simply to launch the game.[1]

---

1. UbiSoft has since picked up *Shadowbane* and plans to release it sometime in 2003.

Take-Two shouldn't feel lonely, because more than a few publishers have underestimated or neglected to consider the costs of launching a PW game, too. Most publishers to date have made the mistake of simply keeping track of development costs, tossing in only some light figures for a couple of server clusters and a few people to answer player email, and letting it go at that. Until recently, it was extremely unusual for even $500,000 to be budgeted for a launch.

Depending on how popular a game becomes during the public Beta test process, simply launching a game can cost $2.5 million easily, and costs of $5 million are not out of the realm of possibility. When you start adding up the costs for launching even 10 server clusters to handle about 30,000 simultaneous players (server clusters currently cost around $80,000 each), laying in the bandwidth, plus employing a 20- to 40-person player relations staff, 3–5 community relations people, a live development team of between 5 and 20 developers, and a network operations staff to watch the hardware, pretty soon you're into serious money.

The test process should give you a good indication of what your actual launch costs will be. In the meantime, at the start of this process, if you expect the game to reach 100,000 subscribers quickly, you'd be wise to budget at least $2 million in launch costs and be prepared to recalculate and scale up several times throughout the Beta test phase.

It is difficult to give specific numbers because some costs such as bandwidth and salaries/wages are variable by geographic region, as are usage levels and a host of other factors. Based on experience, however, we can give rule-of-thumb estimates on the costs for three months of expenses. Table 2.2 includes the two months directly prior to a game's launch, plus the month of the game's launch itself, for a game expected to host 30,000 simultaneous subscribers.

Table 2.2 Launch Costs

Budget Item	Average Cost for Each Item	Number Needed	Total
Server clusters	$80,000	10	$800,000
Player relations	$4,000	12	$144,000
Community relations	$4,000	3	$36,000
Live development team	$6,000	12	$216,000
Management	$8,000	4	$96,000
Billing and accounts management	$4,000	5	$60,000
Office space, PCs, furniture, etc.	$250,000	1	$250,000
Subtotal			**$1,602,000**
Bandwidth	20% of Costs	1	$320,400
Network operations personnel	$5,000	5	$75,000
Misc. overhead	5%	1	$80,100
Grand Total			**$2,077,500**

Rule-of-thumb, three-month costs for a game to support 30,000 simultaneous players. These figures are somewhat low for a game expected to be very popular (100,000–150,000 subscribers in the first three months). Bandwidth is not normally expressed as a percentage of costs, as the charges are normally calculated by multiplying the simultaneous player load by the sustained bit rate. However, our conversations with publishers indicated that this cost normally equaled about 20% of all the costs. Bear in mind that this can be made a variable cost that works in your favor if the team can keep the bit transfer rates from the server to the player and back low.

Note that the figures in Table 2.2 are rough estimates. The employee wages and salaries are monthly and include overhead, benefits, and tax loads. The bandwidth cost may be out of line for some regions, but was calculated at the current industry average of about 20% of total expenditures. The office space, PCs, furniture, and so on. field is an intentionally high one because there always seems to be something you forgot to buy. Also note that most PWs that launched in 2001 sold at least 30,000 retail units on the *first day*, so a load of 30,000 for pretty much any massively multiplayer online game (MMOG) should be the minimum you calculate.

What That $10 Monthly Subscription Fee Pays for Now

One of the often-heard refrains from irate customers is "Spend some more of those millions on more CS and in-game development, you *&%$#&!" Believe it or not, most of the money paid for subscriptions already goes to these areas.

First, there is the matter of how much money these games actually bring in. There is a mistaken belief among the customer base that you can just multiply the number of subscribers by $10 and voilá, you now know how much money an MMOG brings in each month. In reality, an MMOG is fortunate if it can consistently, successfully bill 90% of its subscribers monthly. There are several reasons for this:

➤ Credit card charges run between 4% and 5% per transaction; take that right off the top.

➤ Just because a credit card is valid and has enough unused credit left on it does not mean that Visa, MasterCard, or whoever will actually approve charges to it. In any one month, as much as 1–5% of attempted charges fail for reasons such as data transmission errors, database errors at the credit agency, the card owner changing addresses but failing to make the change in the game's billing database, and so on.

➤ Credit and debit cards expire. Most cards are issued for two- or three-year periods, after which they are automatically turned off and have to be renewed. Even if you assume three-year periods for all cards, when you have a user base as large as that of *EverQuest* (*EQ*) or *Ultima Online* (*UO*), this amounts to thousands of expiring cards and denied charges each month. The percentage on this can be as high as 10% in a month, though that is rare. It more often tends to be in the 1–5% range.

➤ There is outright fraud: the use of someone else's credit card to start an account. This is an extremely variable number, but you can't go far wrong if you estimate 1% of the subscriber base.

➤ The new players coming in and using their free time (normally a free month of play) will be somewhere between 5% and 10% of the total base. While these people may become paying subscribers later, at the start they use your resources, such as bandwidth and any CS help they require.

When you add all these up, a PW publisher is lucky to see 90% of the potential billables on a monthly basis.

Expenses

Of that 90% that is actually billed and paid, what is that money spent on? Most people don't understand just how expensive these games are to develop, launch, and manage.

This may surprise many players, but anywhere from 40–60% of incoming revenue is spent just on keeping a game up and running. This means hardware, software, host sites, bandwidth (which is generally a variable cost that rises as data transmission totals rise, not the flat rate that many seem to believe it is), network operators to watch the game 24 hours a day, people to answer the phones and read and respond to emails, a crew of in-game CS representatives to handle problems and bugs, community relations people, a live development team to fix problems and add features and lands to the game… it all adds up quickly. In a *Wall Street Journal* article in 2000, Kelly Flock, former CEO of Sony Online, noted that *EQ* used 100 employees to do all this at costs of $1.5 million per month. This would be slightly over 50% of the approximately $2.7 million the game probably recorded monthly at the time.

After those expenses, there are the expenses of overhead and other development projects to add in, which can easily eat up another 30% of your $10. These expenses cover things like renting office space for all these folks, computers, desks, and chairs for all of them, office software, bandwidth for all their PCs, a local area network (LAN) to tie them all together, people to maintain the LAN, payroll and expenses for other development teams creating new PWs to create new revenue streams, a quality assurance (QA) department to test software, human resources people to make sure everyone in the company is paid and to track benefits, executive salaries, state and federal payroll and unemployment taxes, pencils, paper clips, stationery, tablets, power strips, heating costs in the winter and air conditioning costs in the summer, replacing the carpet when someone spills a pot of coffee, coffee, tea, hot chocolate, water coolers, copiers, fax machines, CD burners, white boards, conference room tables and chairs, telephones, telephone charges… the list goes on.

At this point, we've spent between 70% and 90% of the money paid in, leaving us with somewhere between 10% and 30% of the take. Where does that last bit go? Most of it goes to the parent corporation as contribution margin, which is then used to help pay overhead expenses there. State and federal governments tax anything left over from that. What is left over after that exercise is amusingly referred to as "profit." If you're very, very lucky (or your accountants are very good), that is 20%. It is probably closer to 5–10% in the beginning, although you should be able to drive this to 30% at the 100,000-subscriber level. In fact, you really have no choice; if you can't drive it to 30%, chances are you won't make it.

To improve margins, new subscription games began charging higher fees in 2001, most often $12.95 per month. Online gamers sucked it right up and kept on playing, as expected. Cost counts less when the player is getting something out of the game. If he/she is happy with the game, the price is fairly fungible up to around $20 per month or so.

ROI Models for the Niches

Naturally, each player niche has its own model for an ROI. Some players are just plain tough to get money out of.

> ➤ **Classics**—Unless you are successful in licensing a number of cheaply developed classic games to a number of sites, there is almost no ROI at this point for new entries into this market niche.

> ➤ **Hybrids**—Common wisdom in the industry dictates that providing Internet play as an option adds 10–15% to sell-through figures. No developer or company has yet provided rationale or evidence for this, but the "fact" is pervasive; this is no doubt justified internally through player registration totals. Common wisdom also notes that Internet connectivity increases add-on sales to around 30–50%.

> There is some public evidence that adding Internet play does increase sales, with Blizzard's free battle.net gameplay site being the best available example. There can be no doubt that play of *Diablo* at battle.net spurred such interest in *Diablo II* (*DII*), of which Blizzard shipped two million units to retail in the first print run, versus an estimated 300,000 for the original *Diablo*. This broke all records for a first print of a PC game—95% of all new games shipped to retail never break the 100,000-unit mark. One would have to say that Internet play certainly provided a good ROI for Blizzard.

> ➤ **PWs**—Here's where things get expensive, but where the rewards can be tremendous. Traditionally, PWs are a 40–50%-margin industry. This means, basically, that after you subtract your expenses of actually running the game, $4 to $5 out of every $10 is left over to pay taxes and other overhead—not bad work if you can get it. Depending on your development and launch costs and assuming the game is sold at retail and is a major hit (200,000+ subscribers within six months), a publisher can start seeing an ROI on a PW as soon as 9–12 months from launch. If the development and launch costs are relatively low, the ROI can begin as soon as six months post-launch, but this is the exception, not the rule. Of course, that assumes that everything is going right, that there are no major problems with your game, and you designed and implemented it correctly. That rarely happens these days.

> Investors and parent corporations love the fact that if a PW game survives its first year or so, then it tends to persist for many more years after that, with dedicated players sending in their subscription fees month after glorious month. *UO* will be

almost five years old at the time this book is published and will have grossed over $100 million for Electronic Arts (EA). *EQ* will be about three and a half years old and will have grossed on the order of $130–$150 million for Sony Online Entertainment. At 40–50% margins, the final ROI for both these products is enormous, matching or exceeding the ROI on the best retail PC games. And they just keep taking in the money.

This illustrates an important point to remember as you go forward with your analysis: The *real* money is in the subscription fees, not selling the retail package. At an average of $9.95 per month for access and trending higher toward $12.95 in 2001, someone who plays your PW for a year is going to pay you the equivalent of three to four retail games. The key is in not trying to gouge the buyer on the retail package, but to provide an incentive to the player to stick with you for years.

Risk/Reward Analysis

Part of figuring out any ROI is determining the risk-to-reward ratio likely from approaching a particular market or niche within that market. Now that overly enthusiastic investors and developers have proven to themselves that just having a product on the Internet is not a business model (the old "just get eyeballs looking at our stuff; we'll figure out a way to make money off them later" ploy), it is time to start looking at the risks and potential rewards presented by the customer.

➤ **Classics**—About the only viable model for this niche right now is to license the games out to various portals at a low cost to the portal. These games are low risk to produce, but also low return.

➤ **Hybrids**—The risks here are low and really depend on whether you plan to ship any kind of real-time strategy (RTS) or first-person shooter (FPS) game. If you do, it doesn't hurt to add Internet connectivity for online multiplay; the cost of entry is fairly low and it can quite possibly help sales. For the most part, pretty much every one of these games developed today ships with Internet peer-to-peer capability.

➤ **PWs**—Because the amount of money needed to develop, test, launch, and support a PW is so high, one has to think very carefully about entering this portion of the market. The basic risk/reward analysis must include the following factors:

➤ **Current and future competition**—What is the genre competition now and at the anticipated launch date? For example, if the proposal is to develop a medieval fantasy PW, how many of those are already on the market and what about your PW will enable it to compete successfully? In this case, the market is flooded with medieval fantasy games right now, with several more scheduled for release in the next year to two years. Unless you have a block-buster license, do you really want to compete in a saturated niche?

➤ **Budget versus expected subscribers**—A PW will probably cost you a minimum of $5 million to develop, $5 million to launch, and $5 million for marketing, for a total of $15 million. Don't be surprised if the total ends up being $20 million. If you only expect to reach 100,000 monthly subscribers at the end of the first year post-launch, at between $9.95 and $12.95 per month each, can your company survive? What level of paying subscribers do you actually need and what is reasonable and realistic to expect for your PW? Hint: Almost every PW by a first-time publisher since 1997 has *under-estimated* the number of subscribers that will try the game during the initial one- to three-month "honeymoon" period. The failures have resulted from games being unready for launch technically, feature-wise, and from not having adequate customer support on launch day.

If you fully expect that your game has a reasonable potential to hit 200,000+ paying subscribers the first year, however, even $20 million in development and launch budgets still looks good on the risk side because the return is likely to be at least $100 million gross over five years.

➤ **Hosting expertise**—Do we have the experience in-house to set up and run a network operations center (NOC) to support the game? If not, can we acquire it? If we blow this portion, what does that do to the subscriber projections? If we do have the expertise, what will it cost us?

Understanding these risks makes it much more likely that you will create a profit margin.

Properties to Exploit

One way to further improve margins is to reuse old code. Most companies just getting into this won't have core code that is of much use for a PW, but code from previous retail hybrids may be reusable for the next original project.

Even for PWs, most developers have a tendency to ignore legacy code and try to build from scratch. There are some good reasons for this, the most important being that darn near every PW that has tried to use legacy code in the past has ended up costing more to develop than a from-scratch product due to reworking and refactoring the code. Training new people on old code doesn't necessarily make a lot of sense.

However, there is a circumstance where it can work. In this, everyone should learn from Mythic Entertainment's successful example with *Dark Age of Camelot*; some of the code in that game is well over five years old and many of the people who wrote the code worked on *Camelot*. The moral here is that if you've got the code and the people, use them.

Talent Pool: Management and Hiring Issues

"Remember the old project manager motto: Check, check, double-check! Do it! And do it again... and then again! (Do you want me to repeat that?)"

Thomas Howalt, project manager, *Anarchy Online*

As is common for most major game software projects, a producer will lead the actual day-to-day activities of the development team. Depending on the size of the company, there may also be an executive producer above the producer, guiding one or more other projects as well. Unlike software projects in other industries, however, project managers are not generally considered vital operations personnel. For the most part, the tasks of tracking milestones and tasks fall on an inexperienced assistant producer who is being groomed for later management. For that matter, because publishers are still young in the online game industry, the top leadership of any project tends to be inexperienced.

However, experience *should* be the common denominator here. If you're starting a project without an executive producer/producer who has actual, hands-on experience with a PW online game and a detail-oriented project manager to keep everything on track, your problems are going to be magnified all the way down the line. Like a pebble rolling down a mountain of loose shale that eventually creates an unstoppable wall of rocks and boulders, one mistake early on can make the test process and launch a living hell. A PW game development project is a place for a project manager to show his or her organizational chops, not a place for him/her to cut his or her organization teeth. "An online game is a huge task, and it is very easy to lose track," notes Thomas Howalt, the project manager for Funcom's *Anarchy Online* (*AO*). "Check everything thoroughly again and again. Do not accept promises; you have to keep track of everything."

The team will be working with widely varied technology that will have to work together as flawlessly as possible on a 24/7/365 basis; because of this, and more so than on any other type of software project, online game teams have to be so rigorously organized and follow-up-oriented from the start that they make a crack emergency room team look positively rudderless.

The problem with this is, of course, that qualified leaders with the requisite experience are not exactly in abundant supply. In particular, finding an experienced and knowledgeable producer, project manager, lead client programmer, lead network/server programmer, lead designer, and director of CS is a non-trivial human resources challenge. There are few enough people with experience on the practical side of commercial online game development that those with experience are generally expensive. Be prepared to pay for expertise.

However, the base pay and benefits expense shouldn't be your only considerations here; not having the right people will cost you much more before development is done. Inexperience causes mistakes and delays, which end up costing more in resources— that is, development money. "There are many mistakes which can and have been made in developing MMP titles," NCSoft's Richard Garriott told us. "Few people have worked on them and been exposed to these problems. Fewer yet are the people who really learned from these lessons. Those properly experienced people will be hard to find, yet essential to saving time and money."

And unlike the common run of game developers, who tend to be somewhat loose with coding procedures and quality control, you need people who respect good software development standards. "One of the top issues I keep in mind when forming a development team is to look for people experienced with formalized development and quality processes," Gordon Walton, the executive producer of *The Sims Online* and someone with over 20 years of experience in game development, told us. This is something that has been missing from game development in general and certainly from the online game world. Mention the concept of "total quality management (TQM)" to the average game developer and he/she will just stare back. Considering the average online game deals with code in a variety of languages and environments that must all work together, but that the industry as a whole is lacking in respect and implementation of solid quality standards, is it any wonder that many online games launch like a 16-year-old driving a stick shift for the first time?

To sum up: Trying to develop an online game without experienced online game management at the helm is asking for trouble. Whatever you have to pay to get them onboard, it is worth the cost because it will save you money in the long run.

The Rest of the Team

Once you have the experienced lead management team of producer, project manager, lead client programmer, lead network/server programmer, lead designer, CS director, and art director in place, the rest of the team will—or should—fall into place fairly naturally. You'll need various numbers of artists and 3D modelers, junior and senior programmers and engineers, network engineers, community relations folks, database people—the drill is fairly well-known and experienced leaders usually know good people they can call on to fill the ranks.

The real issues are timing and numbers; when do you start hiring the various segments of the team and just how many of them do you need? As you'll read in Part II, "Design and Development Considerations," new teams tend to start hiring programmers and artists, and start coding and drawing right away. There seems to be some genetic imperative in game developers to show executives pretty pictures and "walk and talk" demos as soon as possible, even before there is a complete thought about the game. To be blunt: That's dumb.

Think in terms of vehicles: If writing code for a poker or cribbage game is like building a bicycle, then creating and testing *Quake* or *Diablo* might be like building and testing a car (Okay, maybe even a small airplane), and creating, testing, and launching a PW game is on the order of putting together a space shuttle—bigger, faster, more expensive, with more and more interacting parts, and more systems within systems as you go up the scale of complexity. Also, as you get more complex, there are fewer chances to take the project back to the drawing board if/when things don't perform according to the design specifications. You can get back on a bicycle that crashes, and you can survive a sub-specification test drive in a prototype car. Shuttle launches that don't go according to plan are not as forgiving; neither are PW launches.

If you're smart, you won't begin massive hiring until you have the game design and technical documents finished. When asked what mistakes online game development teams make during the development process, one of Richard Garriott's replies was, "Hiring people too soon." He added, "A great deal of groundwork can be done before you need the majority of the staff." That groundwork starts with a relatively small team whose concern is documentation and design, not simply code. The design process should result in documents for the game's design and technical underpinnings. See Part II for more information about these topics.

As to final numbers for team members: It all depends on how art-heavy your game is, and you won't be able to make an accurate assessment of that until the design process is completed. Moreover, the team will vary in size over time. Obviously, art-heavy games will go through a phase of "team bloat," in which the majority of people will be artists and/or modelers. See Table 2.3 for an example of sizing a team by development phase.

While small teams have been able to make some great strides in the past, the current trend is toward larger teams that scale up or down with development needs. Again, art needs seem to be the major culprit in this; online games are starting to approach stand-alone game standards, after having lagged behind for a couple decades. For a large publisher or developer concerned with the concepts of production values and added value, teams moving from the design phase to development have been any size from 12 to over 50, depending on the work needed at the time.

Table 2.3 Development Team Size by Phase

Time Period	Size of Team	General Work
1–6 months	5–6	Design phase
7–18 months	12–20	Tools, game mechanics, initial art
19–24 months	20–50	World building, game mechanics, art-heavy
25–30 months	15–30	Finish development, Alpha tests
31–36 months	15–20	Beta tests

The table depicts an idealized three-year PW development phase. PWs have been consistent for exceeding the staffing numbers of this ideal, or launching on time with problems and spending an extra year or two cleaning up the resulting mess. Notable exceptions are few, *Dark Age of Camelot* with its relatively small team being the most famous.

Differentiation Between Product and Service

Another theme you'll hear over and over again is: online games aren't just a product; they are also a *service*. This is another one of those "Well, duh!" statements that many in the industry give lip service to but fail to appreciate at the gut level.

In effect, developing any online game means developing two competencies: the game and the host site—those processes and procedures by which the game will be managed after launch. This is something few publishers and almost no developers have experience with. They are used to building a game and shipping it out to retail, doing a few bug fixes and posting the patches for them on the Internet, and then moving on to the next project within a few weeks or months.

To date, few development teams have thought in a comprehensive way about how and by whom a game will be run after it is launched. The service portion of a system is composed of several pieces, including all the components of the live team, which includes player relations, community relations, and the live development team, as well as network operations and the host hardware, bandwidth, and an NOC to monitor the machines. They're just building a game; apparently, someone else is going to make all the rest of that stuff magically appear. This attitude is changing, however. Some high-profile miscues since 1997 have begun to drive home the fact that being fully prepared and able to provide a good service, in all its components, is a huge retention factor for subscriber-based games.

And this is where differentiation comes in. It is becoming harder and harder to differentiate games based on mechanics, art, gameplay, ownership of items and "real estate," and socialization factors; developers are beginning to load up online games with those features, whether or not they understand why they are popular. The key differentiator in the future, then, is most likely to be the quality from service, from server and game client stability, right on down to response and resolution time on player-submitted support email.

If you walk away from this book understanding this one point, your chances of having a successful online game just doubled.

Use a License or Go with an Original Theme?

Licensed properties have always been a draw for game development, and some huge licenses are currently being redeveloped for the online world, as evidenced by the movie *Star Wars* and Tolkien's work in *Lord of the Rings*. Historically, publishers have not done well with licenses for retail games; they always seem to under-perform compared to their presumed potential.

This is liable to change in the online world because licenses are, at their essence, shared experiences. Devotees of a license want to gather with other devotees and share the experience; this is what fan clubs and conventions are all about. Obtaining a mass-market license for an online game has some good advantages, then.

However, there are benefits and risks to both sides.

Benefits and Risks of a License

Benefits include the following:

➤ You have a ready-made audience for the game. There is already an awareness built up in the marketplace, which may stretch beyond your game's niche. For example, there will be some people who will be pushed to buy their first PC or upgrade their existing one based on the chance to play a character in the *Star Wars* mythos when they learn that they can interact with perfect strangers who are playing some other character, especially one that made a big impression on them in a gender-related, endocrine-system way when they first saw the character in one of the *Star Wars* movies. This fact comes with its own set of plusses and minuses, but it makes the point that a widely known license has a chance of drawing in brand-new customers who may quickly become moderate or even hard-core enthusiasts.

➤ There are smaller acquisition costs per player due to market awareness of the license.

➤ You have a pre-fabricated universe to play in (which may include years of feature-balancing, if the license is a board or role-playing game, such as *Dungeons & Dragons*).

Risks include:

➤ A license comes with limits imposed by the rights-holder. This is especially true in the case of mass-market properties such as *Star Trek*, where the owner tends to be very protective of the license and sets a "canon" of what can and cannot be done in the universe.

➤ The potential subscriber already has certain expectations about the license, which can be extremely difficult to manage.

➤ Licenses normally require royalty payments, which limit the margin you have to play with.

➤ You are trying to use a license that is character based vs. "world" based. Using LucasArts' *Star Wars* universe as the basis of a PW works; trying to use Obi-Wan Kenobi as a starting point doesn't.

Benefits and Risks of an Original Product

Benefits include:

➤ It has no pesky license to limit what you can and cannot do in the game.

➤ It has no royalty payments to increase margins.

Risks include:

➤ There is no market awareness or built-in audience, meaning higher marketing costs.

➤ It is far tougher to market an unknown quantity than to piggyback on a license.

On the whole, then, obtaining a third-party license is beneficial only if it is a well-known brand name that translates as a "world," not just as a specific character or a closed story with an ending. If one can be obtained, though, it can be a huge boost; *Star Wars Galaxies* from Sony Online is ample proof of that.

On the other hand, building your own brand on familiar themes can create much the same effect, depending on the effectiveness of the marketing and just how much risk you're willing to take to incur heavier marketing costs.

Budgeting the Development and Launch

"MMP budgets almost have to be huge nowadays, but when looking at your budget, make sure that your budget is mostly content (art or world-building). It takes a massive amount of content to create a full-feeling world. If your budget is huge and it isn't mostly content, then your designers/programmers are probably trying to make something that is too complicated, too hard to Beta, and overall huge in risk."

Damion Schubert, CEO of Ninjaneering, who formerly worked on *Meridian 59 (M59)* and *UO2*

Back in the ancient days of 1988–1993, the production values of online games were, to put it charitably, "primitive," and it didn't matter one darn bit. Until around 1996, with the release of the last of the true "garage" efforts, *M59*, online games were between three and five years behind the art and sound production values found in commercial games. *M59* didn't bridge the gap, but it did close the gap a bit.

Similar to what happened with computer games in general, it is no longer possible for two guys in a garage to build and launch an online game. The playing public's art demands alone, which insist on the best possible art and lots of it, make it necessary to employ either a full art team of between 10 and 20 people or a couple of guys with seriously long art delivery timelines.

This was bound to happen once publishers got into the act. Since the release of *UO* in 1997, which featured a CD-ROM packed with art, publishers have been intentionally raising the bar on production values. Part of this was consumer demand for "bleeding-edge everything," and part of it was to make it impossible for a garage team to steal a portion of the market at a critical growth stage in the industry. Considering how bad the art and sound were in online games pre-1996, how loyal players tended to be to one game for years at a time, and how much money the games were making at the time, this was not an unreasonable strategy.

In six short years, budgets have ballooned from less than $400,000 to produce a cutting-edge PW to over $1,000,000 for a relatively easy-to-produce hybrid, and anywhere from $3–$15 million to develop a PW. The costs are heavily on personnel; in the more expensive projects, baseline salary burn rates of $250,000 per month are not unheard of, rising to $300,000–$350,000 during peak art loads. With a three- to four-year development timeline, that adds up.

Development Budget

So how do you budget for development? "MMP games are incredibly expensive to construct," says Damion Schubert, a designer on *M59* and the former lead designer on *UO2*. "The important thing to do is to be sure that you build your team at an appropriate speed and at an appropriate level. For example, don't hire world-builders until you have a tool for them to build with. Don't hire a lot of artists until your art pipeline is well laid out. Given that both of these factors take much longer in PWs than in standalone games, this can save you significantly in the long run."

Richard Garriott agrees that a major mistake some teams make is "hiring people too soon. A great deal of ground work can be done before you need the majority of the staff." It has been our experience that whatever baseline figure the team comes up with in the design treatment, it is probably short by a factor of two or three for a PW, or by around 40% for a hybrid. The first phase is to make the team finish the design and create a master task list in Microsoft Project or some other tracking software.

Your biggest time and money-saver in this process, then, will be completed design documents and project plans. It is impossible to get something approaching a realistic cost figure until that happens. If you're using the proper tracking software and your leads have estimated their development time and cost per task correctly, this should give you a pretty good idea of the overall development costs. An executive producer or senior management should then go over the project plan in detail with the team and not hesitate to ask for more details; the more complete these documents are, the smoother things will run. Clearly noting which tasks have to be completed before the art team is fleshed out is critical at this stage.

Launch Budget

It is becoming common wisdom among publishers that it takes about $5 million to launch a PW, not counting marketing costs. It can easily cost that much, especially when staffing costs for the full live team, hardware and bandwidth costs, and so forth for a full year are figured into the equation. Even a game that needs to support 30,000 simultaneous players at launch (as did the three major product launches of 2001) can cost close to $1.5 million for a minimal setup and the first three months of operations. If you're smart, you'll also ramp up your launch staffing over a four- to six-month period during the Beta tests, scaled to match the popularity of your game during that process.

There is no way to skimp on these costs without being penny-wise and pound-foolish. The best advertising any online game has is a technically smooth launch and a trained, helpful customer relations staff present on the first day. You can always scale down the team if subscribers don't match projections; it is impossible to scale up at the last minute and expect anything except a Type-H cluster bomb of a mess.

In general, the industry hasn't been very accurate at estimating the costs for either a game's development or launch. "After misestimating the completion costs/date, most budgets underestimate QA testing, launch costs, and CS issues," noted Gordon Walton. "It's more a question of what we are good at budgeting for this type of game and the answer is 'not much.'" As a lesson to be learned, this is an important one for the early stages of the process; it will be hard for you to go wrong by overestimating by 25–50%, even after the detailed project task plan is completed.

Chapter 3

Project Management/Manager

As mentioned before, online games are complex creatures with plenty of moving parts. This is a lot to juggle, especially over a two- to four-year development timeline. To finish development in a timely manner, the team must be very tightly organized. This is a factor that has been missing in most online game development projects to date. The main cause has been a lack of institutional training and experience in pure organizational techniques; most producers seem to think that just knowing a bit about Microsoft Project is all they need.

The glue that will hold your online game project together and get it out the door is the project manager. This is the person who keeps the milestone and task list, tracks potential blockages, knows what everyone is doing, keeps records of it, plots it all out, and then follows up by keeping the producer, the leads, and the team informed.

And that's just the start. A project manager looks at the whole ball of wax, decides what is needed to track the project, determines what creates blocks to good tracking and good working conditions, and helps set the team up for success by demanding accountability. His or her responsibility isn't just making marks on a project timeline; it involves anything that presents, or is likely to present, a block to completion. Thomas Howalt, an experienced project manager who was brought on to the *Anarchy Online* (AO) team by Funcom AS to help turn around the game after a disastrous launch, defines the responsibility with this list:

➤ Instill and keep the discipline.

➤ Document decisions, requirements, analyzes, designs, code, and test procedures.

➤ Invest in buying or developing a strong and stable file version control system for *all* your products: text docs, code, graphical assets, and so on.

➤ Invest in buying or developing a strong and stable task management tool—make sure that *everyone* on the team uses it.

➤ Create a configuration and change management process and continue to develop and refine it.

➤ Invest time in creating a common glossary and file-naming conventions. Be strict in the use of these.

➤ Clean out your offices often—no one works efficiently when surrounded by pizza boxes and empty Coke cans.

➤ When you assess your team (as you will more than once), be fair and square—they deserve it.

➤ Create (and document) build routines, and remember the old truth: Build early; build often!

➤ Think QA from day one. This is an issue for *all* on the team. Make sure that every piece of code and world design has a thorough test case that is updated.

➤ Don't be tempted to use the champignon management style! (The champignon style is: grow them somewhere dark, cold, and moist, underground, throw dirt at them with regular intervals, and if any of them sticks up their head, cut it off!)

➤ Make backups often.

When looked at in this light, it should be obvious to the most casual observer that the project manager is a pivot point around which swings the success or failure of an online game development project.

Project Plans

Ah, here's where we contemplate the details. There have been some complex single-player games shipped in the past 20 years, but none of them comes even close to matching the complexity of the average persistent world (PW) game, and few need to be as delicately balanced as most multiplayer retail hybrids.

This complexity is self inflicted; online game designers are in the habit of trying to throw into a game everything they can possibly think of, as a hook to keep people playing—and paying—for years. This approach tends to create more problems than it solves because each moving part created has to link up with every other moving part in the game. Past a certain number of game mechanics, player-usable game items, and the variables that modify them, it becomes virtually impossible to make an alteration to game mechanics or item behavior without touching at least two other mechanics as well. In this scenario, it is very possible to add one new feature or game mechanic that completely upsets the game balance.

In today's online games, the complexity goes even further. Just adding a new rating class to an existing weapon means altering database descriptions to add the new weapon's class, perhaps even adding new art to depict the weapon, and testing the new weapon against every player a character calls, every other weapon, and all non-player characters (NPCs are characters or entities not controlled by a player) in the game to ensure you aren't completely upsetting the game's balance. It all takes code of some sort, of course, and sometimes code of different flavors.

Once you know what the design is supposed to be, everything in the document has to be turned into a series of tasks for assignment and tracking. This is pretty basic stuff for any project, but it is harder for an online game due to the complexity. All this has to be tracked in a project plan and timeline. To get a better picture of what we're talking about, the average retail hybrid has far fewer than 100 player-usable items (usually fewer than 50); fewer than 20 NPCs; and just enough player skills, attributes, and game mechanics to get through a solo game and create a few combinations for a multi-player session. This type of project can be completed by experienced developers in two years or fewer. The average PW, on the other hand, has more than 500 player-usable items; 40 or 50 NPCs of various experience and power levels, with literally hundreds or thousands of them existing in the game at any one time; usually at least 8 player attributes that correlate and modify dozens of different combat, magic, and trade-crafting skills, all of which can grow or decrease over time in a variety of different ways and whose various combinations all have some form of art to depict them; and one or more database entries to track it.

You're probably starting to imagine what could happen if the project plan and development timeline aren't complete and are so chock-full of cross-referenced details that it makes the average person's head spin. Unless you have these details down on paper and turned into the various tasks necessary to complete each detail, it is nearly impossible to be flexible later on, if and when you need to trim back the feature set to get the game out the door before the turn of a new millennium.

The Baseline

When you have all the tasks noted in your tracking software, you'll have created your baseline from the start of coding to finish. Good software, such as Microsoft Project, will lay out a PERT or Gantt[1] chart for you that clearly notes what tasks block other tasks, the order in which tasks need to be completed to move on, and where critical chokepoints exist. This is all pretty basic stuff, but again, it is not yet a firm part of game development culture and is most often observed in the breach. The amazing thing is that more senior executives don't demand this kind of tracking accountability before one penny is spent on coding.

The baseline, combined with the full project plan, should give your management their first true indication of just how realistically the design team is estimating the extent of the work, and it should be a real eye-opener in one of two ways:

➤ The level of detail and the total number of tasks that need to be completed should give them pause.

➤ The lack of detail or number of tasks listed should scare them about the team's judgment in these matters.

---

1. A PERT chart is a project management tool used to schedule, organize, and coordinate tasks within a project. PERT stands for *program evaluation review technique*, a methodology developed by the US Navy in the 1950s to manage the Polaris submarine missile program. A Gantt chart is a horizontal bar chart developed as a production control tool in 1917 by Henry L. Gantt, an American engineer and social scientist. Both are graphic illustrations of a project that note what needs to be done in what order to bring the project to completion. Modern project planning software converts task lists into PERT or Gantt charts to provide an easy-to-see overview of the major events in a project and point out which tasks are dependent on others for completion.

If it is the former, you're on the right track to a smooth development process. If it is the latter, it is time to rethink the whole process; you either need a more experienced team or this just isn't the right project for you and your company.

Flexibility

Flexibility here means being flexible in your feature set and being willing to trim (cut) some features to obtain a shorter and smoother development cycle.

A good producer and project manager will understand at the outset that the design team will always attempt to overreach. If left to their own devices, by the time the designers are finished determining what they want in the game, not even the presence of the 12 apostles on the team will produce any hope of launching the game before you're all ready to retire.

There is nothing wrong with this early in the process; it makes good sense to get as much on paper as you can because it is nearly impossible to add major features later on without upsetting the whole apple cart. At some point before the design documents are completed, however, you're going to have to trim back the feature set to something that approaches sanity. You can take this as a given and, in fact, it is a good exercise for the team to have to prioritize the feature set a number of times before the baseline is pronounced complete.

About six months into ramped-up development, when you begin to see how long the tasks really take to complete and can refine your estimates, you'll probably want to do the feature prioritizing and trimming exercise at least one more time. By this time, even your ramped-back feature set for launch from the first round will be suspect and you'll probably want to give yourself an edge by trimming at least a couple of the lower priority features.

If you find yourself needing to trim features in the six to nine months before the scheduled launch date, odds are that your launch date is already doomed, plain and simple. The smart money says that you're either going to launch poorly or miss the date. You might as well delay the launch, do a full evaluation, and decide whether the game is ever going to be in shape to launch. The worst thing you can do at this point is try to trim out so much that you can launch (poorly, remember) on time. Doing this type of feature triage will add so many bugs and exploits that the game will be unplayable and unstable, creating bad word of mouth. Additionally, there is a good chance that you will have to cut back further than the minimum feature set required for players to have enough fun to stay past their first 30 days.

The moral of this section is this: Trimming the feature set early is good; trimming late is deadly.

Yes, It Really Will Take at Least 2–3 Years to Complete

To paraphrase the elder Von Moltke's famous quote about battle plans: "No production schedule survives contact with reality." This is especially true of PW games because: (a) there is so little experience among publishers and developers in how to make such games and (b) there is only a little more experience in how to construct and follow a proper software development plan. This isn't because publishers and developers are all incompetent—many are and many others aren't. Much of the lack of experience is simply due to the relative newness of the medium. Remember (or if you're much under 40, believe…) that the PC is just barely a couple of decades old. For the first decade or so, there was so much money to be made developing business-related software that most of the best designers/developers were busy trying to strike it rich with what they had hoped would be the next in a line of killer apps that started with Visi-Calc (which made the Apple) and continued with Lotus 1-2-3 (which made the IBM PC). The personal fame, power, and downright heavy loot that attended the market's acceptance of and frenzy about blockbuster titles like those two was enough to keep most creative software folks plugging away in the field of commercial applications. Oh, and for the first decade or so, the graphical capabilities of PCs weren't nearly what they are today, and the Internet was pretty much restricted to text messaging between military or academic correspondents. The gold mine that exists today for publishers and developers of PW games is comparatively new, and we should not be too surprised that some mistakes in the past 5–10 years have been doozies.

Two-year development times are possible for retail hybrids, even starting from scratch, because the feature set and content are generally much more limited than for a PW. Any PW team that tells you they can start a project from scratch and complete it in two years is delusional, trying to delude you, or else they have so little experience in the genre that they just don't know better.

Even if you're reusing old code or have licensed a client/server platform for your PW, plan on a two-year development and test process, minimum. If you're starting from scratch, it can't hurt to plan for as much as four years in the cycle, including six to nine months of scaled testing. Thirty-six months would be the ideal development cycle, but that assumes almost everyone on the project has experience on the commercial side of PWs, knows which features are necessary at launch and which can wait for a later update, and can make those determinations quickly and without a lot of fuss and meetings. Even then, you'll probably find that three years is pushing the edge. Why is it ideal and maybe pushing the edge, you ask? If you've read this far, you probably have at least a passing knowledge of computer hardware. What is just becoming available now that wasn't here 36 months ago? What was supposed to be here last year that now looks like, according to whatever sources you have found to be reliable in the past, it maybe will be coming around in a year or so from now (two years late), assuming the company that is in the lead to introduce it doesn't go out of business first? The point is this: Online gaming technology and features change rapidly. What is cutting edge today may well be obsolete when your PW is ready to launch. It may be a Herculean task, but you have to try to estimate not only the standard technology 36 months out, but also what the players will consider the standard feature set.

You may start with a holy text of a design document and intend to adhere to it scrupulously. You may be able to stick to it, but you may also find that two-thirds of the way through your three-year cycle, some new hardware capability comes out that has the potential of making your game appear "quaint." Do you stay the course (play the cards you have now), or do you expand your paradigm to take advantage of the new reality? One course is at least risky; the other is at least expensive.

So, three years it is, but as the blue-collar folks say about working on Saturdays during a busy season, "I'm only working half a day, but I'm still packing a lunch."

You'll find that most of your time is taken up on two issues: balancing content and testing.

Balancing Content

Balancing a game's mechanics and content is a complex process. It requires exquisite attention to detail in the design stage. As mentioned before, design teams tend to overreach, and even a trimmed-back design will be complex. Design teams will try to shove in everything. This is such an inherent part of the process as seen in many previous games that it is becoming axiomatic. Notes experienced designer and creative director Richard Garriott, "Teams regularly bite off more than they can chew. An MMP can easily become an impossible-to-complete reality simulator."

Even if the team successfully plans for and develops a somewhat limited feature set, it still needs to make sure the features all work together and that no one combination of character race/class/skills/attributes/weapons/armor becomes a virtually indestructible "tank" that can overwhelm the game's other players or the game's NPCs.

Testing

We can't emphasize this enough: Your Beta testing phase must take at least six months and must scale up the number of simultaneous players over the various stages of the Beta to match the load expected on launch day. At that, six months is probably too short for software as complicated as a PW, but it is generally three months more than such games have seen in Beta testing in the past. Hearkening back to the benefits of early-phase design: The more money you save by designing early and delaying the expensive coding part of the process, the more money you can allocate to intensive testing.

This is changing slowly in the industry as a whole, but as 2001's bad launches showed, not quickly enough. If the project plan doesn't account for at least a six-month process, add it in.

The games industry is starting to recognize the importance of scaled testing, but the fact that a number of games premiering in 2001 had serious problems associated with their launches means that it is not yet an inherent part of the culture. If your project doesn't have at least six months budgeted for testing, add it in before you shake your money tree. If you do have six months, don't let the finance people take it away. If necessary, agree to trim a feature, do more design early, delay the code-intensive period, subsist on Tombstone's frozen pizza instead of Wolfgang Puck's, do almost anything. You want to prove your game on adequately scaled testing (footprints in the Sands of Time); you don't want your game to end up the other way (fragments of what used to be a refrigerator in the 46th St. alley outside NBC Studios).

No, More Programmers Won't Make It Go Faster

In fact, panicking and throwing more coders into the mix is usually a guarantee of more bugs and less stable technology at launch. Your best defense here is to make sure the core design team actually takes the time to finish the game design and technology design documents. With those documents to work from, you'll know within a body or two how many programmers, artists, and network specialists you'll need before a line of code has been done.

Why Production Slips Happen

If you've been reading this section carefully, you already know the reasons for most development time slips:

➤ A feature set that was overreaching from the start and needed more time than budgeted to complete

➤ Inexperienced management and senior management that doesn't have a firm grasp of what is possible and what isn't in these types of games, and consequently can't act as a brake on overreaching ambitions

➤ An overly complex set of game mechanics that is tougher to balance than originally thought

➤ Inexperienced (or experienced but overly enthusiastic) developers who overestimated their ability to complete tasks in the time they forecasted

➤ Developers who try to add features on-the-fly, without following a change control process (CCP), which almost always breaks something else in the game or throws the balance out of whack, requiring even more time to fix

Each of these five issues, taken singly, is pretty easy to avoid or fix. Combine them all into one project and the developers might be facing a few sleepless nights and a lot of frustration. "Fix" the five points before development begins and you'll avoid most of the production slips that many online game projects have experienced.

Steps You Can Take to Avoid Common Problems

These steps, of course, require some changes, beginning at the top and working down throughout the entire organization.

Step One: Educate Senior Management

One reason so much money is wasted during development is that it's so darn easy for development teams to mesmerize and buffalo senior management.

The wizard/guru effect is most definitely alive and well at game companies. The wizard effect is the tendency for those with esoteric or hard-to-acquire knowledge to act like wizards and magicians of old, making tricks happen and counting on the laziness of the audience not to do enough of their own research to understand the illusion. The same thing happens today at publishing companies. Very few people at and above the vice president level have even a rudimentary understanding of how Linux, C++, distributed computing, game design, game mechanics, TCP/IP and UDP, and so forth work or what the tradeoffs are. They are held hostage to the knowledge of the wizards. They live and die by the opportunities the wizards present to them and by the choices they make. Without a basic understanding of how the magic really happens, management really has no choice but to approve the wizard's agenda, and that agenda does not necessarily—or even mostly—coincide with the good of the game.

This is easily solved with a bit of personal, hands-on research. You don't have to be a UNIX guru to install it on a machine and walk through a book on working within the UNIX environment. Nor do you need to be a wizard to pick up a book or read online articles on game design theory to understand one or two designers' ideas about the tradeoffs between features and usability. If you are in management, you can probably get the company to pick up the tab if you then take some of your designers to lunch and get them to discuss their ideas. Their ideas may be in line with the ones you just read about, in which case your new understanding of game theory will be firmer. Their ideas may be divergent from the ones you just read about, in which case your understanding of game theory will be wider. In either case, you will know more than you did. Just having a basic knowledge of wizardly lore gives the senior executive a technical edge in this market. You are less mesmerizable. Going to the effort of learning a little, being able to discuss the basic issues, and getting people in the trenches to teach makes you better prepared to make key decisions more quickly and more likely to choose well. On the human side, this activity can garner substantial respect from developers. By being less mesmerizable, interested in their work on a basic level, and willing to learn, the wizards may not invite you into their ranks, but they will be more likely to regard you as a worthwhile part of the overall process.

Another part of the education comes with knowing who the players are and what they want. In more traditional industries, senior management actually gets out of the office on a regular basis and mingles with the customers. Herb Kelleher, co-founder and former chief executive of Southwest Airlines, would regularly fly his own airline and speak to passengers about how they felt about the service. It worked; under his leadership, Southwest won the airline version of the Triple Crown (Best On-Time Record, Best Baggage Handling, and Fewest Customer Complaints in One Month) over 20 times. Being face-to-face with customers, talking with them, and experiencing what they experience about your product or service provides knowledge that is a key advantage.

In the online game world, that means senior management has to get down in the trenches with the players. It isn't enough to have your people hold focus groups and then watch the tapes; you have to play the game consistently and come to understand its strengths, weaknesses, and what needs to be fixed, forge friendships in the game, participate in the action, and get to know just who these people are who are giving you money month in and month out. How else are you going to know what works and what doesn't the next time you have to make a decision on spending millions of dollars on an online game?

Step Two: Foster a Culture of Organization

Equally important as education is creating a culture among development teams that respects the concept of organization. Most development teams don't have that respect. They have just the opposite, in fact; they are cowboys and like to shoot from the hip when an idea occurs to them. They feel that trying to "overly" organize them simply limits their creativity and ability to add to the game and make it "better" during development or during the live phase.

This has to change industry-wide or we'll continue to suffer bad launches and subject players to on-the-fly nerfing and cowboy programming. In this sense, "organization" means a culture that understands that the preparation phase must be fully completed, including the design, technical, and project plan documents and the CCP. Additionally, the culture must understand the need to follow those documents and concepts through to the end of the project.

Because development teams generally regard this concept with antipathy, time must be invested to educate them on the benefits of detailed planning and change control. After seeing evidence that your developers appreciate the benefits of these important processes, you still need to build among (and with) them a consensus for actually using them.

Game developers tend to uphold a code of behavior, prevalent among many early programmers (and not yet eradicated by management), that says that commenting/documenting code is beneath the station of the programmer/artist. There may be a strong correlation between the populations of professional programmers and students who were excellent at getting answers to math problems but hated to "show their work." When programmers are scarce, as they were for general business in the 1950s and 1960s, management is reluctant to insist on program documentation. Usually, the fact that the program or module works is more important to management than how or why it works. Because mystery adds to programmers' financial value and acts as a buffer against being fired, programmers, being human, tend to resist showing their work. As programmers become more available, management can afford to demand to know the technology behind the wizardry. Getting your developers to embrace detailed planning and an organized CCP may be an evolutionary process, and you should be prepared to resell the benefits if old habits present themselves. You may need to reassign, or even remove, "stars" from your team if they do not publicly embrace your view of the necessary organizational culture, especially if they consistently violate key principles.

Just educating senior management and fostering a culture of organization in your process will save you much grief in the short and long terms.

Project Realities

Beyond just plain number-crunching and estimating, there are intangibles that management should be aware of and plan for. Most developers are already aware intellectually or emotionally of these intangible issues, but few work them into development before works begins, feeling they can be addressed if and when they become problems.

Of course, most of these intangible issues become active at some point in the development cycle and can have a significant effect on budget and timeline.

We've already discussed basic budgeting and costs. If you're building a major PW from scratch, you know you must plan for between $5 million and $10 million in a development budget and between $2 and $5 million for the launch. Those are just the basics; what else is involved here?

Budget for Shortfalls, Time Crunches, and Morale Perks

It is almost a given that your project will cost more than you budgeted for. We've seen shortfalls ranging between 5% for well-organized projects to a full 100% from the planned budget for disorganized projects, usually involving inexperienced teams. This is an unusually wide range and the reasons for it are many; if you're just skimming the text, see the rest of this chapter for some examples having to do with the inexperience and culture of the industry as a whole.

You also have to plan for the regular budget-busters that any industry or business can experience: losing key personnel, "crunch" times that require huge amounts of overtime pay, finding out someone lied to the stakeholders, morale perks to keep the team's attitude up, and ridiculously low funding levels from the start.

Have Backup Plans for Your Personnel

If you work in any part of the computer industry, it will come as no surprise to learn that the game sector has more than its fair share of unusual people and personalities. The folks who create spreadsheets and word processors can be rather nontraditional. The people who build software games are like them in many ways, except that game developers are in a sense creating entire new number systems and languages to go along with their products. They are motivated by a need to creatively express themselves through the left-brain activities of designing games and producing elegant art through design and source code, and they have spent time and energy to acquire the right-brain discipline and rigor that is necessary to actually produce that code. There seems to be something about managing/balancing the competing demands on the two hemispheres when operating at a high enough level to deliver the quality that is demanded by today's PW game subscribers that tends to produce half-mad, flaky, iconoclastic geniuses in what would be alarming numbers for any other industry.

Ask any CEO or manager in this business and he/she will have a story that demonstrates how this can work against you. You might hear a story about a key person on a development team who disappeared for days during a critical portion of the project, only to return as mysteriously as he/she vanished, with little or no explanation about where he/she was or what he/she was doing. You might hear about a lead programmer grabbing the only complete copy of the source code and simply disappearing for weeks. That one happened to CEO Brian Fargo of Interplay in the mid-1980s, when the lead programmer on *Meantime*, the sequel to the popular *Wasteland* computer role-playing game (RPG), disappeared with the code. Fargo had to hire a private investigator to locate the man and retrieve the source code. There was no explanation from the lead; it just happened. It took so long to find him and get the code back that *Meantime* basically died as a project. Other stories run the full range of flakiness. On one end, there are the more or less normal tales of critical personnel being arrested for a variety of reasons and the company not finding out for days or weeks. At the other end of the spectrum, there are strange sagas of programmers not leaving their offices for weeks on end and coding 24 hours a day, in the end emerging with code that had little or no bearing on the game and so mentally burned out that they were useless for days or weeks afterward.

Then there is the more normal attrition, such as another company hiring away a key person at exactly the wrong time or someone just plain burning out from overwork. People working in computer games, and the technology industry as a whole, are notoriously mobile; good people receive offers on a regular basis and change jobs often. This often happens in conjunction with burnout; people convince themselves they are burned out because they work too hard for people who don't respect them or their work.

All of this is not at all unusual in the game industry; it happens to most teams. You need to plan redundancy into the team for the key personnel. This is not something most development teams plan for, and it usually comes back to haunt them. Redundancy is expensive. In this business, though, it is also expensive to lose someone at the wrong time and have everyone below them in the organizational chart getting paid for doing less than they would otherwise do while you locate a replacement and bring that replacement up to speed.

You saved money by designing early, waited until the right time to hire the right amount of expensive coding talent, got everybody to document their work, and the one person you have who is competent enough to manage the proper testing that you spent your savings on just joined a cult that preaches against the evils of computer games. Yesterday you were about six months and a day away from launch. Today you're about ready to launch your lunch—or join that cult. Redundancy is the key to building an effective team.

Lies to the Stakeholders

Another characteristic of development teams is that they can and will lie to stakeholders up the chain of command. They lie for a number of reasons, but most typically for the two reasons any executive would or should expect: The project is going to slip the ship date and/or run over budget.

The wizard/guru effect makes lying easy to do, both before and during a project. For example, it should not surprise anyone that project leads and design teams often understand up-front that they can't possibly turn out a game in the time they say they can. It has become relatively standard practice to estimate a development timeline and budget that executives want to hear and are likely to approve, and then later come up with a variety of excuses as to why the ship date has to slip or go under unless the project spends more money. This is not to say that it happens every time or that there aren't legitimate reasons for some slippage in any project. However, it happens with computer games quite a bit more than it does in other software sectors, and under the leadership of people who should know better.

Also, we should note that the lying is not done maliciously; teams have a way of rationalizing the deception by convincing themselves it is for the good of the game and the art, or by convincing themselves after the fact that it wasn't *really* a lie—it was a best-case scenario that had a series of encounters with the typical world. Who could possibly anticipate everything? We gave it our best shot, really.

If senior management educates themselves, such deception is harder to achieve. On the technical side, the managers will know a little more and will be more likely to detect unrealistic assumptions and/or projections. On the human side, if managers really care enough to go to the trouble of learning more about game theory and the technology behind the magic, it becomes more difficult for the developers to rationalize deceiving them. The message to teams is simple: Executives aren't scared of three-year projects and large budgets if you can make a case that the ROI will be there at the end of the day. Executives are scared of being saddled with yet another team that goes over budget, delivers less than the milestones, and lies about delivery timelines.

Don't Pinch Your Product to Death

It is the nature of every business to pinch pennies because every penny spent comes off the profit margin. This seems to be especially true of large online game projects. In the main, this is because of a general misunderstanding of the true nature of the full costs of development and launch. The knowledge of the true costs is spreading slowly and will probably become general knowledge within the next three to five years.

In the meantime, it is important to understand that you need to go into such a project with a full commitment to spend what is necessary for success. As noted more than once in this chapter and throughout the book, understand thoroughly that an online game is both a product *and* a service and plan to act accordingly. Most managers underestimate or completely forget the budget for the launch phase until well into the test phase and have to play catch-up for months, often until well after the launch phase is completed.

In short, you have a major breakpoint on cost control and spending: the planning you do before development begins, which, if done correctly, should give you a number plus or minus 10–15% of your actual costs right up through launch.

Crunch Time

Online games tend to have many more milestone deliverables than other computer/ video game projects, due to the extended development timelines and levels of detailed work that are required. As with any other software project, work tends to lag a bit early into a milestone as delays set in. As the delivery date for the milestone approaches, teams go into "crunch mode," working longer and longer hours to ensure the milestone is delivered on time. Depending on when the decision is made to go into crunch mode, features tend to get pushed back to the next milestone, creating a cascade effect until the team can end up in perpetual crunch mode for the last few months of a project.

Considering that currently almost all milestones in every project tend to lag, this means the team will probably be spending a significant amount of time in crunch mode almost from the start of the project, with serious and predictable effects on burnout and morale. Both of these are high-risk factors for losing personnel mid-project.

There is probably no way to completely eliminate the need for crunch mode because there is just no way to fully eliminate unexpected delays. The best you can do is to make sure the design phase is completely finished before coding begins and be flexible about trimming features earlier in the process, rather than later. You'd also be wise to actually work a number of replacements and their training time into the budget.

Morale Builders and Perks

As previously discussed, two of the recurring problems you'll face over a three-year development cycle are employee burnout and sinking morale. These result in delays and people leaving the project before completion.

If you're smart, you'll budget morale perks into the mix from the start. Most companies do try to have something in the mix, but these rarely go beyond the standards of having meals catered in during crunch time and setting aside a small budget for occasionally buying cheap gifts or dinners for selected team members. On a project as long and stressful as an online game or PW, these aren't nearly enough. Thinking outside the box on this can be a major benefit because a relatively small amount of money spent creatively in this area can save you an enormous sum over the life of the project.

Granting the entire team a four-day weekend for successfully achieving a milestone feature-complete might seem like a wasteful expense of hundreds of person-hours, but it rests and revitalizes the team after a stressful period, rewards success, and gives them an incentive to do it again. Or, you could have a "milestone dinner" and hand out a few $500 bonus checks to people who went above and beyond expectations during the milestone.

Perks are only one part of it. Actively working to build and maintain morale over time is a necessity. Anything (well, almost anything) that breaks the stress and allows people to concentrate again on the tasks at hand is worth exploring. After noticing that the stress in the office was building to high levels where she worked in the mid-1990s, one of the authors stopped at a Toys 'R' Us, bought 20 cans of Silly String, arrived early at the office, and left a can on the desk of each team member. By mid-morning, after a series of battles that are still commented on from time to time, every surface in the office was covered with Silly String and every face was plastered with a silly grin. You can imagine the effect it had on team morale and the leveraged value of the money spent.

The lesson to be learned here: The producer and project manager are in charge of team morale. They need to pay attention to what is happening and should step in before things hit the boiling point for the team or individuals. All too many leaders forget this and pay the price.

Chapter 4

Marketing and Distribution Concerns: Retail Box, Download, or Both?

KEY TOPICS

- Downloading: Not (Yet) a Viable Option

- Buying Shelf Space

- The AOL Model: Do You Need to Actually Sell the Client?

Like any other computer game, the number one requirement for play (and to get paid) is to get the game's player component, the client, installed on a computer. This means distribution, and distribution reach is still king. Two major distribution models have emerged in the online game marketplace: selling the client at retail, as per other computer games, and offering the client for download via the Internet, either free or on a discounted basis.

Of the two, retail sales is still the best method for getting the disc in the hands of the players.

Downloading: Not (Yet) a Viable Option

There has been a lot of hype in the past couple of years about the possibilities of bypassing the retail channel with online games, offering direct downloads of the client as an alternative. Publishers like the idea of bypassing all the middlemen in the retail process and the need to pay marketing development funds (MDFs), creating higher margins on the client.

Unfortunately, the hype is once again overtaking the reality of the situation. While this is a fine idea and will eventually become a reality, we're not there yet and won't be for years:

➤ With over 90% of the US and world market still on 56k dial-up connections, only the most dedicated gamers will even consider a download over 50–100 megabytes (MB). Compare this with an online game client, which has an average of well over 500MB. It is true that hard-core gamers do tend to upgrade to faster Internet connections when they become available and have remarkable tolerance for large downloads, but they are a small percentage of the overall market. Compare this to the download figures for the much smaller 10MB episodes for Electronic Art's *Majestic*, of which fully 91.5% of downloads started were never completed.[1]

➤ Broadband access is growing far more slowly than expected. In 1997, most analysts expected a full 30 million people in the US to be accessing the Internet on broadband connections by 2002; the actual total as of March 2002 is fewer than 11 million connections and, due to the failures in 2001 of cable modem provider @Home and many digital subscriber line (DSL) providers, the rate of new connections slowed throughout most of 2001 and the first quarter of 2002. Broadband access is not expected by the authors to be a major force in the US and Europe until 2005 at the earliest, and possibly not until 2007 or later. And even though Asia is laying broadband fiber far more quickly than the US and Europe, the broadband access numbers in the region are roughly equivalent to those in the rest of the world.

The exception is South Korea, which is, by some estimates, almost 75% broadband-connected. The great bulk of these connections and gameplay happen in cyber cafés, which are unique to that country and are a major force in online games. By some accounts, almost 5% of the total population is registered for one online game, NCSoft's *Lineage: The Bloodpledge*, which sees the great bulk of its revenues from cyber café access fees. Interestingly, however, the number of home broadband connections in South Korea is growing steadily and is expected to reach parity with cyber cafés in the next year to two years.

At any rate, for the foreseeable future, publishers should make plans to maximize retail distribution for the client.

---

1. "Of those who started down the path of registration, only 8.5% completed," EA spokesman Jeff Brown said. The rest quit halfway through, he said, in part because of the lengthy process, which included over 10 megabytes in software downloads." See "*Majestic* Headed for Stores Before Thanksgiving," *USA Today*, October 3, 2001.

Buying Shelf Space

Retailers treat an online game like any other game client. This is both good and bad. On the good side, if the title sells well, like *EverQuest (EQ)* and *Dark Age of Camelot* did, then you can count on shelf space being available. On the bad side, retailers will want what they always want for a retail game package, namely marketing development funds, or MDFs.

MDFs are the retail world's version of the old organized crime protection scheme; if you want prominent (or even *any*) shelf space, room for an end-cap, or to have the retailer show your product box cover in their omnibus newspaper ads, you pay MDFs. MDF costs for a Class AAA project can easily run over $300,000.

Retail chains get away with this because shelf space is limited in most stores to 200–300 spaces and publishers send over 1,500 games to the shelves each year. That makes it a seller's market, and chains are always willing to sell. It is part of the cost of doing business, especially in the US.

Another challenge is keeping that shelf space over time. With persistent worlds (PWs) today, and at least for the next three to five years, until we see how the growth of broadband connections in the home plays out, having a unit on the shelf is critical to the acquisition of new subscribers. PW games tend to settle out at low, but consistent, sales rates. Retailers are accustomed to a three- to six-month shelf life for a product that is selling well; getting them to retain your unit on the shelf after that can be difficult.

This is also a problem you might face with a publisher, who is also accustomed to that three- to six-month shelf life and may not see the need to keep a (relatively) low-selling game client on the shelves.

The AOL Model: Do You Need to Actually Sell the Client?

For a retail hybrid, selling the client is a given; that is the business model and there is no other choice at present. For web-based games, the model is the "free to the player" model and distribution is automatic. For subscription games such as PWs, whether or not to sell at retail becomes an interesting question. If the cost of goods to create a retail unit (typically somewhere between $2 and $6 per unit, depending on the size of the print run) and paying MDFs bother you, you need to ask yourself if you should sell the unit or give it away instead.

Consider: If you sell 100,000 units during the launch period, at an average return of $15 each (wholesale to the distributor minus cost of goods, development funding, and marketing expenses), you'll make $1.5 million. This is hardly an insignificant amount of revenue, right?

If you expect your PW to do even as well as *Asheron's Call* (*AC*), that $1.5 million is equal to 10% of your annual income. Each player who stays with you for 9–12 months will be paying you the equivalent of three games at full retail price, or 7–10 games at your average return per unit, depending on the amount of the monthly subscription fee. The predominant revenue source here is obviously the subscription fees, not the retail unit. In most cases, the revenue from retail sales won't even pay for development costs.

The real money is in the subscriptions, not in selling the unit at retail. The real objective should be distribution, not sales, to get the client in the hands of as many potential subscribers as possible. Obviously, not all publishers can afford to bypass the retail revenue, but alternative distribution means should be considered.

And those alternative methods exist. Consider the AOL distribution model, developed by AOL Marketing VP Jan Brandt back in the early 1990s. Ms. Brandt decided that the best way to increase subscription numbers for AOL was to literally put an AOL client disc in every home in America—not once, but several times and through several means. Remember: This was a time when everyone else was marketing almost strictly online, and maybe including a client disc in one or two magazines per year. She took that an order of magnitude higher and mailed them to US homes several times over a period of years, put the disc as cover mounts on every relevant magazine she could, bundled the client with computers, printers, peripherals, and other software, and put up point-of-sale (POS) displays in grocery stores, software stores, and every other brick-and-mortar retail shop that would hold still for it; in other words, it was impossible for you *not* to have access to an AOL disc, whether you wanted one or not.

It was an expensive campaign, to put it mildly. By most reports, AOL went $1 billion in debt paying for the campaign over five or six years. And it worked. By the time Ms. Brandt was through, there were no viable US competitors to AOL. It remains the top Internet service provider (ISP) in the world with 34 million subscribers as of March 2002. Compare that with Microsoft Network's estimated 4 million or Earthlink's estimated 2.5 million.

You don't have to go $1 billion in debt to distribute your game client. Alternative means exist, but they require highly organized advance planning and a set-in-stone launch date. If you plan to give away the client, you have a number of viable options with which to create a multi-pronged distribution strategy.

Low-Cost Retail POS

In November 2001, NCSoft pioneered a new concept for distributing online-only game clients by selling them as low-cost POS units at Electronics Boutique (EB). The cost of each unit is $2.99, and one assumes that EB gets to keep all or most of that money. The POS version is simply a disc-sized package in a POS display. This no doubt costs NCSoft some money to create the package, duplicate the discs (probably in the $2-per-unit range), and get them to EB retail outlets, but it is an effective way to get in front of the eyeballs of thousands of potential subscribers each day.

Magazine Cover Mounts

Game magazines such as *Computer Gaming World*, *PC Gamer*, and *Computer Games* not only mount CDs on their covers, but they also sell access to them. Prices range from $7,500–$15,000, but the magazine takes care of the disc duplication and, if you "own" that month's disc, your art goes on the disc and the disc holder. This is a cost-effective way to reach 125,000–400,000 hard-core gamers. Remember, however, that there is usually a minimum 90-day lead time on reserving these.

Original Equipment Manufacturer Bundling

Original equipment manufacturers (OEMs) love to bundle software with their hardware as a value-added attraction for potential customers. This runs the full range of hardware, including joysticks, video cards, and on the hard drives of new computers.

Some OEMs do huge buys, in the four- to eight-million-unit range. Traditionally, they pay small fees per unit for Class AAA products and take demo versions of only a few very popular products. If you're willing to take no fee or an at-cost fee for duplicating and shipping the discs to them, however, many OEMs would love to talk to you. Bear in mind that the lead time on OEM bundling is quite long, as much as six to nine months.

Downloads

If you're going to offer the client for free, there is no reason not to have a downloadable version available on your web site. You do need to understand that if your client is as large in size as the average online game client—that is, a full CD-ROM of 500–600MB compressed—the bandwidth needed to download it will cost you somewhere between 50 cents and $1.50 per download. With the cost of goods for a shelf unit now running between $1.50 and $3.00 for most games, this is still significant cost savings, but it is a hard cost that needs to be figured into the equation.

You also need to take into account that you must have registration codes, even for free downloadable clients, or you'll find that the 1% of people in any group who tend to abuse any process will start creating multiple accounts simply because they can, and this can become a significant cost.

Free downloads in general create their own set of problems. For example, how do you limit anonymous downloaders to one download and one account to keep them from just creating new accounts and playing for free on the back of your bandwidth costs? The only way to curb most of this is to insist they not be anonymous and provide a credit card number for registration and issue CD codes, but that also provides a block to entry; many people are still leery of giving away a credit card number in general, and even more are hesitant to do it for something they aren't actually purchasing. Online "pocketbook" initiatives such as Microsoft's .NET and Passport may provide some relief in the future, but only if they become widely accepted.

And that is only one of the problems presented by free downloads today. Like the issue of the commercialization of the Internet in the mid-1990s, companies are rushing in without thinking through all the potential problems.

Chapter 5

Calculating and Expanding the Profit Margins: The Cost of Doing Business

KEY TOPICS

- Some Numbers
- Add-On Profits

Historically, persistent worlds (PWs) have been a 40–50%-margin business. For a developer or publisher, the only niche with significant support costs are the PWs (we're assuming you don't run a web game portal or assume bandwidth or hardware costs for a hybrid).

In an ideal world, PW post-launch support costs would be limited to approximately 40% of the total revenue generated (or 40% of the revenue goal, for newly released games building a subscriber base). Often, the percentage is closer to 60%, due to a lack of concern in the past for providing the customer service (CS) staff with the right tools to do their job quickly and efficiently.[1]

More and more publishers are learning the value of building adequate CS tools during the development process instead of tacking them on at the last minute. Well-designed tools allow each CS representative to do more in less time. During the next three to five years, support costs should go down across the board, and PW games will have a better chance of making the 40% or lower support cost mark.

---

1. Note that former SOE President Kelly Flock was quoted in the press during 2000, including the *Wall Street Journal*, as saying that supporting *EverQuest* cost the company approximately $1.5 million per month, which represented slightly over 50% of basic subscription revenue from SOE's then 300,000-plus subscribers. The last announced subscriber total for *EQ* in 2001 was 435,000. If *EQ*'s support costs have remained stable, SOE is coming close to the magical 40% operating cost number.

Some Numbers

In Table 5.1, it is assumed that a PW will achieve at least moderate to high subscriber numbers by current standards—that is, 200,000–300,000 monthly subscribers at about $10 per month each. Note, however, that subscription fees are on the rise, as with NCSoft charging $15 per month for *Lineage* and Funcom's *Anarchy Online (AO)* and Mythic's *Dark Age of Camelot* charging $12.95. The second column represents the approximate number of employees that ideally would be devoted to the CS task. The percentage at the far right of each line item represents the approximate amount of an ideal 40% of subscription revenue that is devoted to supporting the MMOG/PW.

These numbers vary by company and customer niche; each PW customer niche differs greatly in its needs. For example, an RPG requires a larger player relations staff than a vehicle simulation with fewer RPG elements.

Table 5.1   Support and Operations Costs

Persistent World Support Costs: RPG Model		
Customer Service/Player Relations	**Employees**	**% of Revenue**
In-game support		
24/7 in-game customer representatives	40+	7.00%
Game masters (storyline, quests, volunteers, etc.)	5+	0.75%
Empowered player support team (new player helpers, GM helpers)	5+	0.75%
Other (anti-cheat investigation team, administrative assisant)	3+	0.50%
Community relations (web site, message boards, email)	5+	0.75%
Game Operations		
Live development team (new lands, bug fixes, new features, add-on SKUs)	12–15	6.00%
Network Operations		
NOC staff	8–12	4.25%
Co-located server hardware and bandwidth (Note: bandwidth cost variable, depending on peak usage. Assumes between 10 and 20 player server clusters.)		20.00%
Total Maximum Percentage of Revenue Goals:		**40.00%**

Even at a level of 60% of revenue devoted to support, as shown in Table 5.1, a moderately popular PW (100,000 or more subscribers) will generate significant gross profit over a minimum lifecycle of five years.

Table 5.2 considers broad subscriber income numbers alone, not factoring in revenue from initial stock-keeping unit (SKU) and add-on SKU sales, which can and do amortize a product's initial development and launch costs.

Table 5.2   Moderate Support Costs, Subscription Games

Gross Profit for Subscription Online-Only Game: Moderate Support Costs						
Monthly fee $10						
Monthly subscribers	100,000	150,000	200,000	250,000	300,000	500,000
Annual revenue (approximate)	$12,000,000	$18,000,000	$24,000,000	$30,000,000	$36,000,000	$60,000,000
Support costs @ 60%	$7,200,000	$10,800,000	$14,400,000	$18,000,000	$21,600,000	$36,000,000
Annual gross profit	$4,800,000	$7,200,000	$9,600,000	$12,000,000	$14,400,000	$24,000,000
Gross profit over five-year lifecycle	$24,000,000	$36,000,000	$48,000,000	$60,000,000	$72,000,000	$120,000,000

If support costs can be contained to 40%, as shown in Table 5.3, the outlook for gross profit becomes truly impressive, especially at the 300,000 and above subscriber level.

Table 5.3   Low Support Costs, Subscription Games

Gross Profit for Subscription Online-Only Game: Low Support Costs						
Monthly fee $10						
Monthly subscribers	100,000	150,000	200,000	250,000	300,000	500,000
Annual revenue (approximate)	$12,000,000	$18,000,000	$24,000,000	$30,000,000	$36,000,000	$60,000,000
Support costs @ 40%	$4,800,000	$7,200,000	$9,600,000	$12,000,000	$14,400,000	$24,000,000
Annual gross profit	$7,200,000	$10,800,000	$14,400,000	$18,000,000	$21,600,000	$36,000,000
Gross profit over five-year lifecycle	$36,000,000	$54,000,000	$90,000,000	$90,000,000	$108,000,000	$180,000,000

A game that reaches 300,000 subscribers quickly, as *EverQuest (EQ)* did, will exceed or equal the gross revenue generated by even the most popular home PC SKUs within three years.

The bottom line: With a longer lifecycle than any single SKU and most series (*Age of Empires*, for example), PWs look to be the most profitable PC game products for the next three to five years. The first PW to reach 500,000 subscribers quickly is going to represent a huge windfall to the owner.

Add-On Profits

Until the past three or four years, most online games didn't really look at add-on revenue profits from alternative sources. Lately several games, among them *EQ*, *Ultima Online (UO)*, and *Dark Age of Camelot*, have started to get into the merchandising of peripheral products, such as t-shirts and other clothing, jewelry, cups and glasses, figurines, collectible trading cards, fiction series books, and even paper and pencil versions of the online game. This can all add up to some nice incremental income to add to your margin, and you probably won't have to pay for the creation or production of the items. There are plenty of small merchandisers out there who will pay you a fee and royalties for the right to create and market these items to your customers.

One area of potential income that is currently the subject of controversy is the auctioning of player/characters and in-game items. If you've been paying attention for the past four or five years, you know that players have been using auction sites such as eBay to sell rare game items, in-game currency, and "buffed" characters to other players, sometimes for thousands of dollars. More than one small company has sprung up to do nothing but create and sell characters and items, and that is where the controversy comes in.

Most publishers don't want this activity in their games and don't support it. There are several reasons for this, all tied to CS and player relations resource expenditures:

➤ A significant number of individuals who auction game characters and items are scam artists. The seller advertises an inventory for a character and, when someone has paid the auction price and taken possession of the account, the buyer finds that the inventory doesn't match the auction notes. When this happens, the seller is usually not available, so the player complains to the publisher or developer. This consumes hours of CS resources that can be better spent elsewhere.

➤ Supporting such auctions by third parties, especially companies or individuals that do it as a business, tempts them into using bugs and exploits to grow characters more quickly, as seen recently by the Black Snow Interactive/Funcom *AO* controversy. This not only keeps your security and exploit team hopping, trying to keep up, but it also has the tendency to skew whatever economy exists in the game and to irritate and annoy players who legitimately build their characters and find they can't compete with the doctored ones. In a game that features some form of player vs. player (PvP) combat, this is a very serious issue.

➤ Most PWs have "spawn points," or areas where non-player characters (NPCs) and monsters that may carry rare items or necessary quest items regularly pop up after they are vanquished. As the creation timer on these spawns varies, sometimes being hours between spawns, players tend to "camp" on these spots, waiting for a spawn to occur. Companies making money off auctions tend to bring as many people as possible to camp and monopolize acquisition of these rare items, effectively locking out legitimate players from having a chance at a spawn. Many rare items are needed to advance in certain quests or complete armor or weapons sets, and if a player is blocked from getting them at the spawn points, he/she must either buy them or quit the game in disgust. This costs the publisher players and subscription fees.

The problem with just banning the activity and not supporting it is that it is unenforceable. If you drive the auctions off eBay or other large auction sites, the perpetrators will just set up their own site and the support calls will just continue. One way to have at least some control over the situation is to have your own auction site.

The advantage here is, as the publisher or developer with access to the source code, you can lock down accounts that put up an auction and display the contents for all potential buyers, assuring that auctions run from your site won't be stripped before transfer. This kind of security is good added value to players. You also can bill the buyer and subtract a fee from the sale price before transferring the rest to the seller, effectively making incremental income profit from the activity.

No publisher has yet done this, and there may be legal reasons not to get involved. You also have to consider the intangible effect on your customers, many of whom deplore the practice. However, it is an option for you to consider.

Part II

Design and Development Considerations

Chapter 6

Basic Design and Development Issues

KEY TOPICS

• Practicalities and Advice

• Design

"These worlds are complex, revolve around communities, and require a lot of forethought. It's no longer about, 'Wow, wouldn't it be cool if...' but rather, 'So if we put this feature in, how would it affect long-term balance? Could players abuse it?' and so on. A good, experienced development team will know where the common pitfalls lie, and what precautions to take early on in the development process. Something as simple as having adequate bandwidth and hardware on launch day is often overlooked by first-time developers."

Daniel Manachi, The Themis Group

Online game development teams are weird. Not disturbing weird, like some guy standing on a street corner arguing macro-economics with a fire hydrant. No, it's more like the weirdness of a lovable but dotty old aunt who can immediately take over and manage the extended family when her sister has been in an accident, but has trouble in the morning remembering how to tie her shoes.

The weirdness in development teams comes from the fact that they are pie-in-the-sky creatively and down-to-earth technologically. This tends to produce an effect not dissimilar to multiple personality disorder in an individual: Personality A is the fun, creative one who can design the most complicated, elegant game ever, while Personality B is pretty no-nonsense, task-oriented, and has the nuts and bolts of coding and hardware down to a tee. The problems come in when they fight for control of the body; most times, the fun, creative personality wins out, even if the matter is something Personality B should have control over. It is the age-old conflict between the theoretical and the practical.

This conflict is not readily apparent to outside observers, but it affects everything the team does throughout the development process. Most developers, be they designers, coders, artists, or network specialists, enter the industry because making games is supposed to be a fun, creative activity. Like everything else in life, however, the nuts-and-bolts issues have to be attended to as well; as an industry, we just haven't been good enough Type-B personalities.

One of the common themes throughout this chapter is keeping the two personalities in harmony. Someone has to act as a rudder for the enormous creative energies of the team and must know when to steer them away from the theoretical and toward the practical. These energies are enormous; you'll rarely meet a visionless, incompetent online game development team. Often, though, you will meet teams poorly steered and constantly making emergency course corrections because they forgot to plot the sandbars on the navigation chart.

Someone has to keep things in balance between what co-author Bridgette Patrovsky calls the "esoteric, dream-state BS" that teams can get lost in and the need to actually get things planned, tasked, coded, drawn, and tested. The ultimate responsibility for that falls to both the producer and project manager, the former to keep the team balanced and the latter to keep the producer informed of just what state the development is in. We discussed the project manager in previous chapters; you'll learn more about the producer later on in this chapter.

This chapter will have two focuses: the theoretical (design) and the practical (development). There is plenty of room for movement and opinion in each. Technology discussions, especially, have a tendency to appear cut and dried, and there is always the temptation for an author to lay down what appears to be hard and fast recommendations for development tools, specific languages, operating environments, and so forth. The plain fact is, this industry is still young, and while some good solutions for everyday problems do exist, every new game is different and probably will require a different solution set, especially persistent worlds (PWs).

So, to mangle an old saw, instead of trying to teach developers how to chew technical cheese, what we seek to do in this chapter is give some guidelines and let the reader know what has worked in the past with tools, design issues, and development processes, as well as what hasn't worked.

Throughout the chapters in this section, we'll make some points about console and hybrid online gaming and identify which points about PW development do and don't apply to them.

Practicalities and Advice

"Most good products are designed around the person, not the technology."

Donald A. Norman, author of *The Invisible Computer*, quoted in a *Technology Review* magazine article[1]

For an industry with over 30 years of history and populated by some of the brightest people you'll ever meet, we sure seem to be unable to learn from the mistakes of others. There seems to be an almost emotional, arrogant need to reprise those mistakes, sometimes by the same teams on subsequent projects. A commonly heard refrain from developers is "<Insert feature here> hasn't worked yet because no one has done it right." So, even though non-consensual PvP combat (the player being attacked has no choice in the matter) has been shown in any number of games since 1988 to be extremely unpopular with over 80% of the player base of subscription-based online games, many new development teams plan it into their game on the theory that it just hasn't been done right in the past.

Considering that concept, we thought it would be useful to include advice from other people who have been there too, in the hopes that the information would sink in institutionally. We asked several experienced executives and developers the following question: In your experience, what mistakes do development teams make during the online game development process? The answers we received offered some excellent practical advice for anyone starting an online games project.

---

1. See "Handhelds of Tomorrow" by Claire Tristram, *Technology Review*, April 2002.

Richard A. Garriott, creator of the *Ultima* series and currently a principal at NCSoft in Austin, Texas:

➤ Teams regularly bite off more than they can chew. An MMP can easily become an impossible-to-complete reality simulator.

➤ Teams regularly hire on-paper game designers and/or solo player gamemakers, but MMPs need unique skills not found in other arenas.

➤ Teams often cut corners in code expandability or general quality to try to make schedule. This usually haunts them later.

➤ Companies often hire people too soon. A great deal of groundwork can be done before you need the majority of the staff.

Gordon Walton, executive producer for *The Sims Online* for EA/Maxis:

➤ They don't build for the long term, that is, they don't make the code extensible and maintainable. The live team pays for this for years and the game's financial potential is reduced.

➤ They don't focus enough on quality of service, especially mean time between failure (MTBF) metrics. Failures in the servers deny service to thousands of people, and failures in the client irritate players, raising churn.

➤ They underestimate the complexity of the task. More moving parts drive complexity nonlinearly, and MMP games have a lot of moving parts. Rule of thumb: An MMP game is three times bigger than a standalone game, but 10 times harder to complete.

➤ They underestimate the testing and scaling challenges and end up with a fire drill when their service scales up.

➤ They overestimate the value of the initial game content and overestimate how long it will take the players to consume it.

➤ They forget that some design ideas don't work well within the MMP arena, particularly static puzzles and fixed-content discovery elements. These elements end up on player web sites within days of launch, reducing the value of that part of the game for most other players.

➤ They spend more time on game mechanics than social mechanics. This makes it harder for players to find and play with each other, which doesn't help retention and churn at all.

➤ They forget to bring customer service (CS) in as an equal partner in design and development. Thus, customer satisfaction is lower, and the game is much more expensive to run.

➤ They think they are just building a game (rather than a social venue with gaming elements).

Thomas Howalt, project manager of Funcom's *Anarchy Online (AO)*:

➤ Confidence is good, but control is better.

As stated earlier, an online game is a huge task, and it is very easy to lose track. Check everything thoroughly again and again. Do not accept promises; you have to keep track of everything.

➤ Problems don't solve themselves.

Personnel conflicts have to be dealt with quick and clean. Do not accept discrepancies to pester the atmosphere. Conflict can be valuable if managed well; tension can be fruitful if managed well. It all depends on how mature your team is. Remember: Moss does not grow on rolling stones! Make 'em rock 'n roll!

➤ Everything moves.

Everything in the game may have to change. Be careful what you hard-code.

➤ Repeat after me, please: "Tools! Tools! And more Tools."

You will need tools for everything! Hire lots of tools and library coders. Use money to develop brilliant tools. Make decent and efficient graphical user interfaces, or GUIs. And, force the coders to work with their own tools before they ask anyone else to work with them.

➤ Mountain high, river deep.

Be aware when the "stars" appear. The closer you get to launch, the more need Marketing will have for someone who knows the game and is good at talking marketing-type talk. To all you "stars": Fame is very addictive, but keep your feet on the ground and stay humble! Tomorrow you will be forgotten; that's the way fame works—it does not last. And remember: It is a team effort!

Alex Macris, CEO of The Themis Group and designer of *Spearhead*:

➤ They focus too much on excitement (gameplay) and too little on involvement (the community). Within six months of playing 20 hours per week, any player will find your gameplay boring, period. There is nothing you can do that can make your gameplay more interesting than that of a brand new AAA title coming out six months or a year or two years after your title. But if you have him in the thrall of your community, he'll stay.

➤ Everyone talks about the addictiveness of *EverQuest's* gameplay, likening it to a slot machine, but they lose sight of the meta-game that overlays *EQ* and that makes the achievements meaningful. And I think future games will have a difficult time in succeeding with an *EQ*-style approach because they won't enjoy the network effects that come from being the biggest game.

➤ They focus too much on content and too little on features. Content can be successfully added over time (as *Asheron's Call* proved). Features are far harder to add. The number of game mechanics is a lot more interesting than the number of dungeons.

Andre Backen, former president of Funcom:

➤ The single biggest mistake we make is to overestimate what we are able to get done in a certain amount of time.

Jeff Anderson, CEO, Turbine Entertainment:

➤ The worst thing I have seen repeatedly is a lack of focus. The teams feel compelled to engage in what I like to call "competitivism." Before I was making online games, I worked for a company that made combat flight sims. I noticed that the focus of those games changed from what was "fun" for the general audience to what they have to have on the back of the box "to be competitive." So instead of spending their precious development time innovating, they worried about the physics on the F-22, or making sure they had the latest laser-guided bombs. Maybe it made for an easy marketing angle ("We've got that!"), but it made lousy gameplay. You see a lot of that in the online space already; fervor to make sure that my game hits some kind of feature list—even before there is an idea of what makes the game fun.

Damion Schubert, founder of Ninjaneering and former lead designer of *UO2* and *M59*:

➤ A mistake that I've seen a lot of in the MMP space is a concept I call "ant farming." This is when developers start to envision cool experiments that would be fun to observe from the heavens—but may not be terribly fun for the player base. Usually, these experiments involve ways that players can take advantage of other players' lack of knowledge, experience, or common sense. Developers usually have great defenses for these features, such as "interesting emergent behavior," "case studies in trust," or "fascinating guild tactics," but frequently what they really turn out to be are support nightmares and retention killers.

Design

"The most important issue for me would be fun. How will this system hold up to countless hours of use? How many times can I do X before it gets boring? Online games are built with longevity in mind—no longer are you expecting to just sell the box and move on to the next title, but to keep people entertained for months and even years with a single game. It's not easy."

Daniel Manachi, The Themis Group

One would think that, with millions of dollars on the line, the process of designing and developing an online game would be a detailed, exact, and excruciatingly careful one. Dream on. Here's how most online game projects are developed today:

➤ A small team pitches a project to the publisher.

➤ The publisher looks at some basic spreadsheets and development timelines and approves the project.

➤ The small team begins the design document.

➤ While the design document is still unfinished, the team begins staffing up and coding the game.

➤ The design document still isn't finished, but programmers get way ahead of the designers, so the designers have to go back and change some things in the document.

➤ About a year into the project, the design document still isn't finished, but the programmers have a workable pre-Alpha version of the world-building tools and database finished, so everyone jumps in and starts building, because this is a lot more fun than actually designing the project.

➤ At about month 18, someone realizes that most of the game mechanics haven't been spec'ed out yet and starts building them directly into the game. The design document still isn't finished, but this is explained as, "Hey, it's a living document." The team does, however, have some very cool screenshots and a basic "walk and talk" demo version to show senior management.

➤ At about month 21 into a 30-month development schedule and with the first Beta version due in three months, the team realizes that it is in a complete shambles. People are still designing combat mechanics (or magic, flight, siege, trade skills, the economy, you name it), even though most of the play field has been laid out in the world-builder tool and most of the art is still "programmer graphics." The data for thousands of objects, such as terrain pieces, buildings, weapons, and armor, are in the database. The team panics and decides to tell management there will be delays. They demand 10 more artists and three more programmers to help rush development to a close at month 36.

➤ At month 36, the new release date, the team realizes that trying to design and retrofit game mechanics into a world for which development was well underway was a huge mistake. To make the mechanics work, they are going to have to strip out most of the existing mechanics and start over, including scrapping the database. Management is not pleased, but with $6–$8 million invested, they okay another delay.

➤ At month 48, after having spent almost $10 million and having stripped out about half the features they promised players, the company makes the team launch the game, even though there are over 1,000 known bugs in the game and the technology isn't stable for more than an hour at a time.

This example isn't an exaggeration; it comes directly from the experience of one of the authors, who was called in as a consultant to help clean up this same game after launch. Most game teams and almost all online game teams really have no concept of proper software design practices. What are completed game and technical design documents? Hah! Those things just limit creativity. What about a change control process (CCP)? Don't sweat it; when we think of it, we just change the code and move on. Should we comment the code? Nah, that takes too much time!

In hindsight, the problems with the games shipped to date aren't the surprising aspect. The level of success we've enjoyed in spite of the serious problems is the big surprise!

The Process: Design Twice, Build Once

As we mention more than once in this book, one of the online game industry's peculiar idiosyncrasies (read: "stupidities") is that programming often starts long before the game design document is finished. More than any other single factor, this is why online games in general—and PWs especially—tend to be launch disasters.

How many times have you picked up a hybrid at the software store on release day and then had to sit through a multi-megabyte patch just to get online with it? It is not unusual for hybrids to have a 4–8MB patch waiting for the player on launch day.

At that, PWs in 2001 out-did hybrid patches in a major way. Two games, *AO* and *World War II Online*, each had 75MB patches waiting for subscribers on opening day.

For the purposes of this book, it is generally assumed that an in-house team will be building the online game. We've also split the game design and technical design documents into separate sections. As noted elsewhere, it is not unusual for these two to be combined into one document at some point, if not at the beginning, then at the end of the process.

The Design Treatment

Variously called a proposal, treatment, or game outline, think of this as a "sell" document; you are trying to convince the people with the checkbooks that you and your team know how to build this game and that it will be popular enough when finished and launched to make some money.

The treatment should be relatively short, between 5 and 10 pages. The content will vary depending on whether you are proposing a PW or hybrid, but any treatment should contain the following as a minimum:

➤ **Genre**—Is this a fantasy medieval PW, such as *Ultima Online (UO)*, or a sci-fi shooter, such as *Half-Life*?

➤ **Graphic look and requirements**—Will this be a full 3D interface and require a graphic accelerator card? Will there be a software rendering option? Is the "look" photorealistic, anime, what?

➤ **Interface style**—This is the view the player will see. An interface description for *Asheron's Call (AC)* might read: "A player-configurable first- or third-person perspective using keyboard and/or mouse," while *UO*'s might read: "An isolinear screen, 3/4-raked view, with full keyboard and mouse control."

➤ **Engine**—Are you reusing a current engine, licensing an outside engine, or building from scratch?

➤ **Database**—If you're building a PW, will you be using a commercial database, such as Oracle or SQL Server, or building your own?

➤ **Target audience**—Who will this game appeal to? Is it designed for the hard-core, moderate, or mass-market audience? Will the game tap into multiple markets?

➤ **Client platform**—This item includes the development platform and subsequent port platforms, if any. Is this designed strictly for the PC online audience, or will the game also be ported to one or more consoles? With both the Xbox and PlayStation 2 consoles now in the online game market in a big way, this can be a critical consideration, especially for a hybrid.

➤ **Host platform**—What hardware and software will be used on the server side of the equation, including factors such as the physical machine configuration to be used, operating system and programming environment, database, anticipated peak simultaneous user load, number of server clusters/sets required, and anticipated bandwidth consumption per user and per server cluster?

➤ **Licensed or original world**—Will the background of the game be a licensed world, as with *Star Wars Galaxies*, or an original concept, such as *AC* or *Dark Age of Camelot*?

➤ **Gameplay**—This is a description of the player's gameplay experience. Describe the key gameplay and player interface elements and what will differentiate your game from the competition.

➤ **New player experience**—For a PW, a new player experience that makes the game's basic chat and game mechanics functions clear is absolutely critical. What will this game feature in the new player experience that will help train and hook players in the first few minutes of gameplay?

➤ **Competition**—Are there similar projects on the market already or in the development stage? How will this game compete effectively against those other products? How much money are these other games making, and why will your game do as well or better?

➤ **Staffing and qualifications**—How many people will the team need at the beginning, middle, and end of the development process, and in what specialties? What are the basic job descriptions and qualifications needed for each position?

➤ **Core team**—Who are the producer/project manager, lead client programmer, lead server/network engineer, lead database designer/administrator, art director, and lead designer? Why are they qualified to develop this project?

➤ **Schedule**—This is a preliminary estimate of the development and testing schedule. This will probably be completely bogus; we've yet to see any kind of online game launch within six months of the proposed delivery date with even 80% of the feature set intact. However, executives want to be able to run preliminary figures on when they'll get a return on the investment, so you have to at least try. If you're a smart project manager/producer, you'll pad whatever estimate you make by at least six months.

➤ **Budget**—This is a preliminary estimate of the total dollar cost to build this game and launch it. This should include at the least personnel salaries, software and hardware costs from start through testing to launch, and for a PW, the launch costs in terms of server hardware, bandwidth requirements, and network operations costs. If you can make a reasonable estimate of the CS/player relations costs, do it; far too many publishers have been taken by surprise here. It is rumored in the industry that the reason Take-Two dropped Wolfpack's *Shadowbane* in 2000/2001 was because management didn't realize until late in the process just how expensive it is to launch and host a PW game. You don't have to include marketing funds in here; the folks in executive row will do that. They should already know what it costs to market a Class AAA game.

While it will only take about two days to actually write the treatment, it will probably require between 50 and 100 hours to research it, especially the technology and competition portions. This document then goes to the executives in charge of approving or disapproving projects for development. If they are smart, they'll have a sanity check performed by knowledgeable people not connected with the project. This generally happens, but it makes one wonder why so many obvious non-starters get the go-ahead for a preliminary design document.

In case you're wondering: Yes, the treatment is often used to begin coding a prototype. Yes, this is a huge mistake. Development teams like to have a prototype running at the end of the design process to impress the executives, but this is just a waste of time and resources. So much is going to change during the preliminary design phase that a prototype doesn't make much sense, except to appease leads who would rather be coding than finishing a design.

The Preliminary Game Design

While this is called a "preliminary design," don't let that lull you into complacency; it should be approached in practice as driving toward a complete design document. Remember, the mantra is "design twice; build once." That means you actually have to finish what you think will be the final design, pass it around for comment, and then dig back into the document and make necessary changes, including rewriting the whole document, if necessary.

That sounds like a lot of work, and it is; designs for online games are hideously more complicated than standard retail solo-play home games. Solo games might involve 50 or 60 hours of gameplay, with some limited replay value; online games have to plan on keeping the player occupied for hundreds of hours (hybrids) to thousands of hours (PWs).[2] This means there has to be quite a bit of content in the game at release, plus plans to allow for content additions over time, post-launch.

If the core design team (producer/project manager, lead client programmer, lead server/network engineer, lead database designer/administrator, art director, CS manager, lead designer, and perhaps as many as two other designers at various points

---

2. Both Sony Online and EA claim the average weekly play hours of their subscribers for *EQ* and *UO* is approximately 12–20. This amounts to a part-time job of 1,000 hours a year for the *average* player; the hard-core player in such games can easily rack up 40, 50, or even 60 hours per week.

in the design process) doesn't spend at least three months on the preliminary design document, you can pretty much predict that there will be problems and delays during development, as elements missed in the short design phase become apparent and require fixing or rethinking. Experienced designers plan on at least a six-month design period to allow for two passes ("design twice") before development begins ("build once").

Why so much time? It has been proven by experience and any number of studies that spending more time on the design to finish a complete thought actually reduces development time. Go back to your experience with essay questions. If you took the time to do an outline, no matter how simple, you spent less time erasing and rewriting. The more detailed the outline, the more time saved. If you skipped school whenever there was an essay test given, go back and think about any product you have assembled. Maybe you could assemble it without the manual, diagram, schematic, list of instructions, and so forth, but you could always do it faster with the manual.

No one seriously disputes this as fact, so why do online game projects typically run 20–25% over their development time? The two main culprits are inexperience and game developer culture, which don't generally include best-of-breed development practices, including concepts such as TQM or CCPs. Publishers are not without some responsibility either, of course. So far, they have underwritten a staggering amount of development costs. The more they learn, whether motivated by an interest in gaming and/or an aversion to losing money, the more they will insist on better development practices. In poker parlance, the publishers that learn sooner and better will not only collect more from their winning hands, but they will also fold their losing hands earlier.

If you've been involved in game development before, you know what a game design document is supposed to look like and you also know that such documents rarely get halfway done. At a minimum, this document should include the following:

- The background story—The history of the world and why the player is supposed to be here
- Player interface design
- Character races and/or classes, with detailed notes on the differences between them, special abilities, or advantages
- Character creation and growth processes

➤ World locations and environments, including all natural and "man-made" types of terrain

➤ Full game mechanics, including magic, combat, trade skills, and any other appropriate mechanic

➤ Graphics style guide (the art bible)

➤ Full list of items and artifacts

➤ Non-player character (NPC) types and a list of NPCs and spawn points (if any) to be in the game

➤ Monster types and a list of monsters to be in the game

➤ Static quests (if any), detailed out

➤ Task lists—All the tasks needed to build the game and how long each task should take, from the smallest piece of art to the largest script to be written by a designer

➤ Personnel lists—The number of designers and artists that will be needed, and when they'll be needed

➤ First cut at the milestones, the deliverables for those milestones, and when they are to be delivered

➤ First cut of the overall development and launch budgets

This looks like a fairly short list, but there is a lot of detailed work involved. In fact, this list will (or should) generate a PW design document at least 200 pages in length, including the lists of objects, NPCs and monsters, buildings, and other artifacts. If the team has been thorough, the document will be in the neighborhood of 350–400 pages in length. They'll still probably miss some things, but that's what the review process is for.

The Preliminary Technical Design

In conjunction with the design, your technology leads will be writing the technical design document. This can be either a completely separate document from the game design or included as part of it; it is done both ways in the industry and there seems to be no particular advantage to doing it one way or the other. The important thing is that it be complete.

Also note that this does not take place in a vacuum, apart from the game design; after all, this is a small team and the technology folks have to know what the designers want to do, to be able to tell them if it is even possible. The technical designers will spend a lot of time talking to the game designers before they put even one word on paper.

When technical designers do start writing, their portions of the documents should minimally include the following:

> ➤ **Software**—The operating systems environment for both the client and server, programming and scripting languages, database program to be used (bought or built, and if built, what they'll start with), and graphics and modeling software to be used.

> ➤ **Tools**—What tools are needed and whether they will be built, bought off-the-shelf, or repurposed from existing software. Tools include everything from world-building utilities to CS and in-game gamemaster (GM) powers.

> ➤ **Game server, host farm configuration, and requirements**—This should include the number of physical machines per server cluster, memory and hard drive requirements per machine, how many subscribers each server cluster will be required to host, and the space needed to physically host the machines (if you're building your own network operations center [NOC] for the game).

> ➤ **Bandwidth requirements**—How many bits per second will each player transmit, and the resulting bandwidth required by each server cluster.

> ➤ **Task lists**—Every coding assignment in detail and how long each should take.

> ➤ **Features list**—All interface and game mechanic features, listed in priority order.

> ➤ **Personnel lists**—How many programmers, engineers, and database administrators will be needed, and at what times during the project.

> ➤ **First cuts**—Rough estimates of the milestones, the deliverables for those milestones, and when they are to be delivered. Also, you need a first cut at the overall technical budget for development and launch.

> ➤ **Prototype lists**—What elements will be included in the prototype and what is expected to be demonstrated in the proof of concept?

➤ **Technical risks list**—What elements of the hardware or software could end up being blocks to development and cause delays and slips?

➤ **The CCP**—How changes in the final game and technical design will be submitted, reviewed, approved, and implemented.

By the time the preliminary technical design is finished, it may end up being larger than the game design document. There are thousands of separate tasks to be tracked in a timeline/baseline document. These tasks can easily take up hundreds of pages in a project management chart constructed, for example, in Microsoft Project software. One Project document we recently looked at for art tasks for a role-playing game, for example, was over 200 pages by itself.

The Design Document Review

Now that you have the preliminary documents, what's next?

Most publishers have a design document review (DDR) team to perform a sanity check on projects. DDR team members are pulled from every department in the company to allow every department that will eventually be involved in the project (the stakeholders) to have some input and advance warning. Minimally, the DDR team should include an experienced producer or executive producer, a senior management executive such as the VP of Development, an experienced designer not assigned to the project, experienced client and server programmers, someone from Marketing and/or Press Relations, and representatives from Technical Support (both telephone and email), Player Relations, and Community Relations. Some publishers have separate teams for the game design and technical design reviews.

Once the design team has finished the preliminary design, copies go out to each member of the DDR team for review and comment. Members of the design team then meet with the various DDR team members to get clarification on any question or comment that is not clear. After that, there is also generally an all-day meeting between the DDR team and the game design team to go over the comments and allow the DDR team to ask more questions and get a clearer understanding of the scope and anticipated final outcome of the project.

The relationship between the design team and DDR team is often contentious, and DDR meetings have been known to grow hot. However, it is also a necessary process because teams not only often miss issues—both subtle and obvious—that heavily affect the other departments in the company, but they also sometimes miss gaping holes in their own game's mechanics, technology, or scheduling. You have to remember that design teams are close to their own work, and these games are some of the most complex software products in existence, so it can be easy for these issues to completely escape them. That doesn't mean design teams won't get mad at you when you point out flaws; designers get emotionally attached to their "babies." It comes with the territory.

This is also where you'll start to get an idea of what items on the features list may have to be trimmed to ensure the product ships in a reasonable time period. This is never easy for a design team; after a while, every feature becomes important and integral to the whole experience of the game. In truth, some features can't and shouldn't be trimmed, but design teams also have a nasty habit of letting "feature creep" take over. The whole reason for a prioritized features list is to make the design team complete their thoughts and, as a final option, to allow a producer or executive producer to mandate feature cuts, if he or she feels they are necessary.

For those teams working independently from a publisher, it makes sense to contract with experienced people to go over the design with a fine-toothed comb to isolate just these sorts of issues.

The "Final" Game and Technical Designs

Once the DDR process is complete, the design team holds a series of meetings to go over every comment and every page of the documents, line by line, deciding what changes need to be made and how each will affect the budget, task list, development baselines, and milestone deliverables. There will be meetings with individual stakeholders to discuss the questions and comments from the DDR in more depth and to do some horse-trading to reach a consensus.

It is easy to rush through this part of the process; developers want to get to developing, after all. It is important not to be impatient; take all comments into account and take the time to really put a final polish on the designs. If done correctly, this is the last time you'll have to do a major review of either; rush through it and your chances of ending up in the same boat as the products that experienced poor launches in 2001 are high. The team doesn't have to accept every recommended change, but it does need to give serious consideration to them and be able to adequately defend their decisions.

The other key element of the final design document process is honesty. No matter how emotionally attached to the work a team becomes, each individual on the team knows what concepts and features are truly do-able in the time allotted, which are innovative and worth a risk, and which simply are "neat stuff" everyone has always wanted to try. In a free multi-user dungeon (or MUD, which is usually a text-based Internet adventure game that may also have a hypertext markup language [HTML] or Java graphical component), massive experimentation is allowable; in a for-pay game, innovation and risk have to be balanced with building a game the subscribers will pay for. No one really likes this tradeoff; we'd all like to spend our days in constant experimentation because we want to push the genre forward faster. But with millions of dollars at stake, the people writing the checks expect a reasonable chance of getting their money back someday, and successes pay for further research and development.

So be honest about the tradeoffs. If you're a producer or executive producer, you must constantly remind the team of this and make the hard choices early.

The Second Design Review

Once the team has what it believes are the final versions of the documents, there is a second review process, similar to the first, but shorter in duration. If everyone did his or her job in the first review and asked the hard questions up-front and the design team was honest and patient about the tradeoffs and effective in consensus-building, the second review should go much more smoothly than the first one. There will be last-minute questions and some flaws will be found, but they should be handled easily.

The whole purpose of the second review, in fact, is to just make sure nothing important slipped past the first review and second design phase, and to reach a final consensus between the design team and the stakeholders that, yes, this is the game we're going to build.

The Final Polish

The final polish is simply that: fixing any last-minute flaws that were found in the second review process, making sure that any changes they caused in the budget, timeline, and task lists have been taken into account, and then sending the final documents around to the stakeholders for final sign-off.

For the design team, it is important that you get signatures from the stakeholders. It is not uncommon for questions or comments to pop up at this stage, regardless of whether a consensus was reached in previous stages. Just as you're willing to commit to building the game in the documents within the time and budget noted, you want the stakeholders to commit that, yes, they've read the document, made comments, and understand that this is the game that will be built. Not only is this an important part of the consensus-building process, you don't want stakeholders bothering you later on with questions that should have been raised during the design process.

For stakeholders, it is important to thoroughly read the design documents, understand the implications for your department, and commit to the work if you accept what those implications mean, in terms of work and resources for you and your people. Nothing ticks off developers more than to be submarined 18 months into development by a stakeholder who starts raising basic design feasibility questions.

Chapter 7

Digging Deeper into Development and Design Issues

After some six months, plenty of skull sweat, and arguing with stakeholders about the necessity of this or that feature, the team is finally ready to settle in and begin building the game. At this point, the routine should be fairly easy because the design process has laid out a guide map of what needs to be built when and how many people it will take at each stage.

Naturally, there will be problems; nothing in this industry ever goes exactly according to plan, and changes will have to be made along the way. With the completed game and technical designs to guide you, however, these dislocations should be solved easily so that development can proceed.

As you've probably noticed by now, everything about designing one of these games is a tradeoff between creative design and the plain technical capability to pull off that design. We'll start with the technical considerations, work our way into design issues, and finish up with the testing process and preparing for the launch.

This chapter is not designed to be an exact roadmap of how design and development work. Experienced online game developers will sneer at most of what you'll read as basic and, in truth, it is. As we note elsewhere, this chapter alone deserves its own 350-page book, so it is impossible to be complete and definitive in the space allotted. This chapter, at first glance, may look woefully incomplete to those in-the-know. Thankfully, three of the most experienced people in the industry, Gordon Walton, executive producer for *The Sims Online*, Dr. Richard Bartle, co-creator of the first MUD, and Scott Hartsman, technical director for Verant's *EverQuest*, agreed to look over the book and point out any mistakes we'd made. Any errors remaining in this chapter belong to the authors, not the technical reviewers.

A Note on the Buzzword "Community"

Throughout the remainder of the book, you'll be seeing the word "community" quite a bit. There is a misconception in the online game industry and, indeed, in the online/Internet services industry as a whole, that a product or piece of content builds a community around it. Nothing could be further from the truth; the community already exists and may gather at your game, if you provide the proper tools.

This may seem like nitpicking, but understanding the difference is crucial to success in the online game industry. Many initial game portal efforts, such as TEN (now pogo.com) and Mplayer, failed by assuming they could create a community by just slapping together a portal and some interface software. This was the "If we build it, they will come" mentality.

What they discovered, after throwing nearly $100 million collectively down a rat hole, was that they should have been building tools to facilitate the needs of existing communities—the community center, if you will. A site must build a community center with a suite of tools that is easy to learn and use, and then make sure the customers know they exist. When the customers know that the tools and center exist, whole communities of gamers—be they guilds, teams, or squads from other games or one of the broad market niches—will migrate to see if your community center is easy to learn and use and provides the communications and information tools they require to maintain their existing communities. If it does, and some of the community leaders pick up on them and use them, the community begins to migrate; if it doesn't, they migrate to the best alternative.

Among the current portals and individual online games, Microsoft's Zone (or The Zone, found at www.zone.com) is one of the better examples of providing the necessary tools to facilitate a community. The Zone should be closely studied with an eye toward improving the tools and adding new ones, such as web page hosting for teams and role-playing guilds.

One of the less stellar examples is *Ultima Online (UO)*; the chat tools built into the game at launch were so bad that the vast majority of regular players used AOL's ICQ instant messaging software to communicate during play instead.

What we really hope to accomplish is something that has yet to be done, and that is just list the general, minimum requirements for getting through design and development, show where the quicksand pits are, and give some advice on how to avoid the problems others have experienced.

Technical Considerations

Don't worry; we aren't going to try to make a definitive statement in this section on just what technology you should be using to make an online game. Let it be said that if you're working with some flavor of C/C++ with a compatible compiler, DirectX for Graphics functions, Linux, or Windows NT/2000/XP, and one of several art packages like Maya or 3D Studio, you're in good company.

What we hope to do here is give you some guidelines on what others are using, list some of the tradeoffs they consider when picking software and deciding which world-building tools to use, and discuss whether it matters in what order the worlds are built. The tradeoffs can be critical; for example, do you choose cutting-edge 3D first-person models and objects with many polygons and textures, knowing that these have the potential to create perceived latency on the player's computer, or do you opt for something a little less intensive in the hopes of creating less perceived lag for the player? What you do here and now, at the beginning of the project, determines whether the post-launch live team is going to need a Prozac dispenser in the coffee room five years from now.

There are also business tradeoffs to be considered. For example, consider the Asian market that is heavily into isolinear/God's-eye-view games. The first/third-person style persistent world (PW) is untested there as yet, although *EQ* should be available in Korea and China by the time this book is printed.

Planning to Extend the Game for Years

All other factors being equal, there is no reason an online game can't and shouldn't have years of life. Unless, of course, when you get down to choosing the technology and designing the software, you forget to make it easy to add features and content to the game.

This seems like common sense, doesn't it? Yet you'd be surprised how often this necessity is ignored. Up to this point in the history of commercial online game development, forgetting about making it easy to add content and patch the game has been the rule, not the exception. Some of that has been pure business; a publisher would rather sell an expansion disc than just download little bits of new content here and there. In some ways, that is penny-wise and pound-foolish; the money in PWs is in the subscription fees, not the retail package. Being able to easily refresh content without requiring a trip to the software store can help keep players subscribing to your game for years.

On the other hand, lack of forethought has been the major contributor to this state of affairs. For some reason, developers have had a hard time getting out of the "designed, developed, tested, finished!" state of mind. Since your development team is unlikely to be the same team that manages the game after launch, you have to continually remind them that the process is more one of "design, develop, test, install, wash, rinse, and repeat until retirement."

What this means is that a PW development team must pick core technology and design database arrays that enhance the virtue of content and feature addition with as minimally small client patches as you can get. Without considering this, you'll be creating problems the live team (the people who support and update the game after it goes live) will have to deal with for years.

You also need to understand that if you don't make changes to the game over its lifetime, you are seriously limiting the extent of that life. Constant refreshment of the content, upgrades, and additional features are all necessary to keep the veteran player interested. Without them, you won't have the retention rate necessary to sustain the game long-term, and loyal players will move on to the next new thing sooner than later. That means you have to plan for this in the design and make sure the process of adding content and features is going to be an easy one.

Comments? What Comments?

In this day and age, when most programmers recognize the need to comment their code so that those coming after them know why any particular piece of it was written and what it is supposed to do, you'll find many game developers who don't comment their code at all. This is even more prevalent in the online game industry; there are hideously complex PWs in operation today without a single comment anywhere in the source code. There is a school of thought in the game industry, in fact, that says commenting code is just a time-waster, for sloppy programmers who can't write elegant code that is easily understood. This ignores the fact that most programmers can't agree on what "elegant" code is, much less write an example of it.

It is insanity of the first order not to insist on comments. Ours is one of the most mobile areas of the job market. People change jobs and move to new companies every couple of years, on average. Much of this has to do with the fact that publishers are constantly laying off employees at the end of the year, scheduling many projects to finish just in time to ship for the Christmas selling season. They tend to staff up again for new projects in the spring, and one has to wonder if the reason why so many projects are late to ship is an unconscious (or not) attempt by some programmers to extend the paycheck cycle a bit.

Whatever the reason, it is a safe bet that not every programmer who starts a project will finish it. If that programmer's code is not commented, whoever the replacement is could spend a considerable length of time figuring out the code and its effects on other pieces of code. In projects that can easily exceed 800,000 lines of code, knowing how the pieces interact with each other is a requirement, not a luxury. There is nothing worse than having to replace a critical coder at a touchy stage of development and then finding out it will take three to six months for the replacement to fully understand the legacy code because it is uncommented.

So, a cardinal rule for the team must be comment the code. It is up to the team leaders to establish the standards (Comment algorithms, data, or both? Comment by line or by blocks?) and follow up on them by checking the code and ensuring that the team is, indeed, commenting the code.

Where to Start?

In many ways, choosing technology for an online game starts at the same place as a retail home unit: with the basic libraries and commercial development tools available on the market today. Since you'll be working with both a client and a server complex, there are some interesting additions:

➤ Base (data structures and utilities)

➤ Database

➤ Encryption

➤ Input/Output (I/O) and sockets

➤ Network messaging (TCP or UDP, with UDP preferable in most cases)

➤ 2D/3D sound

➤ 2D/3D graphics

Note that the encryption, I/O and sockets, and network messaging are going to require a different skill set and core competencies than most game development teams normally feature.

What Database, Database Structure, Client View, and Language Will You Use?

Let's approach these topics one at a time.

Database and Data Structures

If you aren't planning to have your online game be database-driven, you're already about to make a huge error. The easiest way to add content over time is to make sure the database and structures support easy, on-the-fly additions of new objects, classes, and art.

Objects and Content Addition

Online games must be refreshed with new content constantly to keep the game alive and exciting for the players. The easiest and most convenient method for this is simply downloading the new content onto the player's computer via the patching process.

If you are going to sanely add content to your game over time, using a 3D client, objects, and a flexible database on the backend are pretty much necessities. Take, for example, *UO*'s situation from launch in 1997 until late 2000/early 2001, when *UO: Third Dawn*, the 3D upgrade, was shipped. Until *Third Dawn*, *UO*'s structure for the art and graphics files used what can only be called the "monoblock" approach: one huge, inherent file that was several hundred megabytes in size. This meant that to add even one piece of new content, the whole file had to be reinstalled, thus producing an impossible patch size for any player. If the live team wanted to upgrade or add content on the client side, it had to convince EA to ship an expansion pack; this hindered content addition for years, until the 3D upgrade was mandated by then Online Services VP Gordon Walton and ramrodded by live team producer and experienced 3D hand Rick Hall.

In most shops, unless the developers are building a database from scratch, a commercial database product such as MS SQL Server, MySQL Server, or Oracle is the main product in use. Either option (build or buy) has its advantages, but in general, it makes the most sense for a team new to online game development to pick a commercially available product; there are more people out there who know MS SQL Server or Oracle than your home-grown alternative.

C/C++, Object-Oriented Language

Is there any PC development group not using C/C++ these days? Most of the shops we queried were using Microsoft C++ and objects. The general consensus seems to be that the use of objects gives far more flexibility in design and makes online games easier to manipulate and change after launch.

The Client

One of the key choices the team will need to make at the outset is whether to go 3D, first person with the interface, like *EverQuest*, or isolinear, like *Lineage: The Bloodpledge*. There are a number of considerations that will go into the decision.

3D First/Third Person Versus Isolinear 3D or Flat 2D ("God's Eye View")   Both interfaces are in use today, but there are more 3D first/third-person online games than isolinear, especially in the PW niche. The 3D first/third-person solution is most popular with developers in the US and Europe (*EverQuest*, *Asheron's Call*, and *Dark Age of Camelot*); the isolinear interface style is very popular in Asia (*Lineage* and numerous imitators). See Figures 7.1 and 7.2 for an example of each view.

Figure 7.1 A 3D, first-person interface, from Funcom's *Anarchy Online*. Most first-person interfaces allow the player to set the camera view to third person (which means the player can be viewed on screen).

Which interface to use is really a matter of design preference and whether or not your team has expertise with one style or the other. Among the player base, the most popular form of interface is the first/third-person, as it is considered more immersive than a top-down view. This may be more a matter of design and game mechanics choice than anything else; *UO* is one of the few major isolinear games in the PW niche, but it has more depth and breadth than any other existing online game, PW or hybrid.

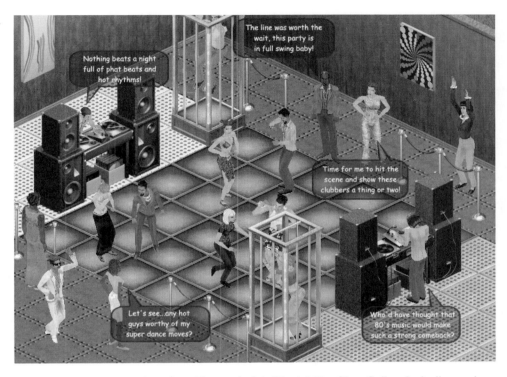

Figure 7.2   An isolinear interface from Electronic Arts/Maxis' *The Sims Online*. An isolinear view shows the player and the surrounding terrain from a god's-eye view, usually in what is called a "raked position," which means the view is not from directly overhead, but from approximately $\frac{1}{2}$ to $\frac{3}{4}$ of the way from ground level to directly overhead.

Designers are beginning to experiment with multiple interfaces, such as combining an isolinear, real-time strategy interface for resource management, but using the first/third-person interface when the player is actually moving about with a character.

Microsoft's DirectX API   Almost every developer working with IBM-compatible PCs today (about 95% of the total market) is working with DirectX, or at least some portion of it. For the uninitiated, DirectX is an applications programming interface (API) that allows programmers to access PC hardware directly in Windows without having to write hardware-specific code. It is somewhat loosely based on the company's component object model (COM), the same technology that drives ActiveX controls. The API includes various modules for dealing with discrete PC functions, such as DirectGraphics (version 8 combined Direct3D and DirectDraw), DirectShow, DirectSound, DirectMusic, DirectInput, and DirectPlay.

While there have been complaints about the clunky, bloated code, numerous updates to learn (eight major version marks in fewer than seven years), and lack of OpenGL support, in general, the API has been well accepted.

Pretty Pictures, Polygon Counts, and Graphic Accelerators: Your Living Hell Has Arrived   Graphic accelerators have become standard issue with new PCs, and there is no doubt they have allowed the creation of ever more realistic and beautiful graphics in all computer games. They have also greatly increased production and development costs because players expect developers to take advantage of the ever-rising on-screen polygon counts, frame display rates, finer textures and meshes, and every bell and whistle imaginable to make a game as visually stunning as possible.

There are two main problems here:

➤ In an online game, the more graphic data you have to load, the more latency the player is likely to experience and the more complaints about lag your customer support (CS) staff will receive. For example, at the time of this writing, *Anarchy Online (AO)* was probably the most visually stunning online game currently on the market. However, when a player zones into a city area, even the most buffed-out PC can take as long as a minute to finally finish loading all those stunning textures and 3D objects—and these are all static objects, built into the terrain. One can imagine the delays if they were dynamic objects that the server had to first identify for the player, then load as he/she came in range.

➤ While most accelerators use the same two or three basic chipsets, mainly being NVidia's Quadro and GeForce and ATI's Radeon, accelerator board makers such as Matrox, ATI, and NVidia have different standards, configurations, and sometimes wildly different software drivers. Toss in Microsoft's DirectX API, which allows developers to access hardware directly through Windows, and the mix can be even more volatile. Since it is virtually impossible for the manufacturers or game developers to test the graphics chipsets and their software drivers with even a significant number of PC hardware and software configurations, there are always going to be conflicts that cause some games and applications to react weirdly or not work at all. The fact that the drivers included with new PCs are probably six months out of date by the time a PC is sold to the consumer (one or more updates have already been issued) also increases the potential for software conflicts.

During the later test phases, accelerator conflicts are likely to become one of the banes of your existence, so be prepared for it.

After launch, conflicts are generally easily fixed by downloading an updated software driver for the chipset. In the meantime, however, it also probably means that your player relations staff will be bombarded with complaints and demands that the problem be fixed.

Building the Right Tools

"You will need tools for everything! Hire lots of tool and library coders. Use money to develop brilliant tools. Make decent and efficient GUIs. And force the coders to work with their own tools before they ask anyone else to work with them."

Thomas Howalt, Funcom

The tools and their capabilities should be fully specified in the game and technical design documents. This is another case where the lead designer and his/her team and the technology builders must work closely together to ensure that nothing escapes notice during the design phase; after all, your designers will be doing quite a bit of the scripting of the game mechanics. It can be hell to realize during development that you forgot to specify the scripting capability to modify a weapon's effectiveness by a character's inventory weight load and then have to try to retool the scripting language to match.

Where most teams get into trouble is in not building the tools to handle those minimal capabilities right at the outset of the project.

World-Building Tools and Editors

The world-builders/editors are probably the most important tools you'll build first. These are what your designers and scripters (collectively called "world-builders") will use to actually construct the world that your players will romp in.

These aren't just graphics tools to lay out terrain and buildings; they comprise a suite of tools to build and edit items, spells, quests, and non-player characters (NPCs), plus a sound editor for sound effects and music.

These tools are no secret in the industry, and their capabilities are fairly well-known. Some of those capabilities are pretty obvious and include the following:

➤ Laying out ground terrain, such as forests, lakes, deserts, and mountains

➤ Basically manipulating and deforming terrain, such as raising mountains, making lakes and rivers, and so forth

➤ Placing man-made terrain features, such as buildings and roads

➤ Placing triggers, such as NPC spawns and weather effects

➤ Creating and editing players/characters

➤ Creating and editing player-usable objects, such as weapons, armor, books, food, gold, and so forth

Bear in mind that these are the minimal capabilities your team will need going forward with the project.

Scripting Tools

What will the designers use to build the world? What capabilities will they need? Most, if not all, PWs support a scripting language. This is mainly used by the designers and world-builders (in conjunction with a home-brewed graphic-oriented tool) to actually construct the game world and mechanics. The whole purpose of using a scripting language is so you don't have to hard-code every mechanic, NPC conversation, or event into your game. It also avoids the need to recompile the executable for the game each time you make a change.

Note that this is not the same scripting you may be familiar with in hybrid games like *Quake*; it can be far more detailed and time consuming and require a language and tool that are far more flexible. The old joke about Ginger Rogers being a better dancer than Fred Astaire (she did everything he did, backward and in high heels) applies here. Bear in mind that an online role-playing game has on the order of 10 times the actual content and complexity of the average hybrid, in terms of player-controlled objects, terrain, and the way inventory objects correlate with a player's skills and attributes. If each change in a PW had to be hard-coded into the executable, none would ever be finished enough to launch, and not many changes and content/feature additions would ever be done.

Python

There are many scripting languages available that work with C/C++, including PERL, JavaScript, Visual Basic, and SmallTalk. However, many shops are now using Python: an interpreted, interactive, object-oriented programming language that is extensible in C or C++ and portable, meaning it works with several brands of UNIX on the Macintosh and on PCs under MS-DOS, Windows, Windows NT, and OS/2. It is also free and has virtually zero compiling time. See www.python.org for details.

Other Tools You'll Need

The other tools include those you'd need in any project with multiple builds and versions:

- ➤ Code building
- ➤ Version control
- ➤ Task tracking

In addition, you'll need a set of tools that just about every online game has neglected to design and build during development and was forced to build at or after launch. These are tools that monitor and log into record files what goes on in the game, including the following:

- ➤ Player activities:
    - ➤ Where do they go?
    - ➤ What do they do?
    - ➤ What do they look at?
    - ➤ What do they buy, where, and how often?
    - ➤ How long does it take them to do it?
- ➤ Client and server statistics:
    - ➤ Who is where, when?
    - ➤ What machines in the server cluster are empty for significant portions of the day?
    - ➤ Which machines are full for significant portions of the day?

➤ Chat logs

➤ Crashes and errors

Some teams actually make the choice not to build these tools because they can add server-side lag into the game—sometimes serious amounts of it. And, truth be told, they aren't "sexy" or fun to work on, compared to cool stuff like game mechanics; in the past, "sexy" has always won out over "necessary."

However, this is a serious mistake because these tools make it easier for the live team to perform a number of critical functions:

➤ **Track player activities and security**—Players who are willing to use exploits and bugs to bypass game mechanics are usually pretty stupid about it. If players find an exploit that allows them to jump experience levels in minutes instead of hours, for example, they'll dig right in and boost their character as many levels as they can in a short period of time. Then they'll start handing out the exploit to their guild mates and friends, who will then spread it out to their friends, and so on.

You can build monitoring tools that know about how long it should take to gain experience, game gold, and so forth, once you feed in the parameters for what is being monitored. These tools can then monitor player activity and create an alert when a character out-performs the parameters coded into the monitor. Once you know which character(s) has located one of these unintended features, your other tools (the ones that tell you where they were and when, and the ones that keep track of character statistics) will make short work of finding and neutralizing the exploits and exploiters. If you don't have the monitoring tools available, you can count on spending literally thousands of wasted live team hours in trying to find and fix them.

➤ **Monitor chat logs**—One of the most prevalent problems in any PW is "verbal" harassment, usually in the form of insults, profanity, racial slurs, or spamming the screen with text to make it impossible for other players to carry on conversations.

Developers aren't keen on keeping extensive logs that record chat conversations and actions performed; they eat up CPU cycles and tend to add lag to the game. If you don't keep these logs, however, it is nearly impossible to create necessary harassment reporting tools for players or to investigate harassment charges at all.

Without these tools, a "live" online game is almost impossible to administer correctly. And without them, the player relations and community management teams will come to curse your name. If you fail to build them, don't be surprised if you're hung in effigy in the lobby of your building.

Host Hardware and Bandwidth

There are a lot of issues to address when trying to determine the hardware and bandwidth requirements. The following sections attempt to address most if not all of them.

How Many Players per Physical Server?

This will depend on the game's design and how the design affects the size of the world, where critical in-game facilities such as banks, training masters, shops, and other player gathering places are located. The tradeoff on this is the more players in one place, the better the socialization, up to some point where there are so many in one location that server-side lag becomes a problem.

This points back to the design and doing your best to anticipate population problems before coding begins.

How Many Servers per World Iteration?

The tradeoff: The more physical machines per world iteration, the more people you can simultaneously host per iteration. More machines, however, means higher hardware costs.

Also, you have to consider how many players to host per physical server vs. the size and popularity of the "world" terrain that server machine hosts. If each physical machine is designed to host 500 simultaneous players, but the region of the world is of such interest that more than 500 regularly congregate there, what is that going to do to performance?

Multi-Processor PCs or Suns?

In most cases, the cheaper alternative is multi-processor PCs, if you have a firm handle on how many machines you need per world iteration. The value of dual-processor PC motherboards is in faster traffic-handling at the server end. Both Sun and Intel announced in December 2001 that they are working on multiple processors on one chip, tied together using simultaneous multithreading to allow each processor to handle two or more application threads simultaneously.[1] This should eventually decrease the costs of server farms, as one physical machine will probably be able to handle more traffic and players.

Just plain clumping commodity, single-processor PCs isn't advised for an application as intensive as a multiplayer game. They aren't designed for this type of job. The higher cost of multi-processor PCs is generally offset by better performance and less downtime, which result in higher player satisfaction.

How Much RAM?

The easy answer here is "as much as you can shove into the machine." You should have no less than 1GB of system RAM for any type and style of online game, and as much as you can reasonably afford is best; there is no such thing as too much.

Will That Be One Hard Drive or Five?

The view on this among developers we've talked to is split. Some prefer having one large hard drive with a backup in a fault-tolerant configuration; some prefer two or more relatively smaller drives with one fault-tolerant backup drive in place.

Purely for redundancy's sake, it makes sense to split the load off to more than one drive if your technical design allows for it. Regular, multiple backups are mandatory in any case; there hasn't been an online game in existence that hasn't had a catastrophic failure that required backup game data to be loaded onto live production servers.

---

1. See the full article at CMP's Silicon Strategies web site:
   www.siliconstrategies.com/story/OEG20011210S0069.

To Linux or Not to Linux...

This one has become almost a religious argument in the community. Microsoft back-end products such as NT/2000/XP tend not to be as stable or cost effective as Linux. Windows NT/2000/XP isn't considered as stable as Linux, can't host as many people per server before server-side lag starts setting in, and costs money to license versus the free use of Linux. On the other hand, NT/2000/XP is generally easier for most engineers to work with, and Microsoft and their affiliated training partners have pretty good training programs and materials available.

In general, most shops are going with Linux because it is free, open source, more flexible, and generally more scalable than NT/2000/XP.

Bandwidth: How Big a Pipe Do You Need?

This is one of the key questions in this whole process. Bandwidth is one of the few variable costs you'll have to contend with; it is also one of your biggest expenses because you pay a peak usage rate; that is, the higher your peak usage, the higher your rate. This isn't like a personal account with your ISP, nor is it like having an account with a phone, water, or electricity provider. It's more like a highway—it's going to be as wide as you build it, and you need to build it for your busiest rush-hour traffic, even when nearly everyone is home sleeping. Going over a peak usage cap is expensive. (Think rush-hour traffic that is so congested that you need a helicopter to evacuate a seriously injured motorist. Compare the cost of a helicopter with the cost of an ambulance.)

Controlling bandwidth usage is critical to the profit margins for the game, yet it is rarely a consideration in the design stage of a project. Designers don't want to be shackled to a bit rate target number; they want to shove as much data down the line as they can because that gives them leeway to add more features to the game. They are rarely challenged on this during the design process because, due to inexperience with the process, executive producers and other leaders rarely even think about it. It is generally during the latter stages of Beta testing, when the data transfer figures are run to determine how much bandwidth needs to be ordered for launch, that executives see the potential cost, realize that bandwidth is going to eat up a bunch of margin points, and turn white with fear.

Thus, one of the first ground rules an executive producer has to lay down is a target goal of how much data is going to be transferred back and forth between the player and the game servers. The bit rate isn't a sexy thing to work on, but there simply must be some common-sense goal to shoot for that won't break the maintenance budget in bandwidth costs after launch. This target can be refined as development proceeds in the testing phase, but not having such a target makes it very likely the game's bandwidth costs will be out of sync with the rest of the budget.

In the US and European markets, a good goal to shoot for is 4–6 kilobits per second (kps)/player or less. You'll find it is difficult to find a living space in that range; several of today's more popular games live in the 8–10kps range. If you can get the bit rate down to 2kps, you're "golden." It's hard to see how that can happen, however, without putting dangerous amounts of data directly into the client, which is just asking for trouble from talented cheaters and hackers. The problem with "golden" is that it's the part of the flame between red and blue.

After you have made your code as elegant, streamlined, and compact as possible, the remaining technique for reducing bit rate is to have some parts of it reside on the client side (each player's computer) instead of on the server side. As code is shifted from server to client, players have access to more critical functions. Most players just want to have fun with your game, but some players would just love to "have fun" with your code. Their definition of "fun" will cost you money and time.

Asian markets generally have more tolerance in bandwidth because the governments there tend to lay a lot of fiber-optic bandwidth and offer price supports to keep it inexpensive. South Korea is the best example of this, and it shows in how Korean PWs use bandwidth for games; the average seems to be a 30MB connection to support a server that can hold 1,000–3,000 simultaneous players. This is also one reason why few Korean games will be appearing in the US market until massive recoding and optimization are done.

Then there is the consideration of the player's connection to the Internet. Hard-core gamers tend to upgrade hardware much faster than moderate or mass-market gamers. In general, they are seeing better Internet performance right now, especially in the US, where less than 8% of households have broadband access as of February 2002. There are plenty of myths abounding about that access, however.

Bandwidth Will Not Save You

Bandwidth: It's a clarion call, a wizard's chant to create the spell of no-lag. All we need is more of that super-big, mystical stuff, "They" say, and all will be well.

More bandwidth, "They" say, translates to more speed for data. You know the line: big pipes, no waiting, and an end to the nefarious lag monster. Imagine 50–80-millisecond latency rates for everyone! We could play all those Internet action games and flight simulators and the frame rate might actually match the data transmission rate.

And cable modems and DSL lines, those deity-blessed saviors known collectively as "broadband," will give us that access, "They" say. Why, as soon as everyone is on a cable modem or DSL line, we'll all experience low ping times, and playing a session of *Quake III* or *UO* will be a lagless exercise worldwide. Broadband, the experts trumpet, shall save us all.

Understand something up-front: What you hear about broadband these days is marketing fluff, and it's about as honest as marketing fluff ever is. That is to say, it is riddled with misdirection, incomplete information, and lies by omission. All the marketers want you to see is the perfect case; the reality of the situation can wait until after you've plunked your money down on the table.

What "They" want you to see and believe is that broadband in the form of cable and DSL will remarkably improve your Internet performance; what "They" don't want you to see is that bandwidth is only one part of the puzzle and that all parts have to be fixed for broadband to have any lasting effect on lag.

If you believe we're saying that certain cable companies, cable access providers, DSL providers, and content providers—the ubiquitous "They"—are fudging the truth about the efficacy of broadband access for their own purposes, score yourself a 10. Let's have a little reality check:

> ➤ Lack of bandwidth alone is not the cause of lag. Yes, lack of adequate bandwidth is a major cause of latency. The US Department of Commerce estimated in 1999 and 2000 that the amount of data sent out over the Internet doubles every 100 days. Compare that to the amount of fiber and copper that is laid on an annual basis and you will find that only about 12.5% of the needed bandwidth is being laid every year.

However, that is not the whole story. Other major contributors to latency include obsolete routers, obsolete and badly configured servers, badly programmed databases and applications on those servers, and the existence of certain critical data-routing chokepoints on the Internet, such as at the metropolitan area Ethernets (MAEs).

What this means, my friends, is that you cannot control lag at the end user's home. It doesn't help just to open the broadband spigot into the home; in fact, without fixing the other parts that create lag, it hurts more than helps. All those additional bits and bytes are going to be crowding the lines at those obsolete routers, badly configured servers, and data chokepoints, and that will just make the problem even worse in the short run. By "that," I mean over the next three to five years, overall lag for the majority of Internet users is actually going to get worse, not better.

If you think lag during multiplayer games is bad now, just wait two years.

➤ Massively multiplayer (MMP) games can and will take advantage of broadband to reduce lag. We're not talking about a one-time shot of 20k of data from a web page, which can then be cached and redisplayed. PWs (and retail hybrids such as *Tribes* and *Quake III*) are dynamic; the information needed, such as player locations or the effects of combat or magic, changes quickly.

It can be bad trying to shoot out data for a twitch game such as *Quake*. With massively multiplayer games (MMGs) such as *EQ* and *Air Warrior*, significant lag can be—and usually is—caused by the backend server programming. Look at it this way: If 1,000 simultaneous users are sending in commands to the server, and those commands each effect anywhere from 1–50 other players, the amount of data that has to be correlated and sent back out is tremendous. At the risk of making some enemies, most programmers in the MMG arena haven't been doing it very long, and they can be sloppy about how much data needs to be transferred in these situations.

In other words, this is a technical design issue, not a broadband access issue. Just opening up the bandwidth pipe is less effective than improving the programming on the game's server or PC client. In most MMGs today, much more data than necessary is being transferred. This may be one of the easier problems to solve, although it won't help that much if Internet lag is still bad, which it will be for some time to come. Read on.

➤ Cable modems can deliver speeds of up to 100 times standard telephone modems. Well, yes, they can—occasionally—on a perfect day, in a perfect situation, if you are the only person on the line, or if you wave a dead chicken over the cable modem and invoke the correct spirits, and if other factors outside the user's control don't intervene.

Sarcasm aside, a cable modem is a pretty good deal—right now. This will not last. Unlike DSL, in which you lease a certain portion of bandwidth that only you have access to, cable modem users share the bandwidth. The usual configuration is 500 users to a neighborhood "head end," sharing something like 10MB of bandwidth. Now, if only you and a couple other people are using that bandwidth, which is the case today at many head ends, you can get pretty good performance on downloads. I know; I've used cable modems more than once since 1998 and I love them for pure downloads, especially late at night. I can grab a 30MB file in 5–8 minutes.

But imagine the situation two or three years from now, when all 500 slots on your head end are filled, with all those people downloading huge movie files and MP3s and 30–200MB game demos. Ten megabytes divided by 500 equals 20,000, according to my calculator. That's about 20k in tech-speak, give or take some hexadecimal reasoning. When that happens, you'll long for the days when you had 56k worth of bandwidth all to yourself.

This is a shell game with rapidly diminishing returns. The cable providers know this and they hope you are not smart enough to realize it. This is one of the reasons why they are so resistant to open the lines to other ISPs, such as AOL and Earthlink. If all those millions of users clog the cable lines too soon, their best marketing fluff blows away like a dandelion on the wind. This is also why they are placing governors on their systems already, so they can limit how much bandwidth you actually use. They are also quietly altering their user agreements to note that they can limit your bandwidth use at any time, for any reason.

➤ DSL is a good alternative to cable modem access. Well, it would be, if the stupidly greedy telephone companies would drop the price today. Right now, it costs about $40 a month for a DSL line that provides about 360k of bandwidth into the home and about 128k of uploading from the home to the Internet. This is not that great a deal. Even though you don't have to share that bandwidth with 500 other subscribers, it's only about six times as much download power as you get from a 56k modem, and you still have to deal with the traffic jams elsewhere on the Internet. As a result, DSL users are starting to see traffic jams at trunks, those nexus points where many telephone lines come together.

However, two or three (or five) years from now, when the cable lines are clogged like an 80-year-old saturated fat eater's arteries, this could be a great deal—*if* the stupidly greedy telephone companies don't raise the price after a few hundred thousand users subscribe to it, which is exactly what they did with ISDN broadband lines. This is why ISDN hasn't grown into the millions of users the phone companies predicted five years ago.

So before you plop down $40 or more a month for broadband access in the expectation of superior gaming, understand this: Broadband will not save you—not for a long while anyway, and not until a lot of routers and servers are replaced with newer equipment, pressure is relieved at the chokepoints of the Internet, and more programmers learn how to code games for more economical data transfer. Yes, you probably will see a performance increase, but it will not be the Nirvana-like experience promised, and it will get worse over time as more people subscribe to broadband outlets.

What does all this mean? It means that programming a game (or web site) to appeal to broadband users is going to actually cost you more in bandwidth. If you are willing to suck up this cost and can afford to pay for it, that's one thing. Just make sure you go in with your eyes open; more data transfer might make for a better online game, but it also might drain your pocketbook faster than you expected.

Co-Locate Your Servers or Set Up a Big Farm at Home?

Where to place your servers is a question you need to consider because it will have an impact on how much physical space you need and how many operations employees you need to hire to launch. If you're planning on being published/hosted by a third-party publisher, you'll want to know how they do it because it will have an impact on their bottom expenses.

To "co-locate" simply means to place your hardware at someone else's network operations centers (NOCs). The big Internet backbone providers, like Sprint and Exodus, have them all over the country and either own NOCs internationally or have cut deals with firms overseas to provide that capacity.

This one is a toss-up and may depend greatly on whether you're going after an international market right away or sticking with home territory for a while. You can see examples of both methods in the US: EA's *UO* co-locates servers in each US time zone and in the international territories it services, and Sony Online Entertainment's *EQ* uses one large farm in San Diego for US players.

Another major tradeoff here is in the potential for player-side lag versus close-at-home control of the hardware. By co-locating hardware at the NOCs of a major backbone provider, you give the option to the player to reduce the overall number of Internet data transfer hops from home to a game server, which generally reduces lag time.

The big issue is cost. Setting up your own NOC can be expensive, and not just in hardware, software, building a clean room to house the servers, and leasing bandwidth to connect it to the Internet. You also have to have operations people to monitor the NOC 24/7/365 and fix problems as they arise. At a bare minimum, you need at least 6 people to cover the 21 8-hour shifts in a standard work week, and that doesn't take into account vacations, sick time, or emergencies like having to take the dog to the vet or picking up ill children from school. Most companies try to slide by this by having the servers page an on-call operator at home if they go down, but this works about as well as you'd expect; in the truly critical incidents, when thousands of customers can't connect to the servers, the Law of the General Perversity of the Universe dictates that the server paging software will fail. This is especially true on holidays, patch days, and for highly anticipated scheduled events in a game.

Co-locating at a backbone NOC can solve many of these problems. It isn't a fail-safe solution, but at least you don't have to build a NOC; you can spend that money on operators to watch the servers and correct problems.

Player Hardware and Software

While choosing which player hardware configurations and operating software will work with the game software may seem like shooting ducks in a barrel, it is actually one of the toughest issues to address, due to the speed with which PC technology changes. One almost has to have a crystal ball to know what the standards will be in 24 to 36 months.

Push the Envelope or Design for Today's RAM and Processor Standard Configurations?

There has been constant growth in personal computing power over the years. About every 18 months to 2 years, CPUs take a 50–100% leap in processing speed and the standard amount of RAM pre-installed in new PCs seems to increase, although standard installed RAM has been slowing down of late and there are some early indications that processing speed is reaching a plateau as well.

In the late months of 2002, the standard configuration for new PCs seemed to be a 1-GHz Pentium processor, 128MB of RAM, and a video accelerator card with 32MB of video RAM. A "buffed out" game machine is a 1.2- to 2-GHz Pentium processor, 512MB to 1GB of RAM, and a video card with 64–128MB of video RAM. If the trend continues as in the past, today's buffed out machine will become the standard configuration sometime in late 2003 or early 2004.

To date, the habit in the industry has been to push the technical envelope as far as it can be pushed and still have an audience with the computing power to buy and run the game. Up through 2001, almost every new online game required an upgrade of the processor, RAM, video card, or all three, to get the fullest measure of the game. This is the "hardcore" or early adopter model of gaming (see the player market definitions in Chapter 1, "The Market"), appealing to those with the money and inclination to spend on gaming.

So, Who Are You Designing For?

The problem with the early adopter model is that it tends to limit your potential audience to that 10% of the market; most people aren't willing to spend a lot of money upgrading their hardware just to play a game. This is why it is so important to select, early in the process, which market niche(s) you'll be appealing to with your online game. If you're going after the sweet spot of the hard-core market, then you'll definitely want to anticipate what the buffed out PC configuration will be as you enter public Beta testing and take every advantage of the capabilities of those machines.

If you want to spread subscriptions among two or more of the niches, however, you'll need to scale back your aspirations and design either for the buffed out machine of today or, if you hope to have a mass-market product, design for today's standard configuration.

Broadband or Narrowband Access?

Over 90% of the world is still using 56k dial-up for access, and that figure is not likely to change significantly in the next two to three years; why would you limit your market by designing now for broadband access only?

Designing for broadband will likely cost you more in bandwidth leasing after launch than you planned for. If you plan to scale your game to broadband needs, be prepared to open your checkbook a bit wider. Also consider what broadband scaling might do to the RAM and processor speed requirements of your game servers; with all that extra data flowing back and forth, you'll probably want to increase both to prevent as many bottlenecks as possible.

Never Forget: The Client Is in the Hands of the Enemy

There is a phrase used quite a bit in the online game development industry: *The client is in the hands of the enemy.* The first known public use of it was in 1989 by Kelton Flinn of Kesmai, after a cheat hack of the *Air Warrior* player client appeared on the GEnie online service.

The phrase is not exactly a secret among developers; we've all heard it multiple times at conventions or seen it used in email or in developer message groups. Before the popularity of Internet auction sites, cheat hacks such as this were done purely for the twisted need to win at all costs, or because players got tired of getting their heads handed to them by other players. These folks were containable for the most part because there were only a few of them, and gamer populations were small compared to today.

Now that use of the Internet has exploded and web auction services such as eBay exist, there is a whole new incentive to cheat. One can make a tidy sum auctioning off items or characters in an online game. Some buffed out characters with lots of loot have sold for $3,000 and more on eBay. One company started by a couple of enterprising young capitalists once claimed to be making $400,000 a year selling *UO* characters and items. This is not chump change. It has become such a part of the current gaming culture that one of these companies is unabashedly suing Mythic Entertainment over halting their eBay auctions of *Dark Age of Camelot* items and characters.

The "enemy" phrase was not meant as an insult to players, but as a warning to front-end client developers: Once you distribute the front-end client, the enemy has access to it, not just the good guys. It says, "If you leave important, modifiable information in the client, the modification of which would give an individual an advantage over other players, it will be modified." It is a clarion call to make sure you don't leave important information on the client, to protect the integrity of the game for the 99.9% of your players who will never attempt to hack you.

It's significantly worse in these Internet days, as it is pretty easy to acquire software that can sniff the data packets going in and out of a modem. All it takes is one pretty decent code mechanic to sniff the packets, decrypt them if necessary, write an application to use that information in some way, and voilà! You have interesting little applications like *ShowEQ* or *UO Extreme* that give some players a huge advantage over everyone else.

This kind of thing isn't just a headache for developers. Such activities have a debilitating effect on legitimate players; if others are speed-hacking or exploiting holes and bugs to build characters or monopolize rare or necessary game items, denying others a fair chance to succeed and build their own legends, the honest players tend to get mad, then discouraged, and leave the game for more congenial—and secure—playgrounds. This is a hit directly on your pocketbook.

The prudent course of action, then, is to keep as much of the game as possible on the server side of the process and as little as necessary on the client. As we said previously, streamlining your code to lower the bit rate is good. Lowering the bit rate by putting important, modifiable information on a few hundred thousand PCs (remember, whatever dangers it comes with, wide distribution of the client is your goal) means that somewhere, someone is going to "have a little fun" with your code—then they are going to tell their very best gamer buddies. The next thing you know, you are on the wrong end of an expensive lesson in exponential growth.

You also need to make sure your monitoring and security tools are in place at launch because you can't possibly catch every bug or exploit.

Localization: Talk to Me, Baby!

Developers and publishers are starting to realize that Internet gaming is a truly global market. The example of NCSoft's *Lineage: The Bloodpledge* in South Korea, which has some 5% of the country's total population playing that one game, opens whole new vistas for gaining new subscribers. It also opens up a whole new set of problems, not the least of which is the localization of language to allow conversations in the local tongue. Thankfully, there is a solution to make such localizations easier: Unicode.

What Unicode does is provide a unique number for every character in virtually every human language used on computers today, as well as some historic and classic languages. These numbers are platform- and program-agnostic, meaning they work on just about every computer and software application imaginable. The Unicode standard currently supports over 94,000 characters, and its implementation is controlled by the non-profit Unicode Consortium.[2]

The beauty of Unicode is that when it's implemented on a client/server basis, it becomes much easier to implement new languages, especially if you keep as much display text as possible on the server (always a good idea for an online game, as it is much easier to add and modify text on the server than on the player's client, which requires a download patch).

There are other solutions available to use in place of or in conjunction with Unicode, such as the enterprise translation software provided by Systran Software,[3] but establishing a facility among your developers with Unicode seems to provide the most cost-effective and useful solution overall.

Which Languages, Then?

Which languages to support at launch depends on the publisher's willingness to branch out into the territories. We recommend the following as a minimum set to be supported, as it covers the most active online gaming populations in the world (as well as most of the world's population):

---

2. See the Unicode Consortium's web site at www.unicode.org/ for membership details. Membership is not free, but it is low cost ($2,000 per year or less for most corporations and commercial enterprises).

3. See www.systransoft.com/ for information.

> ➤ English

> ➤ French

> ➤ German

> ➤ Spanish

> ➤ Korean

> ➤ Chinese

> ➤ Japanese

Customer Support: Dude, Where's My Tools?

One of the reasons online games have lousy reputations for CS is because, so far, they have tended to *have* lousy CS. One of the reasons for this is because development teams neither design nor build tools to facilitate the process. In most cases, lip service to the concept may be expressed, but what the CS reps end up with is whatever the developers use to check and manipulate character stats, abilities, and inventory via the database. If tools are actually designed during the game and technical design document stage, they are almost always the first features cut when crunch time hits.

Quite aside from the incredibly scary and non-secure concept of giving lots of employees access to modify pretty much anything in the game database, there are important tools needed by GMs, account reps, and technical support folks—tools the game as a service just cannot function without. See Part III, "Launching and Managing a Game," for more information. Among the more important tools and commands normally left out are these:

> ➤ **Kick out and ban**—There are always "bad actors" in any online game, and this is not a reference to poor role-playing technique. Grief players, jerks, chat spammers, bug exploiters, and racial harassers will all make appearances. GMs need a way to kick these players out of the game and lock their accounts from access to the game. This should be a minimum, default power of all GMs and game management personnel. Amazingly, most games have to retrofit the command in after launch.

➤ **Squelch or mute**—Simply turning off a player's ability to chat with other players in the game for a time works wonders for calming down the temporarily deranged player, unhinged by a frustrating experience or just having a bad day. Use of a "Mute" command can prevent the need to simply ban a player from the game, which is a touchy situation in the best of times.

➤ **Account management**—Billing and account management people need to be able to look up billing histories, access a player's name, address, and phone, make reimbursements and charge-backs, and so forth. You'd be surprised at how many games launch with a billing module that was built, literally, two days before launch day. You would not be amazed at how unstable such a module is, with only two days of thought and coding put into it. For example, Funcom's *AO* launched with a web page billing module that didn't use secure socket layers, basically opening subscribers' credit card numbers to any so-called script kiddie or bush-league hacker with the proper—and easily available—script. This deficiency was corrected quickly, but you can imagine the public relations nightmare it created.

➤ **The harassment button**—As discussed earlier, there is a portion of the online population that thinks nothing of harassing other players "verbally" in the game, simply for their own amusement or to take advantage of the anonymity of the Internet to act out their "anger issues." This most often takes the form of racial- or gender-based slurs, extreme profanity, or simply "spamming" the screens of everyone in the local gameplay region to prevent anyone from holding a public conversation.

If the live team doesn't put a clamp on this type of activity from the outset, the game can quickly become inhospitable to the average player and drive him/her to the competition. Since no one can afford to have enough personnel on-board to monitor all conversations and nip this in the bud, clamping down is tough if you don't give the players a tool to record and report harassment. At a minimum, this tool should grab the reporting player's last two to five minutes of chat and activities logs and send them as an email to your support team for later investigation.

Chapter 8

Getting into the Design

KEY TOPICS

- Acquisition and Retention Features

- The Themis Group Player Satisfaction Matrix

- The Critical "New Player Experience"

- It's the Socialization, Stupid!

- The Importance of (the Other Guy's) Storytelling

- World-Building: Just What Is "Content," Anyway?

"(Design) teams regularly bite off more than they can chew. An MMP can easily become an impossible-to-complete reality simulator."

Richard Garriott

"They (design teams) underestimate the complexity of the task. More moving parts drive complexity nonlinearly, and MMP games have a lot of moving parts. Rule of thumb: An MMP game is three times bigger than a standalone game, but 10 times harder to complete."

Gordon Walton

These comments by Richard and Gordon express a fairly common theme we found among the experienced people we interviewed for this book. Design teams tend to walk nose-first into a wall of complexity by trying to shove every feature they can into a game or by not fully understanding, at the start of the process, the complexity of the interlinking among the game mechanics, player skills, and attributes, the player-manipulable objects, and the fields that can modify the objects and players themselves. Much of this comes from not actually completing the game design before major coding begins; designers rarely move into development with a full and clear understanding of just what the player experience will be on a day-in, day-out basis over a long stretch of time.

The other major contributor to over-complexity is that designers can rarely articulate just who, exactly, the game is being built for. If you ask that question, the answer you're likely to hear is, "Uh, the hard-core gamer." If you ask a designer to define who the hard-core gamer is and why he/she should pay money for this game, you'll see a lot of finger-pointing at *EverQuest (EQ)* and *Ultima Online (UO)*, without much substantive detail. They instinctively understand that they don't know who the real customer will be and, to make up for that lack, they cram in every feature they can think of or have seen in another game. Designers who do not have a clear idea of what their target player's profile is—especially designers who are inexperienced in a commercial atmosphere—are liable to revert to this shotgun approach when they would benefit more from marksmanship.

The solution to this problem is a relatively easy one, but it does require an experienced producer or executive producer to exercise "tough love" right from the start of the design process:

➤ Make the design team list the acquisition and retention features for each customer niche, including feature sets that take into account the calendar lifecycle of each niche.

➤ Require the team to prioritize those features for development.

➤ Make the team dig in with a cutting tool and trim the set down to a list that it believes doesn't require divine intervention to complete before the new millennium.

➤ Go through the list yourself, reprioritize the features, and make the team defend why each feature should be in the game.

We guarantee it will be a sobering exercise, at the least. It will probably also create some true anger among some members of the design team, which is where the tough love comes in. As a team leader, you'll probably have to cut one or more features that the team considers crucial or to which they have formed an emotional attachment. Be ready for histrionics and fireworks,[1] and use the tools and information in this book to back up your decisions.

---

1. It may seem that throughout this book that we're hard or "down" on designers and design teams. In truth, we are, but not out of any disrespect for individuals or their responsibilities. To make these things work right, they have to be the brightest, most educated, and versatile people in the process. Designers have the hardest job in the industry because, at the end of the day, the game succeeds or fails financially and as a *game* by what they do. If you think having $10 million in development funds and the jobs of 30-50 on your shoulders is an easy responsibility to carry, you're in the wrong business.

Acquisition and Retention Features

"I try and think of what every feature does in terms of acquisition and retention. More specifically, I try and rationalize every feature on how it ties a player to (1) other people within the game environment and/or (2) an in-game reminder of a valuable game accomplishment. There are dozens of other variables, but these are the big-ticket items in my opinion."

Gordon Walton

Most computer and video games have only one distribution problem: how to acquire customers—that is, how to get the customers to walk into a store and buy the box. This includes retail hybrids, as most publishers don't provide an online distribution or multiplayer support solution for customers; they depend on the players to do that for themselves, or for one of several online hybrid gaming portals such as GameSpy or The Zone to do it for them. In neither case does online in-game support become a factor. Hybrids today are a product, but they are not yet a full service in most aspects.

Online games in the persistent world (PW) category, being both a product and a service, have a unique problem: They not only have to acquire customers, but they also have to retain them. If a subscription fee is involved, the retention factors have to work for a minimum of some months or, preferably, years.

It makes plain sense, then, to know just who it is you want to play and pay for the game and what features those people want that will keep them coming back month after month. If you accept the market demographic niche definitions found in Chapter 1, "The Market," you have a pretty good idea of who will pay a subscription fee, who might pay a fee, and who you're going to have a devil of a time getting to pay you a penny.

That puts you halfway home; now you must nail down the details. Before we can really start listing the features, we have to know who we want to, and/or is likely to, play the game after launch.

Prioritizing: Who Are We Designing This Game For?

Design/development teams proposing expensive PW projects tend to engage in a bit of (mostly) unintentional obfuscation toward executives; the teams treat the PW market as a solid whole and fail to mention that there are identifiable sub-populations within the genre. In effect, they engage in lying by omission because they either don't really understand the different sub-populations' motivations or they just assume the executives won't understand the difference between someone whose primary play motivation is hanging out and chatting and one who is going single-mindedly to gather every cool possession in the game.

Some experienced online game designers don't want to admit to the "suits" that there might be a significant percentage of players (25%, in fact) who care as much or more for socializing than about the game or its mechanics. They might put a limit on all of the neat stuff the designers want to load into the game in favor of more chat tools, for instance, and where's the coolness in designing chat tools?

There is nothing wrong with building a PW game that appeals only to one or two of the four main player niches; for example, *EQ* appeals directly to the achiever class of gamer, with a nod or two to the socializers, and one could hardly call that game unsuccessful. To appeal to the broadest possible cross-section of potential subscribers, however, a PW should contain elements that appeal directly to the four main Bartle player types. Before that can happen, everyone—from executives paying the bills to the most junior designer—needs to agree on just what those types are.

Thankfully, a pretty good definition and model set exists, written by the good Dr. Bartle.

The Bartle Player Types

Dr. Richard Bartle was the co-creator of the first MUD in 1978. Over the years, as MUDs proliferated on university mainframes and eventually as commercial products, he noticed certain types of common play behavior in MUDs and made the first attempt to categorize those behaviors. The categories he defined were achiever, explorer, socializer, and killer, and he explained the behavior patterns in an article titled "Hearts, Clubs, Diamonds, Spades: Players Who Suit Muds."[2] The article was first written in 1995 and gained widespread recognition quickly. Over the years, Dr. Bartle has periodically edited and revised the article to keep it current.

---

2. See Dr. Bartle's full article and the new introduction to it in Appendix D; used by permission of the author and *The Journal of Virtual Worlds*.

Here is how Bartle described what he saw:

The four things that people typically enjoy personally about MUDs are:

i)   Achievement within the game context.

Players give themselves game-related goals and vigorously set out to achieve them. This usually means accumulating and disposing of large quantities of high-value treasure, or cutting a swathe through hordes of mobiles (i.e., monsters built into the virtual world).

ii)   Exploration of the game.

Players try to find out as much as they can about the virtual world. Although initially this means mapping its topology (i.e., exploring the MUD's breadth), later it advances to experimentation with its physics (i.e., exploring the MUD's depth).

iii)   Socialization with others.

Players use the game's communicative facilities, and apply the role-playing that these engender, as a context in which to converse (and otherwise interact) with their fellow players.

iv)   Imposition upon others.

Players use the tools provided by the game to cause distress to (or, in rare circumstances, to help) other players. Where permitted, this usually involves acquiring some weapon and applying it enthusiastically to the persona of another player in the game world.

So, labeling the four player types abstracted, we get: achievers, explorers, socializers, and killers.

This was the first attempt to define general player and gameplay types in a virtual world, and these motivations still hold up well in today's market, where games with 20,000–100,000 simultaneous players are no longer unknown or even rare. These types more than adequately explain the gross motivations of the general player base and provide a good framework from which to start designing a massively multiplayer (MMP) game world.

Moreover, players rarely exhibit just one form of play behavior; they tend to mix and match styles and change behaviors over time.

Several years ago, Erwin Andreasen put up on the web a survey of questions, the answers to which would allow MUD and PW players to rate their own play styles and discover how much of their play time was as an achiever, socializer, explorer, or killer. Table 8.1 includes some of the results from the Bartle Quotient Survey[3] on the web, showing how players rate themselves in various combinations of those four general categories created by Dr. Bartle, sorted by response rates, combinations of play in the categories, and percentages of the total respondents. The responses to the survey gives you an inkling of how players see themselves and their own playing styles in PWs.

Table 8.1   Survey Results from "Measuring the Bartle Quotient"

Overall Totals	Combination Play	Combinations of Three
1. E 30% (33967)	1. SE 16% (18043)	1. SEA 12% (13727)
2. S 25% (28027)	2. ES 14% (16549)	2. ESA 10% (12044)
3. K 22% (25016)	3. KA 12% (13760)	3. EAS 9% (10318)
4. A 22% (24916)	4. EA 12% (13606)	4. KAE 6% (7433)
	5. AK 8% (8994)	5. KAS 5% (6327)
	6. AE 7% (7962)	6. AKE 4% (5194)
	7. AS 7% (7960)	7. AES 4% (5180)
	8. KE 5% (6588)	8. ESK 4% (4505)
	9. SA 4% (5554)	9. SEK 3% (4316)
	10. KS 4% (4668)	10. ASE 3% (4312)
	11. SK 3% (4430)	11. KEA 3% (4226)
	12. EK 3% (3812)	12. AKS 3% (3800)
		13. SAE 3% (3741)
		14. ASK 3% (3648)
		15. EAK 2% (3288)
		16. SKE 2% (2835)
		17. AEK 2% (2782)
		18. KSE 2% (2686)
		19. KES 2% (2362)
		20. EKA 1% (2116)
		21. KSA 1% (1982)
		22. SAK 1% (1813)
		23. EKS 1% (1696)
		24. SKA 1% (1595)

From the "Measuring the Bartle Quotient" web site, `http://www.andreasen.org/bartle/`, March 4, 2002 at 2:28pm EST. Abbreviations: E= explorer, S= socializer, A= achiever, and K= killer. The numbers in parentheses represent the total number of respondents scored in that percentile. The Combination Play column represents the total percentage of players scored by combination players, such as socializer/explorers (16% of the total respondents). The Combinations of Three column represents an even finer gradation of play, such as 12% of the total respondents showed elements of socializer, explorer, and achiever in play style. As of the date and time this sample was taken, there had been a total of 111,926 respondents included in this composite.

---

3. All stats used by permission. For more information, see Erwin S. Andreasen's "Measuring the Bartle Quotient" online test at `www.andreasen.org/bartle/`.

Despite the fact that the survey is unscientific, it has been the experience of the authors that these percentages fairly closely match the reality of the customer base in current commercial PWs, with the exception of the "importance" of the killer class of players. The importance of that class has been overblown by a vocal minority and by PvP combat-oriented designers. For example, check out the specific survey results for the top five commercial PWs[4] in Appendix C "The Bartle Quotient Survey and Some Results," and you'll find few people rating themselves as pure killers in most games.

The takeaway from this exercise should be obvious: 55–60% of players in both the general population and those playing for-pay games classify themselves primarily as socializers and explorers. These are people who form and join guilds and teams, spend quite a bit of time in-game chatting or engaging in social events, and wander about the world, exploring its secrets. For three of the five commercial games, 20% or fewer of the players rate themselves as killers, with 26% for *UO* and 25% for *Dark Age of Camelot*, two games that are attractive to the killer class of player due to the faction-based conflict inherent within their designs.

What this says is that, even if you build a game heavily weighted toward the killer classes via PvP and faction or team/guild conflict, chances are you're going to be attractive to only 20–25% of the total player base. The dichotomy of this is that most of the PWs that launched in 2001 or are being developed today for launch in 2002–2003 are heavily weighted in design toward the killer class. This is likely to cause increased churn rates for the socializer and explorer classes, whom the killers look at as their intended victims by virtue of that same design.

Unless you're firmly set on appealing to one player type and you're comfortable with the thought that such a design may greatly limit your subscriber total potential, the idea is to have a balanced design that appeals to a number of player niches.

Features: Acquisition and Retention Over Time

For purposes of the following discussion, we're going to assume that you want to appeal in some fashion to all four Bartle types, in an attempt to maximize the subscriber total of your game.

---

4. *Lineage: The Bloodpledge*, which claims four million subscribers, was not included because fewer than 30 *Lineage* players had rated themselves in the survey at the time the sample was taken.

Now that you have a general idea of the size and scope of the basic customer groups, you can take the design treatment discussed earlier and begin to match up the vision of the game with the features the players will want to have available.

Exactly what those features are, however, is a matter of some controversy within the industry. Some general features that apply to all four player types, such as secure player-owned housing and no-conflict safe zones, are unanimously accepted among the design literati as required to attract and retain customers for the long term. After that general feature set, however, few design teams actually give much thought to applying features to player types. They have a general understanding of the features they want in the game and which features have worked or not worked in other games. They rarely dig very deeply into player needs and motivations or list them out by the Bartle types, or any other analytic measurement for that matter. Thus, the features list tends to be scattered and a bit incoherent for the design as a whole, and that usually comes back to haunt the team later on.

The Themis Group Player Satisfaction Matrix

"As we talked with various developers and publishers," says Alex Macris, CEO of The Themis Group,[5] an online game consulting and full-service support company, "we began to notice a trend: The teams had no firm grasp of who the potential customers were or how their feature set appealed to those customers. They just assumed that everyone played for the same reasons and wanted every possible feature. Trying to make the teams understand the differences between the general player types and what they wanted in a game was frustrating at times."

To get a handle on this problem, Macris devised an unusual and innovative solution. What he realized is that, although many people in the industry knew what the separate features were, no one had taken the time to plot them out in a logical, easy-to-see manner. He also knew that development teams understand issues and concepts best when

---

5. Disclaimer: One of the co-authors, Jessica Mulligan, was president of The Themis Group at the time this book was being written.

arranged as data points in a matrix; trying to just explain features to them as concepts made things more difficult, not less. So he sat down and drew out a basic matrix chart that correlated the Bartle player types against the game features they needed or wanted at various stages in their lifecycle for an online game.

The format Bartle arrived at was one of those simple solutions that the industry has needed but somehow missed for years. Table 8.2 shows how Macris expressed the player lifecycle and satisfaction factors in a simple matrix.

Table 8.2   Basic Player Satisfaction Matrix

Bartle Player Activity Types				
Lifecycle	**Socialization**	**Accomplishment**	**Discovery**	**Conflict**
Confusion (0–1 month)	Features	Features	Features	Features
Excitement (2–4 months)	Features	Features	Features	Features
Involvement (4 months–4+ years)	Features	Features	Features	Features

The Player Satisfaction Matrix is copyright Themis Group 2001–2002 and used with permission.

Down the left side of the matrix are the first three periods of the average player lifecycle, as noted in Chapter 1. Across the top run the major activity types that parallel the four Bartle types: socializers, achievers, explorers, and killers. The boxes that cross-reference each lifecycle period with a player type list the features those players want or need at that stage of their "career" in the game.

What The Themis Group does for a game is first fill in all the relevant features for the "complete" PW, with the features prioritized from highest to lowest needed, as shown in Table 8.3.

Table 8.3 The Player Satisfaction Matrix, First Step

	Socialization (Socializers)	Accomplishment (Achievers)	Discovery (Explorers)	Conflict (Killers)
Confusion (0–1 month)	2. New player greeters	3. New player greeters	3. New player greeters	1. Clear us vs. them hooks
		2. Detailed online game info		
				4. New player greeters
Excitement (2–4 months)	5. Enhanced chat	3. Clear path to growth	2. Exploration is rewarded	1. Team PvP
				3. Grow combat skills
Involvement (5 months–4+ years)	5. Mechanisms for creating social events	4. Quests	2. New lands to explore	2. Faction vs. faction combat
		5. Events	3. New dungeons to explore	

Examining Table 8.3, you'll see at the left are the first three phases of the player lifecycle. At the top are the four main PW player types according to the Bartle index. In each box are the general features each player type needs or wants at each phase of the lifecycle.

Within this matrix, any experienced design team member at Themis can go through the filled-in features boxes and highlight the features that exist in the game, as denoted by the bolded features in Table 8.4.

Table 8.4   The Player Satisfaction Matrix, Partially Filled

	Socialization (Socializers)	Accomplishment (Achievers)	Discovery (Explorers)	Conflict (Killers)
Confusion (0–1 month)	2. New player greeters	3. New player greeters	3. New player greeters	1. Clear us vs. them hooks
		2. Detailed online game info		
				4. New player greeters
Excitement (2–4 months)	5. Enhanced chat	3. Clear path to growth	2. Exploration is rewarded	1. Team PvP
				3. Grow combat skills
Involvement (5 months–4+ years)	5. Mechanisms for creating social events	4. Quests	2. New lands to explore	2. Faction vs. faction combat
		5. Events	3. New dungeons to explore	

When the work is finished, the team has an invaluable tool; it can tell at a glance which features are currently planned or existing in the game and which features are missing for specific player types.

This method has proven to be of enormous help in focusing design and development on just what should be in a game at launch to help acquire subscribers and which features are needed to retain subscribers long term but can be added at a later date, say, through an expansion pack or server-side patch.

The trick is to know what feature set is needed for your game to function competitively at a base level in the marketplace and build from there. Table 8.5 is a partial list of features we believe necessary for the acquisition and retention of subscribers at all levels, from hard-core gamers to mass-market non-players. Bear in mind that while many acquisition features are also retention features, a retention feature does not always work for acquisition.

Table 8.5 Basic Acquisition and Retention Features

Acquisition	Retention
Easy to install	**Technical stability**
Easy to register account	Servers up 95%+ of time
Cutting-edge graphics	Client doesn't crash
Easy-to-use interface	Patches are stable
Easy to get started	**Player-owned housing**
New player help	Individual housing
Intuitive game play	Guild/team halls
Rapid rewards at beginning	**Advanced social features**
Character individuality	Player-configured chat channels
Multiple races	Guild/team/race channels
Alter size/shape of body	Regular guild/team events
Many apparel options	**Frequent content addition**
Many combat & trade skills	Expansion packs
Make/sell items	Content downloads
Learn new skills over time	Player-created content

The Critical "New Player Experience"

Designers love complexity; nothing gives them more of a sense of satisfaction than watching interlocking game mechanics work together or providing an interface that can do anything and everything, including walking the dog and making coffee. There is also an element of competition among designers to provide more features than the previous guy did, under the assumption that more is better.

What many designers forget to plan for is how long it will take a new player to learn how to operate the necessary features in a game compared to the average new player's patience level. Designers play games for years before they get the financial go-ahead to work on their own game. Then they spend dozens of months building their game. Naturally, they know how everything works (or how everything is supposed to work). By the time they get funding approved for their game, they are strangers to the sense of wonder and frustration that a new player experiences.

Space shuttles are wonderful, but the number of people qualified to pilot them is small. The average middle-school youngster could drive you to a hospital ER these days— seat, mirror, ignition, gas, brakes (maybe), and you're there. If a new player has to be fairly adept at using most of the capabilities in your everything-under-the-sun feature set to grow a character's stamina, wealth, skills, and so forth fairly quickly in the game world, then the only players your game will retain over time will be from the hard-core segment. Remember: These customers are not buying a car for $15,000—they're test-driving a virtual world that costs $25–$50 to enter and $12.95 a month to rent a life in (and you're giving them the first month's rent as an incentive to stay). You have 30 days, and often less time than that, in which to hook them.

Having nothing but hard-core players can still be a winning formula, assuming that within the next 3–5 years, nobody develops an interface that walks the dog, makes coffee, kills spiders, and then takes out the garbage. If you could keep 50% of the hard-core gamers playing your PW for a year, someone would probably come along and try to seduce your shuttle pilots with their newer, better feature set and interface. As you will see, what you drive is important (getting there may be fully half of the fun, indeed), but so are where you go, what you do when you get there, and with whom.

Another thing that is often ignored is whether the new player experience is compelling enough and entertaining enough to make the player stick around, or whether it is a frustrating experience that causes him/her to churn[6] out and go looking for entertainment elsewhere.

The quality of the new player experience is your key retention factor. The player has already decided to try you out; if he/she can't figure out the interface easily, or the environment is so hostile the player can't succeed at something early on, you'll probably lose the player in the first month. Historically, the churn rate of new players from online games, after garnering the hard-core players in the first three months of the game being available, is well over 80%, and in some cases, exceeds 90%. Overall, long-term retention (two months or more) varies, but 40% retention of all those who try the game is pretty standard.

There are a number of reasons for this churn; fixing these reasons during the design phase should be of paramount concern. Following are some of the worst offenses:

> **Complexity of the interface**—If the client interface is cumbersome to use, employs non-standard commands or methods for everyday issues, or employs so many buttons and capabilities that even a shuttle pilot would have trouble figuring out how to use it effectively, you can expect only a small, dedicated core of players to bother learning it.

---

6. "Churn" stands for "change-turn." It is most often used in the industry to describe players who change from customers into non-customers.

➤ **Complexity of the game mechanics**—Sure, lots of interlocking moving parts are cool and represent a triumph of design; they also tend to limit your subscriber base to those players with the determination and sheer grit to work through them. Experience has shown that this is a limited market. It is fine if your game world is interesting enough that hard-core players spend time on Internet sites sharing special hard-won information, but new players should not need to go to those sites to master the basics quickly.

➤ **A hostile new player environment**—If the new player represents nothing more than a crunchy snack to experienced players, or NPCs, or the environment, you can expect a lot of churn. For example, *UO*'s environment on launch was completely hostile to new players because player killers (PKs) had free rein. Those who were trying the game tended to get "ganked" by the PKs repeatedly. This is not conducive to creating "fun" in the minds of most players and caused tremendous churn from *UO* in the early days. It was only when EA reined in the PKs and provided more of a safe haven to allow the new players to get to know the game that subscription growth began to rise again. It is important to provide protection to the new player, to allow him/her to get to know the game and learn how to gain protection.

➤ **An unsatisfying initial experience**—If the new player can't achieve something memorable pretty quickly or be rewarded in some fashion, the game is simple drudgery and unentertaining. Some quick reward, one that preferably teaches something about the game or interface, can provide an accomplishment "hit" and keep the player hooked for more. SSI's old Gold Box series of *Advanced Dungeons & Dragons (AD&D)* computer games solved this one by starting the level-one characters within a few points of level two and advancing the player within minutes of starting through some simple, easily completed actions.

➤ **A lack of information or training in-game, in context**—Most players never read the game manual; they just jump right in and start playing. If they can't figure out how things work or have easy access to that information in-game, they are soon gone to try the next guy's product. Our history has been that we tend to dump the new players into our complex games without even an interactive tutorial to get them started; we just leave them to sink or swim on their own. The first game to actually provide a tutorial was *AC*; players were led through a series of training actions to get to know simple commands such as walking, running, chatting with other players, arming weapons, and so on. Few online games since have followed this example, though one or two have retrofitted tutorials post-launch.

Additional devices, such as interactive tutorials, tool tips, NPCs standing at new player entry points to provide information, or even human players or gamemasters (GMs) to provide an immediate welcome and offer of help, are not luxuries anymore. Some of the other factors that are listed, such as the complexity of the interface and game mechanics, can be blunted with thoughtful and timely tutorials, training, and assistance to the new player.

Consider every feature you want to design into the game as a potential block to new subscribers, and make sure you build in mechanisms to let the new player learn the basics quickly and easily and survive long enough to start enjoying the game.

It's the Socialization, Stupid!

In the end, an online game is really just a mechanism to allow players to socialize in a context. In the industry, we are fond of saying, "They come for the game and stay for the socialization." There is more than a little truth to that statement. Past a certain point in a player's "career" in a game, being with friends and associates online is more important than the game itself, or at least equally important. If both elements aren't present, the player really has no reason to stick around.

This has manifested itself in the form of guilds and teams that stay together for years and sometimes move from game to game as whole entities if they find a game offering better tools for socialization and togetherness that enhance the bonds players form. Many designers go wrong by assuming that the gameplay will always be the primary reason for being there and pay more attention to adding content than to refining tools for establishing and maintaining social bonds.

All Players Socialize...

So why aren't developers building better socialization tools? For games that depend on good communications and affiliations between the players, the industry seems to have real trouble coming up with decent chat and teaming tools. They are so bad, in fact, that most people use a third-party tool, such as AOL's Instant Messenger (AIM) or ICQ, for in-game communications whenever possible.

This has been an issue for something as basic as chatting, as some games, such as Sony Online's popular *EQ*, used to take over the main loop of the computer and prevent the game from being windowed or the use of <ALT+TAB> to toggle out to a separate application such as AIM or ICQ. This was done for security reasons (it is easier to hack a client that can be run in the background and allow the use of other applications), but with in-game chat tools being, on the whole, so bad compared to the third-party utilities, it makes it more difficult for players to coordinate among themselves.[7]

Interface designers need to take fully into account the need of the players to socialize and communicate on a variety of levels—from two people whispering to private team communications—and build such tools into a game from the outset.

Robust Chat Tools

Many games still hearken back to their text MUD roots and require players to use "slash" commands to talk (they need to type the slash character (/) to communicate or issue special commands). In these days of graphic point-and-click interfaces, this seems absurd and is yet another indication that designers and developers tend to build games for themselves, not for the players.

If you want to know what an in-game chat utility should look like, look at some good models that already exist: the interfaces and feature sets of AOL's Instant Messenger and ICQ. Most of the features of these chat utilities are not very difficult to implement, and they center on the twin concepts of ease-of-use and being intuitive/easy-to-learn.

Some games with fairly good chat tools include *Asheron's Call (AC)* and *Anarchy Online (AO)*; they allow not only the use of standard MUD "slash" commands, but they also use a point-and-click interface as an alternative method.

Figure 8.1 is an example of *AC*'s chat bar. Clicking on the Chat button at the lower left allows the player to assign another player as the default recipient.

---

7. Sony Online is making a run at fixing this problem for their games. They launched their own version of Instant Messaging software for *EQ* in late 2002, and one can assume that *Star Wars Galaxies*, scheduled for an early 2003 launch, will either have IM software at launch or shortly thereafter. *EQ* also now supports windowed mode.

Figure 8.1 The *AC* chat bar, located at the bottom left of the screen.

Figure 8.2 shows a different chat method used by Electronic Arts' *The Sims Online*, known as "barking." The chat text is typed in by the player and then displayed near or above the player who is "speaking."

Figure 8.2   The chat method of *The Sims Online*. Note that what the player types appears over the head in a balloon. This is known in the industry as "barking chat."

At minimum, your chat tools should allow players to do the following:

➤ Chat locally with other players in the same general game locale, be this line of sight or a set region. (This is generally the default in a game.)

➤ Chat globally with one specific player in the game (generally known as a "whisper").

➤ Chat globally with team or guild members only.

➤ Create a private channel for two or more players to chat globally.

Other features may be added at your discretion, but each should allow the player more freedom to create customized chat groups and, in general, make communication easier, not more difficult to use or understand.

Full-Featured Guild/Team Organization Commands at Launch

The capabilities to form and control permanent guilds and create temporary teams on-the-fly (usually for a limited game session to hunt, share loot, and experience awards) are going to appeal to the core, critical mass of your game players. Of all the games launched since 1997, only two have had good and fairly easy-to-use guild/teaming tools: *UO* and *AC*. Other games have managed to get them in place some time after launch, but this is the band-aid approach; the many players looking for team support at the outset may have already left to find another community for themselves and their friends.

Guilds should have some inherent advantages, such as the ability to contribute to a common fund of equipment or game "gold," share or designate player-owned housing as a guild hall to store extra equipment for common use, and have private chat channel capability (if the use of private channels is not inherent within the game).

These commands are important because they allow existing micro-communities to support themselves and recruit new members; they are both acquisition and retention tools in that sense.

At an absolute minimum, your guild commands should include the following. Note that the term "guild" used here can also mean any form of permanent team structure, such as a squadron in a flight simulator:

➤ Create a guild (using some minimum number of members to allow the formation, or you'll end up with 50,000 of them; we recommend a minimum of 10 members to allow creation).

➤ Name the guild—You might want to consider a profanity filter for this one.

➤ Invite a new member.

➤ Approve a membership request—If a player requests entry into the guild, this command approves that request.

➤ Deny request—Denies membership to a player who has requested it.

➤ Expel a member from the guild.

➤ Create and/or name guild rankings and/or titles—Players love to be able to rank or title themselves inside their micro-community. This capability is usually left to the guild leader or three or four appointed guild members.

➤ Request membership in a guild—A player can request to be admitted to a guild.

➤ Accept membership—If a guild leader extends an invitation to a player, he/she uses this command to accept the invitation and become a guild member.

➤ Leave a guild—A current member leaves his/her current guild affiliation.

➤ Disband the guild—The guild leader disbands the guild and all members are automatically expelled.

➤ Transfer leadership—The current guild leader transfers that status to a different player.

➤ Designate a guild hall—Allows a player to designate his/her housing (if it exists in the game) as a guild hall or house, allowing guild members to enter and leave at will.

You probably can't go overboard in providing customization or utilization commands to guilds or teams. This is the heart of the game for these players; anything that allows the heart to beat more efficiently becomes a retention feature.

Other Tools That Foster Micro-Communities

Since the presence of micro-communities such as guilds and teams is critical to a PW game's success, plan extensive features that speak directly to their needs. Following are some of these needs:

➤ **Team housing**—Teams like to have a secure, private space to gather to plan missions, train new members, be safe from the opposition (be it other teams or game monsters), and store excess inventory items for later use by the "extended family." Few PWs have had this feature at launch, although many games, seeing the effect housing has had in other games, are now in the process of adding it.

If you really want to go all out, make sure you have several different sized houses available, from cottage-sized rooms for smaller teams to multi-story structures capable of housing goods for dozens of players. Teams grow and shrink over time and have different housing needs; they also like the accomplishment of upgrading housing for "snob appeal" reasons.

➤ **Multiplayer/multilocation inventory storage**—Houses are great retention and acquisition features, but they suffer from being fixed locations in what is probably a large world. At some point, team members generally end up scattered across the world for various periods of time, with only limited access to the team's shared inventory. Creating some form of sharable storage lockers in various locations allows teams to explore the world and set up caches for later use. As socializing and exploring make up over 50% of PW players' gaming style and preferences, this does a lot to facilitate their play and overall satisfaction.

➤ **Team-based events and quests**—The events portion of this feature will be discussed more fully later. However, if your game includes a mechanism to provide dynamic quest/mission generation and/or adventures, don't neglect to build in parameters and rewards that provide clear benefits to those who successfully perform them collectively. Teams don't just gab among themselves; they also want to accomplish things together. Give them that opportunity.

➤ **Special team chat commands**—Like a moderator for a web chat, team leaders occasionally find it useful to be able to gag some team members, turn off speaking ability in a channel for all but the leader(s) for mission coordination purposes, or even boot rowdy or uncooperative members from a team chat channel. Providing these capabilities is one of those extra touches that teams talk about with non-subscribers, and good word of mouth is what this industry is all about—sometimes.

The Importance of (the Other Guy's) Storytelling

This is another one of those sections that would require its own 350-page book to really define, explain, and provide advice on how to do it correctly. That isn't possible here. What we can do is give you some general guidelines on what to avoid and a few examples to illustrate those points. Anything deeper is going to have to wait for another time and another book.

At the 2002 Game Developer's Conference, an audience member asked the panel on "Building the Next-Generation PW" how he, as a writer, could ensure the integrity of his story in a PW. The reply came from panel member Raph Koster, the creative director on *Star Wars Galaxies* and former lead designer of *UO*: "Get over yourselves; the rest of the world is coming. Okay? People value self-expression. Is 'story' going to go away? No. Is careful crafting going to go away? No. Are the professionals engaged in that going to go away? No. Well, except that IP—the concept of intellectual property—may, but that's a whole other side discussion. The thing is that people want to express themselves and they don't really care that 99% of everything is crap, because they are positive that the 1% they made isn't. Okay? And fundamentally, they get ecstatic as soon as five people see it, right?"

This illustrates just one of the habits picked up from the designers of standalone games: the need to tell a linear story. To put it another way, linear stories can be a good thing in a standalone game, but it is never a good idea in an online game, if that's all you have. There is also the issue of self-expression, which Raph nailed in his response and which many online designers ignore or forget.

Designers also have the mistaken impression that they *have* to tell a story and guide the ignorant and silly player through it step by step to a logical conclusion. Few players want a linear story, and even fewer of them want you, as the designer, to tell the entire story; what they want you to do is give them an environment within which to act: set the stage, provide the props, speak the first paragraph, and then sit back and watch while they provide the middle and end of the tale.

In other words, players are there to create their own legends and tell their own stories, both as individuals and as part of group; they are there to interact with the world, not solely to have the world act upon them. It doesn't make a lot of sense to spend inordinate amounts of time and resources building tools to allow the designers to tell an ongoing but hermetic story after launch, when what many players want are the tools to create and tell their own stories.

Note that providing a background story, the history of events, politics, diplomacy, and so on in your world to date is an absolute must, if only to assist the player in suspending disbelief and deriving more entertainment value from your game. There is also nothing wrong with providing ongoing events and situations that the players can pick up on and run with. This involves some work and resources on your end, but can be hugely popular with the players, provided they are "winnable." Don't fall into the trap of setting up a huge scenario with only one possible outcome, regardless of player actions, such as co-author Jessica Mulligan did with the Trinsic city siege in *UO* in

1999. The players don't like them and, more importantly, they find ways to block that one possible outcome, requiring you to use *force majeure* to settle the issue.[8] This leaves an incredibly bad taste in the mouths of the players.

Mostly, though, the players want to create their own fun and stories within your world, to the extent that your interface and player-usable tools such as guild and teaming mechanisms allow. For the most part, this involves situations that let them change the face or nature of the game world, such as a war with another team that allows them to control territory or banding together to rid the area of a particularly nasty creature that you have introduced and they have encountered.

However, the most compelling kind of content in your game is likely to be player-created stories and situations that don't spring from a plot you provide and which also change the game world in some fashion. An example of this might be two members of separate guilds getting "married" in the game, thus ending a faction war that had made the area dangerous for all players to move around in without getting killed; or players banding together to hunt down and eliminate PKs from a game, as the KOP guild did on *UO*'s Pacific shard ("shard" is *UO*'s term for a game world iteration); or even just a number of players or teams pooling their resources to buy a large castle they can place on the terrain and use as a base.

The takeaway from this section should be simple: No matter what tools you want for yourself to tell stories to the players, also provide tools to allow players to create and tell their own stories and provide their own amusement. You must be flexible and willing to change your game and story to take into account the actions of the players over time. "Interactive" should refer not only to the players acting within the context that the designers create, but also to the designers then reacting to the players' activities.

---

8. In our own defense, my team and I were basically lied to by a programmer on the *UO* live team when we designed for separate outcome possibilities of the Trinsic siege—that is, the players successfully defended the town or they didn't. If they were successful, certain conditions and events would not happen on that shard. However, we were told by the *UO* programmer that this wasn't possible, so we had to settle for the lesser design of a forced ending.

About one week after the conclusion of the event on all shards, at an online services team post-mortem of the event and in the midst of being roundly criticized for the way it was conducted, I noted what we had been told by the programmer, who was sitting right there. His somewhat embarrassed response was, "Oh, was *that* what you meant?" It irks me no end that, to this day, the Trinsic scenario is used as *the* exemplar of bad online game story event design.—Jessica Mulligan

An excellent resource to learn more about this is Raph Koster's personal web site at `www.legendmud.org/raph/gaming/index.html`. Read his articles under the sections titled "Essays" and "Snippets." They are well worth the time.

World-Building: Just What Is "Content," Anyway?

For most designers and development teams, "content" is the world they create and whatever they put into it. Content comprises the size and shape of the environment, monsters, houses, trees, rivers, weapons, and transportation (as opposed to "gameplay," which is the game's mechanics and interface).

While a good argument can be made that this is all just environment and that the players are the real content, for purposes of easing through this section, we'll go with the basic preceding definition, with a few changes.

Tools

What tools do you need to build a world? The necessary software capabilities are well known, even if development teams are not in universal agreement about how to use them, as you'll read about later. For now, we need a description of the basic tools and their general capabilities:

➤ **Natural terrain editor**—If you're going to have a PW, you need some form of persistent terrain for the players to interact in. This tool creates and places or modifies natural terrain features such as mountains, rivers, grassland, forests, boulders, caves, and the like, or the equivalents for other genres, such as planets and asteroids for a space-based game.

➤ **Man-made terrain editor**—This builds or modifies things such as houses, roads, shops, castles, space stations, and the like.

➤ **Item/object editors**—Build or modify anything that a player can hold, such as a weapon or jewel, or interact with, such as a door that opens and closes, animals, or vehicles that can be mounted and ridden.

➤ **NPC editor**—This will make non-player characters, give them an inventory, and ideally allow you to assign behavior patterns to them. NPCs and their behaviors can range from vendors that players can use to buy and sell from to monsters and guards to which you have assigned particular attack and patrol zones. This will probably end up being a sub- or super-set of your player/character editor.

➤ **Script editor**—This allows the creation or modification of game mechanics that aren't hard-coded into the source code. If done right, most game mechanics, be they associated with magic/psionics, combat, or trade skills, can be created, modified, modeled, and tested using the script editor.

➤ **Sound editor**—This allows the insertion of sounds that play out on action triggers or as ambient background noise. These sounds will include everything from animal noises, wind and other weather sound effects, weapons sounds, footsteps, and so on; if it makes a noise, there will be a trigger and sound associated with it.

➤ **Quest editor**—For the term "quest," you can also substitute "mission" or "adventure." Most PWs have either built-in or dynamic quests; some have both. These usually involve the player or a team requesting a mission, being told what has to be accomplished to get credit for the quest, and usually, being told where to go to perform it. Most of these, especially dynamic quests, are relatively simple and usually involve fetching some object or animal, talking to an NPC, giving an object to an NPC, or going someplace, getting a bit of information from one NPC, and delivering it to another. Static quests are usually much larger in scope and complexity, normally require more than one player, take more time to complete successfully, and not surprisingly, eat up plenty of designer and world-builder resources.

Thus, the capabilities of a quest editor generally need to be complex and extensive, including the ability to assign quest reward conditions, assign trap and NPC triggers that go off as the players attempt to complete the quest, and keep track of time for any quests that have a time limit.

With these tools and general capabilities, pretty much anyone can be taught how to technically construct a PW. What they should actually *do* with the tools has more to do with the game design document and design philosophy.

"Space" Doesn't Equal "Content"

Just because you have good tools and can lay down terrain, NPCs, and objects at a pace unmatched by mere humans doesn't mean you actually should. More important than "Do I have absolutely every tool ever conceived?" is "What am I using the tools to do?" More is not necessarily better; in fact, in persistent games, the opposite is often true.

For example, consider a comparison of pure size and space in the "more is better" frame of reference. In some ways, Turbine's *AC* is an innovative game, especially the allegiance system, which has the effect of causing established players to court new players (sometimes to utterly ridiculous lengths, but that's another story). One of *AC's* features is the huge world players can explore, usually juxtaposed against *EQ's* smaller and more quickly traversed "zones."

If all that players wanted was a huge space to travel around in, it would be game, set, and match for *AC*. So why is it that *AC's* massive expanse of territory is generally considered more boring than the smaller, zoned *EQ*? It's simple: Space is not equivalent to content. *AC* may be a huge world that takes hours of real time to walk across, but there is little to do in much of that space *except* walk and look at the same scenery and terrain for long periods of time. We appreciate beauty. *AC's* scenery is *beautiful*. We have played in *AC's* world and enjoyed it. But, *AC's* world-space is larger than it is beautiful. There are vast expanses that have no creatures, towns, buildings of any sort, and more importantly, no other players out there wasting hours of their time walking around in an empty space.

EQ's zones, on the other hand, may be relatively smaller, but they are packed with content. Each one is significantly different from the others, from terrain to building and artifact types to the creatures that inhabit them. And because the zones are smaller and more interesting, there are generally other players hanging about, which makes for a more interesting game session.

This general rule has been well known in the industry for years, going back to the early experiments on GEnie in the late 1980s, but somehow it continues to be violated by developers with new entries. If there is nothing interesting to do or experience, or the "happening" places are widely scattered and hard to reach except through many minutes of boring travel, you're just wasting server space and the player's time.

"Mass" Doesn't Equal "Content"

Conversely, you can go overboard by creating an unnecessarily high density of world stuff (known colloquially in many areas of endeavor as "just shoving too much crap into too small a space"). Some games tout thousands of weapons or armor pieces, but achieve these numbers simply by assigning a large number of levels to each basic weapon type. Most don't even bother to turn out original art for each piece, but just assign a text descriptor and change the capabilities on the server side. Another device designers use is to overpopulate the space with so many NPCs, monsters, buildings, roads, vendors, shops, outhouses, what have you, that a player can hardly move without having a collision with something.

Among developers, this kind of "piling on the density" is regarded as a reaction to the lack of an interesting or cohesive design concept from the very start of the process. If your world is based on the American West and you notice that you have 5-, 6-, 8-, 10-, and 12-shot revolvers but have omitted Derringers on the low end of the spectrum and Gattling guns on the high end of the spectrum, you have a problem.

Okay, What Is "Content," Then?

Speaking in generalities can get us into trouble. So, look both ways, here it comes: In general, if something in the game doesn't serve a planned, useful purpose as either an advantage or disadvantage to the player, it isn't content. One boss troll guarding a cave entrance is content; hundreds of trolls running around the countryside for the sole purpose of being killed by players is not content; it's a badly planned, useless riot. One or two vendor shops at a crossroads are content; having dozens of buildings there is a waste of your server's space and the player's time if only a few of them serve any use.

Someone will automatically point out that the cities in *UO* are large and filled with buildings. The difference is that almost every building in each of *UO*'s cities serves a purpose. It is almost impossible to walk into a building in Britain, for example, and not be able to conduct some sort of business. Contrast this with Omni-1 in *AO*, which is far larger than Britain and has several times more buildings, the overwhelming majority of which are window-dressing that perform no function beyond creating client-side latency with the time it takes to load them all and using up player minutes to pass them by and get to the useful content. Content is a balancing act that needs to be carefully thought out, based on how many players you expect to be in the area at any one time, what they are expected or allowed to do there, and whether the game is flexible enough to allow the players to create their own "content" there.

This balancing process doesn't stop at the design and execution of the design. You have to monitor the actions of players over time and modify the content to suit. If so many players are using the shops in one location that it is tough to get in and out in a timely manner, you need to open more shops nearby. If crucial NPCs are in scarce supply and this is causing boredom, you need to add more of them, or create new NPCs, or add some other activity that can occupy players' gameplay.

There is plenty of room for interpretation of these general rules; there is no perfect solution to balancing content versus usefulness. On the whole, however, less is more, if it is well designed. If you are careful not to waste the player's time with meaningless yet required travel or actions, you'll have a much better chance of turning out a flexible, interesting content set.

It all boils down to this: You can't have just depth or just breadth. You need a balanced helping of each to maintain equilibrium between excitement and involvement and to avoid boredom. A shallow game with no depth will get stale quickly; a narrow game with no breadth will see players maxing out characters and possessions almost before you're rested up from launch day.

Player-Created Content

If you have depth and breadth in the design that allow players to have an impact on the world, you'll find players will be more than happy to create their own content. Player-created content does not mean giving them tools to build anything they want. That way presents a nightmare of possible copyright and trademark violations. Imagine a precocious adolescent male building Porno-Disney for him and his friends to romp around in. If the parents don't sue your pants off, rest assured that Disney will do so, or worse. For a commercial enterprise, the chance of a violation and resulting lawsuit is just too great. What player-created content does mean, however, is giving the players access to tools that can be used to enhance their own gameplay and socializing online:

> ➤ **Change the physical landscape within certain rules**—That is, build houses, space stations, stores, whole cities, or whatever makes sense for your game.

➤ **Change the political landscape**—That is, run for mayor, create a faction of teams or guilds, influence tax rates, or start or end faction wars.

➤ **Change the economic landscape**—That is, own and run a store, affect the economy by creating shortages, and so forth.

➤ **Change the social landscape**—That is, perform diplomatic functions and activities from a micro to a macro level (think tribe to empire), create and run guilds or teams, or explore and claim new lands for the team, faction, or empire.

These capabilities allow the player/character to become involved in the larger game world, beyond the strictly personal activities of combat, trade, exploration, and so on. These kinds of functions are not that difficult to plan, execute, and test, but many current games are missing them. These are the tools that allow the players to have a "game within the game." Be prepared to see players playing the game in ways you never expected or intended. They will create their own content with whatever is available.

One example of this happened in the medieval fantasy *UO* in 1999. One group of enterprising players put together a theater company and rewrote and performed plays. Their online presentation of *The Wizard of Oz* featured numerous costume changes, special effects via in-game magic powers, and even a spell to make one player into a dog to play Toto. They were so successful that the support team for *UO* helped create and reserve characters for them on various server clusters so the troupe could "tour" *UO* with their shows.

Another example would be the bridge-diving contests in *Air Warrior*, a World War II air combat simulator. Kesmai's game featured rivers that separated the three main factions and bridges across them to allow tanks and jeeps to cross. One night, while pilots were bragging in-game about their skill, they decided to test it. The challenge was to fly at top speed under the bridge, as close to the water as possible. When that became passé, they added the difficulty of diving from great height. And when they had mastered that, they added the difficulty of diving from great height, attaining top speed, and flying under the bridge *upside-down*.

These are only two examples, among many we could have chosen from, of player-generated content. Neither required GM intervention; the rules were by the players themselves within the context of the game's capabilities, and they were managed by the players. Again, after you launch *your* game, be prepared to see players playing *their* game. Recall the advice of Raph Koster to a writer trying to ensure the integrity of his/her story in a PW; in a significant way, this applies to designers, too.

Chapter 9

Other Design and Development Issues

There are a number of other design and development issues that have to be addressed somewhere along the line. We've collected and will discuss those in this chapter.

Console: Oh, Brave New World!

Analysts have been predicting for years that millions of gamers would be playing online via game consoles. All throughout the 1990s, the likes of Jupiter Media Metrix, Datamonitor, and Forrester Research made wild guesses of anywhere from 12 million to 30 million online console gamers by 2001. Obviously, that did not happen.

Not having learned their lessons from the mid-1990s, the analysts' predictions on this have just kept getting wilder. For example, Datamonitor predicted in November 1999 that 45 million console gamers would be playing games via the Internet by 2004, compared to 28 million PC online gamers. Datamonitor also estimated a total of 165 million consoles sold worldwide by 2006, but failed to make clear whether that number was all boxes sold in years past or just next-generation consoles. Other estimates are of a similar vein, and they haven't become any more realistic in 2002.

This kind of inflated guesswork is good for selling reports at $2,500 a copy to people who want to convince the guys with checkbooks to cut loose, but it has little to do with reality.

Our take on this: These guys are smoking crack, and damned pure crack at that. The good news: There is no expectation in the console of free gaming, as there is on the Internet in general and "casual" game sites such as Pogo in particular. As Jupiter analyst Billy Pidgeon said in a recent news article, "It's going to be easier to make money there because in the PC space, there are all these people giving away stuff. People don't have those expectations on the console side. I think Sony and Microsoft are going to structure the online services so that there's going to be a service charge that includes some basic content and a real push to upgrade to premium services."[1]

The obvious question here is whether the Internet gaming experience will be good enough to promote online console gameplay. It is an open question at this point whether the synergetic effect of combining console games with the Internet will be a net positive for the console market, neutral, or worse. In the next sections, we'll try to give you an understanding of the main factors that are involved: the Internet backbone, game design, and some peculiarities of console games.

> **NOTE**
>
> For purposes of this discussion, we are assuming that most online gaming for consoles is going to be a pay-for-play proposition in some form or another, such as paying for the overall network connection service. Considering recent actions and comments from console company execs, such as Square announcing that *Final Fantasy XI Online* will cost 1500 yen ($15 US) a month when launched, this is probably going to be the case for most online console gaming. Offering free online play is a totally separate market; it may sell some extra SKUs, but you have to be a really good developer to get away with it. To date, only Blizzard has had noteworthy success with it in the PC market.

Reaction Times and Latency

From issuing a command on the controller to seeing the reaction on the screen, console gamers are used to experiencing consistent split-second reaction times. By split-second, we're talking on the close order of 60 milliseconds. Loosely translated, that comes out to less than one-tenth of a second, or in lay terms, "really damned fast." That's why they are called "twitch" games.

---

1. See "Online Game Makers Seek Key to Profits" by David Becker, January 25, 2002
   (URL: http://news.com.com/2100-1040-823258.html).

The Internet is a bad bet for online versions of twitch games because the Internet can be about as split-second and consistent as your average presidential candidate. Estimates of average Internet latency—the time it takes the average piece of data to go from point A to point B—vary from 125 milliseconds to over 500 milliseconds. Worse yet, the latency is not consistent. It is not unusual to have a data packet stall for several seconds during a trip, giving rise to the web's cynical nickname: the World Wide Wait. Can you imagine trying to duel another human in the average boxing or martial-arts arena game and having to wait a second or so for a punch or kick to update on the screen?

Okay, so the Internet has a high vacuum index now, but how about in the future? Pundits and experts are telling us that broadband will solve these critical issues for us "real soon now." Without going into another rant that questions their sanity, they are wrong. Latency rates and inconsistency are getting worse, no matter how backbone providers fudge the figures to show "improvements." Broadband makes the problem worse, not better; each new broadband customer represents an escalating demand for ever more data to flow over increasingly clogged lines. We just can't lay fiber fast enough—only about 12.5% of what we need each year just to stay even. It's going to be this way for a long time, maybe 10 years or more.

What does it all mean? With inconsistent latency being a critical issue, publishers are going to have a hard time charging for online console games that are optimized for split-second reactions. This means they'll probably end up giving away online play for free for most games, just as Mpath, Pogo, TEN, and The Zone had to for the PC twitch games.

Microsoft may have solved some of these problems by signing an agreement with Level 3, a large broadband access provider, to provide a closed loop network for the Xbox Live service and by requiring broadband connections for any Xbox Live subscribers. This will have the effect of reducing much of the latency that dial-up users see; once a subscriber enters the Level 3 network, much latency is eliminated. At the time of this writing in December 2003, with Xbox Live less than a month from launch, the results look good. The real test will come as more players sign on to the service and more bandwidth is in use.

Design and Controllers

Console controllers mandate that these games be designed with two- to four-player games in mind. The biggest hits in the online world right now are the 8- to 32-player retail hybrids, such as *Quake III*, *Tribes*, and *Unreal Tournament*, and the MMP PW games, such as *EverQuest (EQ)* and *Ultimate Online (UO)*. The 2- to 4-player games— and most 8- to 32-player games, for that matter—just don't draw a long-term audience.

This would seem to argue that you'd want to give away two- to four-player online gaming for free as a loss leader in hopes of selling some extra units, unless you can offer some other benefits and perks that make paying a monthly fee worthwhile. The only benefit known to be worth anything to an online gamer is some persistence of the character, like racking up permanent win/loss scores and gaining power and attributes. That's where the game design comes in and why most online console games are going to fail hideously in a pay-for-gaming environment, especially in the first two or three years of widespread online console availability.

Console developers will have to design with the Internet's less-than-wonderful latency in mind, something they've never had to do before and that is completely antithetical to their industry. They will no longer be able to write game design documents using a template that starts with something like the following line: "This is a twitch combat/sports/fantasy battle/arena duel/whatever style of game (please pick only one; we don't multiplex here) that will appeal to the male teen market." We suspect that the only change to that template at some companies will be to delete the word "twitch," which pretty much guarantees some spectacular and expensive failures.

Remember: Console games and online games are not only games that are played on different platforms, but they are also different markets with different needs. Unless the console publishers understand up-front that more is required than just porting video console games to an online platform, they are in for a rough ride and we're going to see some online console games that would appeal only to the devil's ugly sister. Online gamers expect a wider, deeper, and longer experience for their money and are quite vocal when they feel they aren't getting it. Developing a game is only the first part of the puzzle; most of the work happens after the game is shipped.

Again, Microsoft is going a slightly different route by requiring all Xbox Live console games to have voice chat capability built into the game, and by adding a microphone and headset to the Xbox Live retail unit. So far, this has proven to be a big hit with the players; it frees up their hands to control the game, instead of having to type to "talk" to the other players.

Naturally, there have already been problems with "grief" players spewing profanities just to get a reaction, and players are already starting to wonder out loud how to protect the younger set from verbal predators. There have also been complaints about the low quality of the voice filters, which are designed to allow people to disguise their voices during the in-game chatting. Overall, however, these are problems that are likely to be solved over time; it looks like voice chat for console online gaming is here to stay.

One Problem: The Designers

"You need a visionary who can dream up fantastic gameplay. A visionary who can write and talk like few. A person who is charming, committed, and efficient. A visionary who understands enough technology to include this aspect when he or she creates designs of fantastic worlds and gameplay functionalities. And very important: This person's greatest talent should be the ability to listen. To the development team, to marketing, management, and most important, to the players."

Thomas Howalt, Funcom AS Oslo

Yes, it sounds strange. These guys—and they are overwhelmingly guys; very few women actually get to be one of the "Chosen"—are your bread and butter, the people who decide the background story, how the game mechanics will work, what features will be in the game, even how your client interface will look and work. You'll have anywhere from two to six on your development team, and their productivity is the first link in the chain that determines whether or not you'll actually hit your milestone dates.

If you have an experienced lead designer (experienced in the commercial, for-pay side of the industry), one with a level head who understands that paying customers have much different expectations and needs from free-play MUD habitués, that person is worth his/her weight in platinum. He/she will be your best friend because he/she won't waste a lot of time trying to throw every imaginable feature into the design, spend months designing intricate and ultimately doomed player-administered justice systems, or argue the virtues of consenting versus non-consenting PvP combat with other hard-core players who happen to be on the design team. He/she will get to the point, design an overall environment that contains the features most loved by the greatest number of players, and go on from there with innovation.

Unfortunately for you, there aren't that many experienced for-pay online game designers around. In all likelihood, you'll start out with designers who got their experience as implementers (imps) on a MUD. If you are in development on a PW and this is the case for you, now is the time to get very scared.

Why? Simply because MUD imps, as they are called, no matter how clever they are with code or design, do not have experience with paying customers. Being a MUD imp does not give you any clues about what paying customers want or about what works/does not work in a for-pay online game. MUD imps have never had to concern themselves with these issues, and most of them don't care to do so. Their whole experience and training with online design has been with experimentation and playing around. So what if the MUDders howl and scream if a new game mechanism installed with no notice goes horribly wrong? The whole purpose of a MUD is, really, to experiment and learn. If a player doesn't like it, well, the price is free; let him/her go somewhere else and moan.

That works fine in a university atmosphere, where many MUD imps get their first taste of being game gods. There is absolutely nothing wrong with this attitude in a non-pay situation. It is a problem, however, at the for-pay level, and for obvious reasons.

If you're ramrodding an online game, then you need to be aware of some of the hidden dangers designers bring to the table and what you can do to ameliorate them.

"The Vision Thing"

A tall hurdle you'll have to leap with your designers, and the development team in general, is "The Vision Thing," as in, "Hey, this is The Vision and we will stick to it, dammit!" Designers normally have a tremendous amount of pride of ownership in what they are doing. Many of them consider themselves on a par with movie directors and novel writers, delivering a story to an audience and expecting everyone in the audience to get the same thing out of the experience.

Unfortunately, that does not take into account the dynamic and ever-changing nature of play in a PW. The overriding problem with The Vision Thing is this: It does not normally allow for flexibility or change based on the actual play styles of for-pay gamers. No designer or team of designers could possibly hope to close all the holes or find and fix all the flaws in a PW design; the collective intelligence of a player base in the thousands or tens of thousands dictates that any design hole or flaw will be found and exploited. On top of that, the collective intelligence of the players also dictates that they will find ways to play your design within the rules you have set and coded, but in ways you never expected.

The Vision Thing has caused more problems for existing online games than just about any other issue. Overadherence to The Vision can allow concepts that are not appropriate for online games to be inflexibly locked in during the early design stage, and it can also breed inflexibility in the post-launch stage. While a moderate sense of inflexibility toward basic concepts can be a good thing—what designer would be worth having if he/she weren't passionate about the work?—complete inflexibility of view is rarely a good thing: In a PW, it can be disastrous.

You rarely see this problem in designers who have at least one commercial MMOG under their belts; once you've experienced the problems The Vision Thing creates, you tend to accept the lessons and learn from your mistakes. For example, note the recent improvement in flexibility on Verant's *EQ* live team, now that some highly experienced online game veterans such as Scott Hartsman, Rod Humble, Robert Pfister, and Rich Waters are part of the process. This is just one more example of how critical experienced MMOG people are to a successful and smoothly running post-post-launch stage.

If your team is lacking in this experience, the time to nip this in the bud is during the initial game design document process, when you can exercise more control over the process and before anything is set in stone. If something seems suspicious or just not appropriate to an MMOG, we've found it a helpful exercise to require the designers to write an analysis and justification for the suspicious design feature or concept, explaining why it would be good for the game and players. This tends to focus a designer on the immediate issue: Will this have a reasonable chance of being fun, interesting, or entertaining, or is this just a cool-sounding idea that would be fun to work on?

After launch, strict adherence to The Vision Thing has the tendency to cause ossification, especially if the live team doesn't take ownership of the decision-making process right away. There is no doubt you'll have to make some changes to the gameplay over time; getting past the legacy of the development can be a block, especially if the developers are still around and working on the next game. Developers tend to become emotionally attached to the game during the development process; proposing to make changes to their "baby" can cause howls and anguish.

The MUD Imp Syndrome, Also Known as Cowboy Programming

The MUD imp syndrome, or cowboy programming, is a serious problem. Paying customers expect a certain amount of consideration and consistency; that's hard to achieve if the designers are experimenting with the design after launch. The development or live team member can call it "innovation," "refreshing the game," or anything else they like; if it isn't in the design document and it hasn't been vetted by the change control process (CCP), it is experimentation and who knows what it can screw up?

Cowboy programming usually takes the form of one developer coming up with an idea for a new feature or a fix for a problem and implementing it on-the-fly with no documentation or notification to the team. This also means little or no testing, and changing any moving part in one of these products requires complete testing to ensure you haven't thrown a monkey wrench into the gears of some other mechanism. No matter how easy or uncomplicated a change may seem, something as simple as changing a weapon from a +4 modifier to a +5 can completely upset the balance between classes of players, creating an uber-class when the weapon is wielded. Doing the reverse—taking away a capability—is seen as wasting hundreds of player hours; it tends to tick off the player base.

This is bad enough during development and testing, but cowboy programming on a live product can ruin your reputation because it almost always causes problems. Even if a change doesn't unbalance the game, the players will find out about it (you wouldn't believe how many players test everything after a patch), and your community relations staff will be immediately beset with charges of nerfing ("nerf" is a generic term used by the community to describe the act of changing an ability or feature in such a manner that it takes away power from players) and arbitrarily penalizing players. Nothing irritates the players more than having their time wasted, and cowboy programming usually results in that happening to a significant portion of the player base. This causes huge problems for customer relations; even one undocumented change can result in dozens of hours used by the customer relations team to try to control and manage the situation.

Even if you have a four-step program in place during the live phase to notify players of upcoming changes, as discussed in Chapter 12, "The Live Development Team," it has been our experience that every team has a cowboy who believes it is his/her right to bypass the CCP as a time-waster or not regard it as necessary for "small" changes. You'd be amazed at how many of these "small" changes are coded right into the live production servers, bypassing the test server altogether. You'd also be amazed at how many cowboys continue to make the same mistake over and over again, regardless of the cost in pain and frustration to other members of the team.

The best place to curb cowboy programming is during development and initial Alpha testing by rigidly enforcing version control and the CCP. The development team leader has to make a point of it, consistently and constantly, emphasizing how being a cowboy affects the other members of the team. It might be necessary to rein in a developer who consistently goes rogue by having his/her version patch addition privileges revoked, making him/her go through a supervisor to document and demonstrate changes before they are placed on the test server. At some point, it may even be necessary to remove a repeat offender from the team, just to drive the point home.

The important thing to note is that cowboy programmers are rarely malicious just enthusiastic and very goal-driven to fix or add as many things as possible. You just can't ignore the fact that maverick coders will cause you unending grief if allowed to exist on the team.

The Player Must Die!

For some reason, designers as a class love to punish the players. They spend inordinate amounts of time devising clever and fiendish methods of penalizing players for straying outside the boundaries of The Vision. This is not necessarily a bad thing, as long as there is a concomitant system of rewards. Unfortunately, for too many designers, a good reward for the player means not inflicting punishment, so a vicious cycle develops in which the design continually punishes players for straying outside The Vision and the main rewards are for playing exactly as the designer wants you to play and no more. This tremendously limits flexibility and freedom in a medium that professes to emphasize these attributes.

An example of this attitude is the whole consenting versus non-consenting PvP controversy that is currently raging within the community. Non-consenting PvP basically means that anytime you are playing, you're subject to being attacked and killed by other human players. There are three main sides to the controversy:

➤ There are the adherents of non-consenting PvP, who believe that being open to attack without warning by other players creates the drama of conflict and brings communities of like-minded players together to battle the fiends. They believe the only reason non-consenting PvP hasn't worked in 30 years is that no one has done it "right" yet. This is the "non-consenting PvP is good" approach.

➤ There are those who oppose non-consenting PvP on the grounds that, historically, it has never worked and tends to drive a large number of players away from the game, as in *UO*'s early days. This is the "non-consenting PvP is bad" approach.

➤ There are those who think non-consenting PvP can work, as long as there are plenty of ways for players to advance without placing their characters in danger and as long as PvP regions of the game are clearly marked. This is the "opt-in" approach to non-consenting PvP; you opt into it by crossing some boundary or voluntarily tripping a flag; thereafter, you're fair game. In a sense, it is both consenting and non-consenting.

Currently, there are several major games due out in 2002 and 2003 that feature PvP as a major component of the game, including Wolfpack's *Shadowbane*, Verant's *Star Wars Galaxies*, and EA/Maxis *The Sims Online*. *The Sims Online* is slated to be a more mass-market online game, so the opportunities for PvP will be extremely limited. *Star Wars Galaxies*' creative director, Ralph Koster, was also the lead designer of *UO* and learned many lessons with that game, so *Star Wars Galaxies* will be using the opt-in approach.

Shadowbane, on the other hand, seems to be leaning toward the "non-consenting PvP is good" approach, at least at the time of this writing in late 2002. This should not surprise anyone, considering that their motto since 1999 has been: "I don't play to bake bread, I play to crush!" They have since claimed that the motto was only a joke and public relations stunt, but online chats with development personnel over the past few months seem to indicate that the non-consenting PvP mentality is alive and well at Wolfpack.

Note also that of the three projects listed, *Shadowbane* is the one team with no real-world experience in designing and developing PWs. What the team sees is its own vision, not the vision of the bulk of the players. Thus, players who don't want non-consenting PvP are presented with a hard choice: Live with it or leave. It seems likely that the inexperience of the *Shadowbane* team, combined with their own bias toward non-consenting PvP, is about to teach them a hard lesson about the number of players willing to indulge them. As it states in their frequently asked questions (FAQ), "On the other hand, we expect large areas of the world map to basically become a 'No Man's Land.' If you decide to travel in the Badlands, do so at your own risk."[2]

This is exactly what happened to *UO* in 1997, and there is no reason to assume that the result will be different in *Shadowbane*. It is also an example of punishing players who don't conform to the developers' bias of how the game should be played. The result for *Shadowbane* is likely to be the same as it was for *UO*: a mass exodus of the estimated 80% of the player base that doesn't like or want non-consenting PvP.

Other general examples of "The Player Must Die!" include loading a world with large monster spawns to make the world "exciting" for the player (read: dangerous) and consistent nerfing to take away power and capabilities from specific player classes.

The best way to handle this problem is to ensure that team leaders act as a brake on the designers and ensure that there is something to do in the game besides fight and die. This problem usually starts with an incomplete design, or one not completely thought out or considered. After all, these games are supposed to be PWs, and that means more than persistent death.

The Neat Stuff Syndrome

The neat stuff syndrome (NSS for short, and also known by a more scatological term than "stuff" inside the industry) occurs most often after the game design documents are completed and development has begun. It starts when someone on the team says, "Hey, wouldn't it be *neat* if…" and goes on to expound on some feature or mechanic the team didn't think of during design meetings. More often than not, there follows a half-hour of, "Oh, yeah, that would be so cool!" followed by a designer making a notation to add it to the design as soon as possible.

---

2. See `http://Shadowbane.ubisoft.com/gameinfo/strategyfaq.shtml` for more information.

If this happened only every once in a while, it wouldn't be an overwhelming problem; however, with developers being creative types, it happens *a lot*. You can hardly go to lunch with the team without hearing some variation on the theme. Even worse, there are some leaders and senior management folks who just love to pop their heads into a lead designer's or producer's office and say, "You know, I was thinking about your project, and wouldn't it be *neat* if…." When senior execs start pulling this trick, their subordinates generally feel obliged to at least study the issue, and the deadly spiral begins.

This is a major contributor to "feature creep," the tendency of software designers to keep adding features under the rationalization that new features are needed or will enhance the finished design. The problem is that adding features adds moving parts to an already complex mechanism and usually occurs without full thought being given to the ramifications on the design, individual features, and game mechanics.

During the design stage, team leaders have to be sensitive to the NSS and remind the design team that a mistake everyone else has made has been to overreach in the design. As an interesting exercise, you can ask the team at various stages to pick 5 or 10 features to cut immediately, whether you actually intend to cut them or not. This will give you a good indication of how focused the team really is.

If you institute a CCP, controlling the NSS after the design process begins is easily accomplished by simply insisting that the CCP be used to request any change.

Okay, What Can You Do?

It isn't that hard to fix these things; all it takes is some research, logic, and analysis. The research comes from playing competing products as a paying customer and noting what does and does not work, reading as much literature and as many Internet postings from experienced designers, producers, and executives as possible, and making notes about what they say. The logic and analysis come in when you then review your own game's design based on your research and point out any discovered flaws to your team. Most designers and producers aren't stupid; if you point out a problem, they'll generally understand.

Consider this: If you laid out $5 million for a house, would you just turn the contractor loose and tell him/her to come see you when the house was done? Of course not—you would check in periodically to see for yourself how construction was coming along. If you had any doubts at all about the progress or quality of the work, you'd hire a second contractor to come in and inspect the work. After all, if you're committing $5 million, what's another few thousand dollars to increase your comfort level?

Amazingly, in the past 15 years, I have yet to see this happen during the development of a large PW project—and those projects now routinely cost more than our mythical $5 million house. Call it the "not invented here syndrome," or cheapness in the front office. The fact is, all that money is being spent without a second opinion from an uninvolved outsider. This is where most teams get into trouble, in not having an independent analysis done and depending on the designers to be perfect. This is a bit like letting the fox guard the hen house (or like letting the inmates run the asylum). That kind of administrative approach doesn't work in many situations. The Founding Fathers worked checks and balances into the Constitution of the US, most newspapers have fact-checkers and editors to backstop writers, and doctors insist on second opinions for critical, life-threatening diagnoses.

The point is, your designers need "fact-checking" and an oversight committee, too. If no one on the team or in the company is qualified to do it, hire an independent designer to do it. In fact, you're probably better off hiring a designer on a short-term consulting basis to do this, if only to avoid political divisions within your own team and get an honest opinion from an uninvolved third party.

Development Issues

We assume that your development team has actual knowledge in programming, art, and the other basic tools necessary to actually build something. It has been our experience that most development teams are fairly proficient in these arts, with the possible exception of the server-side programming and administration, which still have some way to go to develop standards for the niche.

So, if the people involved have the basic skills, why do these games always seem to ship late, with critical bugs and design flaws?

Why Are These Games Always Late to Ship?

It seems to be the rule that online games start with a 24-month development schedule and ship somewhere between month 36–48. Some of the past delays can be attributed to inexperience of the teams and/or developing new technology for a new market, but that isn't the whole story.

The biggest reason we've noticed for development delays is the tendency for online game teams to start building before they've finished designing. This is particularly true of projects that start from scratch, where the creators want to get busy creating (a project's version of youthful folly: hexadecimal-gram 123456, an ironic numerical version of "first things first"). It can also be a difficult-to-resist temptation for teams that use legacy code in a project. They can easily get the impression that since they have a "head start," any mistakes or changes based on executing before design completion will be more easily fixed (a project's version of misplaced trust: hexadecimal-gram 2B2B2B, in which the lead designer questions the value of existence, and in some cases, decides that cult life has something to be said for it). These perilous exuberances bypass the necessary step of completing and vetting the design to create a coherent and completed thought. It is like beginning development of a new car without knowing exactly how many parts you'll need, what they will cost, and where each will fit onto the car. One could start building the next Corvette, end up with the next flame-prone Pinto, and have to scrap all that work and start again.

Like all such situations, this creates more work later on, not less. For example, as noted by the quotes from experienced professionals throughout this book, most teams tend to overreach from the start in terms of the number of features and mechanics they try to pile into a game. If the team starts building without a finished design, imagine what happens later on when the designers discover six months into development that certain game mechanics can't be made to work. As you've probably guessed, they find themselves forced to strip out pieces and rebuild them, which affects every other piece of content already built in, probably causing many of them to have to be redeveloped as well. Instead of being six months ahead, the team can find itself back at square one (which would be a fine place to be if it were the start of the project, but that was half a year ago, and where they are now is more like six months in the hole). If the team had a cohesive design before starting execution—one vetted for overenthusiasm, overload, and with the features prioritized—its time savings from avoiding redevelopment would likely be enormous.

Two other major contributors to development delays are the NSS and its associate, feature creep. As the whole concept of an enforced CCP is foreign to most game developers, teams prone to the NSS and feature creep quickly find themselves falling behind in milestone development as they try to add in all the "cool" things that spring from those two attitudes. Later, they discover that adding moving parts to the equation without fully modeling them beforehand is breaking other parts, causing even more delays to fix them. To torture the car analogy a bit more, it would be like deciding six months into development to use a more powerful carburetor and finding that it needs more space than the old one. Married to the idea of the new carburetor, the team starts stripping apart the engine to build more space for the new part, only to discover that, with the engine in pieces on the floor, 15 old parts will have to be redesigned to be smaller or have a different shape to accomplish the task, at a significantly higher cost per part and adding six months to the project. Now, not only is the team not six months into the project, but they've also added six months, effectively losing a year—oops!

The Vision Thing can also create delays in the sense that designers and developers who become enamored of and married to an idea are extraordinarily resistant to changing it, even when it is obvious that change is needed. You wouldn't believe the lengthy, circuitous rationalizations developers are capable of spinning to keep from having to yank or rethink a cherished concept. They'll keep pouring more time and skull sweat into it in the belief that they just haven't quite figured out the nuances yet, but it is only a matter of time, just around the corner, or subject to an impending epiphany. By the time it becomes obvious that the concept or idea is going to have to wait for another project, literally months can be expended.

Balancing Creativity with a Schedule

Recognizing and dancing with the factors of creativity and timeliness requires a delicate balancing act on the part of management. Knowing when to put a lid on creativity to maintain a schedule (because time *is* money in the business of online games, in the form of salaries, overhead, and missed sales) is a management skill comparable to defusing a bomb or playing high-stakes poker. An appreciation of the technical aspects involved with the decision can be a lifesaver. A delay of a year means additional costs of somewhere between $1 million and $3 million; capping any possible unnecessary delay becomes a matter of profit versus loss.

The other side of that coin is that you can't be sure when a designer's crackpot idea might not be the next big thing that makes the company filthy rich. Not very many companies would have taken a chance on a game like *The Sims*, for example; the idea is just too "out there" for many of us to grasp as a design concept. In most companies, the design proposal would have been laughed out the door. Yet the game has sold more units than any other PC game in history since it shipped in 1999, and the expansion packs continue to sell like there is no tomorrow.

The question becomes, then, how to balance creativity to a schedule. Unfortunately, there is no hard and fast rule; if there was, there would rarely be production delays. However, there are some things you can do to limit the risk.

The Importance of a CCP

The front line in controlling potential production delays is the CCP, making all additions and changes to the design go through a vetting process to make sure you aren't breaking something or adding inordinate amounts of time to the schedule. Establishing and, more importantly, enforcing a CCP will cause developers to think in-depth about a change or addition before it is brought up seriously as a proposal. Once such a proposal is run through the process and other team members get to respond to it, you'll often find hidden traps that prohibit its addition or, conversely, convince the team and management that the change is worthwhile, even if it costs more time. The important thing is that the process is controlled and structured, instead of getting the team into a situation where designers or developers are throwing features at a wall to see which ones stick.

Enforcement will be an issue. You can take it as a given that most of your team will loathe the very idea of a CCP until they see how it works and recognize the benefits of less wasted time and a more stable product. The opposition will probably take the form of just ignoring it, with one or more of your people figuring they'll slip in a feature or change and no one will be the wiser. Besides, when people see how utterly cool it is, no one will care, right?

Most times, the bad side-effects of this kind of activity will be apparent, and it will be relatively easy to point out to the offender just what was broken or delayed by skipping the CCP. Sometimes, the feature will be very useful and popular, adding to the game without breaking or delaying anything. What do you do then? The answer is: You keep the feature *and* reprimand the offender for bypassing the process, and then you have a talk with the team about the process. It doesn't matter how good the feature is or how valuable the team member; without enforcing the CCP through both reward and punishment, you might as well not have one and accept that there will definitely be delays, not that there *might* be delays. Everyone has to know that the ultimate penalty for violating the CCP can and may be termination.

And what about the reward? How about bonus checks, or something else special and unique to the team, when milestones are hit on time and the CCP has not been violated?

Do You Know What Your People Can Do?

Another part of controlling delays is knowing what each of your people can accomplish in a given period of time. You start by understanding that game developers almost always overestimate their own productivity, and then ratchet down on their expectations and assertions based on your experience with them specifically and your experience in the industry in general. That may sound callous and jaded, but it has also been the experience of the industry to date. To be perfectly blunt, most developers are pretty arrogant about their own abilities, whether that arrogance is warranted or not. It comes with the territory, and you need to understand and be aware of it. It doesn't make game developers bad people; it just makes them game developers.

For a scratch team composed mostly of people you haven't worked with before, this can be hairy until you've seen what the people can do. It can be a nail-biting exercise as you try to limit the amount of work the team member is responsible for until he/she shows his/her capabilities, balanced against the need to keep the project moving forward. The only advice that can be given here is: Make sure your team leads are highly experienced, can recognize chronic non-productivity, and are willing to pull the trigger on a non-productive team member early. The longer you wait, the worse the damage. Pulling the trigger may take the form of a private conversation to make sure everything is all right at home, or worst case, replacing the team member if there is no good explanation. Much as we hate to face it, some people just don't fit with a team and sometimes have to be fired. No one likes to do it, but it is necessary, sometimes.

For a hand-picked team, basic non-productivity or inability to do the work probably won't be an issue; you've worked with them before and know what they can do. Any lack of productivity or delays are probably due to outside factors and can likely be remedied just by talking through it and perhaps giving the team member some time to get things worked out.

Task Slippage: Who Really Controls the Project Timeline?

This is as much a command and control issue as anything else. Depending on the composition of your team, either the producer or project manager controls the milestone timeline. This includes the responsibility of keeping the task completions, progress, and dependencies on the tracking sheet fully updated and keeping the leadership and team informed of where the blocks and potential blocks are or are likely to be.

If this responsibility is being fulfilled, even a casual glance at a Gantt or PERT chart will clearly show what tasks have been finished, which are delayed, and what other dependent tasks those delays are slowing or halting. The whole purpose here is to provide ongoing tracking and accountability and prevent sudden surprises. There's nothing worse than reaching the first Alpha test and realizing that the developer who was supposed to spend two weeks writing the login server code wasn't able to because other small delays slowed down his/her other tasks. With a properly maintained and tracked timeline, this kind of surprise won't happen.

This also assumes that the producer or project manager is actually in control of the timeline. All too often, one or more of the leads is allowed to informally control what is actually worked on or is a current priority, regardless of the plan or CCP. The responsibility and authority remains with the producer or project manager, but the accountability factor becomes skewed. Individuals remain accountable for their own tasks, but the overall accountability for tracking and planning is now in question.

Nothing can rip a team apart faster than fuzziness or lack of control in the command chain. If an individual feels that the accountability and responsibility are being unofficially shunted sideways, it becomes tempting to realign the workload to the more "fun" stuff with an equally informal, "Hey, I thought I'd work on this instead; is that okay with you?" to the "informal" leader. It doesn't take much of this to undermine the integrity of the timeline altogether.

Game development teams are notorious for this, based on the theory that everyone is friends with everyone else and it is (or should be) an egalitarian system. There may be the occasional team that can work this way, but not often and not many. It is nearly impossible for 30 people to decide on what to have for lunch, much less come to a consensus on priorities and work tasks.

Hammer-Time: Does Crunch Mode Really Make Up Time?

Inevitably, for a variety of reasons, work on milestones slips. As the date to deliver the slipping milestone approaches, teams try to make up for lost time by going into crunch mode. To go into crunch mode means to work more days per week and longer hours on each of those days. It is the game industry's answer to the question, "How do we make up the time we lost fiddling around with neat stuff three months ago?" It has become so endemic that producers actually plan crunch mode time into the schedule. This is akin to the old saw of losing money on each transaction but making it up in volume; it doesn't work very often.

No one ever wants to go into crunch mode; it is a debilitating exercise that, at its peak, sees developers sleeping on the floor of their office for days on end, gulping chips and Jolt at the keyboard, and staring at the monitor with exhausted, baggy eyes. On a personal level, the exhaustion leads to more bugs that need to be fixed, wasting even more time. It also takes days to fully recover from crunch mode—days of lower productivity that add up to more crunch mode time at the end of the next milestone.

On a team and project level, more time spent in crunch mode tends to lead to more time in the test-fix-test cycle, which means—you got it—more delays.

Crunch mode can be useful if used in moderation, and it may be necessary at the end of the development and test cycle just to clean up unanticipated problems. Planning crunch mode time for every milestone, however, or being forced into it continually to make your milestones should tell you something about your design, planning, work load, or team culture/team psychology. If you're in the middle of development and in crunch mode continually, it is time to step back and take another look at your plan and design.

The Test Process

Know this going in: You have probably already underestimated the amount of time and number of people you need for testing your PW. Because these games are so complex and have such different yet interlocking technology, there is a lot that has to be stressed, broken, and fixed. Teams that haven't been through this at least once don't really understand this. "They underestimate the testing and scaling challenges," according to Gordon Walton, "and end up with a fire drill when their service scales up."

There is a process you can use to minimize the risks, but it requires some redefinition of what the standard test phases are testing for compared to their common use today. The process involves time and patience.

As discussed in Chapter 1, "The Market," the process also involves spending money because you'll need to add bandwidth and server hardware to anticipate the increased number of testers you'll need and ramp up your customer service (CS) and player relations staff at the same time. Over a 6- to 12-month period, and assuming you'll need to handle at least 20,000 simultaneous users at launch, you'll buy and install enough bandwidth and hardware to handle that load and hire and train somewhere between 20 and 50 player relations staff to service them at launch.

Develop, Test, Fix, Scale Up, Wash, Rinse, Repeat

"You can never start testing too soon. We've now instituted the process of monthly test builds, which go through a rigorous testing cycle. We then stabilize the build and check for performance. This is giving us a big edge as we prepare for testing this time around. Likewise, you will always try to cheat at the end and give up testing time for new features. Don't do it. The problem just gets worse with every feature that you add."

Jeff Anderson, CEO of Turbine Entertainment

What Jeff remarks on is a process that is coming into use more and more among experienced teams, though few yet go to the quality control extent that Turbine now uses. In the past, teams tended to do no or only minimal testing of their code before it went into a version build, and then depended on the QA department to test the build while they moved on to the next build.

Do you see the problem here? Developers were (and in many cases, still are) working on the next build before the current one was debugged. That means more content was added before the debug was finished, which can and usually does mean a lot of wasted work as the new code becomes inoperative after the fixes are deployed. I know this sounds utterly insane and self-defeating, but this is exactly how it was and is done today by most online game development teams.

Thankfully, it *is* changing, as the industry as a whole watches high-profile failures, gains experience in online games, and begins to understand that more moving parts mean more and better testing procedures. The key elements to keep in mind are time, numbers, and patience.

Rarely does the testing process for a PW take enough time or involve enough testers. As Gordon Walton has noted, almost every team underestimates the scaling and testing challenges for a PW. Up to early 2002, for example, the average announced time for full Beta testing of a PW was about three months.

This may seem adequate on the face of it, until you understand that what the MMO industry refers to as a Beta test is what most other industries call Alpha *and* Beta combined. This is one of the bad holdovers from the early days of MMO development for the old online services; teams were totally inexperienced with the whole process of quality testing procedures and just made them up as they went along. They knew Alpha and Beta tests were standard, so they just figured that the testing they did themselves was Alpha and the testing with players involved was Beta. What none of us understood at the time, of course, was the distinction should have been made by *what* was being tested, not who was involved in the testing.

Now that many MMO products are being developed in (relatively) more professional settings, combined with managers having experience with more than one MMOG development project, this is starting to change. The test periods are segmented by content to be tested, no matter who is involved, and are starting to stretch, although if 2001's launches were any indication, not by nearly enough. To give credit where it is due, most of the bad launches in this industry have had more to do with short-term financial pressures than development teams believing buggy products are ready for paying customers. This is being penny-wise and pound-foolish; more on that in the later section entitled "Patience."

Time and Numbers

Until you've done it once, it can be difficult to grasp the concept that some bugs happen at 2,000 simultaneous players, but not at 1,000, and vice versa, or just how many network and server-related problems can be revealed simply by scaling up from 500 to 1,000 simultaneous testers. Teams also tend to greatly underestimate how long it will take to fix and retest bugs, balance problems, and flawed mechanics and systems.

In addition, you may find that your game and social mechanics, balancing, non-player character (NPC) and monster populations, and overall world size and design work quite well at 500 simultaneous players at the end of the Alpha test series, but become completely inadequate for 1,000 simultaneous players. For an industry that designs server cluster technology to hold 2,000–3,000 simultaneous players on average, this can be terrifying.

It all starts with a proper test plan that emphasizes enough time to actually do the job correctly, notes specific testing targets for each phase (what systems, mechanics and/or load are to be tested), allots the time to truly fix each major test build before moving on to the next, and scales up the simultaneous player numbers far beyond the norm.

As you can see from Table 9.1, you shouldn't be skimpy on planning test phase durations. It is a good idea to schedule longer periods than you believe you need; you can always cut back the duration if things go well, but adding more test time tends to upset everyone from management right through to the players. As a general rule of thumb, a test period that lasts two weeks will take at least another two weeks to debug and retest. At an absolute minimum, the Alpha and Beta tests should be planned at no less than six months; for a major, highly anticipated game, they should be planned to last at least one year.

Table 9.1   Testing Time and Numbers

3 Months			3 Months			
Alpha 1	**Alpha 2**	**Alpha 3**	**Alpha 4**	**Alpha 5**	**Alpha 6**	**Alpha 7**
Dev. team	Dev. team	Dev. team	Dev. team	Dev. team	Dev. team	Dev. team
QA dept.	QA dept.	QA dept.	50–100 PT	50–100 PT	50–100 PT	50–100 PT
All hands	All hands	All hands	QA dept.	QA dept.	QA dept.	QA dept.
			All hands	All hands	All hands	All hands

3 Months			
Closed Beta 1	**Closed Beta 2**	**Closed Beta 3**	**Closed Beta 4**
Dev. team	Dev. team	Dev. team	Dev. team
500 PT	1,500 PT	3,000 PT	5,000 PT
QA dept.	QA dept.	QA dept.	QA dept.
All hands	All hands	All hands	All hands

3 Months			
Open Beta 5	**Open Beta 6**	**Open Beta 7**	**Open Beta 8**
Dev. team	Dev. team	Dev. team	Dev. team
10,000 PT	20,000 PT	50,000 PT	50,000 PT
QA dept.	QA dept.	QA dept.	QA dept.
All hands	All hands	All hands	All hands

This table represents an idealistic progression of a one-year test period for a highly anticipated PW. "QA dept." represents the QA testers, "all hands" is the entire company, if the development team is part of a larger organization, and "PT" stands for player-testers, or outside players who are brought in to assist at various stages. The various phases represent major systems and stress loads to be tested. The player-tester numbers represent total testers in the program, not simultaneous testers.

Internal, Closed Testing

What Jeff Anderson refers to in the quote at the start of this section is what you should be doing for pretty much all your milestones: build, test, fix, repeat until completely fixed, new build, repeat until you hate your life. The testing will be easy for early milestones, will get somewhat elusive and nonlinear for middle milestones as the code and content become more complicated, and will smooth out again approaching Alpha.

This kind of testing takes place within the team and QA group, with the occasional all-hands testing involving the company as a whole. No one really expects to find all the hidden bugs or flaws, although you will find many of them (Some bugs won't show up until hundreds of people interact with the code and each other simultaneously.) The purpose is to sterilize the apparent bugs and anomalies from the build before complicating matters with new content and code.

Most teams have some sort of procedure in place for this, however informal; where the teams often fail is in not formalizing the procedure and completing the testing before moving on.

Alpha Testing

Alpha testing is your first attempt to start really testing distinct systems, such as the combat system or magic, for balance, utility, and functionality. You'll also be testing how systems work together to eliminate conflicts and fix flaws in design or balance. The purpose of the Alpha test is to move the game to a "feature-complete" status in preparation for the Beta phase. By the time you're finished with Alpha testing, you should have in hand a game that you believe is feature-complete and ready to be fully played by outsiders, with no more features or content to be added, and which has had some stress and load testing.

If you are going to add features or systems to the design, the Alpha test phase should be considered the last chance to do so, and the attitude and work should be aimed more at completing the set design than thinking up new bells and whistles to go in. There is always the chance someone forgot a critical feature or tweak, however, so the team managers shouldn't necessarily close their minds completely to the possibility.

In general, early Alpha tests should include inside testers, not outside testers. In the past, Alpha testing, or the first rounds of major tests, took the place of the closed Beta, with a few interested players invited to pound on certain mechanics, systems, or features, while other systems, features, and mechanics were still being finished for testing.

While it is enticing and sometimes necessary to invite potential players in to an early Alpha test, the primary purpose is to test and debug distinct systems, mechanics, and features. Players, on the other hand, are notorious for playing builds, not testing builds. It takes careful selection of outside testers and even more careful management of them to ensure that meaningful testing is done. Left to themselves, outside testers will play the game to the extent possible and ignore such niceties as bug reports. This may be acceptable when it comes to open load/stress testing; it is not acceptable when the game isn't feature-complete.

At some point in the Alpha phase or later in the Beta phase, however, you will want to scale up the simultaneous player load, and this will require you to bring a select group of outsiders into the fold. Most teams accept applications for testers online and sift through the thousands they receive to choose 50 or 100 who seem to understand the process. Actually, finding outside volunteers experienced at game testing isn't difficult; managing them and getting them to actually report bugs can be. It is helpful to have someone on your QA team as the main point of contact for test volunteers, tell him/her specifically what needs to be tested, and charge him/her with monitoring and compiling the reports. This person should be utterly ruthless about dropping testers who aren't making reports. Regardless of how well your team sifted through applications to get what appeared to be a worthwhile group of 50–100 testers, you'll probably find that some of them are just taking up server space and bandwidth for the notoriety of being in the test and leaking information to their buddies. They are expendable and replaceable. You are selecting a jury of sorts, so you should select alternates in case some of your jurors develop human traits, like laziness, the inability to keep a bargain, and so forth.

Finally, you'll want to make sure that at least minimal load and stress-testing is done to ensure that the simultaneous user numbers don't break your network code or the game's mechanics. You'll want a minimum of 200 simultaneous testers, as anything less won't put a serious strain on the servers. This might be a good time to pull out some of those old tester applications, pick another 300–500 for Beta, and invite them in to the last Alpha stress and load tests as a bonus.

Beta Testing

Beta testing is not a design phase! Burn that phrase into your brain.

Beta testing *should* mean: "We're feature-complete, there is no system or feature in the game or technical design document left to add, and no more original design work will be done on this game until after launch, period. Now we're going to find the bugs and flaws that we missed in Alpha, fix them, scale up the load, and then do it all over again until we have a stable, balanced game fit for paying customers."

That's what Beta should be; what actually happens is that most online games use the Beta test process to finish the execution of features and systems that were part of the final design, add entirely new features and systems, and make major code changes. In fact, most online games are finishing up the game design document's features and systems right up to launch day, which is why so many of them launch with balance problems, technical instabilities, and major bugs. Every feature, system, or other type of game element requires extensive testing; trying to add things at the last minute guarantees that they won't be tested properly and won't work right. In this context, there is no such thing as a small feature or change; anything you do is liable to affect one or more other moving parts in ways you never dreamed possible. If you've burned the opening phrase into your brain, you won't have as many problems during Beta as other games have had. It is a simple rule; enforcing it will save splitting headaches in both the short and long runs.

Moreover, understand that this is not as short a process as most people think. The Alpha test may have gone swimmingly, but adding numbers tends to break things. In fact, that is the whole reason to scale up numbers and stress-test; break things, fix, scale up, break them again, fix again, repeat as necessary.

Closed Beta

Before starting Beta, you're supposed to be feature-complete. That means everything you expect the players to have access to at launch is in the game and tested through Alpha. Don't make the mistake of rationalizing the meaning of "feature-complete" as, "We're *almost* there, except for combat and that magic stuff" just to get into the Beta phase. The time to add (or cut) features is before Beta begins.

Now is when you'll really start ramping up the number of testers available, tracking the simultaneous user load, and gearing up some test sessions specifically to get as many people as possible online, until the technology breaks. The process of "scale up, stress, break, fix, and repeat" is a vital one if your servers are going to be stable for launch, and it is one that you can't skimp on. Too many teams make the mistake of thinking that load stressing and balancing can be completed at the end of the process, just before launch, instead of stabilizing at each step before proceeding. This kind of deferred maintenance will compound the problems and workload you'll face at the end of the process, when you should be making a final polish before launch.

Although you've just come through the Alpha test and the game is feature-complete, don't get complacent. With more people involved in the testing process, this is where the bugs you didn't find in Alpha will start to show up and any flaw in your network, mechanics, or overall design that slipped through previous tests will become painfully obvious.

The first objective of the closed Beta phase should be to scale up the tester numbers to equal the maximum planned simultaneous player load for one or two server clusters/ world iterations. This is the first highly critical chokepoint of the Beta; you'll find out if your technology can handle the physical load and if your design is balanced enough and has enough flexibility to keep the players occupied when a server cluster is full. You'll also be looking for exploit holes you missed in Alpha. As Kathy Schoback, Director of External Development and Publishing, Sega of America, put it to us in an interview:

> *Beta testing can reveal many detrimental player behaviors before launch.*
>
> *For example, NFL 2K2 for Dreamcast was widely hailed as extremely player friendly, and the experience of playing against a real person completely exceeded the artificial intelligence (AI) experience—that is, until players began to realize that they could just "hang up" on their opponent when their beloved Raiders were getting whupped 49–0 in the first quarter. This could have been identified by extensive and truly "public" Beta testing, and rectified by more aggressive community management.*

Your community management team will probably be the first to spot these kinds of activities, either through postings on tester forums or through direct observation. The problem is not so much in identifying them as it is in fixing them; some, like the problem noted by Kathy Schoback, are tough to solve. How do you tell the difference between a random disconnection and someone bailing out to keep from losing? If you can't, what kind of stop-gaps or penalties can you reasonably program that won't unduly penalize the poor person who was randomly disconnected? And this is only one problem of many you'll encounter.

There will also be problems with both technology scaling and game design. Beyond just finding bugs, fixing them, and retesting, you will be doing fine-tuning on class, skill, and mechanics, balancing issues as flaws become apparent and retesting those, too, and they can be far more difficult to fix.

The final objective of the closed Beta phase is to stabilize the technology and design to the point that they work consistently and well. This means no known but unfixed client or server crash bugs ("We'll get it in the next phase, really; time to move on now, we're wwaaaalllking, we're wwaaaalllking…"), a stable login server, and mechanics and gameplay that are as balanced as you can reasonably make them.

Security Issues

"Players love to cheat—especially in online games. Based on this information, it is important to properly Beta-test online games before they go out to market—this extra exposure will give you valuable feedback and may also help identify items that you may not have anticipated. Also be ready to add server-side support to prevent user cheating with methods that you were not able to predict."

Scott Hawkins, consultant for Sega of America

Some players are just lame and like to cheat for bragging rights. It may seem weird that a significant portion of the player base is willing to do anything to win, but that's the reality of the situation. Worse, some of the outside testers you bring in for this phase are there for one reason only: to find bugs and exploits and *not* report them. What they are hoping is that no one else finds them and they can reserve them for their own use after the game goes live to the public. In these days, when players can auction off characters and items for hundreds or thousands of dollars, there is great incentive to use bugs and exploits to cut the time necessary for character development or object acquisition to improve cash flow from sales.

This has worked in the past because developers haven't understood the need for monitoring, tracking, and logging tools to identify and stop this activity. From experience, the players willing to indulge in this kind of thing understand that their chances of being caught are slim because most online games have no or only rudimentary, hard-to-use tools and because developers initially place little emphasis on finding and stopping the activity.

To save yourself a mountain of headaches later, take the time to build the tools, assign one or more people to be "security specialists," and use the testing period to debug and refine the tools, the process, and the people. See the following sections for more detail.

Open Beta

By this time, if you've been diligent about the test, fix, retest procedure, your technology is probably fairly stable up to 2,500–5,000 simultaneous players and the feature set is working adequately. Now is the time to *really* put stress on the product by adding several thousand more testers to the mix.

Stability is the goal here; the games that failed the launch process in 2001 lost the bulk of their customers due to unstable technology. There were certainly content and feature problems, but most players are willing to work through those kinds of problems—for a while at least. What they have little patience for is not being able to log in, getting disconnected constantly, server-side latency, and bugs or crashes that interrupt gameplay and/or negate hours of "work." These things interrupt immersion and socializing and dilute the very permanence of character that helps attract and retain players for the game.

To reach that goal, you're going to need to load the servers with far more bodies than you have previously. Yes, you'll still be finding bugs and doing some rebalancing, but these activities should be minimal if closed Beta was successful. The real objective is to constantly "break" the technology, fix it, add more warm bodies, break the technology again, fix it again, add more bodies. Repeat this process until you cannot only clearly demonstrate that the technology can handle the simultaneous player loads you expect at launch, but you can also develop a sense of confidence that it will be capable of handling the growth of the first three to six months post-launch.

Stressing Out

The goal here is numbers; recruit as many testers as you can get for your servers and aim for as much testing up-time as possible between fixes. If you refer back to Table 9.1, you'll note that the number of outside testers for the first round of open Beta takes a huge leap from 2,500–5,000 to 10,000. This may strike you as a difficult number to achieve, but it won't be; these days, even relatively unknown MMOs receive Beta applications in the tens of thousands. The real problem will be in deciding which ones to allow in. Since you'll be looking less for formal bug reports from these people and more just to get their warm bodies into the game, the easiest method is just to select the additional 5,000 at random and email them sign-up codes for the test.

Now it is time to repeat the closed Beta process of test, break, fix, retest, repeat as necessary. The only significant difference to the process is that you'll be adding testers in numbers you probably didn't consider before starting development.

What you're liable to experience will be scary; your technology will break down constantly. If it isn't the login servers choking on the number of simultaneous players trying to get into the game, it'll be one or more servers in a cluster crashing unexpectedly because too many players tried to crowd on to one physical machine, or all the clusters going down because the database tried to do too much, too quickly, and choked on its own output, or a zombie process eating up the system memory until a server grinds to halt, or… you get the idea.

It may be scary, as well as incredibly frustrating, and you may take some very vocal beatings from testers carping in public about your "bad" technology. (Warning: This does tend to cause executives to get nervous and worry about the company's reputation.) However, problems like these are *exactly* what you want in this phase. If you don't find them now, imagine how bad a public relations beating you'll take after launch, when they will surely show up (probably during a four-day holiday weekend, with the five critical people you need to fix the problems out of cell phone range in the Alaskan wilderness, and with three-quarters of the player relations staff under quarantine from a freak outbreak of some unknown virus).

There will be incredible pressure from executives to fix things *now*, which translates as, "I don't care if you have to use chewing gum and chicken wire; just stop the screaming!" If the technology is particularly unstable under load and the volume of complaints and nasty comments from players rises to unbelievable levels, you can expect morale on the team to plummet. In other words, things are going to get hairy.

Patience

All of which brings us to patience. With all that pressure and screaming going on, there is going to be the temptation to rush through the process with stop-gap fixes that stem the problem but don't actually provide a permanent solution. If the pressure gets too high, you may be ordered to do it by some higher-up with no foresight but tender sensibilities and a highly evolved "fight or flight" survival instinct. This may solve the immediate problem, but it's like using duct tape on a leaky pipe instead of welding the hole closed; there will be a constant dripping until the duct tape is thoroughly soaked, the gum fails, and the water explodes out again. Better to bite the bullet, cultivate patience, and provide the right repair the first time.

Doing a fix when you should have performed a repair postpones the problem until the worst possible time: when paying customers are coming in the door. The idea is to find and solve problems so the launch is as smooth and trouble-free as you can make it. A stable, trouble-free launch is the single best method you have of creating good word of mouth and getting a lot of customers in the door quickly.

Some people in the company may not understand this, however, especially if this is the company's first PW and their first real exposure to just how vocal—and downright mean and nasty—online gamers can be. If they haven't been properly prepared beforehand for how superficially ugly the situation can get, that first exposure can be a real shocker. The lesson to learn here is: Patience begins with preparing everyone before the worst happens.

That means the expectations of everyone involved, from senior management to the players, have to be properly managed throughout the development and test process. Proper management of expectations for this means talking about them long before you get to the open Beta phase:

- ➤ The producer(s) needs to brief senior management and the company as a whole on the process and expectations, beginning from the very first day all the way through the Beta process, including the possible reactions from the players when you start stressing the technology.

- ➤ The team leaders have to educate their people during development on what the Beta process is all about and why it is a good thing that the technology is being made to break so much.

- ➤ QA and community relations have to continually brief the players involved in open Beta that one of the specific goals of the phase is to continually break the technology, and encourage them to leap into that wholeheartedly.

- ➤ Community relations and public relations have to use the web site and interviews to brief the press and general public on the purpose of open Beta testing and why it is a good thing that the game is breaking.

Why do all this? Without this kind of management of expectations on the front end, a development team can expect their lives to be a living hell all through the open Beta test phase. Unless you're a card-carrying sadomasochist with a desire for gratuitous pain, why would you want to go through that?

The Freeze: Closing the Loop to Launch

Okay, you're in the last stages of the open Beta, the game is stable, and it's time to prepare for the official launch day. Now what?

Now is "the freeze," meaning you stop messing around with changes in both the client and server code. They don't necessarily have to be frozen at the same time; it depends on your client distribution model.

The Client: Retail Box

Since you're going to need a minimum of 30 days from the time you send the client to the duplicator to the time it shows up in a box on retail shelves, you have to finish up any last-minute polish on the client and freeze it at least six weeks before launch day.

Why six weeks instead of four? Shouldn't you keep working on the client right up to the moment you have to send it to the duplicator? If you're going to be selling the client in stores, you'll want at least two weeks of "frozen" status to test the retail version for any missed client-side bugs and just to ensure that it is truly stable. You'll also want to do fresh installations on as many different machines as you can get your hands on. QA will already have done as much machine configuration and compatibility testing as they can, but it can't hurt for everyone on the team to do fresh installs of the frozen version, work with it for two weeks, fix any lingering bugs or anomalies, and make sure it actually works correctly and intuitively.

Once the frozen client has been tested for two weeks and is shipped off for duplication, *don't touch it*. In the past, teams have continued to work on and add to the client after it was shipped to the duplicator, on the cheerful assumption that hey, we can just download the changes to the player with a patch, right? The problems come with the size of the patch downloads; they tend to be large. *World War II Online* and *Anarchy Online (AO)* both had 75MB downloads waiting for new players after the install process. For a dial-up user running at 56k, which still constitutes the majority of US and European connections, this can easily be a 7- to 10-hour download, depending on the quality of the connection.

The hard-core gamer tends to be more philosophical about large patches; just as price is of small object to them, so too is a 10- or 20MB download, for the most part. However, any patch for new, registering players larger than about 4MB can be a serious block to entry. Learn from the example of EA's *Majestic*, where more than 90% of 100,000 potential players abandoned a 10MB download of the free episode before completion of the download.

If at all possible, it is better to hold off on client patch downloads for two to four weeks after launch. By that time, you'll be past the initial rush for the doors and things will have steadied out a bit. Of course, if serious client-side bugs pop up during that period, you'll have no choice but to fix and patch them; just keep them as small as you possibly can.

The Client: Self-Publish Online

Bypassing the retail channel to publish the client online is a hot topic these days. We don't currently recommend this, mainly because most people still don't have broadband connections and forcing a long download is more market-limiting right now than requiring someone to walk into a retail store. That will certainly change over time, maybe as soon as 2005, but it is the reality of the situation right now.

If you're still determined to publish the client via online downloads, you'll need at least a two-week freeze period to establish stability, and it is recommended that you hold off on patches as much as possible for the initial two- to four-month post-launch period.

The Server

When the client is frozen, it is a good idea to also freeze the server code, but that might not be realistic; there always seems to be some cleaning up and tweaking to do. If you're going to make changes after the freeze, it is generally a much better idea to make server-side changes; they are easier, don't generally require a download to the player's client, and mistakes made in the patch are easier to fix.

In general, the name says it all; if you're going to freeze the software, *freeze* it. Every change after that greatly increases the chance of a problem at launch.

Wiping the Database Clean and Rewarding Testers

After 6–12 months of testing, the PTs who stuck around for a few months will have become attached to the characters they created. This is only natural; if some people didn't form emotional attachments to their characters, we wouldn't have a business.

However, this can present a tricky situation, as most games wipe the player database clean at the end of Beta, and this represents a loss in the minds of the testers. As the Beta phase draws toward conclusion, you'll start hearing talk from the testers that, you know, maybe you should be different from all those other guys and not wipe the player database clean for launch.

The players don't seriously expect you to leave the test characters intact; that would have the effect of unbalancing the game heavily in favor of them from day one of live operations and they know it. Long-term testers will already have the advantage of knowing the game better than new players, and that can be a pretty hefty headstart. What you can do is plan in advance how you will reward the testers for helping you out. This can take several forms that don't impact the gameplay directly, which should be your goal:

➤ **Reserved character names**—Allow testers who were active a certain minimum period of time to reserve a character name for use after launch. Since persona names are key "fame" identifiers in PWs, this is considered a great reward.

➤ **Special tester sigils or items**—Players love to brag how they were involved with a game "since the first Beta, before you punks even knew the game existed!" Unfortunately, most games have no way to easily acknowledge that status, so plenty of poseurs pop up. You can make this a meaningful status; if the game features unique clothing or jewelry pieces, character titles and ranks, or some other way to uniquely mark an online persona, create one specifically for testers and make sure they each get one. This is almost never done, yet it would be remarkably popular.

➤ **Extended free play**—The industry-standard reward is to offer some amount of free "tryout" time for newly registered players, usually the first month of play. You can thank your testers by extending this time, although you have to weigh this option carefully; it can eat into your margins if your tester numbers were high.

The point is to reward your testers in some visible, recognizable manner.

Ramping Up Player Support

One of the industry's consistent mistakes is to underestimate the extent of player support needed for a PW. As discussed elsewhere in this book, the total number to bring on-board depends on whether the proper support tools exist and whether the game is stable. The questions of "How many?" and "When?" support personnel need to be hired, trained, and deployed are at the center of vigorous debate within the industry, with proponents of different solutions displaying zeal and intensity more typically associated with religious belief. Ask any professional in the industry and you'll probably get a different answer each time.

What we end up with, then, are cases that contrast wildly, such as *UO* versus *EQ*, where *EQ* has two-and-a-half to three times as many support personnel as *UO* to handle about twice the number of subscribers, or *Asheron's Call (AC)*, which has less than 20% of the support personnel as *UO* to handle about one-third of the subscriber base. Everybody does it differently; the only consistent element to support is that players in almost every game agree that it is done badly, inconsistently, and it takes too long to get help.

When to bring on support personnel and in what numbers have no standard answers, either. To control costs, most companies try to ramp up support in the 30 days before launch. While fiscally reasonable, this ignores that PWs are complicated beasts with unique idiosyncrasies that take a great amount of playing time to truly understand. In most cases, it is virtually impossible to train gamemasters (GMs) to provide adequate support in 30 days or less; you need more like 60–90 days.

While you'll have one or two people assigned to support the game during Alpha, probably from QA, the time to start seriously hiring and training your support staff is during the six-month Beta phase. At that point, the game should be feature-complete; no new systems or mechanics will be added that will require trainees to have to hurry to keep up with the players. The model to use is the same one General Von Steuben used to train the Continental Army during the Revolutionary War: Start small, train a select group, and use them to train more people later on.

Using the Von Steuben method, Table 9.2 shows how such a ramp-up can occur. The idea is to add people as you increase the number of testers, until you have enough trained GMs at launch to adequately support the expected load. Estimating how many subscribers you'll have at launch is still something of a black art, but you should be able to make a reasonable estimate based on how many testers you have, how many Beta test applications you've received, and how well the buzz has created pre-orders for the retail unit (if there will be one). The example in 9.2 is based on a game launching after reaching 50,000 testers at the end of Beta and reaching 100,000 subscribers within six months of launch.

Table 9.2 Player Support Ramp-Up

	Month 1	Month 2	Month 3	Month 4	Month 5	**LAUNCH** Month 6
Testers/subscribers	1,000	2,500	5,000	20,000	50,000	50,000
Senior manager	1	1	1	1	1	1
Game masters	3	5	10	15	20	20
Lead GMs	1	1	1	3	3	3
Community relations	1	1	2	2	3	3
TOTAL PERSONNEL	**6**	**8**	**14**	**21**	**27**	**27**
	Month 7	Month 8	Month 9	Month 10	Month 11	Month 12
Testers/subscribers	60,000	70,000	80,000	90,000	95,000	100,000
Senior manager	1	1	1	1	1	1
Game masters	24	28	32	36	38	40
Lead GMs	3	4	4	4	5	5
Community relations	3	3	3	3	3	3
TOTAL PERSONNEL	**31**	**36**	**40**	**44**	**47**	**49**

An example of ramping up player and community relations during the Beta phase to achieve 1 GM per 2,500 subscribers at launch, plus leads and managers.

Based on our experience with many online games over the past 16 years, and assuming all the requisite tools are in place and functioning and that you intend to provide 24/7 service, the best recommendation we can make is to have a minimum basic ratio of one frontline GM for every 2,500 total subscribers you expect at launch and be ready to add personnel quickly if the game sells like hotcakes. You should reach this number at least one month before launch, to give most of your support personnel time to become familiar with the game.

The costs of hiring and training shouldn't be your only consideration here; you also have to consider the intangibles, such as how speed of response enhances your reputation for good CS and acts as an acquisition tool, to bring in more subscribers through good word of mouth. With a smooth launch being such an important factor in the acquisition of subscribers, a smart company that expects a game to do well right out the gate (and can afford the wage, salary, and benefits load) should take the GM totals in Table 9.2 and increase them by 50% to ensure better response times to player help requests, both in-game and via email.

It will be a balancing act between your need to have an adequate staff and the size of your launch budget. The best advice we can give is not to treat this area as disposable; good customer support is *the* main differentiator between PWs today. Having good support through a trained and adequately sized team is both an acquisition and retention tool; poor or sloppy support costs you subscribers in the long run.

Part III

Launching and Managing a Game

Chapter 10

Launch Day

"When we launched UO, we expected some problems. That being said, there was a whole class of issues we did not expect at all and were entirely unprepared for. Think of it this way: Suppose you built a real city from scratch. At first, you build the roads and houses but have no citizens. Then one day, you say, 'Ah, the city is ready. Okay, 100,000 people, come move in!' That is basically what we did when we launched UO.

"In a real city of 100,000 people, there is a huge amount of social and political infrastructure. We had none. Thus, everyone who wanted to complain about things that could be parallels of how often the trash is picked up, or pot- holes, or school boards, or penalties for laws, or laws themselves, had no formal way to voice their thoughts. Thus, they all complained to the few creators. The creators who number a mere few dozen cannot possibly respond to queries of 100,000 citizens; thus most went unanswered, thus most felt we were ignoring their plights, thus they hated us. In fact, we did hear them, we were working diligently to rectify their issues, but we likewise had no way to respond to them, as they had no way to voice to us their needs.

"It took over one year to evolve a proper community struc- ture. Creators should grow their online communities well before launch."

Richard Garriott

If you aren't scared of launch day, you ought to be.

Of the seven major persistent worlds (PW) launches and several minor ones since 1996, only two have avoided significant levels of tragedy. On the other five, servers crashed, critical bugs abounded, and customer service (CS) was overwhelmed or non-existent; in other words, they were a mess.

You're probably thinking: "Hey, we planned for this ahead of time; didn't we just go through a test period? We'll be different from those other guys, really." And you may be right; stranger things have happened.

Chances are, though, you aren't as ready as you could be, especially if this is your first time out of the gate. Like real combat, until you've lived the hell, it is impossible to truly comprehend just what is about to happen. A good launch is absolutely critical to your long-term success. *Ultimate Online (UO)* and *EverQuest (EQ)* were able to get away with poor launches because they had first-mover advantage in the marketplace. That luxury is no longer available for games entering the market today. Every player who tries your game and then flies away after a bad launch seems to make it known on one Internet rant site or another these days, which means several other players won't be giving you money, either. The ones who don't bother to post on the Internet are still subject to using traditional word of mouth to spread knowledge of their dissatisfaction to interested parties.

Launch Philosophy

Your launch philosophy should encompass plans for both the long and short terms. This is not like simply shipping a product to retail; this is an ongoing service that must be maintained long after the player buys or downloads the game and starts playing. Short-term thinking on your part will almost certainly leave money on the table for others to pick up, in the form of players who leave during your free trial period for other products and services.

There are a few simple guidelines you can follow to make things go more smoothly during this process. We cover those in the next several sections.

Don't Launch Before the Game Is Ready

Your concept may be explosive, capable of blowing the doors off the gaming world like a nuclear weapon. If it isn't quite perfect yet, you can survive, provided you can deliver it safely. But, if it isn't complete or if it is technically unstable, it is likely to blow up in your face. You only get to launch once. You only have one shot at a good first impression with someone you meet on the street. Here, you have but one chance to impress the highly motivated players checking out the game during the first two weeks. If you blow it here and players leave the game, it is almost impossible to recapture them later. Don't be tempted to launch with serious, known problems just to get it over with; that is short-term thinking that will cost you millions in the long run.

There *Will* Be Problems, So Be Prepared

This is the period in which the most problems are likely to occur, in fact. You'll experience them technically with the host/client platforms, service, and administrative tools, and emotionally with some players and player support personnel. If there is ever a good time to overinvest in player relations and overall support, this is it. It is far easier to scale back support to adequate levels once the crisis has passed than it is to try to scale up quickly to meet an emergency.

Just because there will be problems anyway does not mean you should launch prematurely; doing so will only scale up your difficulties to unmanageable levels.

The Game Is a Service, So Treat It Like One

Be service-minded, not product-minded. How you handle the customers during the first week or two of the post-launch phase will set the tone of the relationship for months to come.

Being service-minded means preparing ahead of time. Before accepting your first player's subscription payment, have these items in your toolbox, not on your to-do list:

➤ Policies and procedures on dealing with customers, written out, vetted by all relevant departments, published to the team, and thoroughly discussed before the launch.

➤ A well-trained player relations staff who exceed the expected need, who are familiar with the game and policies, who understand that 50% of the job consists of taking shots from abusive players (and not taking it personally), and who do their jobs with compassion and speed.

➤ Middle- and senior-level managers experienced with online game player relations who are empowered to make decisions on the spot, who are guided by the policies and procedures, and who feel the need to be best-of-breed in online service and support.

➤ Rehearsals with the player relations and community management teams on possible crisis situations and methods for handling them.

Fumbling here means losing the trust of the players, and that trust takes months or years to recover, if you recover it at all.

The Importance of a Technically Stable Launch

When the industry speaks of the launches of games such as *World War II Online* and *Anarchy Online (AO)*, the comment heard most often is, "What made them think they were ready to launch???"

Those two games have become the epitome of the bad launch, and it has cost them dearly in long-term revenue. Neither game was ready to launch when it did and, compounding the problem, both games sold over 40,000 units at retail in the first two days, well above the final simultaneous user levels in the final tests. This created an extreme, yet untested, load on the login and game servers. Both crashed and burned on launch day, experienced ongoing technical problems during the initial two weeks post-launch, and ended up with a lot fewer paying subscribers because of these issues.

So, why did they launch? From public statements made by company representatives and a little deduction, the main reason was apparently financial—the desire to start generating cash flow (or in PlayNet/Cornered Rat's case with *World War II Online*, the *need*, as evidenced by their later bankruptcy) and see a return on the investment after a long and expensive development process. The results were obviously not what they expected: poor word of mouth and initial customer retention rates far below the industry average.

The lesson: Learn from the mistakes of others.

Some of the problems others have seen at launch are listed here:

➤ The game gets swamped by too many players trying to log on during the first day of service; login servers and the game itself slow to a crawl or crash repeatedly from the load.

These days, it doesn't take much to create enough hype on the Internet to get 25,000–35,000 people to buy the retail package on day one. Of course, these are the motivated buyers; they are buying the retail SKU because they are going to log on to your game. If you aren't ready to handle 25,000–35,000 simultaneous players, you're already in the hole, trying to climb out.

To state the painfully obvious, nothing drives away potential subscribers faster than not being able to log in and play.

➤ The guys upstairs want to start seeing some cash flow, so they order a launch, regardless of the state of bug fixes and technical stability in general.

This problem comes in two forms:

➤ **Developers or QA misstating the situation**—Most executives today don't fully grasp the technical or support problems of these games. They realize that they don't know, and they depend on the developers and QA to state accurately and clearly whether the game is ready to launch. Whether from pressure, fear, inexperience with the process, or overestimating their own ability to fix problems quickly, developers and QA often misstate the actual condition of the game to give executives a "feel good" moment about ordering the launch. In a sense, this comes under the heading of lying to the stakeholders.

➤ **Executives ignoring the advice of the developers and/or the QA department**—Even when the development team and QA give accurate reports and recommend a delay in launch, executives have been known to order it anyway, based on the mistaken belief that any cash flow is better than none or just the plain need to start getting some cash in the door.[1]

_____

1. One of the authors uses an example of a persistent world project she consulted on a few years back. "What the company wanted was to improve acquisition and retention of subscribers. They had a horrible launch that generated some controversy, so I started by trying to back-track the reasons for it," she says. "One of the documents I was shown was the Quality Assurance book listing the unfixed bugs. There were well over 400 pages of them, including known crash bugs in both the game client and server. On the first page of the book was a letter from the head of QA recommending a launch delay, countersigned by the Producer and the Lead Tester and receipt of which was acknowledged by a senior management person. That letter was dated only a few days before the launch actually took place. Senior management obviously did not understand at the time the ramifications of launching in that state." She added, "This kind of thing is not at all unusual in the industry."

Don't launch with bugs just because you want the income flow. A bad launch actually costs you revenue in the long run because it creates bad word of mouth and reviews for the game. Launching too early hurts the return on investment (ROI), especially in the short and middle terms.

➤ The client is shipped to retail with known, sometimes serious, problems because the development team is certain it can fix the problems by the time the game hits the shelves.

While we admire the confidence of coders in their abilities to fix problems quickly, this borders on arrogance because it hasn't happened yet in any of the poor launches seen since 1996. It takes far more than 30 days to find, fix, and test a couple dozen bugs, and most PWs have launched with *hundreds* of known bugs, never mind the hidden, unexpected ones that lay in wait for launch.

We have yet to see a situation where a development team was able to come through on this promise. Based on that experience, development teams shouldn't fool themselves that they can do it, and those responsible for green-lighting a launch shouldn't believe it can be done.

➤ Player relations is swamped by email and in-game help requests due to under-staffing and/or the number of technical problems in the game.

How you publicly handle technical instability with the players is just as important as how you deal with it internally. Assuming you don't launch prematurely and don't hit many unanticipated technical snags, there will still be some technical problems due to the sheer load of people trying to access the game at the same time and, in a perfect example of Finagle's Law According to Niven,[2] some hidden systems and game mechanics bugs will reveal themselves only when the billing clock is ticking.

To our knowledge, no PW launch since 1996 has featured an adequately staffed or trained Player Relations department; everyone keeps getting taken by surprise by the sheer load of email and in-game help requests.

Here are some guidelines to help you plan for the load:

---

2. "The perversity of the universe tends to a maximum."

➤ As a general rule of thumb, your direct, individual contacts with the player base per month, meaning in-game help requests, emails, technical support requests, and billing and account management issues, can very easily equal the total number of subscribers. In other words, if you think you'll sign up 40,000 subscribers the first month, you should plan for 40,000 separate help requests.

➤ Each help request takes time to resolve. Most of them should be fairly easy to resolve, especially common issues such as, "I'm stuck on the game map!" However, those minutes can add up quickly, as you can see from Table 10.1.

Table 10.1   Support Hours

Help Requests	Avg. Minutes/ Request	Total Minutes	Total Man Hours	8 Hour Shifts Needed	Minimum Employees Needed
40,000	1	40,000	667	83	17
40,000	2	80,000	1,333	167	33
40,000	3	120,000	2,000	250	50
40,000	4	160,000	2,667	333	67
40,000	5	200,000	3,333	417	83
Help Requests	Avg. Minutes/ Request	Total Minutes	Total Man Hours	8 Hour Shifts Needed	Minimum Employees Needed
100,000	1	100,000	1,667	208	42
100,000	2	200,000	3,333	417	83
100,000	3	300,000	5,000	625	125
100,000	4	400,000	6,667	833	167
100,000	5	500,000	8,333	1,042	208

As you can see from Table 10.1, even at an average resolution time of one minute per player help request, the hours required to deal with those requests stack up quickly, as does the expense of hiring employees to deal with them. As it is standard in the industry to give the first month for free as a trial period, the more successful you are in attracting players in the first month, the higher the expense will be in personnel for what amounts to freeloading players.

If the game is technically stable and the game mechanics don't present many unanticipated problems, or as you find and fix problems, the number of requests should steady out to a lower level after the first two to three months. If they don't, the team needs to sit down and figure out why and make recommendations on what should be fixed to lower those request totals. Also, once the player relations and other support people have some experience under their belts, you'll find that resolution times will drop, sometimes dramatically. However, every game is different and, depending on the complexity of it, help requests and resolution times may remain at high levels for a long time, perhaps the life of the game.

Examining Table 10.1, you can see why emphasizing a technically stable launch, including monitoring and logging tools, and having full-featured tools for the player relations and other support staff can be critical to the profit margin. Keeping careful track of these metrics, striving for stability at launch, shooting for quick resolution times, and adjusting support service where and when it is needed can mean savings of literally hundreds of thousands of dollars in the first six months of operations.

➤ Your Beta phase will help you determine the number of support people needed at launch.

You aren't just testing the game through Beta; you're also testing your assumptions about workflow and staffing levels for player relations, community relations, and billing and account management. Actual staffing levels are discussed in other sections. We mention it here because the warning signals on staffing levels given out during testing are often ignored or misunderstood. There is a general tendency to assume that when Beta technical problems are fixed, no other serious ones will reveal themselves, causing a drop in the number of player help requests at launch. History has shown this to be a somewhat enthusiastic assumption, not grounded in experience.

If the staff is overwhelmed by 20,000 simultaneous testers during the final load testing and you expect to ship 50,000 units to retail on the first day, one should assume that most of those 50,000 units will be sold in the first week and the buyers will try to connect to the game. If the staff was hard-pressed with 20,000 players, imagine how it will be for them with 30,000–50,000 simultaneous players.

➤ It is highly recommended you "overstaff" for the first month to two months.

Since you're likely to see the biggest rush of new customers and the most problems with your service during the first month to two months of live operations, it is better to overspend than underspend on personnel during this time. Better the additional cost of an extra 15 or 20 gamemasters (GMs) for a couple months than to risk having bad word of mouth ruin the reputation of the game during this critical period. The idea is to be able to respond faster to player help requests, especially in-game and via email. More rapid player relations response times result in higher player satisfaction, resulting in higher retention rates. They also act as an acquisition tool through good word of mouth ("Hey, these guys really know what they are doing!"). If you are successful in this strategy, you may find your subscriber numbers soaring beyond even inflated expectations and the temporary support personnel becoming permanent.

How many, with whom, and when to begin the overstaffing is a matter of theory, not established fact, because no one has done it yet.[3] Much also depends on whether the game is technically stable; if the game has serious connection or server crashing problems or serious in-game bugs that affect the performance of characters, no number of GMs is going to be able to keep up with the email and in-game petition load.

Assuming that a launch is technically stable and has no serious game-impeding bugs, our experience with other launches indicates that a basic formula of one player relations person at launch per 1,000 retail units in the first shipment is probably a good number to start with. Following this formula, if you are shipping 50,000 units to retail in the first print run, you should have 50 player relations people on-hand on launch day, 100 for 100,000 units shipped, and so on.

Next let us consider when and with whom. This is where it gets stickier. It takes time to train a GM for any particular product; these are complex products and you can't just drag someone in off the street and expect him/her to do even an adequate job. That means you have to bring these people in, at an absolute minimum, 30 days ahead of launch, and 60 days would be much better.

Considering the expense, we'll assume that most publishers will choose the 30-day option. The only viable venue for finding temporary employees for a three-month contract quickly is, of course, temporary worker agencies, any number of which can be found in most metropolitan areas. Using "temps"

---

3. *Star Wars Galaxies* Creative Director Raph Koster and Executive Producer Rich Vogel have both mentioned this concept in seminars and lectures. Sony Online's *Star Wars Galaxies* is expected to launch early in 2003, so we may see the first instance of it then.

allows you to scale quickly for the launch and then scale the support personnel numbers to meet the actual need after the launch phase has settled out. While in most cases we would not recommend temporary assignment workers for a duty as critical as player relations, the risk is acceptable for a launch phase under the following conditions:

➤   The temps are used for Tier One help requests only, meaning the easiest problems to resolve.

    All other problems are escalated to the permanent staff, who are better able to resolve them quickly and efficiently.

➤   Access to in-game powers is extremely limited to maintain security.

    Temps should not be able to manipulate or change player/character stats, create or delete objects from the game, remove or place objects on player/characters, or have any effect on non-player characters (NPCs). At most, temps should be able to "unstick" players from game terrain by moving them a very limited distance, and they should have the power to teleport themselves to any location within the game.

➤   All temporary worker in-game actions and "chat" messages are logged, and those logs are reviewed on a daily basis.

    This helps you maintain quality control during the launch phase; even the limited powers noted here can be abused to give the temp's friends an advantage. For example, a temp who can teleport anywhere in the game can "scout" out locations or other players for friends, giving them the advantage of knowing where good treasure or vital NPCs are located or where enemies might be located for ambushing. As temps have no overriding loyalty to the company or the game, you should assume that at least one of them will try to get away with this.

How Much Hardware and Bandwidth?

Previous sections in this book have discussed technical stability and the importance of achieving it before launching a game. "Technical stability" for launch doesn't just mean that the software code works well; it also means making sure the physical infrastructure to handle the load is in place and tested before the paying customers hit the front door. In this case, "infrastructure" means having enough servers and server clusters, routers, and bandwidth capacity to handle the load, and to be able to grow gracefully if the load outstrips expectations.

The key phrase is "to grow gracefully." If the number of subscribers creating accounts outstrips the ability of the available infrastructure to handle them, the game will see increased latency on the game servers due to player overload on the machines and the bandwidth's capacity, traffic jams and delays on the login servers, and refused player connections as login servers or server clusters either hit their assigned peak connections or just plain give up and "die" from the overload. If this occurs, it doesn't matter if you launch with the most stable code and balanced game mechanics ever seen in the PW market; the players' perception of the game will be that it is buggy, was launched too soon, and/or is not ready for prime-time.

To prevent this from happening, you have to plan for both expected load and unexpected overload at launch and have the resources on hand to deal with it. At minimum, you need the extra hardware and bandwidth capacity on hand to set up and integrate a new server cluster on-demand. How much more you'll need depends on a couple factors.

How Many Servers/World Iterations?

Most server clusters for current PWs are configured to handle between 2,000 and 3,000 simultaneous users, out of a total of 10,000 or so paying accounts per server cluster. The actual numbers vary between games; for example, the original server cluster for Funcom's *AO* (a "dimension") was designed to host 10,000 simultaneous players and all of the game's subscriber accounts. On the whole, however, a configuration of 2,000–3,000 users/10,000 accounts per cluster is the most common.

Depending on how many load testers participated during the open Beta tests, you probably had between two and five server clusters running at any one time (20,000–50,000 load testers). Most publishers assume this is the launch load they'll have to handle, but that doesn't take into account the following:

> ➤ The number of potential players that don't generally participate in testing. A significant number of people don't want to put time into the game until it is launched and supposedly stable. There are no hard and fast numbers for this category, but you can generally get a pretty good idea from retail pre-order numbers.

➤ Players that subscribe multiple accounts for themselves, friends, and/or family members. This is another number that is tough to anticipate. As a self-protection measure, a publisher should assume that a minimum of 10% of the peak number of open Beta testers will open multiple accounts.

➤ Marketing "buzz" around the game versus retail pre-orders and the number of units being shipped to retail in the first print run. Marketing and Press Relations departments have a bad rap for being "weasels" and not even playing the games they market, but they are usually quite good at creating a sense of anticipation for a PW release. In fact, they are generally so successful and so far out in front of the development team that the latter gets taken by surprise when the subscriber load quickly outstrips their own estimates and growth schedules.

The only way for publishers to protect themselves in any of these situations is to look at the initial print run and pre-orders.

How Many Units Are You Shipping to Retail?

Boxed goods publishers want to ship as many shelf units (often called SKUs) to retail as they think the market can handle. It makes sense, considering the normal business model for publishers; build the game, hype the game, and then sell as many units as possible during the "sweet spot"—the first three to six months of a game's normal shelf life.

This makes perfect sense for a solo-play home game, but it can present problems for a PW game service. The problems a service can experience scale up with the number of total and simultaneous subscribers. The trick, then, is to correctly anticipate the launch load and add both additional server and bandwidth capacity to allow for graceful growth. There are two good metrics that can be used to estimate planned overcapacity levels: the first is the number of testers that took part in the final open Beta phase load tests; the second is the number of retail pre-orders and planned first print-run for the game.

➤ **Total simultaneous testers**—The testers that come in during the open Beta are generally the motivated players interested in playing the game. The number of simultaneous testers is pretty self-explanatory; if you hit 50,000 and the load tests went smoothly, you can assume that most of them are interested in the game and will purchase the retail unit.

There is no way to truly gauge just how many of them have or will pre-order the retail unit, plan on being in line to buy it on launch day, or how many people they talked to who weren't in the test but whom they've convinced to buy the game (such as friends, a guild, or a team from another game). The best "fudge factor" to calculate is to just assume that at least 80% of them will buy the game and participate in launch week.

➤ **Retail pre-orders**—A somewhat more precise indicator of the number of people that will try to play during launch day is the number of pre-orders at retail chains. If the tester load is scaling up to 50,000 during open Beta but the retail pre-orders are at 75,000 two months before launch, you have a happy problem: the need to lay in more hardware and bandwidth. You can assume most of them will be picking up their copies in the first couple days of launch and getting online.

About two months from the projected launch date, you should look at the pre-order and total open Beta tester numbers and make a determination on how many server clusters you're likely to actually need on launch day. If you have 75,000 pre-orders and you can comfortably hold 10,000 accounts per cluster, you'll need 8 server clusters to handle the expected load. At this point, you must decide how much over-capacity to stock up for. As stated earlier, a minimum of one extra server cluster on-hand is a necessity, not a luxury. Depending on the hype surrounding the game and how the estimates are fine-tuned during the last two months (if marketing is doing its job correctly, pre-orders of the retail unit will continue to grow), you may want to add one or two more extra clusters in reserve.

Staged Launch

One way to cut the risk of being overwhelmed during the launch phase is to stage out the launch. This is accomplished by not shipping all available retail units from the warehouse to the stores, but breaking them into three or four shipments and parceling them out in daily or weekly allotments. For example, instead of sending 100,000 units to retail on the first day, send 25,000, and then send another 25,000 a few days later, and so on. This effectively limits the number of people who can sign up new accounts at any one time, greatly reducing the chances that your hardware and bandwidth will be overwhelmed. Even just three days between major influxes of new players can give you much-needed time to do emergency troubleshooting; it is much better to incon- venience 25,000 subscribers than 50,000.

Staging your launch also allows you to gauge the "last-minute" sales and pre-orders caused by the enforced shortage and decide if you need to order server clusters and bandwidth over and above your current reserves.

A last warning on this: If demand outstrips resources, there is going to be the temptation to install your test server cluster as a live production server "just until we can get in new test hardware." Don't do it; without a test server, you'll be in the position of having to test fixes and changes on a live production server cluster, and this is completely unacceptable. Not only will the players on that cluster howl like banshees (and rightly so; they aren't paying money to be guinea pigs), your reputation will suffer as well. All it will take is one major crash of the "test" server for you to lose all trust from the player base.

How Much Bandwidth Capacity?

By the time open Beta is in full swing, you should have a good idea of the bandwidth consumption per connection to your game—that is, the total bit rate per individual user and per distinct server cluster. These metrics, combined with your estimation of the number of production and reserve server clusters needed on launch day and the peak number of simultaneous users you'll have to support, will give you a pretty firm idea of the amount of bandwidth you'll need to have available.

Beyond that, you'll need to estimate a growth rate for the game for the first three to six months and make sure that the bandwidth capacity to handle that growth is on hand. The best recommendation we can make is to estimate your need at launch (plus the reserve clusters) and tack on enough extra capacity to handle at least one additional server cluster. If you are co-locating clusters at the network operations centers (NOCs) of an Internet backbone provider, such as Exodus, this isn't a problem; most backbone NOCs have plenty of capacity and can step up availability in an instant. If you plan on hosting your own server farms and laying in your own fiber, this is more problematic; getting the local phone company to actually lay in the phone line can be like pulling teeth. Average wait times in major metropolitan areas are running over 30 days; this isn't something you can wait until the last minute to get done.

Who's in Charge on Launch Day?

At this point, just before launch day, you should have in place both a game development team and a live development team. The live development team may or may not be fully rounded out, but by this point, your mission-critical positions are filled and they've been working with the game development team for some time. For that matter, they may be working *for* the game development team, as part of the final crew bringing the game to the launch stage, and some members of the game development team are probably slated to move to the live development team to help maintain continuity and a keen knowledge base of the code.

If you've done as we've suggested, at this juncture the game has two producers and, at minimum, some duplicate sets of lead designers, client programmers, server/network programmers, and maybe a few duplicate junior designers and engineers in the mix, too. At the same time, the rest of the overall live operations team, including community relations, player relations, and network operations, have been ramping up and getting to know both development teams.

With such a mixed command structure, communication links and responsibilities may become an issue, especially in knowing which "duplicate" is responsible for fixing bugs and publishing changes and who communicates them to community relations, player relations, and the players. It is important to maintain a clear chain of authority, both within the company and with the players, to avoid misunderstandings ("Hey, I thought you were fixing that bug!" or "What are you doing answering questions for the community guys? That's my job!") and create a smooth pathway for transitioning the live development team into operations later on.

Who Does What, and When?

How long a launch phase lasts depends greatly on how many problems the game and service experience on launch and how long it takes to fix those problems and stabilize the product. Even though the live development team has been slowly ramping up during the testing process, the game development team is still far more familiar with the code and design and can do this job more quickly and more efficiently.

Ideally, a launch phase for a fairly stable product and service can be planned to last for three months, at which time the live development team takes over from game development, which then goes on a long vacation to rediscover what that "sun" thing looks like. For that three-month period, the game development team hierarchy should remain in charge and have sole responsibility for assigning, tracking, and testing fixes for patches. They should also be the people that community relations taps to provide "official" answers for public distribution.

If the game and service experience a load of serious problems from the outset, however, the duration of the launch phase should remain flexible, as long as six months. By the end of this time, the service will either be stabilized or you'll be trying to come up with an alternate strategy to stave off impending disaster.

Introducing the Live Development Team

It should be the responsibility of the community relations team to keep the subscriber base informed as to who is in charge and maintain the communication flow between the teams and the players (see the later section titled "Disaster Control"). This includes managing the public transition of the internal leadership and teams to prevent a sense of confusion, instability, or trepidation among the players. A sudden or abruptly announced transition can easily be mistaken for firings or replacements for incompetence and may be blown out of proportion by that portion of the player base that lives for such drama.

If it hasn't happened before this in the open Beta test period, community relations should begin smoothing the way for the public transition to the "new" team at the end of launch by introducing the live development team to the player community. This is in addition to any community relations activities with the game development team, such as online developer chats and regular team postings monitored by the community relations team. Community relations' purpose is to maintain the game's public chain of command in the hands of the game development team, while simultaneously making the players accustomed to hearing from the people who will eventually be in charge of the game. There are a number of strategies that can be employed, such as a series of regular "Letters from the Live Team" that discuss issues of concern to the players or note some of the combined activities of the game and live development teams, and live team online chat sessions to let the players get to know the live team's personalities.

If the live team is being introduced for the first time during launch, it is probably a good idea to wait until the initial two-week "rush" period is over. If there are issues with the launch, the great bulk of them will occur during this period, and there may be a sense of confusion and chaos among the players; there is no need to amplify that by introducing new people and perhaps creating a perception that confusion reigns internally, too.

Transition Ceremonies

When the day arrives to move from launch to live operations and make the official transition from game development to live development, the occasion should be noted with two ceremonies: an internal one within the company and one that is held publicly, with the players. This is a critical milestone in the life of a PW and it is important to let all concerned know that not only have the game and service moved into a new phase of the lifecycle, but the baton has been passed to others to carry.

The Company Ceremony

For the game development team, this has been a long haul, certainly at least two years and perhaps as long as four years. For some of your team members, this will be the longest sustained activity they've experienced in their lives and the most significant project in which they've ever been involved. Some of it will have been fun and exciting, basking in the adulation of players who appreciate the effort; some of it will have been pain, sweat, and sleepless nights, suffering the ingratitude of that small section of the player base that likes to carp and criticize at every little bump in the road. As the team comes to the end of the trail, there will be mixed emotions, including satisfaction with the job done, some sadness and happiness that it is finally over, and probably a little depression, too; they will no longer be the cocks of the walk. For people who have just spent years being the online game industry's equivalent of rock stars, this can be a bitter pill to swallow.

Conversely, it is a new beginning for the live development team, as they prepare to take on the huge responsibility of maintaining a game and service that may have taken $20 million to develop and launch. They will probably be both excited at the prospect and nervous that they may blow it.

To help ease the transition of both teams into the new situation and set a demarcation line for the rest of the company, it is important to have an all-hands company ceremony that acknowledges the hard work and success of the game developers and clearly and cleanly passes the responsibility torch to the live development team. This can be as simple as a company meeting one afternoon, with a small ceremony thanking the game development team, introducing the live development team, and having short speeches by the two producers, or it can be as elaborate as a formal company dinner, complete with plaques, awards, and speeches.

The Public Ceremony

Equally as important is a ceremony for the benefit of the players, again to scotch potential rumor-mongering and let the subscribers know that the change from development to live operations has been made.

If at all possible, this "passing the baton" ceremony should be done in the game and at least somewhat in the context of the game, with players invited to attend. It is recommended that you don't throw open the doors to any and all who wish to be there; that is practically a guarantee that the physical server will be swamped and probably crash, because *everyone* will want to be there. Imagine 2,000–3,000 simultaneous players trying to crowd onto to a small region of the game and you'll get the picture.

Rather, pick or create a closed location in the game for the ceremony and hold a drawing, raffle, or some other random, non-partisan selection method to fill the player attendee slots for the ceremony. At the appointed time, have your GMs transport the player/characters to the correct spot, conduct the ceremony, and then have some kind of event, such as a banquet or skill contest. This kind of ceremony and event really charges the players and puts a "human face" on the live team; it makes them part of the family, so to speak.

If it is just not possible to effectively hold the ceremony in-game, hold a web chat and/or post "in-character" announcements on your web site, announcing the change of leadership and the movement from development to live operations.

Disaster Control

Technology can be a perverse creature. Most PWs experience a few bumps during the first couple of weeks of the launch period. If it isn't a piece of hardware failing catastrophically at exactly the wrong moment, it is a hole in the design that no one caught during testing that plays havoc with the player base, or a hidden bug that decides to pop up the day after launch and start crashing the client or servers. Even if you have an incredibly stable game service at the end of open Beta and it is apparent to you that there will be no huge problems with the code or service on launch, it just makes sense to have contingency plans in case disaster does decide to strike. You have to consider weird and unlikely scenarios, as some things are completely out of your control. What if your Internet access provider goes down for an extended period on launch day, as happened to one launch in 2001? Or, what if one or more key team members become unavailable for some reason, or your test server cluster refuses to boot at exactly the wrong moment because someone on the cleaning crew was messing with it the night before? What if something as simple and uncontrollable as the weather suddenly turns nasty and the power in the building goes out?

These situations may be out of your control to stop, but that won't be the way the players will see it. If the Internet access into the game servers goes black, it is going to be your fault, plain and simple. It's your game, isn't it? Fix it! What am I paying you chumps money for, anyway? How you handle these problems internally and with the player base as they crop up is going to be a key factor in the retention rate—that is, converting trial players into paying subscribers. Therefore, it makes sense to do some contingency planning on how disasters will be controlled.

Internal Disaster Control

The producer, network operations manager, manager of player relations, and manager of community relations should form the core of the disaster planning team and start meeting well before the launch to construct a disaster control plan. The plan should include the following elements:

➤ A notification process that puts everyone on the various teams on full alert for a possible all-hands drill for 16–24 hours on launch day.

➤ A meeting or publication schedule that informs everyone in the organization that, if the worst happens, all teams may have to provide round-the-clock staffing until the crisis is over.

➤ Bug lists—Understand just what bugs remain and publish that list internally to be prepared to deal with them.

➤ Customer support ramp-up—Make sure the CS staff is fully staffed and trained and ready to pull double shifts if necessary.

The policies, procedures, FAQ sheets, and problem-response answers that player relations will be using should be double-checked. A series of meetings with the staff should be held to go over them one more time.

➤ Communications plan—Have the community relations team create a communications plan for linking with the producers, getting updates from them, and constructing timely public messages to inform the players of the problem, what is being done to fix it, and a general estimate of the time when the fix is expected to be completed.

As launch day approaches, the disaster planning team should meet regularly with development, player relations, and community relations to go over the plan, make or note any necessary changes, and discuss the plan in-depth with the teams. There should be a final all-hands briefing on the disaster control plan the day before the launch is scheduled to take place.

If Disaster Happens

If disaster does strike: Pause. When the adrenaline starts flowing in reaction to a problem, the first reaction is usually to do something, anything, to start making things better. In this situation, unorganized action is a recipe for creating another disaster. Instead, slow down and take the time to get organized and follow the process and plan you've developed.

➤ **Use the plan**—Don't hesitate to put into action those elements of the plan that apply to the situation, even if the situation doesn't seem to warrant a disaster reaction. In a less-than-disaster situation, the extra organization and galvanization provided by the plan can only help; your team will feel more comfortable knowing there is an organized response to the problem, and everyone will know how they are supposed to respond.

➤ **Get organized**—If there is more than one problem to be solved, prioritize them and assign people to start the investigation and fix process on the top priorities. Top priority should be given to those elements that prevent players from accessing the game, such as bugs that crash the client, game servers, database, or network servers. After those are dealt with, bugs that can be used to exploit the game mechanics or duplicate game items should be handled, followed by lag or latency issues. After those issues are dispatched, get together with the team, go over all the remaining outstanding issues revealed by the launch, and prioritize the fix schedule.

➤ **Communicate**—While all this is going on, the community relations team should be meeting briefly but regularly with the producer, getting updates, and constructing messages to post for the players. While problem-solving is ongoing, it is a good idea for community relations to be posting on a regular basis, such as once per hour or half-hour, even if progress is minimal. The players will be much more responsive and patient with the process as long as you make the attempt to keep them informed. Whenever possible, substantive information should be relayed; for example, if the game servers need to come down for a reboot to install a fix, give the players both a warning before the reboot and an all-clear signal when it is safe to go back into the game. If a client crash bug fix is being tested on the internal test server, note that in a message.

➤ **Follow up**—Keep the players informed as to the overall progress. Once or twice a day, community relations should post a message from the producer, noting which problems have been worked on, which have been fixed, and which are still in the fix/test process. If the producer has scheduled game downtime as part of the process, make sure this is part of the message, even if you've posted about it elsewhere. This will give the players the opportunity to plan their game time and gameplay, which is really what they want to know about the process, as well as that the team is working hard to fix problems.

Chapter 11

Managing a Game Post-Launch

KEY TOPICS

- Barbarians, Tribesmen, and Citizens

- Transitioning from the Development Team to the Live Team

- Managing the Expectations of the Players

- Player Relations: The In-Game GMs

- The Service Philosophy: Acquiring and Retaining Subscribers

- Security: Keeping Honest People Honest

- Community Relations: Processes

"Probably the most frequent mistake I've seen live teams make is that they don't listen to their player base when deciding what new features they want to add. Live teams are under the delusion that the game is theirs, as opposed to that of the player base, and often they will try to muck with systems that are just fine, thank you very much."

Damion Schubert

Now the *real* work begins.

Okay, you've launched; now what? It may surprise you to learn that, if you're to be a success, 90% of the work to be done on this game is still ahead of you. Anyone can build a persistent world (PW); maintaining technical stability and managing it effectively are the hard tasks. Just ask any developer who has launched a game since 1996 which was harder—development or post-launch management.

If you ask most developers with experience on an online game about launch and game management scenarios, you're likely to hear about a scenario similar to the following:

> ➤ Millions of dollars of development money have been flowing out of the company coffers for two, three, or four years.

➤ The announced launch date has come and gone between one and three times, meaning the game is already six months to a year overdue.

➤ The people who write the checks and would like to see a return on their money are putting pressure on the development team to get the damn thing out the door already.

➤ The developers decide to cut a bunch of features that have been promised to the players, including features already listed on the back or inside cover of the retail box.

➤ Even by cutting a bunch of features, there are hundreds of bugs still to be fixed, but the money guys order the box shipped and the game launched.

➤ The game is hugely unstable, the servers and client crash constantly, features are missing or don't work as promised, and the team is working 20-hour days to try to catch up.

➤ The players are up in arms and ready to hang the developers in effigy.

➤ Bad word of mouth circulates about the game, killing subscriptions and sales.

➤ The development team members start printing résumés on the company printers and faxing them to the competition on the company fax machines.

Refer to the section in Chapter 10, "Launch Day," titled "The Importance of a Technically Stable Launch" for an overview of what makes a good launch. Sadly, the industry hasn't seen very many of them in the past five years.

Once the launch period has come and gone, it is time to settle in for the long haul of managing the game. That starts with understanding the players.

Barbarians, Tribesmen, and Citizens

One of the biggest issues you'll have to contend with is the players. This issue is unavoidable. You must manage player expectations, have respect for your players, and listen to them as well. You can and should care deeply about them, too. After all, these are your customers. Every time they log into your game, they make a decision. With a few clicks of the mouse, they choose to continue supporting you.

The player issue will cause an unsuspecting developer more grief than anything else he or she can imagine. This is definitely not for the faint of heart. You may pay for, design, and create a world, but at the end of the day, if you want people to pay you their dollars, yen, and francs to play in it, sear this fact into your brain:

It isn't your game; it's the player's game.

Developers spend years focused on making a game. If they're not careful, this will breed certain assumptions, such as the world they created will remain their world and the players will play the game the way the creators want it played.

That will not happen. Players have their own motivations and objectives. We're talking about hundreds of thousands of people with different personalities—yet there are only 30 or so people who make a game. When a game goes live, the developers have to view it as a new game and a partnership with the players to make that world thrive. To do this, the developers need to understand who the players are, why they show up, and what makes them stay.

Who Am I?

The psychological makeup of hundreds of thousands of players could be broken down into any number of groupings and categories to help explain behavior and objectives. For the purposes of this book, we'll simplify and break it into three broad categories. Players who don't fall into one of these three areas are usually considered "general" players. General players are fairly neutral. They obey the rules, play the game, and might help out when they see someone who needs help. They aren't nasty and they aren't pillars of your community. They're regular "Joes."

It's important to note that there is gray area between these types. The categories that follow are generalizations. Please don't expect all your players to neatly line up into the areas we've listed. It won't happen that neatly, we promise.

Barbarians

The barbarians are the "problem children" of online gaming. Their objectives vary, but one thing is consistent: They don't care what you or anyone else thinks.

Barbarians don't care about your intricately conceived game mechanics or your well-thought-out player justice and accountability systems, or whether or not exploiting a bug is cheating. These are the "griefers," players who love the anonymity of the Internet and whose main enjoyment comes from ruining other players' experiences. They are the bug exploiters who don't care if duplicating gold, weapons, armor, or whatever requires them to flood attack your routers and crash a server. It doesn't bother them that thousands of others have their game interrupted.

Barbarians are the cheaters, script kiddies, account hackers, client hackers, and "k&wl d00ds," whose objectives are not socialization with friends in a game, but making sure they and their small group of other social misfits can giggle behind their hands as they stare at the monitor, happy to have caused heartache and pain to someone else.

Identifying barbarians is a critical task, one easier said than done. PWs, or those with servers under company control, have the advantage of logging activity. Problems can be verified and dealt with at a later time. In free-play peer-to-peer games, such as *Diablo II* or *Age of Empires*, it is almost impossible. The collective intelligence of client hackers and the anonymity of the Internet make it difficult for a developer to take action. This is why peer-to-peer games have such poor attendance online compared to sales; when the client hacks show up, the honest players give up in disgust. The same is true for PWs when bad behavior goes unchecked.

For some, the raw intensity of the "virtual psychopath" that many barbarians represent can be refreshing in its novelty. At first, some who encounter them react as though they are cute online versions of Hannibal Lecter. Soon after meeting barbarians, they notice what is missing from the comparison: education, erudition, and the ability to function in society. In fiction, Dr. Lecter's victims had some reason for becoming his entrees. Barbarians will eat your customers without any provocation or remorse. They are more akin to the mass murderer in the Richard Pryor movie who, when asked why he murdered all those people, replied, "They was home."

Barbarians are a statistically small group. However, they do a lot of damage to games. Reroute them or get them out of the game. It's that simple. The only players who will shed a tear at the banishment of griefers are other griefers.

The bottom line: Barbarians will drive customers away faster than Attila could jump on his horse.

Tribesmen

The objective of the tribesmen is to ensure that they and their personal micro-community (guild, team, squadron, clan, or Saturday morning coffee and killing club) have a great time. They are very team-oriented; it is not unusual for them to call each other in the early morning hours to get the tribe online for some objective. They help each other out, and at times, are pillars of the community, helping new players and generally trying to be a resource.

They can still cause problems in-game. For example, tribesmen have no trouble organizing "camping" parties. This is much like the big kids staking out the basketball court and not letting anyone else play. They put groups of players in an area and prevent others from utilizing it. This way, only the tribe reaps the benefits.

If another tribe or player annoys them, they can organize quickly and for long periods to attempt to drive that tribe or player out of the game. The tribe may use a variety of intimidation tactics. The goal: Make the game unplayable for the group or person they are angry with; in other words, drive them out.

Group dynamics can cause people to view rules differently. What players might not think is acceptable as individuals can change when it's for the good of the tribe. There can be a bit of mob mentality. If something is seen as an affront to the tribe, you could wind up with an entire group retaliating against the game, breaking rules as a way of fighting back, or the whole group may decide to pack up and move to another game.

There is beneficial power to the tribe as well. When happy, the entire tribe stays where it is. Listen to your tribes. Give them tools to facilitate group management and communication. Keep in mind that your tribe leaders are your political lifeblood in the game. They influence large groups. If you disrespect them, you can turn entire tribes into barbarians.

Citizens

The citizen is the crown jewel of any online game. Think of these players as the good people you know in the real world. In a game setting, these are the people most likely to take new players under their wing, take part in role-playing events, lend their in-game cash and resources to a greater cause, and always have a civil word for passersby.

Moreover, they are willing to obey the rules and play the game "realistically" (according to your vision) and in-character and encourage others to do so as well. Their objectives are to create a legend for themselves, but not at the expense of the game or other players. They want the whole game and all the players to survive and thrive within the world you've created.

The citizen usually strives to become a community leader. If there is no political or diplomatic portion to the game, they'll create one from whole cloth and convince others to participate. They become player advocates, game advocates, and at times, can create around themselves a cult of personality that becomes more vibrant and important than the game itself.

Citizens are pure gold. They keep others in the game. Please remember that the citizens deserve your attention. They aren't your squeaky wheels (like your problem children), and it's easy to overlook them. Attention given to the citizens has a huge impact on the world. It benefits the entire community. Do not fall into the trap we've faced before. You spend so much time responding to the fires caused by your problem players that your good players feel neglected. Over time, the neglected good players become barbarians themselves.

We've been there and we've done it. It hurts the game. Learn from our mistakes.

Now What?

Now that you know the three broad categories, what do you do about them?

When it comes to barbarians and upstart tribes, two words are key: logs and reports.

Create logs for everything you can. Log player transactions and transfers above a certain size, character traveling speeds, player inventories, you name it. This is the best method you have for catching cheaters, dupers, speed hackers, and other exploiters.

As an illustration of how this can save you plenty of time and heartache, Damion Schubert, former lead designer for the groundbreaking *Meridian 59* (*M59*), tells this story from his 1996 experiences:

I had coded guilds into M59 over the weekend, shortly before we were supposed to go gold. It was a rush job, but I took uncommon care and felt pretty confident that I had implemented something that was fairly bug-free. So imagine my consternation when a group of players told me something was totally broken.

One aspect of guilds was the guild halls. Players could conquer another player's guild hall by sneaking into the guild hall and flipping a switch. If it wasn't unflipped inside of 10 minutes, that guild hall was considered conquered. The key—the only way to sneak in—was if you snuck in the front door behind a player who belonged to the guild. Once inside, it was trivial to open the door, allowing the rest of your guild in. This simple design was such to ensure that players could only conquer guild halls while the defenders were actually online.

Except that the guild members yelling at me were swearing up and down that no one was online when their hall was taken over.

The way they figured it, the math was simple. They had 10 members; all 10 of them swore up and down that they hadn't entered the hall in the last day, nor had they gotten the ominous "Your guild hall is being raided!" message. I began to crack open code, pore over logs, and try to calm them down. Unfortunately, none of them showed me anything wrong.

Until one of the guild members, one who had been quiet up until this point, took pity on me. She sent me a private message saying, "It's not broken." She went on to explain that she had waited until the rest of the guild was offline, then she opened the door for another guild. I understand she got 30 pieces of silver for her trouble.

With that news, I coughed and told the assembled angry mob that I had explored all available information and discerned that the takeover was in fact legal and that there was no bug. I refused to give more information than that. I never found out if they discovered the Judas in their ranks.

As for me, I learned my lesson: LOG EVERYTHING, and offer a robust system for reviewing the logs. When hunting down bugs and/or reviewing player cries of foul, nothing makes the job of the GM easier than knowing that he/she has perfect information and can state with 100% accuracy when a player isn't telling the whole truth.

Logs are fairly useless unless you can create coherent reports from them. Incredible as it may seem, most companies simply dump logs into a UNIX file and the poor schmuck investigating an infraction has to use *grep* and other commands to tediously look through them, hoping to find the relevant portions. (Note: *grep* is a common search tool used on UNIX systems. The manual page for this simple search program runs about six pages. It's a beast. You can tame it, but why should you when better tools exist that mere mortals can use?) Talk about a waste of time! Data is useless unless it is relevant.

The best method is probably a searchable database that allows a comparison of various fields by date and time, size, and so on, with regular daily reports on some transactions. For example, if the game features "gold" as the cash medium, receiving a daily report on all accumulations or transactions above 1,000,000 gold (or whatever size makes sense for your game) can help you pinpoint dupers quickly. If the same character suddenly gains 20,000,000 gold, you know to investigate further.

Transitioning from the Development Team to the Live Team

"I think most other publishers are going to be reactive rather than proactive in developing strong CS for their games, and if they minimize the importance of CS, their games will suffer enormously."

Kelly Flock, former president and CEO of Sony Online Entertainment[1]

If you organized things correctly during the development phase, your live team is already trained and in place, ready to take on the task of post-launch management. The basic team will look something like Figure 11.1.

---

1. See the full interview at http://EverQuest.station.sony.com/hht/features/standards.jsp.

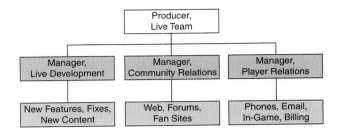

Figure 11.1 Live team composition and general responsibilities.

A live team has three main responsibilities:

➤ Manage the expectations of the players by carefully managing the flow of communication between the live team and the players.

➤ Respond to and resolve player help requests quickly and efficiently.

➤ Continually refresh the game content and features and fix problems in the code.

Experience has shown that the most efficient structure for meeting those responsibilities is the one shown in Figure 11.1. Let's look at each of the three areas in more detail.

Community Relations

"One of the huge problems that faces online community relations personnel right now is when players get information from bad sources—rumors—or from a GM who was just thinking aloud, or (and I've seen it happen a lot) a player makes a suggestion that other players feel is so exciting that they feel entitled to its implementation (no matter how crazy, unfeasible, or inappropriate that idea may be). A huge, often hidden challenge for the community relations department is gently defusing these ideas without the players charging your offices with torches and pitchforks."

Damion Schubert

The Community Relations department is probably your smallest in terms of personnel, but it is the single most important group on the team. These are the frontline troops that set the tone of your dealings with the players. The team is responsible for the web site and message forums (where players get the official word on changes and additions to the game and have questions answered by the community relations and development teams), and coordinates with unofficial fan sites to keep the buzz and word of mouth about the game constant and good. They also collate important information about players' wants, needs, and attitudes and pass it on to the other members of the live team.

Most large online games have a community relations staff of between two and five employees, and may use volunteers to help moderate various categories in the message forums, especially those relating to guilds and other player organizations.

Player Relations

This department contains most of the employees on the live team. It includes the in-game support people, commonly called GMs, technical support via email and telephone, and billing and account support.

Gamemasters

Gamemasters (GMs) almost certainly make up the bulk of this department. The total number of them varies from game to game, but the larger games featuring 100,000–500,000 subscribers and 20,000–80,000 simultaneous players should have at least 30–100 of them on-staff. The GM has to be a number of things, not the least of which are: (a) comforter: being sensitive to the attitudes of the paying customers when problems occur and providing commiseration and a venting point; and (b) air-traffic controller: quick on the uptake in handling the problem/help request queue quickly and efficiently.

While each game has specific needs and peculiarities, general GM responsibilities include:

➤ Helping players who are "stuck"; for instance, a character is physically stuck somewhere within the game and can't move or escape

➤ Investigating and dealing with harassment issues, such as "grief" players intentionally ruining gameplay for others, racial slurs, extreme profanity, and so on

➤ Investigating bug reports and passing them on to the development team

➤ Assisting with player-run events such as weddings and skills competitions

The GMs also represent one of your greatest danger points. Along with the community relations team, they are on the front lines, dealing with your players on an intimate, live basis each day. What they say and do impacts the attitude of every player in the game because the players talk among themselves and post on fan sites. If one or more of your GMs is regularly rude, caustic, or insensitive, the whole game suffers.

GM corruption is another problem. Most GMs are gamers; many come from the very community you service. It is very easy for them to retain community loyalty and do favors for in-game friends, such as scouting other players for them; creating and giving friends "uber-items" such as excellent or rare weapons, armor, or lots of in-game "cash" such as gold or credits; and taking part in raids on in-game quests or other players' property, if PvP combat is allowed in the game. They can also use their GM powers to create items or characters that can be auctioned off on Internet auction sites such as eBay.

The players always find out about these incidents, and it is always damaging. How you handle the inevitable incidents—and there *will* be incidents, count on it—can have a major impact on your players' confidence in the company and the fairness of the game.

These problems occur because GMs for most games have full access to all commands, including access to the database that allows creation of new items or manipulation of character statistics. Most help requests in games are of a basic level and don't require such broad powers. You can limit the scope of this kind of problem by structuring several levels of GMs and GM powers and by adding a knowledge base that allows players to help themselves to information.

Gamemaster Levels   GM levels can be implemented as in the following:

> ➤ **Level 1 GMs: The easy stuff**—Somewhere between 50% and 80% of all in-game issues are going to be fairly quick and easy to handle, requiring only one or two minutes to deal with. They won't require deep thought or intricate solutions; they'll be as simple as cutting and pasting a pre-written answer or moving a player a short distance to take care of a "stuck" issue.
>
> Thus, Level 1 GMs should only handle issues that can be dealt with almost exclusively with basic communication tools, not with database manipulation such as changing a player account or creating or deleting items. The Level 1 group should act as traffic cops and gatekeepers, addressing the simple issues themselves and routing the more complicated issues up to Level 2 or 3 GMs.

As the knowledge base grows and standard responses for issues are written and included, the issues that the Level 1 GMs can handle will increase.

Level 1 also includes GM trainees.

Level 1 responsibilities include the following:

➤ Reviewing and classifying help requests in the queue

➤ Handling any issue that has a pre-written response

➤ Routing more complicated issues, such as player name changes or problems that require database access, to a Level 2 or 3 GM

➤ Making small changes that affect player/characters, such as moving them short distances to deal with "stuck on the map" issues

➤ Evaluating terms of service and rules of conduct violations and complaints

➤ **Level 2 GMs: Dealing with problems**—Level 2 GMs deal with issues that require some action on a player, such as kicking the player out of the game, suspending gameplay privileges, changing offensive names, temporarily squelching a player's ability to "speak" in-game, or "jailing" a player/character to stop harassment of other players.

In the main, Level 2 GMs handle those issues escalated by Level 1 GMs and have a broader set of tools and/or permissions to work with. They are expected to work customers through issues that require more than the one or two minutes generally needed for a Level 1 problem.

Level 2 GM responsibilities include the following:

➤ Handling issues escalated by Level 1 GMs

➤ Changing offensive player/character names

➤ Squelching, suspending or lifting a suspension, jailing or unjailing, or submitting an account for permanent ban from the game to the Level 3 GMs

➤ **Level 3 GMs: Making changes**—Level 3 GMs handle issues that require manipulation of the game database in some way and are the final arbiters on player bannings, in-game reimbursements of items, skills, and/or abilities, and changes to the game state, such as database rollbacks.

They are also responsible for the GM training program and maintaining the GM policies and procedures.

Level 3 GM responsibilities include the following:

➤ Banning player accounts

➤ Reimbursing game items or data that players have lost due to bugs or a GM error

➤ Making game state changes, such as removing or adding terrain, rolling back the database after a bug is found and corrected, and so on

➤ Developing and revising GM support policies

➤ Developing and revising the GM training program

Knowledgebase   One reason why PWs see high help petition rates in-game is that official information about gameplay, player/characters, goals, game mechanics, and so on is not readily available. Players should at least be able to research their own issues out of the gameplay environment on the game's associated web site. Even better, if the knowledge base is accessible in-game, many basic questions can be answered immediately by the GMs by either cutting and pasting the proper link to the player or by the player searching it out on his/her own.

Technical Support and Billing/Account Support

Your out-of-game support will generally be composed of two main elements: phone support and email support. Generally, this type of support will cover three subjects:

➤ The player can't get into the game. Usually this is an installation or connectivity issue and is generally handled on the telephone or via email.

➤ Email that is used for bug, harassment, or account/billing issues.

➤ Billing and account management issues, which normally entail telling a customer on the phone that charges on his/her credit card were denied, which is why his/her account was suspended.

The bulk of this support is done through email, and many publishers find that offering no or little phone support works well for them. It is certainly more cost-efficient to perform email or online chat support; phone support takes time and has a hard cost attached to it, especially if you offer 800–number, toll-free service.

Gamers are social creatures, and some gamers are *really* social (and at times, a tad lonely and in need of a human voice). These people, though loyal customers, will eat up the time of your telephone representatives with small or even nonexistent problems, just to have some company and social contact. Some will call you several times each month, each time with a different problem or complaint.

Between the cost of telephone services and the time taken by the service representative to handle the call, it only takes 15 or 20 minutes on the telephone to turn a $10- or $12-per-month customer from a profit center to a loss item; another 10 or 15 minutes, and that one caller has just turned some other customer into a profit loss for the month.

If you're going to have telephone support, we suggest you use a local number, not a toll-free one. This will at least do some pre-qualifying of support calls; people tend to think twice about frivolous calls if they have to spend money to make them.

The Live Development Team

The development team should be your second largest division on the live team. These are the people who will fix bugs, fix balance issues, create new tools for player and community relations as needs become apparent, and add content and features over time to keep the game fresh and alive.

The number of developers will vary, depending on your particular needs. For example, *Ultima Online (UO)* in 2001 had about 20–24 people on the live development team, including 2 producers, a couple of content designers/scripters, several client and server programmers, 2–3 artists, and 3 "story events" designers. Other teams have as few as 5 and as many as 30 to 50.

The responsibilities of the live development team will be discussed in greater detail in Chapter 12, "The Live Development Team."

Managing the Expectations of the Players

"What it means is that they (the developers) are planning ahead to set expectations with consumers such that they can meet or beat the implied contract present with them. If you don't set player expectations, they still have them, and often beyond the level of your ability to deliver."

Gordon Walton

Now that you have the right people in place and everyone knows who is supposed to be doing what, just how do you manage this thing, anyway? The first step is getting a handle on just what you're doing and relaying that to the players.

This is one of the critical issues facing any online game post-launch, and it involves an arcane black art known as "managing the expectations of the customers," otherwise known as your players. It's very easy for your Marketing and Public Relations departments and player relations, community relations, and development teams to speak separately to the player base or online press and promise or imply different features, fixes, and changes. There is one cardinal rule to always remember when communicating with your players: Anything and everything posted or mentioned in public by a member of the team, no matter how amorphous, will be taken as gospel. Everything said by any employee will be immediately taken by your subscribers as being set in stone and in the development track pipeline.

Take, for example, *UO*. At the game's launch, there was no coherent policy or procedure for communicating with the players. For the most part, the developers and designers posted what they wanted to post, whenever they wanted to. The various members all frequented different player-run fan sites and engaged in "theoretical" discussions on features and changes to the game and almost never relayed these discussions in whole to the rest of the live team. When these discussions didn't result in changes to the game, this led to charges of unfulfilled promises and gave a black eye to the game.

Once, one of the designers on the live team was asked by a player online if necromancy and alchemy could be added to this medieval fantasy RPG. The designer, before consulting others on the team, said he liked the idea and would bring it up with his associates. Within 24 hours, the *UO* fan sites were abuzz with the news that necromancy and alchemy were coming to the game. The designer tried to stem the tide by saying, "Hey, we're just thinking about it," but it was already too late. Soon, it was announced that the features were on the development list—and there they sat for years. The designer wrote a check that Origin Systems had to cash, gave another black eye to the reputation of the game, and incidentally, created a running joke at *UO*'s expense that still exists today.

The Four-Step Notification Program

So, what is a poor live team to do? You can't *not* talk to the players; open communication is a necessity in this market, not an optional exercise. It looks a lot like a "damned if you do and damned if you don't" situation, doesn't it?

It's actually much easier than it looks from our examples. What you need is a cohesive internal organization that controls the flow of information from your own people on the live team to the players and back, and a process that allows the *controlled and managed flow* of information to the players.

What the players want to know is: What is broken, what is being fixed, and what cool, new stuff will be added, and when? They want to get inside the heads of the live development team and understand what they are thinking and planning, so they can plan their own in-game time and strategies accordingly. In other words, they want to feel like they are a part of the process. That means they want current information, they want to know that their opinions are being delivered and considered by the development team, and they want some advance notice regarding major changes.

Delivering this kind of coherent short-, mid-, and long-term information and coordinating player responses starts with a four-step process managed by community relations on the web site and in the message forums. The following process has proven successful in helping to manage player expectations in several games:

> ➤ **In Concept (Long Range)**—This web page is used to list additions or changes that are under consideration for implementation in the coming months, but have not yet been decided on. These are presented as concepts only for player comment, with links to a message board topic dedicated to the specific concepts or changes mentioned.

There is no timetable given for possible implementation; these are simply discussion subjects. It should be made clear to the reader that any line item in this section that is subsequently cleared for development work is weeks or months out from implementation, and that some, none, or all of them might be cleared for development at some time.

Any concept previously discussed but later junked by the live team should also be noted in this section.

➤ **In Development (Long Range)**—After the live team has made a decision to begin work on a concept, change, or feature addition, it is noted here, along with some minimal explanation of how it is expected to function in the game and what the overall effects of the change will be.

Again, no timetables for release are given.

➤ **In Testing (Short to Mid-Range)**—Listed on this page are line items from the "In Development" section that have been added to the internal and/or public test server and are now being run through the QA testing process. Each line item should have a detailed explanation of the functionality and use of the change, feature, or addition.

➤ **In the Next Patch (Short Range)**—Here you'll find line items from the "In Testing" section that have cleared the QA process and will be installed in the next scheduled patch, with a date and time given for that patch. The text describing the functionality and use of each line item should be reproduced here, along with any changes made to the line item during the test process.

There are several variations on this process that can be used; for example, the "Update Center" web page from *UO* is shown in Figure 11.2.[2]

---

2. This is a good example of a player notification system. Note the four-step process at the top of the page, along with a fifth link for "General" testing issues as they occur. Note also that the *UO* live team expands on the concept by posting regular update letters from various internal departments.

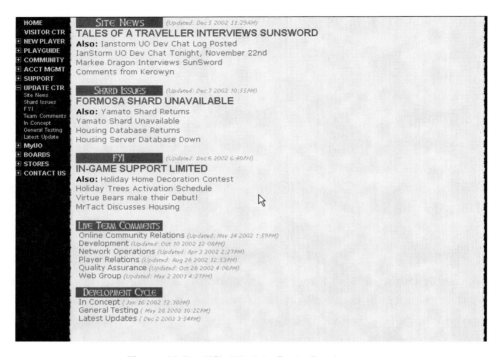

Figure 11.2   *UO*'s "Update Center" web page.

Using the basics of the four-step process, the community relations team for *UO* coordinates with the producer and other team members to get information and post it on the correct web page. Then, on the message board forums, they coordinate the discussions concerning these posts and relay the critical discussions. Thus, they *expanded* on the minimal four-step process.

Instituting such a player notification process right from launch day will save the live team from plenty of grief down the road. However, there is a major caveat: All members of the live team have to buy into the process, and that means instituting a general prohibition or restrictions on which team members can post, when they can post, and on what subjects.

In other words, team members have to be willing to gag themselves and clear all communications with the players through community relations. This can be as drastic as requiring all team members to refrain from posting without first clearing it with the community relations team or as loose as community relations establishing strict rules and guidelines to be followed when posting and working with the team members over time to refine the process. Whatever is instituted, it must be acknowledged that community relations is in charge of this aspect of player expectation management and that what they say goes.

The Rules of Managing Player Expectations

PW gamers have a wild and wooly streak to them and are quite capable of being caustic and rude in posts. This most often happens when they perceive that a live team has treated them, as a class, with disrespect and dishonesty. Nothing will inflame players more than an unannounced change in a game mechanic or character ability that erases dozens or hundreds of hours of play time. Lying or being evasive about it before or afterwards only compounds the problem. The whole concept of unannounced and/or hidden changes is considered disrespectful, as if the time a player puts into a game means nothing to the company and can be wasted at a whim.

For some reason, many developers feel the need to hide takeaway changes. Much of this is probably to avoid predictable player outrage before the change takes effect. They'd much rather just face one huge blast of pain than have to discuss it for several days or weeks with the players. The problem with this method of making changes is that each instance causes the players to lose some trust in the game and the developers, and that trust is the most important asset any team has.

Building trust means building loyalty, and loyal players become loyal subscribers for months and years. It builds patience, and patient players will work with you on just about any change you want to make. It is a karma bank; the more good karma you deposit, the more you can pull out when you need to make really drastic changes.

In that sense, building trust by managing player expectations simply means following these rules:

> ➤ Always be 100% honest in all communications you choose to make with your players. Don't "hide" nerfs or anything that will be seen by the players as taking away capabilities or features from them. The players will discover them and feel betrayed. Discuss any takeaway, or any change that could be perceived as a takeaway, openly and at length before it is actually installed in the game.

➤ Never promise a feature or create an action item you can't deliver or which hasn't been 100% cleared for addition to the game by the live team.

➤ Never promise or even speculate about game mechanics, features, or *anything* without discussing it with your own people first.

➤ Enforce a policy of an integrated, "single official voice," so that only designated community relations individuals may post freely on the web or in a chat and others may post only with prior approval or by following the rules and guidelines that community relations sets down and under their supervision.

➤ Ensure that the live team producer and head of community relations review all official postings and communications before they are made available to the public.

➤ Keep the player base continually informed of what the live development team is currently working on by means of the web and message boards.

➤ Never promise a "due date" for a fix, feature, or other content until it has been thoroughly tested and is scheduled for a specific patch.

➤ Insulate your developers from nonofficial communications with the players. Knowing when to come down on development team members for breaking the "single voice" rule is a key—and they will break it; you can bank on that. Developers love to communicate with players because the players make a point of conferring the status of gods on them. It is an almost irresistible temptation for them to get out there and bask in the glow. What they don't realize is that the players are playing them, in hopes of gaining favors down the road. This is one of the toughest problems the community relations team will face in the live phase of the game because developers love to gab with the players.

➤ Know when to sit on the marketing/public relations folks and keep them from getting too far out in front of development's actual feature additions and other content enhancement efforts.

➤ Remember: You can't win an argument with a paying customer. Even when you win on points, you lose in the court of public opinion. The lesson to be learned is not to argue. When you have something to say, say it and don't get drawn into a long argument about the supposed merits.

Figures 11.3[3] and 11.4[4] demonstrate how community relations managers (CRMs) can create an "in-depth defense" that insulates the developers from direct contact with the players on a daily basis, yet allows for the free flow of information between the two groups when needed or desired. Following these rules will allow you to avoid most of the heartache your colleagues have already experienced.

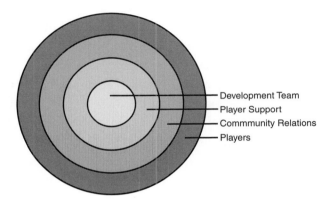

Development Team
Player Support
Commmunity Relations
Players

Figure 11.3   Post-launch communication loops.

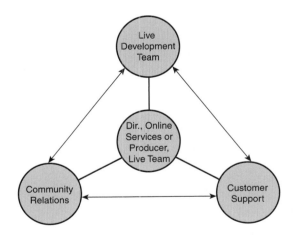

Live Development Team

Dir., Online Services or Producer, Live Team

Community Relations

Customer Support

Figure 11.4   The live team's communications flow.

3. To insulate the developers from nonofficial "chats" with the players, the information and communication flow must work from the development team in the center out toward the players. The direct link between the players and the organization is community relations, which passes information back inside the target to customer support and the development team.

4. All information flows into and through the overall head of the live team. The three departments of the live team also communicate with each other, while keeping the head of the live team fully informed.

Player Relations: The In-Game GMs

No online game launches without some problems or fails to experience them later on. There are so many issues involved in games this complex and containing this much data exchange, they can't all be listed here. As an example, almost every PW of any size will experience "stuck" issues, spaces on the game map where player/characters become physically stuck and can't move or become stranded in a sector from which they can't remove themselves back to the rest of the world. If a player is "stuck," someone has to go there and teleport him/her away from the area and *fast*, or you just lost a customer. Consider some other examples: A grief player may be harassing other players by standing in a crowd and spamming the screen with obscenities, just because he/she can; or, you may be experiencing login delays and/or player disconnects from the game; or, you can have any one of a dozen other issues, all of which players expect to be handled as fast as possible—not first thing tomorrow, not even later today, but *right now*, dammit! What am I paying you jerks $10 a month for, anyway?

Someone has to be around to help the players when the problems show up. That someone is a GM.

How Many GMs Do You Need at Launch?

This is the big question for any supported online game. If you plan to support an online game, this will be your largest department, by far. Determining how many GMs you need at launch, and how to grow the number of GMs gracefully as the subscriber base grows, can determine whether or not you have a respectable profit margin. Hybrids and free web-based games don't have this issue; any support beyond pure technical support and bug fixes is left for the consumer to find from other consumers.

The effectiveness of your marketing and the participation in and response to your open Beta tests should give you a pretty good idea of how many GMs you will need on day one of commercial access. As a gauge, even marginal, niche games such as *World War II* are seeing retail sales of 35,000 and more on launch day; that means 35,000 people are going to be trying to crowd your login servers on the first day. Or, you could be like Blizzard's free service, battle.net, which shipped two million units of *Diablo II* in 2000 and saw sales estimated by some sources at over 200,000 units on the first day. Needless to say, battle.net had a hard time staying stable for a while.

The size of the GM crew should also be relative to the stability of the servers and client during the Beta tests. If you experienced a bunch of "stuck" and harassment issues during the Beta and weren't able to fix most of them, you'll need a larger crew. Also, remember Patrovsky's Rule: It isn't just that you have to make a good first impression; in a crowded market, you only get *one* chance to make a good first impression. Historically, *most players churn out of an online game in their first month of play*. If you short-staff the GM team under the misguided notion of early cost savings, players will have to wait longer to be helped and more will leave early. Short-staffing means you're simply leaving money on the table for some other developer to pick up.

So, how many GMs will you need? For a game that expects to hit 100,000 subscribers fairly quickly, say, within the first two to three months, you must expect a heavy load of potential subscribers to check out your game in the first two weeks and be prepared to meet that load. The experience of most games launched in the period of 1997–2001 has been sales of 30,000+ units the first day of availability, reaching 100,000 sales in the first month to six weeks. Experience has shown that launching with one GM per 5,000 paid (or anticipated) subscribers, or 20 GMs trained and in place at launch, is the absolute minimum necessary to do the job for most such games. One GM per 2,500 anticipated subscribers is much better, especially for the first month, and most especially if your game runs into technical problems at launch.

How Many GMs Do You Need to Add Versus Subscriber Growth?

How many GMs to add during the initial growth stage depends very much on the technical stability of the game. If the game is fairly stable, "stuck" issues will be the bulk of your calls initially, followed closely by harassment help calls. In this stage, one GM per 2,500–5,000 subscribers should work fairly well. If the game is very stable and the stuck and harassment issues are few, you can trend toward one GM per 5,000 subscribers.

Figure 11.5 shows a basic flow line of GMs to players, based on both optimal and unstable game conditions.

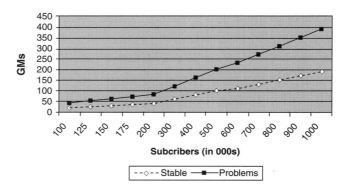

Figure 11.5   GMs needed versus the subscriber base of an online game.
Note that instability equals more GMs.

Instability on Launch or Patch Day

If the game is unstable at launch, all bets are off. Hire temps, dragoon management and chain them to a computer monitor, and train the janitors and get them answering calls, too; you'll need all hands and then some. If your game remains unstable for two to three weeks from launch, even this probably won't help; about the only thing that can save you at this point is the direct intervention of a deity, which is well beyond the scope of this book.

If the game is fairly stable during normal operation but tends to become unstable on patch days, which is not a rare occurrence these days, you'll have to figure out a rotation for adding GMs for the hours immediately following the reboot and activation of the patch. You should also consider putting the GMs on the phones, answering emails, and in chat rooms, if you have them, in case the patch takes longer than expected. This is another fairly regular occurrence, unfortunately.

Scheduling Issues

Online games have peak hours of play. These peak hours are centered around common societal leisure time; not surprisingly, that means most play happens during off-business hours. You can count on the weekday hours of 6 p.m. to 12 a.m. local time and about 9 a.m. to 12 a.m. Saturday and Sunday being the busiest.

Check that phrase, "local time," again. Now that the Internet has made online games a global phenomena, a publisher has to be sensitive to the fact that "local time" in Asia and Europe means the game servers will see usage spikes several times a day, not just in the evening and weekend hours in the US. Not only does this make it more expensive to staff, because you have to have GMs available for these international players too, but the scheduling can become a nightmare. Do you have call centers in Asia, Europe, and the US? Do you centralize in the US and try to have American GMs handle the language difficulties? Can bilingual or multilingual GMs be hired for $9–$13 an hour?

These are questions a publisher must answer in the design stage and implement gracefully in the Beta and launch phases. Experience has shown that it's better to have local language speakers service the local community, but not everyone can afford to do that. At the minimum, it pays to make certain that all hours, 24/7, are covered by GMs.

Another good reason for 24/7 GMs: Any GM downtime is when exploiters and grief players will plan and implement their reigns of terror. If you have no GM coverage from 12 a.m. to 8 a.m. local time, you can expect substantial abusive activity during those hours. It won't stop completely even with GM coverage, but having some GM presence will give the abusers pause.

Handling Email

It is not unusual for a PW with 100,000–200,000 subscribers to receive an *average* of 500 emails per day.

Now that you're properly scared to death, you have to figure out who is going to deal with all that email. Usually, no one wants to do it, especially if the game has problems, so this duty normally falls on the GMs by default. Online game email tends to fall into four categories:

➤ Frontline Technical Problems (FTPs), or "Hey, I can't get this *&^%$! thing to work!"

FTPs involve any technical problem that prevents the player from installing the game on his/her home computer or from connecting to the game via the Internet. Among the problems faced are conflicts with the Windows operating system and peripherals such as video and sound cards, and conflicts with other software on the computer that have taken over a piece of required memory or IRQ switch.

These emails are time-consuming and often involve an exchange of several emails and/or a phone call or two to figure out why the game client won't install or connect. It is not unusual for FTPs to account for the bulk of trouble tickets, especially during the first three months post-launch.

➤ Billing and Account Management, or "You bastards double-billed me!"

About 90–95% of all billing for subscription games is done by credit card. Credit card billing is a funny and touchy process, and all subscription games have had trouble with it. The emails in this category normally fall into two categories: (a) claims of apparent double- or multiple billing on the card in any one month, and (b) the card was denied by the bank and the player's account was suspended.

Game company billing programs are horrible. This is because they are often built at the last minute before launch, when someone suddenly notices they don't have one. You can imagine how stable something flung together at the last moment would be. If the billing program doesn't burp and cause a chunk of the player base to receive notices they've been billed twice for the month and thank you very much for playing, someone notices that some player's card hasn't been billed for four months and hits the card for all of it at once.

Bear in mind that double-billings almost never truly occur and, when they do, publishers are quick to refund any overcharge. You are more likely to see the second issue: charges denied by the bank. This happens every month and it really upsets the player to whom it happens. In almost all instances, it is not the fault of the publisher, but caused by two other reasons.

Just because a credit card is valid and has enough unused credit left on it does not mean that Visa, MasterCard, or whoever will actually approve charges to it. In any one month, as much as 5% of attempted charges fail for reasons such as data transmission errors, database errors at the credit agency, the card owner changed his/her address but failed to change it in the game's billing database, and so on. In these instances, automatic player account suspension procedures usually take hold until the publisher can retry the failed card number, in effect locking the player out of the game for hours or days.

Credit and debit cards expire. Most cards are issued for two- or three-year periods, after which they are automatically turned off and have to be renewed. Even if you assume three-year periods for all cards, when you have a user base as large as that of *EverQuest* (*EQ*) or *UO*, this amounts to thousands of expiring cards and denied charges each month. The percentage on this can be as high as 10% in a month, though it more often tends to be in the 1–2% range.

Even though neither of these problems is the fault of the publisher but that of the bank, the player, or random chance, that doesn't matter to the players. After all, they don't deal with your bank—they deal with *you*, and isn't the customer always right? They aren't going to call or email the bank; they are going to call or email the publisher.

These emails are usually easy to handle technically (although the customer may have a right to be irate), but they do take five or fifteen minutes each. These should go directly to accounts management; if they come to the GMs first, they should be forwarded to accounts management, along with a quick GM reply to the player that the mail has been forwarded to the right people.

At the end of the monthly billing cycle, when most of the billing and account management problems appear, it can get quite hairy and strained around the Accounts Management department for a few days.

➤ Harassment, cheating, and reimbursement issues, or "Johnny called me a wanker, and then used a hack to kill me and steal my horsey. Please kill him and give me back my beloved Trigger."

This category will drive your GMs buggy. Some players are problem children. The number of them is usually small—only one or two percent—but the problems they cause are legion and each instance affects a number of honest players. If the problem kids aren't harassing other players with racial or sexual epithets or spamming the chat screen so other players can't get a word in edgewise, they've gotten hold of a cheat program someone wrote for the game and used it to kill other players and loot the corpses.

Harassment is easily dealt with if you use the method Gordon Walton set up for *UO*. He had the live team create a "harassment button" in the client interface; when used by a player, it saved a block of the chat text going back several previous minutes. This log was then sent by email to the proper GMs, who investigated the matter and issued a ruling on who should be suspended.

Without such a mechanism, you either have to ignore the harassment issue, which is not a good idea if you want to keep your player base happy, or spend hours tracking down witnesses and trying to pull the relevant text out of the server log files, which is not an efficient use of your GM's time. See Part II, "Design and Development Considerations," for further advice on this.

Cheating through hack programs and reimbursing lost or stolen items are trickier matters. Unless you've built the code into your server and client to track and report unusual events, catching a cheat hack is a very tough proposition. Worse, claims of cheat hacks by other players are almost always false, either due to not understanding how a player legitimately used game mechanics to gain an item or just outright lying to gain revenge on a player who bested them. Unless the GM recognizes the problem immediately and determines that no hack was used, you have to investigate the matter, just in case, because nothing erodes player trust in the game and company faster than the feeling that the playing field isn't level. The lesson here is this Design logging and tracking features on everything you can think of into the game during the design and development stage. It is the best way to track unusual events that might be cheat hacks.

The best advice that can be given on reimbursement is this. If your game is of sufficient size, say over 150,000 subscribers, you probably aren't going to be able to reimburse lost or stolen items except in select cases, in which a programming bug or flaw was the cause of the loss. Make sure your policy on reimbursement is published widely and frequently to the players, and that the GMs handling email know that policy.

➤ Second-line technical problems, or "A bug teleported me across the game and now I'm stuck in a cave!"

If you have your tools set up correctly, technical support and billing and account management questions will go to the right departments automatically and the GMs will never have to bother with them. On the other hand, there will always be plenty of bug and exploit reports, "stuck" issues, and other items that the GMs can and should deal with.

Most of these can be resolved fairly quickly. Some, such as bug reports, take longer because an investigation needs to be done. But, most bug and exploit reports can usually be handled with the customer with a simple, "Thanks, we're on it," and passing the report on to the security team or the developers on the live team.

The 24-Hour Response Rule

Many online GMs ignore the importance of answering email in a timely manner.

Most issues can be handled by a GM—especially in-game issues. Remember that the GMs probably know the ins-and-outs and idiosyncrasies of the game far better than anyone on the staff, with the possible exception of the leads on the development team. They are certainly in-tune with player concerns and know which problems are recurring issues. The GMs are a damn good resource for the whole live team; just talking to them to get the top five issues of the week can determine what fixes the development team should make to reduce the email and in-game petition queue loads.

Sadly, email tends to be a low priority for most game managers. They allow player mail to stack up in the queue for days at a time while attending to other, more "important" tasks. This creates player angst and anger; no one likes the feeling that he or she is being ignored. A point to remember is that your players talk to each other; if one player's email goes unanswered for 24 hours, 30–100 other players will know about it at 24 hours plus 1 minute.

And the 24-hour rule is only the minimum guideline; following it will keep you out of trouble. To help create good word of mouth about the game, you need to be much faster in responding. A good methodology to follow is the response/resolved method. It takes a bit more work but achieves incredible results in terms of good word of mouth:

➤ Each shift, one or two GMs are dedicated to email. The email GMs prioritize the incoming email and answer the priority issues first. Priority issues are things that prevent the player from being in the game or moving about the game world (stuck issues).

➤ At the very least, each player email should receive a short, personal note within two hours, even if it will take longer to resolve the player's issue. This can be as simple as a cut and paste of, "Hey, we received your email and we're working on it, and I'm the guy following up for you," signed by an actual person. It is important that such "response" emails not be signed with "From the <game> Team" or similar impersonal signatures. The player will just assume it is an auto-generated email. The personal touch is vital here.

> ➤ If the GM cannot handle the issue, he/she routes it to the proper person.

> ➤ Within 24 hours of the first response, the player receives a second email with either a resolution or an acknowledgement that the trouble ticket is still open.

Follow-Up!

It is extremely important for whoever gets an email to follow up with the player as soon as possible. Even a simple, "Hey, we haven't forgotten you!" email will work wonders in gaining player patience when a problem takes some time to resolve.

The keys are quick response, follow-up response, and resolution response. Note that this means, after the initial player contact, actually communicating with the player before the player finds it necessary to email you a second time with an irate, "Hey, what's going on?"

Phone Support

How many phone representatives you need is an interesting question that really depends on how stable the game is. If the game is fairly stable and you have fewer than 250,000 subscribers, you can probably get away with five to eight phone reps during normal business hours. If the game is in a perpetually unstable state, all bets are off; you'll probably need to constantly dragoon GMs into the phone queue to help out.

Technical Phone Support

Your technical phone support will closely mirror your FTP email and billing and accounts management email requirements.

Accounts Management and Billing

You'll receive the greatest load of billing and account questions at the end of each month, when the end-of-month billing is run and expired credit cards cause some accounts to be suspended for non-payment. The end-of-month billing resolution cycle will probably require some temporary help from GMs or others for two or three days. It is important to handle these problems quickly; the sooner you get new credit card information from the player, the sooner he/she is back in the game and paying you a subscription fee.

The Service Philosophy: Acquiring and Retaining Subscribers

Nearly every online game developed by a retail computer game publisher to date has made one error during design and launch: They have treated the game as if it were any other computer game.

That has been their experience and forté: building a game, launching it, patching it a couple times, and then moving on to the next project. This is akin to Safeway or Albertson's opening a new grocery store, stocking the shelves once or twice, and then ignoring the store and moving on to the next town. Eventually, the shelves will become empty and shoppers will stop going there.

Unlike other computer entertainment products, however, massively multiplayer role-playing games (MMRPGs) require more forethought during design and more work after launch. Knowing this now, your game has (we hope) been designed and developed with two cardinal rules in mind:

➤ This isn't just a product; it is also a *service*. Just as much work goes into the game *after* the launch as *before* the launch.

➤ The game itself is a vehicle that allows existing communities to congregate and socialize. Therefore, both *acquisition* and *retention* features have to be built into it, just like any other service.

Most MMRPG developers don't build following these rules and end up paying for it later on. For example, take volunteer organizations. Until recently, these were a standard part of every PW and most games launched with a volunteer group in place. However, three of the top four MMRPGs—EQ, UO, and AC—all launched without adequate tools or organizations built for recruiting, training, and monitoring/logging the actions of their volunteer support corps, which are good retention tools. They have paid for this error in sometimes very slow response times to player help requests. Players can wait hours for a request to be attended to. They are all playing catch-up in this regard.

Understanding from the start that you are providing a service, you need to keep in mind both acquisition and retention features, you need to build the tools and features necessary to support the five critical elements necessary for the success of any online PW, and post-launch, the team needs to pay attention to these tools and use them. The following elements are interlinked necessities for any MMRPG. They can each be built separately, but they work best when all are built into a game and inter-react with each other.

The Five Elements Necessary for Success

The five elements include Talk Soup, Band of Brothers, the Living Organism, Welcome Wagon, and Help Me!

Talk Soup

Your PW needs many methods for players to communicate, individually and in groups, and both in and out of the character of the game. Yes, this is a game that will allow tens of thousands to play simultaneously; players, however, will naturally segment themselves into smaller community groups (guilds, teams, towns, races) for their own ease and comfort.

If this communication is facilitated, the communities will be able to grow more easily and more quickly, and the game will have a much greater chance of becoming the player's primary entertainment vehicle. This is done by ensuring that there are many easy and intuitive means for players to contact and communicate with each other, and making sure the community relations and player relations teams take advantage of those tools to communicate effectively with the players. This encompasses everything from instant messaging between individuals, to player-configurable in-game chat channels, to special message boards for guilds and teams, to in-game email between players and groups of players.

This sounds like a very common-sense element that every game should have. However, most online games have had only minimal communications tools at launch and, after a hue and cry from the players, were forced to build decent communication features into the games later.

Lack of these capabilities has also limited the ability of the live team to communicate effectively during their support missions for the players. The essence of supporting the player is being able to communicate effectively. Being limited to web posts or 80 characters of text at one time slows down support and makes it more difficult to communicate.

Band of Brothers

In the final analysis, players don't continue to play a game because it is cool; they continue to play because their buddies are there. Once they join some kind of guild or team organization, the emotional attachment to that group of friends, that band of brothers (to paraphrase Shakespeare and HBO), makes it very difficult for them to leave the game for a competing product.

To facilitate this, you'll need to build in full-featured "guild" functions, allowing players to set up, manage, and control the membership of teams. The team element is critical; it allows friends to congregate logically, easily, and within the context of the game. They will do this whether you provide this service element or not; by providing it, however, you add to the acquisition and retention features of the game. Only *UO* and *Asheron's Call (AC)* currently have easy and intuitive mechanisms for accomplishing this.

The community relations and player relations teams also need to understand how the "band of brothers" phenomenon can play into enhancing the retention of new subscribers by providing ready-made, player-run support mechanisms. Many guilds are willing to train new players and recruit them into the fold to increase their own size and power within the game. This is a powerful means of locking in loyalty.

However, many games pay no particular attention to the needs or desires of the teams within their product. Providing them with the tools to create their own content, such as team events, faction wars, or in-game parties and weddings, should be a top priority for the live team.

The Living Organism

A subscriber's play style will change over time. Some customers churn out and stop playing, others move in with new ideas about how the game should be played, and new content and features are added. The longer someone plays, the more likely it is that his/her goals within the game will change. Someone who started out as an explorer may transform into a socializer, or a socializer may transform into an achiever.

This type of change contributes to the dynamic nature of a PW, but it can also cause problems if the live team isn't changing pace and objectives along with the customers. A responsive and flexible service philosophy takes into account the major playing styles and how they change over time, and then adds content and features that match.

Historically, the opposite has happened more often; live teams have watched how the players play and then made changes to try to force them back into a cloistered vision of how the game *should* be played. Considering that these are virtual worlds as much as anything else, this is like Ford telling Taurus owners the car was never built for Sunday afternoon drives in the country and the vehicles are not to be used that way.

Inflexibility such as this will tend to set a live team into conflict with the players, as designers try to shoehorn players into a particular style and players keep trying to break the chains and move on with their virtual lives. The service philosophy should take into account the changes that will happen and work with them, not against them.

Welcome Wagon

Online games and other PW environments can initially be confusing for many users. How many times have you entered a new online environment for the first time and wandered around aimlessly for hours, trying to figure out the simple basic mechanics of how to move, talk, and interact?

Our experience in online gaming over the past decade has shown that games that have a human greet the new player within a few minutes of logging in for the first time have an extraordinarily low churn rate (20% vs. 50% for the industry overall). In-game tutorials can take up some of this slack, but nothing beats having a human drop by and say, "Hi! Can I help you get started?"

To get the most bang for your buck, the game should have a staff of paid or volunteer helpers specifically to greet new players and help them get to know the world. With the proper backend tools to allow them to support the players and then ensure that new players have someone to talk to and help them get started, the churn rate will be lower than average. Supporting the GMs and new player greeters by giving them the proper administrative tools and some leeway and discretion to solve player problems on-the-fly will lower initial churn faster than almost any other feature.

Help Me!

For some strange reason, some developers and publishers who are banking their future on games accessible from the Internet and web are failing to use them fully for support. No game currently has dedicated chat and message assistance available on a 24/7 basis; at best, such assistance is available for a few hours each day.

This ignores the 24/7 nature of the web's subscribers, who exist in all time zones and geographic locations. The live team can solve this problem by implementing a root structure that includes the following elements:

➤ A dedicated message board for use by the game's subscribers

➤ In-house and volunteer "sysops" to monitor the message board on a 24/7 basis and respond within two hours to all questions and inquiries

➤ A dedicated chat system capable of supporting a significant portion of the subscriber base

➤ In-house and volunteer chat hosts to facilitate the chat rooms and service the subscribers in them

➤ A complete and detailed knowledge base database dedicated to the game and available to both subscribers and volunteers on the web, and (perhaps) within the game as well

By implementing this structure, human beings will be available at all hours to assist your subscribers and direct them whenever possible and feasible to relevant portions of the web site and knowledge base.

The Volunteer Organization

There has never been a shortage of players willing to donate some time to the other players. Until about mid-2000, it was standard practice for online games—indeed, for online services as a whole—to have a large volunteer corps to assist in helping the other players or developing and managing online events and quests. These volunteers were recruited by the live team into loose "management" structures run by other volunteers; they set their own training programs and schedules, and generally, the specifics of their own "duties."

Recently, however, because of civil lawsuits by former volunteers against both EA and AOL,[5] the long-term use of volunteers in US-based for-pay online games is in question. It may be that only European and Asian publishers will be able to utilize them post-2002. See "The Joys and Dangers of Using Volunteers" later in this chapter.

---

5. In late October, 2001, the Department of Labor dropped an investigation against AOL in this matter. Two civil suits, one in New York filed in 1999 and another in Cailfornia filed in 2001, continue. See "Labor Department won't pursue AOL complaints," *USA Today*, October 29, 2001.

For those companies planning to use volunteer organizations, note that these players have typically been unstructured, unsupervised, and not supported with the proper software tools and in-game abilities to truly help people. A good method for correcting this deficiency is by implementing an organization similar to that in Figure 11.6.

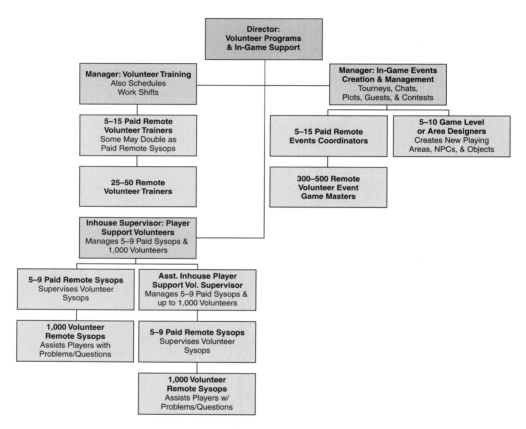

Figure 11.6 Volunteer organization chart.

If you expect your PW to have 100,000+ subscribers, the "very loosely supervised" model organization should use the matrix in Table 11.1 as its base for recruiting and meeting service goals.

Table 11.1   GameOp Time-Slice Chart

	Greeters and Hosts	Volunteer GMs	Junior Event GMs	Senior Event GMs	Volunteer Actors/Events Helpers	
	1–1 game help and guidance for new players	In-game help requests; chat and forum maintenance	New to intermediate events/quests	Intermediate	Actors and assts. in plots and events	
	Number: 200	Number: 1,000	Number: 500	Number: 300	Number: 1,000	% of Total Volunteer Time
New Player 0–20 Hours	100%	25%	50%	0%	25%	40%
Beginner 20–50 Hours	0%	25%	25%	0%	25%	15%
Intermediate 50–300 Hours	0%	25%	25%	50%	25%	25%
Advanced 300+ Hours	0%	25%	0%	50%	25%	20%

The Joys and Dangers of Using Volunteers

Whether or not it is legally allowable in the US to use volunteers in the online space is an issue still to be resolved by the courts. There are two court cases in progress, which, if taken to the bitter end, have the capacity for delivering an answer:

➤ HALLISEY and WILLIAM versus AMERICA ONLINE, INC. and AMERICA ONLINE COMMUNITIES, INC., Docket #: 99 Civ. 3785 in UNITED STATES DISTRICT COURT SOUTHERN DISTRICT OF NEW YORK.

Filed in May of 1999, this one continues to drag on with little news about any progress in the case itself. In late 2001, however, the Department of Labor dropped an investigation into the matter with no action taken against AOL.

➤ KATHERINE R., GAIL LEE G., STEVEN J. F., and IAN R., (names edited) versus ELECTRONIC ARTS, INC., and ORIGIN SYSTEMS, INC. Civil Action No. 00 – B – 1839 in United States District Court, District of Colorado.

Filed in September of 2000 by Katherine Reab, a former contractor and previous volunteer for EA's *UO*, and three former volunteers. There has been no news on the case since late summer of 2001, when Ms. Reab announced that depositions were being taken. Class action status has been applied for, but no word has been given on whether it has been granted by the courts.

In both cases, the Plaintiffs have alleged that the Defendants violated the US Fair Labor Standards Act of 1938[6] by having a volunteer perform duties that a paid employee should perform, and are seeking back wages and penalties. There is no indication at the time of this writing when either case might actually go to trial.

Both cases have had a somewhat chilling effect on what had been a standard practice in the American online community. EA and Microsoft (publishers of *AC*) have withdrawn support for their US game volunteers, and other publishers and developers have said privately that they are awaiting the outcome of one or the other suit to decide whether volunteers are a good idea for their products. Sony Online Entertainment continues to provide volunteer support for *EQ*. Publishers outside the US, not restricted to US law, continue to feature volunteer programs. For example, Norwegian publisher Funcom has a large volunteer program for *Anarchy Online (AO)*. Other European publishers and developers are also exploring the use of volunteer organizations.

Whether or not a volunteer support organization violates US law is not your only worry, though. The dangers of supporting volunteers in an online game are not restricted to legal matters; there are the personalities and psychologies of online gamers to consider as well. While some volunteers are extremely helpful and truly add to your game, there are some who want to be volunteers for different reasons, and those reasons generally have little or nothing to do with helping others.

Screening is necessary to try to eliminate the deadwood and abusers before they are turned loose on an unsuspecting player base. It is not all bad, however; there are a significant number of players who sincerely want to volunteer and give something back to the game and help others get started more quickly and easily.

Some suggestions follow for separating the wheat from the chaff.

The Chaff   Start by identifying the chaff:

> ➤ Me! Me!
>
>   The players clamoring the loudest to be leaders in the program are, by and large, the last people you want to pick.

---

6. The FLSA is US Title 29, Chapter 8, Sections 201 through 219. See the Legal Information Institute's US Code Collection pages at `http://www4.law.cornell.edu/uscode/29/ch8.html`.

A significant number of players love to have a title and a little power to exercise over other players but have no inclination to actually help support those players in the game. They love to construct elaborate organizations with themselves at the top, handing out assignments, holding court with their lieutenants, and generally doing nothing except basking in the glory of being the leader. Or, they may be micro-managing martinets, haranguing the troops at every turn and causing turnover in the program.

For these "leaders," being top dogs in the program is part of a game within the game, becoming influential through contact with the "devs." Things may run smoothly for a while; these people do tend to be organized. Eventually, however, the temptation to exercise that contact power with the devs becomes too great; what use is power if you don't exercise it occasionally, right? Usually, they begin keeping volunteers in line with veiled threats of denunciation to the live team. ("You better watch your step with me. I have friends at the top, you know.")

Soon thereafter, they begin using this tactic on the players, and then things begin to fall apart. The last thing the players want is some petty virtual bureaucrat threatening them, and they aren't afraid to point fingers publicly. The program then becomes a bit of a joke as the abuses are pointed out, the other volunteers start taking a raft-load of abuse, and turnover in the program shoots through the roof. If not handled in a timely manner, this abuse of trust can mar the program for months.

Thankfully, the "Me! Me!" people are relatively easy to pick out. They are normally among the first people to queue up to be in a volunteer program. Before you even begin calling for volunteers, these people will be emailing to let you know they can "help" by organizing things for you with, you know, some of their friends. All through the test phases, they'll be posting messages of almost fawning support on your testing forums, shouting down anyone pointing out a problem or taking the design to task for flaws. They know that getting their names out there as avid supporters is flattering to the developers and makes it more likely they will be picked as volunteer leaders. Eventually, they manage to have regular and private contact with one or more of the developers through instant messaging or email, solidifying their positions even more.

If you pay attention to these warning signs, you won't have a problem separating this kind of chaff from the mix.

➤ Thanks for the Toys, Boys!

Some players will abuse any powers you give them. It is not uncommon to set up a series of volunteer-only commands to allow the volunteers to perform simple functions, such as teleporting across the world and going invisible. While these powers are nice for volunteers to have and make it easier for them to help other players, bear in mind that many player-volunteers are loyal to their friends, not necessarily to the game. Some people volunteer just to get the powers because they have already scoped out how to abuse them to their and their buddies' benefit. Using teleport powers to move friends around the world is one fairly common example.

As with the "Me! Me!" people, any abuse of this nature will create an air of distrust among the players. The "Toys" people themselves are hard to spot up-front because they are generally smart enough to be polite, quiet, keep their heads down, and initially, not be too obvious with their abuse of power. The more they get away with it, though, the broader and more obvious the abuses become, until players start sending email that point them out. By that time, it is too late; you've already taken a "trust" hit.

The abuses themselves are easy to detect if you have the proper logging and reporting tools in place. This has been discussed in detail elsewhere in the book; there is no need to further belabor the issue here.

➤ I'm one of the 10 best dungeon masters (DMs) in the world, no matter how many player/characters have to die to prove it!

Every game sees a large stack of these types of applications. As volunteer programs are normally involved in helping set up and run in-game events and storylines, there is always a surfeit of wannabe game designers who feel, given the chance, the live team will recognize they are the cat's meow when it comes to writing and running them. These players have probably been running campaigns as DMs in pencil-and-paper role-playing games in their local area for years and are positive your game is the place to let the world know of their sublime talents.

While they are well-meaning, the problem with these players is that the majority of them are not nearly as talented at writing and running online scenarios as they think they are. They almost always devolve into situations where the volunteer DM just keeps throwing more and more powerful mobs of creatures at or springing more powerful traps on the other participants until they all die or run. Their objective is to make sure they personally achieve satisfaction, not that the players necessarily have fun or are entertained.

The only way to weed out the worst of these types is to hold auditions—that is, make the prospective event volunteer write, cast, and run one or more scenarios; then observe and grade them, and only take the very best of them.

The Wheat   There is wheat out there if you analyze the players carefully:

➤ Not Me, Please!

The already-helpful players who least want to be official members of the program most often turn out to be the best volunteers.

These are the quiet players who always seem to have time to answer "newbie" questions, or give them some gear to help them get started, or even teach them the ropes for a few hours or days. They are often mature, "speak" in measured tones, and maintain an even keel. They just quietly go about their business, playing the game and helping other players, and never apply to be official volunteers.

There is a school of thought that these players shouldn't be recruited; they are already helping other players, so why fix something that isn't broken? On the other hand, with proper tools to spot and immediately assist a new player or someone who needs help (even if the powers are only in escalating the request higher in the queue), they can help more people, more effectively, in a shorter period of time.

Convincing "Not Me!" players to become part of the organization is tough, but well worth the effort. Even if they decline, they will be flattered by being asked.

Empowering Players: Alternatives to a Volunteer Program

Organizing a volunteer program can be a long and resource-intensive task, at least in the initial stages. For some teams, it can make better sense to spend that time on tools that allow players to empower themselves and their teams to provide help in-game.

The essence of any PW game revolves around the micro-communities that develop: factions, teams, squadrons, guilds, and the like. Many such micro-communities last for months, even years, as friendships build and the team has adventures together and creates for themselves a bond of history and legend. For any such micro-community to survive long-term, however, new people must be recruited into the family on a regular basis.

And this is where empowerment can have a huge effect on the game without a volunteer program in place. Except for problems associated with patch publishing and any ongoing player harassment issues, most help requests tend to come from new or less experienced players. Player micro-communities use new player training as a recruitment tool; hang with us, we'll train and equip you, and you get to be part of the security of our little family. Providing tools to help in-game communities identify and assist new players hooks these "newbies" quicker, provides more of a chance to make them long-term subscribers and increases overall player satisfaction.

Such tools can be as simple as a guild-specific command to list all players with less than a certain amount of time in-game, or new player chat channels that all new accounts default to. This allows communities to find the people who most need help and provide them the answers they need. There are some issues with these capabilities that require well-thought-out solutions; for instance, what if a guild or team uses these commands to locate and attack new players? How do you prevent that? The idea is to make it easy for micro-communities to find and help people, while still protecting new players from predators.

This does not need to stop at pure help functions, either. Volunteer programs also help out with in-game events such as player weddings, tournaments, and other competitions. Providing some basic event creation tools allows micro-communities to provide their own content. This also allows the live team to spend more time concentrating on higher priority items, which end up providing more varied content to the player base. As an example, the Atlantic server Mage's Tower Guild in *UO* used to offer regular skills tournaments with prizes of gold and rare game items. To assist, the *UO* GMs would set up a secure area for the tournaments, complete with communications crystals to allow non-participants to observe. Imagine if the Tower Guild had access to those tools themselves? How many more events could and would they have run if they didn't have to wait for scarce GM resources to become available?

The point is that there are alternatives to using volunteers, but they require the developers to give up some control of the game.

Security: Keeping Honest People Honest

Never forget that the collective intelligence of your players is far greater than your development team's, no matter how brilliant that team may be. The average time in-game for PWs varies from game to game, but it is between 12 hours (*UO*) and 20 hours (*EQ*) per *week*. You'll find that is more time than your developers spend actually playing the game. If there is a hole, flaw, exploit, or bug, the players will find it.

In these days of eBay and other auction sites, in which digital possessions from PWs have been sold for thousands of real-world dollars, these issues transform from irritants to huge problems. If 1,000,000 game "cash" can be sold on an auction site for $20 but requires the "dupers" to continually crash your game servers to create the duplication, then that is exactly what they will do. It won't matter to them that they are depriving a few hundred or thousand other players the chance to be in the game. They just don't care.

That kind of money can also tempt your own people to use GM administrative powers and database access to create characters and items to sell for cash. It has happened at least once before in *UO*, with one $10-per-hour GM creating game gold and other character inventory items and selling them for over $8,000 before being caught. While this kind of internal corruption is thankfully rare, each incident has effects on the player base all out of proportion to the reality of the situation. The first thought in the players' minds becomes: Who knows how many times it has happened and not been detected?

These issues make it imperative to have a security team that does nothing but investigate these incidents and take action when they occur.

The Security Strike Team

The prime responsibility of the security team is to coordinate with network operations and the live team developers to investigate anomalies for nefarious activity. Such anomalies can include repeated server crashes late at night, characters suddenly jumping multiple experience levels in a short timeframe, or one character suddenly coming into possession of thousands of one valuable item. These are indications that players have found that are exploiting bugs to duplicate items or fool the database into accepting nonexistent player/character accomplishments.

This is where your logging and reporting tools come into play. The only way to make a security team cost-effective and efficient is by ensuring that they have access to everything that happens in a game, in a convenient manner. This means logging all transactions that exceed or break certain levels and conditions, automatically creating daily reports of major anomalies they can check each morning, and providing full-featured search functions they can use to create their own reports.

Internal Investigations: Keeping Your People Honest in the Era of eBay Money

It is also necessary to have internal investigations to ensure your own employees aren't exploiting players and the integrity of the game by creating items for sale on eBay or helping out some buddies in the game by using their powers for their buddies' advantage (or their enemies' disadvantage). This happens far more often than publishers are willing to admit, and GMs and others with administrative access can get away with it because most games don't have adequate logging and reporting features to help catch the offenders. Most games can't even run a report on the character names created the night before to check for intentionally offensive names, such as "F***you<company-name>." You can imagine how hard it is for them to investigate possible dupe bugs.

Regularly and secretly investigating your own people is a touchy area, but if your logging and database reporting functions are as complete as they need to be and independent of GM control or modification, it is worth the time to do spot-checks on GMs on a regular basis and tell your GMs that they are being done and why.

It is also a good idea to hire your security team from outside the company, not from the ranks of the GMs themselves. Not only do friends and coworkers find it hard to fink on their buddies, but it can also cause resentment toward former friends when they do. Or, as in the case of the above-mentioned *UO* GM caught selling game items on eBay, it can cause friends to want to find and initiate a real-world assault on the offender for betraying their trust as well as that of the players. Thankfully, the offender was whisked out of the building before his firing was announced.

Community Relations: Processes

"Less is more. What I mean by this is that communication with players should be clear, consistent, and focused. A larger quantity of unfocused communication is inferior to consistent delivery of focused messages. I'm a big believer in memorializing information in a single place that is easily accessible to the player base. Duplicated information is error-prone."

Gordon Walton

"Tell them less than you are initially inclined to, but never be dishonest. Treat them like adults. Reach out to people who will happily build community sites and be cheerleaders for you. Be sure you let them know when you change something due to their input. And, most of all, be sure that you never let them feel like your communication with them has grown stagnant."

Damion Schubert

Managing the expectations of players starts with and revolves around the community relations team. They have the primary responsibility to ensure that a consistent, focused, honest message is presented to the community, and that the concerns of the community are relayed back to the other members of the live team for comment and consideration.

However, they can't do that without the cooperation of the live development and player relations teams. In that sense, customer relations is a consensus-builder within the live team and between the live team and the player base. They drive the processes that keep information flowing.

The Three Principles

The processes of managing a game community start with the three principles discussed in the next three sections.

Constantly Design for Growth and Change

If an online game is successful in building a subscriber base, participation in both the in-game and web communities will grow over time. Features and support not required at launch will be required months down the line. As much as possible, those features need to be planned at the outset to allow for a graceful, structured growth. It also means there have to be regular reviews of the community relations features set and changes made to ensure that growth and change within the community are being met successfully.

This also means that there has to be open communication among the player relations team, community relations team, development team, and the publisher, so everyone knows about and buys into the plan developed to support the game over time.

Create and Maintain Feedback Loops

As discussed earlier, the communication among the players, community relations team, developers, and the publisher needs to be carefully managed to protect the reputation of the game and the company and to keep even small incidents or rumors from being blown out of proportion and creating a mess. At the same time, the players want unfettered access and input to the game developers.

Creating and effectively maintaining feedback loops between the players and community relations and between community relations and the developers and back again is vital to creating an atmosphere of contribution, while at the same time protecting the developers from having to answer every question or comment the players might make on message boards or in chat.

Empower the Players over Time

Players change their own roles over time. Some become leaders and need tools to help them lead their people; others become opinion-makers in the out-of-game community; while other players create roles they find interesting for themselves. Each requires different tools and capabilities; if they have them, they'll help you increase the size and role of your game community over time. It is necessary to ensure that this is tracked carefully and that players are empowered at the proper times.

The Cult of Personality

The point person on these principles and processes is your community management, specifically the lead CRM.

If there is one thing players hate to see on message board postings, it is a communiqué from the developers or company signed "From the <game name> Live Team." Nothing is quite so impersonal or noninteractive as a faceless, human-less message. This whole industry is based on interactivity, with the game and between the people who play it, make it, and publish it. With the human touch so important a factor, why would anyone go out of his/her way to de-humanize the process?

Amazingly, that is exactly what many online game publishers and developers do, in spite of the abundance of publicly available evidence that it does not work and that the players dislike it. You need the human touch.

One effective way to keep the human touch is to set up one person as your contact point with the community and create a cult of personality around him/her. If you pick the right person as the lead, day-to-day CRM, this won't be a problem; it will happen naturally. For example, take Jonathan "Calandryl" Hanna. Jonathan began as a player of *UO* and, over time, became an influential opinion-maker in the forums. When Origin Systems began looking for someone to come in and take over community relations for their sloppy and disliked public face, he applied for and got the job.

Within weeks, he had the players eating out of his hand. Not only was he one of them, but he also made a concerted effort to take player questions, track down the answers, and post them. He also took the time to post chatty messages and dealt with the players with respect and humor.

This is the perfect type of community relations person—a gamer who knows the player base, likes them, and considers himself/herself their advocate to the live team, without losing sight of the fact that he/she still works for the company. This minor kind of cult of personality, when the right person experienced with the product is the center of the cult, serves a number of functions:

➤ It enhances player comfort and trust in the game and company. Having a real, live person interacting with the players, instead of a faceless corporation, creates the human connection that Internet game players live for.

➤ It makes insulating the rest of the live team from daily player pressure easier and more amenable to both sides. Developers worry about losing contact with the player community and understanding their issues, and players worry that they won't get the straight skinny from the developers. A trusted intermediary can negotiate these waters and satisfy both sides.

➤ It provides a control mechanism when problems develop. It is not unusual for the patching and publishing process to create temporary problems due to bugs or balancing issues. This also causes a temporary spike in complaints and a rising swell of player dissatisfaction, confusion, and anger. If not handled correctly and in a timely manner, this can quickly get out of hand. A trusted and effective CRM can ride the swell and control it, keeping the players appeased with a constant flow of information on the web, in message forums, and through "Letters from the Developers," and reining in the natural inclination of the developers to get out there and defend themselves (that is, argue with the players).

This takes a person of particular qualities. It isn't enough to just drag someone out of the community and throw them into place. All too often, the loudest supporter running a fan site is picked for this duty, in a modern-day demonstration of, "He who raises his hand first gets the job." While this is certain to get a loyal "wannabe" on the staff, one who will not often question the developers, it might or might not get you the person with the qualities you actually need.

The qualities you need include the following:

➤ A person who can see both sides of the issue and isn't afraid to challenge the developers—Live team developers tend to get too close to the game and forget that proposed changes won't just alter the game, but also affect the experience of the players. If the players are a vocal and not particularly complimentary lot, the developers may actually come to resent the players and unconsciously make changes designed to irritate them further.

➤ A good CRM knows the game inside and out and is willing to take a stand for or against changes that will affect gameplay, both publicly to the players and privately to the live team. This doesn't mean the CRM denigrates the live team to the players; it does mean the CRM is willing to be vocal privately about proposed changes and, if overruled, still "owns" the change publicly with the players.

➤ Someone who understands the unique sense of humor of online gamers—Players have a somewhat twisted and dark sense of humor, full of sarcasm and innuendo. If your frontline CRM doesn't understand the humor, it will be impossible to make a connection with the players.

➤ Someone who understands the power of the word "us"—The players want to be involved in the game as members of the community, not just as anonymous players who send in $10 each month to get access. As such, they want inclusion, and responding to them with the word "we," meaning the live team, just draws a line in the sand that some of them are more than willing to cross. A CRM who can include the whole player base by making the whole into "us" already has half of the potential "bad actor" problems solved.

➤ A person who understands that you don't argue or get snappy with the players— Some players are barracks-house lawyers and will endlessly debate the fine points, if you let them. To them, this is just part of the game and part of the fun. Nothing pleases them more than trolling for a CRM on the message boards, getting the CRM to take the bait, and then making a fool out of him/her by frustrating him/her to the point where he/she snaps.

➤ The CRM should be a person who maintains an even keel, remains polite in the face of the most horrid or derogatory posts, and knows when and when not to continue a debate and how to close one off gracefully. This is someone who understands that expressing disappointment over a rude message and apologizing for not being able to satisfy the offender sends a far stronger message than lashing out and getting into a fight.

➤ Someone who understands the player bias on issues and can sort his/her player contacts accordingly—The vocal minority of any PW tends to come with built-in biases. Some are self-serving; everything they say or do will be focused on improving their personal role in the game. Others are subject matter experts; they know the subject (the game) in minute detail and will continually argue for more hard-core game mechanics and options at the expense of other players.

➤ A CRM needs to be able to identify and track the bias in discussions and posts and weigh and respond to them accordingly.

Daily Activities

The daily activities of the community relations team will revolve around the message boards, email, and maintaining the community relations portion of the web site.

Message Boards

Message boards, often called forums, are a vital part of the community relations team's online presence. Much of the team's daily interaction with the players comes through this medium. There are pros and cons to offering open message boards to your subscriber base. On the pro side, having open forums gives the team access to a broad range of player opinions and affords them the opportunity to build compromises and consensus around sticky issues.

On the con side, less than 15% of a subscriber base ever posts on forums, and that <15% represents the vocal minority of the game. They have their own agenda and, by answering their concerns publicly, you tend to get more of the same, a sort of vicious positive feedback loop on the concerns of the biased few.

Even facing these potential pitfalls, if you don't have open forums, how can you expect to communicate effectively with the players or correctly manage their expectations? Even rude or uncomplimentary message posts can contain a grain of truth; it is important to acknowledge those and make certain they get into the right hands on the live team for consideration.

The community relations team's daily activity surrounding the message boards mainly consists of reading the new messages, responding to them, and collating and forwarding interesting or important threads to the various members of the team for answers to questions or clarifications.

At some point, the community relations team collates those answers from the live team and posts them in the proper message board threads. Unless you want the live development team spending a couple hours a day just responding to posts, you'll want to establish a regular routine of one or two days per week in which those answers to player inquiries are posted. If the response days are clearly noted, the players' expectations of answers will be managed to those days. It also makes sense to have a dedicated forum category or thread titled "Answers from the Team" or something similar, so players know where to go to get the responses.

The community relations team should not necessarily limit itself to just those message board activities. Players like to banter with team members and know that they are human and have senses of humor. Indulging in some of this goes a long way toward keeping the vocal minority under wraps.

Email

Another major portion of the day will be spent reading and replying to community relations-specific email. Some of this will come directly to the community relations mailbox and some will be forwarded from the player relations team. For the most part, this email will deal with in-game balance issues that require answers from someone else on the live team, or will need to be forwarded to player relations for action on account management, harassment, or billing.

It is easy for the email load to community relations to get out of hand. The more you answer specific concerns or inquiries, the more they'll send. The best use of the community relations team's time is to get as many of the emailers as possible using the web site and forums. The team should "push" as many answers as they can to the web site or forums by referring the emailer to a FAQ sheet, knowledge base entry, or specific forum thread.

Whether responding or referring to email, it is important to follow the 24-hour response rule. You don't want to get a reputation for "ignoring" emailers.

Web Site Maintenance

The community relations team is responsible for maintaining the content on the web site, which includes maintaining the front page of the site to draw readers in to important information, adding new content such as news, links to interesting forum threads, regular articles, letters from the team, and archiving older content.

As a general rule, the community relations team should put up some new piece of content on a daily basis, even if it is just a link to an interesting forum thread. With careful organization of features such as "Letters from the Team" and new content to go into the four-step player notification system, this won't be difficult to accomplish. The important thing is to keep the site fresh and new; it is as much a living organism as the game itself and needs to reflect that.

Player-Run Communities

A PW's subscriber base isn't just a great big blob of a community. Imagine 100,000 or 200,000 subscribers trying to organize activities around the whole group; it would be virtually impossible. Rather, player-run communities consist of smaller, more easily managed micro-communities. Variously called guilds, teams, squadrons, fellowships, and allegiances, these micro-communities band together to provide the members with in-game assistance and a regular social group within the world. There is safety and power in numbers, after all.

The activities of player-run communities encompass not only the in-game actions of micro-communities such as teams and guilds, but also the web-based interaction of these teams and other interest groups based around the game. Many of your player teams will host web sites for their members, complete with message boards, Internet Relay Chat (IRC) chat rooms, and news areas. Moreover, more general communities based on character classes, specific server clusters (especially if they are specialized clusters, such as PvP or role-playing-only servers), factions, or character skills are also likely to spring up.

While much of what goes on in appealing to these leaders will have to do with maintaining the illusion of immersion with the game ("in-character"), there will also be plenty of out-of-character (OOC) exchanges to discuss game changes, policies, and the like. These communities can be a live team's best resource for helping to set opinions and gain support for game changes, additions, and what might otherwise be unpopular policies and procedures.

Supporting these communities with in-game and web resources is becoming a must for publishers. Figures 11.7[7] and 11.8[8] show one method, using the web, which Sony Online and EA use to support player teams and create a sense of inclusion.

---

7. Sony Online Entertainment's *EQ* has begun supporting micro-communities of their premium-priced servers, called *Legends*, by providing them guild pages. This is a good example of outreach to potential opinion-makers.

8. Note that the guild names are hyperlinks to further information about the guild and specific members, including hyperlinks to private guild web sites not hosted by EA.

Figure 11.7 A guild page for Sony's *EQ Legends* premium server.

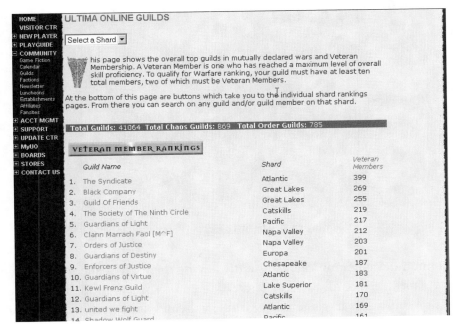

Figure 11.8 *UO*'s guild page.

Leadership Roles for Micro-communities

There is no particular average population size for a micro-community; it can be anywhere from a couple friends to several dozen. Some micro-communities become quite sizable, recruiting hundreds of members and organizing several team-related activities each week. Many are highly organized, with a motivated leader or leader council, and are operated like a going concern, with an internal ranking hierarchy and members required to support the team on-call. They usually write and distribute a team charter to the members, laying out the mission of the micro-community and the requirements to join and remain in good standing. Some of these teams are so organized they make organizations like the Shriners look positively chaotic, as shown in the *AO* player guild training screenshot in Figure 11.9.

Figure 11.9 An *AO* guild in group training.

These communities communicate constantly among themselves and with other communities via message boards and email, creating and resolving conflicts and reaching consensus on important in-game issues. These activities are normally left to the team leaders and the members go along with their dictates. Like every group, there are leaders and followers.

The leaders of these player-run communities are among the influential opinion-makers of your overall community. There may be 200,000, 400,000, or more subscribers to the game, but probably fewer than 1,000 of them are setting or managing the opinion for many of those subscribers. The leaders of the larger groups probably represent a number of sub-groups within the game and have regular contact with other community leaders.

Keying into these leaders and "massaging" that relationship is the job of the Community Relations team. It will be somewhat symbiotic; the leaders will derive more authority over their own groups from their contact with the team, and the team will be able to have greater influence over the leaders, who wish to continue siphoning off some of that power. They will also be something like amateur politicians, used to the process of give and take to reach a compromise within their own groups and with other factions.

The Policy of Inclusion

There are a number of ways to include the leaders in your strategy, but they all depend on drawing them into the decision-making process. This allows them to cement their authority over their own people and, in the best of times, makes them advocates for you with a large segment of the game population.

The best approach is probably a combination of some of the following elements:

➤ **Email lists**—The simplest way is to set up one or more email lists of the micro-community leaders and send regular updates and messages to them, drawing them deeper into the storyline with in-character messages or delivering timely OOC news for inclusion on their team web sites.

The lists can be derived from the game's own list of guilds/teams. If your particular game doesn't make provisions for such lists, it isn't hard to set up a web page to allow the leaders to register for one.

➤ **Guild leader web site**—In addition to a standard news area, this should include forums and a chat area, as well as in-character and OOC posting forums and pages.

If possible, this should also be password-protected or accessible via invited accounts only, if just to add to the feeling of inclusion and "specialness." You can bet money that the password won't stay secret for long or that someone will allow another player access to their account to check out the area; that's not the point. The point is to recognize the leaders.

➤ **Council of leaders**—Banding the leaders together into a council and holding regular chat room meetings will help seal the bonds of loyalty. This is most useful for helping push a storyline or series of important in-game events forward. However, it can also be used to help set a player consensus on items posted to the four-step notification program discussed earlier or to allow leaders to bring forward concerns from their own micro-communities. On controversial issues where the player base is up in arms, the council can be the spearpoint of keeping a lid on the situation while the issue is discussed.

There will probably be too many such leaders to pull them all into one large council; a smaller council of 10–20 chairs, with leaders rotating in and out of the chairs at set periods between 30 days and 3 months, is more doable.

It is important to understand that, if you choose to use the council method, you have to listen to them and take their suggestions and recommendations whenever feasible. If the leaders ever get the idea that they have no influence (that is, they are not truly included in the process), the council will fall apart amid loud complaints and loss of trust from the player base as a whole. Only go into this if you're serious about the policy of inclusion and are willing to let the council have a bit of power and influence.

This doesn't mean you have to let them vote on every little feature or change; if most of the leaders—and, through them, their constituencies—are opposed to some proposed change or feature, it bears looking into.

➤ **In-game meetings**—The leaders can be included in the process by conducting in-game meetings in which their power and influence within the "world" is acknowledged and demonstrated to other players. For example, the event GMs of Funcom's *AO* regularly host in-game, in-character meetings with organization heads (*AO*'s version of guilds). The GMs pose as main characters from ongoing storylines and consult leaders from the various organizations about in-game events and actions to be taken in response to them.

What You Are Really Doing

Appealing to micro-communities through their leaders doesn't mean just including them in the process and enhancing overall player satisfaction. What you are really doing is practicing self-defense and creating goodwill by somewhat Machiavellian means. These folks are very passionate about what they do; that's why they are playing your game in the first place. In effect, what you are trying to do is get them to buy off on dreams they are already in the market for and then help fulfill them.

What the community relations team has to be careful to avoid is not trying to sell them *its* dreams outright or too forcefully. The team may believe that the background story is the greatest piece of literature in the history of mankind, but if the players are insistent about taking it in a direction not conceived of by the writers, then you have a problem. Trying to force such ideas down their throats will only cause dissension and bad feelings. Using the leaders to create a consensus and following through, however, creates a tremendous store of goodwill.

And you may need that goodwill later on, in case you screw up in heroic proportions and need all the goodwill and patience you can get from your players.

Chapter 12

The Live Development Team

Sometime from one to six months after launch, the live development team will take over responsibility for the game from the development team proper. By this time, the game should be stable, the initial crush of subscribers absorbed, and the intake of new subscribers settled out to a low, but consistent, level. The live development team should have a relatively calm environment in which to begin its work.

And there is a lot of work to be done. The overall responsibilities of the live development team are three-fold:

➤ Maintain the game's current content and tools

➤ Design and add new content and tools on a regular basis

➤ Design and develop major game expansions (either retail or download)

Live Development Team Responsibilities

Let's explore each of the responsibilities in a little more detail:

➤ **Maintaining the game**—Maintenance is a fairly simple process: Identify and fix bugs as they are reported, monitor the game servers for stability and anomalies in the code, and make sure the administrative tools used by player relations and others continue to work as intended.

➤ **New content and tools**—The live development team designs and develops new content and features for inclusion in the game on a regular basis (every two to six weeks) and confabs with the player relations and community relations teams to identify new tools or capabilities needed by those worthy of them. This is the meat of the matter for both the players and the team; regular refreshment of the content is vital to the good health and growth of the game.

➤ **Expansion pack development**—For games with a retail component, it is necessary to keep a steady flow of expansion packs on the shelf. This not only keeps a presence at the retail level to attract a steady stream of new potential subscribers, but allows the retail software to be recompiled and updated, avoiding exceptionally large downloads for new players.

How often to ship a new box to retail is a matter of resources and how quickly the world-building tools allow for new content to be built. The available evidence seems to suggest shipping an expansion every nine months to a year as optimum. As examples, Sony Online's *EverQuest* (*EQ*), the largest US game, has been out for a little over three years and already has three expansions with a fourth in development as of January 2002; *Ultima Online* (*UO*), out for almost five years, has shipped four of them; and *Asheron's Call* (*AC*), the smallest of the three examples, has been out just over two years and only recently shipped its first expansion.

With all this activity going on, it is necessary to be organized and coordinated to avoid a constant process of "patch, freak out, fix all the bugs that should have been fixed on the test server, and calm down the players who want to hang us all again." The heart of all of this is the publishing process.

The Publishing Process

Patch day: These words strike terror into the hearts of players all over the world and with good reason; the industry doesn't have a great record of stable patches, nor one of informing the players just what changes will be made in each one. More often than not, patches aren't well-tested, they are filled with bugs, and they contain wagonloads of unannounced changes, some of which look like bugs to the uninformed players.

In previous chapters, we discussed cowboy programming and other bad development practices that foster this kind of self-defeating chain of events. If the producer of the live team can manage to control the team's cowboy programming and its equally noxious, shoot-from-the-hip cousins, it will be by strict enforcement of a publishing process. The publishing process structures fixes of the current/old code, design changes, and additions that represent new code, plans for QA testing, and lays out when and when not to do an emergency patch.

The Publishing Plan

In some ways, the process for creating and publishing a game patch should resemble the initial development process discussed in Chapter 2, "Planning." Such a thorough process has not been the standard to date, resulting in unstable patches that crash games and nasty bugs that sometimes corrupt entire character databases. This often necessitates a rollback to a backup version of the game, which results in the loss of many hours of player in-game time and accomplishment. Now you know why players dread patch day.

A patch should be meticulously planned, developed using best-of-breed version control and CCPs, and thoroughly tested and debugged on a live test server before being inflicted on the subscribers. Patches published online to the player base won't be as large as the initial development, but they still need to be charted in a task schedule program by a project manager. And the live development team, like the initial development team, tends to bite off more than it can reasonably chew for a patch.

Patch Creation and Publishing Schedules

The steps that should go into the publishing process can be outlined as follows:

1. Creation of a live production plan. The plan should include the following:

   ➤ Bug list: Bugs detected and to be fixed

   ➤ Balance issues: Fixing out-of-balance regions, items, and classes

   ➤ New features: Interface capabilities, bells, and whistles

> ➤ New content: New mechanics, dungeons, skills, crafts, and so on

> ➤ New tools: To assist members of the live team

> ➤ Tentative schedule of patches by date

>> ➤ Regular schedules for fixes

>> ➤ Regular schedules for new content

2. Development and documentation of changes. This phase should include the following:

   > ➤ Version control of changes and additions to the code

   > ➤ Change control process (CCP) documentation of changes

   > ➤ Commenting of new code, recommending of changed code

3. QA plan. This includes the following:

   > ➤ CCP vetting of new content and features

   > ➤ Internal test server implementation

   > ➤ Live test server implementation

   > ➤ Fix problems found in testing and retest

4. Publishing the patch: Patch day! Substeps include the following:

   > ➤ QA sign-off

   > ➤ Producer sign-off

   > ➤ Authorization to initiate a publish

   > ➤ Emergency patch procedures

Step 1 is the planning and design stage: when the fixes and new content are planned, prioritized, and scheduled for publishing. It is important to note that this document will change frequently as problems are fixed, new concepts and content are planned, and previously planned content and features are created, tested, patched to the game, and removed from the schedule. There is also some tentative scheduling of when the game patches will be published and what will be in each patch.

> **NOTE**
> It is recommended that you schedule "fix" patches separate from new content and feature addition patches. Mixing them can be convenient, but imagine what would happen if a "fix" isn't really fixed or causes unanticipated problems and has to be rolled back to an earlier version? If the new content is critical to the ongoing storyline or is highly anticipated by the subscribers (as it almost always is), being forced to revert to former versions will cause a major hoo-rah, guaranteed.

Step 2 is the development phase, when the changes and additions are developed and documented.

Step 3 is the testing process, controlled by QA. QA should perform initial tests in-house on a closed server, perhaps assisted by a small crew (25–50) of trusted outside testers. Once problems detected in this testing have been fixed and retested, the changes can be placed on a live test server, with open access to the subscribers. The process should be fairly rote from that point: find the bug, fix the bug, retest to make sure the bug is really fixed, repeat until finished.

Step 4 is the actual publishing of the patch to the live player servers. Once QA and the producer have signed off on a patch, authorization is given to initiate the "publish" according to the schedule.

Occasionally, nasty problems with the code will develop out of nowhere and require an emergency fix to stabilize the game or eliminate a particularly nasty bug. Following the dictates of The Law of the General Perversity of the Universe, an emergency will usually happen at 3 a.m. on the Saturday morning of a four-day holiday weekend. If an emergency patch is needed, there should be an authorization process documented, even if it is just a panicked junior engineer calling the producer for permission to make a quick fix and reboot the servers.

The Live Test Server

Some teams like to hide upcoming changes from the player base. As discussed earlier in the section about managing the expectations of the players, this generally causes more problems than not. Remember that the players are stakeholders, too, just as much as any executive or member of the team. Their input is important, if only so they can say they had some.

Aside from the consideration of not taking the player base by surprise with changes, live testing with as many people as you can get is a necessary component of the live phase development procedure. Remember the bugs that were found when thousands tested in the late stages of open Beta, on code that you were *positive* was stable? Why would anyone believe, then, that making changes to code interlocked with many other moving parts can be done successfully with just a few dozen testers?

So, a live test server is needed. There are a few guidelines to follow:

➤ Players who regularly inhabit a test server can become proprietary about it, in the same manner they do with their characters and possessions on the production server. It is recommended that you wipe the character database clean often, just to get players in the habit of it.

➤ It can be difficult to attract and retain players on the test server; they only have so much time to play, and the testing doesn't develop into a permanent character. A system of rewards can go a long way to attract people onto the server. For example, you can offer a tester-only item of clothing for use in the live game after a certain number of hours of testing is completed; players enjoy this kind of recognition among their peers, as it implies close contact with the god-like developers.

➤ Something that many teams forget is that the player base exists at all levels of experience and character growth, and with all manner of item inventories. After wiping a database clean, all characters are back to zero in growth and inventory, so the main testing is done by low-growth characters with "newbie" items. Be sure the live test server has player-activated options for raising and lowering test characters to various stages of growth and easily adding items to the inventory, so balance and bug issues can be tested in all ranges. This will also help attract players to the test server, as players love to test out character classes and items they haven't touched before.

➤ Listen to what the testers say. One of the most common mistakes teams make is to ignore what the testers are telling them. The communication has to flow both ways for the test server to be of any real use to the team.

How Often Should You Publish?

After the initial launch phase, when the game has settled into a stable state, you should institute a regular publishing schedule of patches. With a regular schedule necessary to manage the expectations of the players about patch publishing, the question becomes how often you should publish a patch.

We've seen every schedule from once per week to every two or three months. In our experience, once per week is too often and once a month is not often enough. A happy medium, depending on the resources available, is every two to four weeks, not counting emergency patches.

The important thing is that publishing patches happens on a regular schedule and that schedule is kept, if at all possible. There will always be exceptions; some scheduled publishes won't make it through QA. Constant communication about the state of an upcoming patch with the players will help you manage these occasional situations.

Critical Bugs and Exploits

What is a critical bug or exploit? When it comes to bugs, anything that crashes either the servers or game client has to be fixed as soon as possible; that's just plain common sense. We don't know any developer who wouldn't work as long as it takes to find and fix a crash bug. Some exploits, especially attempts at duplication of items, require players to intentionally crash servers through the introduction of lag or what looks like a denial of service attack (streaming huge amounts of data at a server until it slows to a crawl or crashes from the load) and should be treated the same as crash bugs.

The same criticality goes for duplication bugs that don't require crashing the servers to implement; anything that allows a player to duplicate game items outside the context of the gameplay should be found immediately. Whether you close it right away is a more interesting issue; live teams have been known to put in logging code just to see who is using the dupe bug consistently, so those people can be removed from the game at a later time.

Beyond that, we get into the realm of theory and speculation, at least from the developer's point of view. What may be a critical exploit or harmful bug to the community relations or player relations team—one that must be fixed right now—might not be a priority at all for the live development team. Is being able to stack flour sacks around a boss monster to prevent him from moving and making him easier to kill a critical exploit that must be fixed immediately, or can it wait until the next scheduled patch? How about players using a teleportation spell to strand non-magic users on an island? You certainly want to stop that kind of activity, but should it be fixed right now, or can it wait?

These are tough areas for decision makers, and the best guideline we can give is this: If a bug or exploit thoroughly screws up the balance of the game and/or is used to prevent other players from playing normally and requires gamemaster (GM) intervention to set right, it probably ought to be fixed as soon as possible. In other words, if it generates help calls to the GMs, it ought to go to the top of the "fix" queue.

Bug-Fixing Versus Nerfing

"Nerfing" is a generic term used by the community to describe the act of changing an ability or feature in such a manner that it takes away power from players (for example, changing crossbows into Nerf crossbows). While the term "nerfing" existed before 1999, it came into general use by subscribers to describe the actions of Verant's live team early in *EQ*'s lifecycle, when it was nerfing a character class, skill, ability, or weapon seemingly on a weekly basis. Nerfing does not include vital bug fixes, although the players may perceive them as such if not properly forewarned.

Developers most often use the term "game balancing" to describe this activity. They are pretty much the same thing with the same effect: They neutralize dozens and even hundreds of play hours for individuals. There's nothing like working for weeks to achieve a skill level and having the developers change the rules overnight because they feel it unbalances the game. It may even be true that a skill or ability is horribly unbalanced and a change is necessary; doing it without warning and discussion with the players, in a for-pay game, is guaranteed to cause outrage and the occasional death threat.

It is also a mistake that almost everyone in this industry makes. For some reason, developers seem to delight in springing takeaway surprises on the players, as if knowing about them in advance will somehow neutralize the change or give the players an advantage. However, nothing angers players more than being presented with a surprise nerf. Predictably, developers seem shocked at the ticked-off reaction from the players every time because they believe they are doing good things for the game.

Some changes are necessary—even nerfs—but there is no excuse for not utilizing the community management team to prepare the players for them. If the players know a week ahead of time that a certain change is coming, they can avoid wasting their time playing to advance skills, weapons, or whatever is about to become less useful. And, in the end, it is all about not wasting the player's time.

Planning and Implementing Major Expansions

Throughout the whole process of regular patches and adding new content, the team needs to be planning the major expansion packs. Most often, these expansions are developed as new retail units to retain vital shelf space and keep the "buzz" about the game alive. Most expansions are also far too large to conveniently download, which is another recommendation for planning them as retail offerings.

The computer/video game press will almost never rereview an online game simply because new content has been added on a regular basis. However, the press is in the habit of reviewing new retail units. Issuing an expansion as a retail unit is almost certain to get it reviewed by the major game press.

These expansions should cover two main areas:

➤ All the fixes and content/features additions to date, to bring the shelf unit as close to the current code base as possible

➤ New content and features found only in the expansion

What kind of new content and features should be added? Following are the considerations you should ponder:

➤ Do you want to primarily appeal to new players or service your current players?

   Remembering that most new players will churn out before the expiration of the free trial offer, you get your best return on investment (ROI) from your current players. Keeping current customers around should be a primary concern, so heavily weighting new content to retain current customers is not a bad idea. The idea is to keep them in the involvement phase of their lifecycle and not let them slip into the boredom phase. Be careful not to add just top-level content; those in the mid-range, who are most likely the players who want to stay but don't have 20 hours per week to indulge, can use some refreshment, too.

If you're keeping a unit on the shelf, you'll have a steady influx of new customers anyway, so don't sacrifice the satisfaction of current players on the altar of higher numbers. That doesn't mean you can't add content for newer players, especially if you need new tutorials or should redesign the new player experience. This is important to look at in the first major expansion but less vital in subsequent ones.

➤ What are the customers asking for and what needs to be added?

If the community relations team has been doing its job, you should have an ongoing list of the major features and additions requested by the players and know which items in the envisioned or upcoming section of the four-step notification plan are most discussed. By now, you should have also set up your own player satisfaction matrix (PSM), as discussed in Chapter 8, "Getting into the Design."

Both should figure heavily in planning the features and content for an expansion, as long as the bias of the vocal minority on the forums is being accounted for. If something is called for by both the players and the PSM, you should probably include it. For example, if both the PSM and the players are calling for player-owned housing, it should be in the expansion.

Implementing an Expansion

Turning on an expansion looks a lot like the original launch day. The current players will be rushing out to buy the expansion on the first day, to get their hands on the new content, so the servers will see an unusual spike in the number of simultaneous users, similar to what happened the day the game went live.

Thus, the day an expansion hits the retail shelves should be treated like launch day, and the two to four weeks afterward should be treated like a launch phase: Rest the team beforehand, anticipate server and bandwidth overloads, and dust off and review the emergency plans from launch day.

IV
Articles from the Experts

Even though online games have been around since 1969, the industry is still in its infancy. As this book is being finished in the winter of 2002, there are well over 100 for-pay online games in development, but only about two or three hundred people who have gone through the development process from soup to nuts. That isn't a lot of frontline experience to go around for an industry that is expected to grow in the double digits every year for the next three to five years.

It was our intention from the start to include some supporting articles written both by us and a few of those 200 people. The purpose was not necessarily to back up the text of this book; some of the points made in these articles take a decidedly different tack. Rather, the purpose was to provide post-mortems, opinions, and alternate views from other experienced developers so the reader could see more than one side of some these thorny issues. Some articles, such as Damion Schubert's "The Lighter Side of *Meridian 59*'s History," amuse while demonstrating some of the issues that can rise up out of nowhere and slap a developer in the face. Others, such as Talin's "Managing Deviant Behavior in Online Worlds" and Jonathan Baron's "Glory and Shame," contain serious discussions on elements of persistent world (PW) management that are often overlooked by developers and which have killed more than one game post-launch.

Some of the original articles were months or years old, so we asked the authors to update them, which they kindly did. A couple of them, including the post-mortems on *Anarchy Online* and *Dark Age of Camelot* by Gaute Godager and Matt Firor, respectively, are original to this book. The key to understanding what this section is all about is simple: The authors all have direct experience developing and managing PWs. What they write contains information that will be invaluable to those developing or managing PWs. In other words, the reader is getting the benefit of direct experience, straight from the horses' mouths.

Is there anything more valuable than that?

Chapter 13

Microsoft's UltraCorps*: Why This Turn-Based Game Failed*

by **Jessica Mulligan**

KEY TOPICS

- Turned-Based Conquest Games Are Not Mass-Market

- Too Easy to Exploit the Game Design

- Constant Bugs and "Hacks" Destroyed the Game's Credibility

- Lack of Publicity and Marketing by Microsoft

- Failure to Refresh the Game Often Enough

- The Zone's Sysops Were AWOL.

AUTHOR NOTE

During the week of June 1, 1999, Microsoft and VR-1 (www.vr1.com) closed down *UltraCorps (UC)*, a turn-based MMP game of space conquest and resource management, and one of the first premium, for-pay games to debut on Microsoft's Gaming Zone (www.zone.com). It was also the first of the crop of "new" (post-fall 1996) for-pay online games to be closed down. In this context, I define "new" as online games developed by inexperienced but well-funded shops since 1996, as opposed to experienced developers such as Kesmai or Simutronics, which developed online games during the period from 1978–1995 on shoestring budgets and a lot of passion.

I noted in print at the time that it would not be the last such game to fail, and 2001 showed me to be all too correct. Why this attitude? Some of the reasons *UC* failed are being repeated by others. As I read over the case study in early 2002, I found that most of the lessons are still current, showing how little has changed in three years in this industry.

Here are the main points from the original case study. The lessons to be learned still apply today.

Turned-Based Conquest Games Are Not Mass-Market

I liked *UC*, but I seem to have been in the minority. Nor does this surprise me; in a niche market, turn-based conquest games are a niche within a niche. Like the war game market, turn-based strategy players are small in numbers, but they are usually willing to pay a premium to play.

On a mass-market game portal such as The Zone, this practically the guaranteed financial failure of *UC*. Even during the free Beta campaigns, it was tough to get more than 5,000 or so of The Zone's well-publicized two million plus subscribers (then) to try a campaign. After *UC* converted to $9.95 a month for unlimited play, this dropped to about 1,800 players, and slowly slid to about 800. Even the most recent campaign, which in an uncharacteristic fit of generosity and common sense by Microsoft was offered free to the community, only attracted about 1,500 players.

Too Easy to Exploit the Game Design

As anyone with even a modicum of experience in this industry knows, some players will do anything to win, including cheating and finding and using the holes in the game design. Such players are completely unrepentant about such play. They argue that if an action isn't blocked by the design and code implementation, it's a feature, not an "exploit." On one level these players have a point; it is up to the developer and designer to plug such holes.

Turn-based conquest games lend themselves to these holes. In essence, they are number-crunching games; the number and power of attacking units versus the same for the defending units determine the outcome of battles. Once you get past even odds in a battle, very little is left to chance or random factors. Think of it as *Risk* on a somewhat grander scale.

When *UC* was designed, too little thought was given to how these relatively few players could exploit design flaws to create unfair advantage. Especially in the early stages of a campaign, *UC* was weak in preventing one person from having multiple accounts to feed one master account to exploit the design.

Referred to as MACs by players, multiple alias cheaters were perceived as one of the biggest problems of the game. Using this exploit, one player would establish several game aliases on The Zone then use them all to join a single *UC* campaign in the hope that two or more would be within supporting distance of each other on Turn 1. The "mule" accounts would send starting military units as trade fleets to the "master" account. Even with the random starting placement inherent within the game code, a player using four or five accounts had a pretty good chance of having at least two accounts within mutual supporting distance. Those "mule" accounts that were too distant to be of help could be restarted to try for a better placement closer to the "master" account.

This would give the MAC player a huge advantage at the onset of a campaign, effectively doubling or tripling his/her military units and planetary building resources. It would be like one player in *Risk* receiving 50 armies starting on Turn 1. No other nearby player could compete with that kind of power.

A similar design exploit could be and was used constantly by teams of players. Instead of one player with multiple accounts, teams of players—with sometimes as many as 10 participating—would designate one player as the "master" account and would "feed" his/her home planet with fleets, which also effectively stripped their planets of defenses for an easy capture. Those players would then restart the campaign and, if luck placed them in range, repeat the procedure. In this way, teams would rotate who got to win or place highly in a campaign. Even nastier, sometimes teams of MAC players would band together and totally overwhelm the local competition within 10 turns of a 30- or 60-turn game.

This type of exploitive gameplay drastically altered the odds for a few players in campaign after campaign. Players who relied on diplomacy to try to create alliances with other players just couldn't compete. Thus, the "fair" players would participate in one or two campaigns, not make the top-50 rankings (and thus not be eligible for the occasional Master's Tournaments), and then just not play anymore.

Constant Bugs and "Hacks" Destroyed the Game's Credibility

Since day one of MMP games, a small percentage of players have made it their business to find and exploit bugs in the game code. They are very good at finding these bugs; they can and do find every bug in a game's code. Some players have even gone so far as to hack the frontend or backend of a game, although this is rare.

UC was no exception. Bugs not only cropped up; they tended to be persistent. It was rare but not unknown for players to find ways to move resources from one campaign to a completely different one. This happened often enough that a warning about it was put in *UC*'s player code of conduct.

During one early campaign (it might even have been one of the Beta test campaigns), it was discovered that a player had found a bug that allowed him to create an unlimited number of one type of military unit on any planet he controlled. Thankfully, like most such cheaters, he was stupid and created far more than his resources would have allowed, so he was discovered quickly. The *UC* programmers handled this one creatively; rather than just ban the player, the programmers created and launched some very large fleets to all his planets and destroyed them, and then the programmers publicized the event as a warning to others.

As another example, check out this notice in the rules for the most recent Master's Tournament for *UC*:

Battle Algorithm Abuse

There is still a known bug that can affect battle outcomes when fleets are configured in particular ways. Players who take advantage of this anomaly know what they are doing, since there is little other purpose for configuring fleets in this manner. This strategy will not be permitted in the Master's Tournament. All battles will be monitored and offenders will be penalized or disqualified. This policy was enacted in the Alliance Game and virtually all such abuse came to an end, so let's hope there will be no need to enforce any penalties in the Master's game.

This particular bug has plagued *UC* since it was made available to the public. While VR-1's developers tried to manually monitor and stop it, that's a lot of work—and isn't that what a computer is for, anyway?

The persistence of these bugs and exploits, and the fact that some players in every campaign were abusing them, made it impossible for the reasonable and responsible player to truly enjoy the game.

Lack of Publicity and Marketing by Microsoft

Microsoft's goal on The Zone is to push its brand names. That it does, with great zeal. After the initial launch of *UC*, it was tough to find ongoing promotions for the game, nor did I ever see the game marketed in banner ads on other game information sites, as I did with The Zone in general. For goodness sake, there wasn't even a link to VR-1's web site from any of the game's pages on The Zone, and I looked hard.

We learned a long time ago in this industry that "If you build it, they will come… *not!*" You *have* to get the word out. With a small niche market such as turn-based strategy games, you *really* have to get the word out. That wasn't done here and was a major contributor to *UC*'s failure, I believe.

Failure to Refresh the Game Often Enough

VR-1 did try, adding the occasional new units and some campaigns that varied the rules a bit. Unfortunately, it just wasn't enough; the new units were just minor variations on existing units, and the rule variants didn't go far enough. There just wasn't enough new about the game on an ongoing basis, and that is the death knell for massively multiplayer online games (MMOGs).

Supposedly, *UltraCorps Version 2.0* was in development at the time the game was scotched. It might have been interesting to see what changes were planned. For the other reasons in this article, a new version probably would not have saved the game, but it would have been nice to try.

The Zone's Sysops Were AWOL

UC had a semi-tough learning curve. When this is the case with an online game, you need to have a human available online and in the game's chat room to advise prospective and new players on how to get started. Early in *UC's* life on The Zone, there was a constant stream of interested prospective players in and out of the chat rooms.

Not once in over a year did I ever see a sysop from The Zone on duty in the chat room for any campaign or to help someone wanting information about the game or wanting to know how to get started. Occasionally players helped them out, but that was somewhat rare; the chat room would stay open while the player was in the game, so it basically looked like questions were being ignored.

However, I *did* occasionally see a sysop from The Zone in a chat room planning strategy with a paying customer ally. My holdings in a game were also attacked more than once by sysops from The Zone playing the game competitively.

This is inexcusable. Microsoft was/is in charge of sysoping most of The Zone's games, *UC* included. One of the major reasons *UC* failed so completely to draw new players over time was the total lack of attention paid to it by The Zone's sysops. And if the sysops are going to play competitively, the least they can do is pull some duty in the chat rooms and help out the newbies.

Most of the items listed in this article add up to a constant, sad refrain: ignoring the service side of this business in favor of development. It doesn't seem to matter how often we harp on the issue; the service side of the online game market continues to get short shrift.

I suspect the first company or game to really pay attention to these issues is going to get rich, while the rest of the pack languishes.

Chapter 14

Anarchy Online *Post-Mortem*

by **Gaute Godager**, Game Director for Funcom's *Anarchy Online*

AUTHOR NOTE

The first time I met Funcom's co-founder and game director for *Anarchy Online (AO)*, Gaute Godager, it was across a conference room table in Oslo, Norway. He was holding a report about *AO*, which my company, The Themis Group, had written for Funcom's president. He was not very happy with us; he had no idea we were writing the report until he'd been handed a copy and was wondering why we hadn't consulted with him and his team. He felt ambushed, somewhat justifiably so.

From that rocky start, we grew to appreciate each others' talents and experience and dug in on the game. Using some of the recommendations Themis made and adding in their own talents, ideas, and agile minds, he and the rest of Funcom's team performed that rarest of feats: turning around a persistent world (PW) that had become synonymous with the phrases "bad launch" and "failure," making it a successful enterprise. These days, I proudly tell my friends in the industry that Funcom may have used us as advisors, but the work—and the sweet smell of success—is all theirs.

And because *AO* is one of the very few examples of a turnaround in our industry, I thought it important to have Gaute write a post-mortem on what he and the rest of the Funcom crew experienced and what lessons they learned. I think you'll find this article fascinating; I did.

"Every man should get a terminal disease, and, in fact, we all will. It makes us realize how much we take for granted—sunshine—the laughter of grandchildren."

Desmond Tutu, Archbishop and Nobel Prize winner, December 2000[1]

I would like to start out saying this is not a regular post-mortem. It does not follow the normal "form" of such a document, and we have just begun! *Anarchy Online (AO)* should hopefully run for several years. This is a personal chronological tale of the events that shaped the game.

Looking back on the years of work on the game that came to be *AO*, it leaves me now with a feeling of melancholy. It would be a bold lie pretend *AO* so far has become the success we, Funcom, yearned for. Be that as it may, we shall nevertheless search history to find the battles won and also try, like any pirate on the Caribbean sand, to hunt the buried treasures. We will hopefully uncover some invaluable lessons learned. I put the quote from Archbishop Tutu at the top to try to remind me that some of the lessons we learned might have seemed like stuff we take for granted.

Also, I think it is a bit early to talk about the after-death of this game, as it has only just been born. But then again, birth and death are forever intertwined. Let us thus go back in time, to the very beginning…

The Foreplay

The history of *AO* is also the recent history of Funcom. I need to tell you some things about Funcom, here at the very beginning. If you do not understand this, the making of *AO* could seem absurd. Funcom (and yes, this is the right way of spelling it) was founded in the spring of 1993 in Oslo. This was back in the "Klondyke" years of game development, or most likely in their ebb. Anyway, we quickly grew from 5 to 100 in one and a half to two years.

Developing original console games and doing "conversions" was our trade. (To "convert" a game meant basically taking a very complex game, on, for instance, an arcade platform, and reverse-engineering it—trying to make it run on a home game

---

1. Speaking about his cancer in an interview with BBC World Radio, December 2000.

console [back then, one such system was the SNES] with one-tenth the processing power and memory.) I daresay it was not a very creative process on a gameplay level. It was more a matter of engineering craft—and there is a lot of creativity there—at which we were pretty good. (Have a look at the published games on our home page, www.funcom.com).

We had a young crew. The mean age was 24 or so. We quickly learned that being a *developer* in the game industry was like being a bitch in the food chain. I don't easily use that term. I have thought many hours about this. Of a game sold on the shelves for $50, we would normally get $1–$3. This was, of course, after a history in which we took more than half the risk ourselves, funding the development to a large extent.

Anyway, Funcom for 4–5 years was a very interesting witch's cauldron of successes and disasters. We made some decent games (*Casper* for Interplay and *Pocahontas* for Disney), we made some terrible games (*Dragonheart*), and we learned.

But look at what we did. We were faithfully trying to squeeze a good game out of half-digested ideas, based on creative material from totally other areas—that is, movies. The combination of the lack of any real prospect of success due to the business model, combined with the lack of creative freedom, left everyone with a hunger for something else.

Funcom was ripe for making something on its own. The whole company wanted badly to give birth to something where we took an even bigger chance, took even bigger risks, but had greater chances of doing it big!

And we were ripe with misfortune. The publishers we contracted with went bankrupt. Publishers would buy the rights to our games simply to delay them since they had an in-house competitor (which they launched like a bombshell when our game unexpectedly stayed in the polishing phase for half a year more than expected). Unfaithful engineers would steal the most promising piece of technology Funcom had ever made and start their own company—shortly after selling it for major money to some other greedy publisher who did not, six months earlier, want to buy it from us. That particular incident led to a 1,000,000-kroner out-of-court settlement, which, by the way, may be a Norwegian record for stolen technology. We had people from other game developer companies standing outside our entrance trying to recruit key personnel. It was absurd.

Thus, making *The Longest Journey* was like kindling a flame of hope in the darkness to us. First off, we became our own publishers. It was also our first major 100% in-house production! It became a great game, albeit within a fading genre. (Please head over to www.thelongestjourney.com and check out Ragnar Tørnquist and Didrik Tollefsen's great game.) Being a "normal" PC game, it still had slim chances of making Funcom a successful company. I think I've heard somewhere that only 50% of all PC games started make it to market, and that 2% of the market eats 90% of the revenue. It might be hearsay, but it contains something very true: we needed another platform—a platform of gold and honey.

The Conception

It is easy to name the father of *AO*. It was Marius Kjeldahl. He was at that time our vice president of new technology. I say he was a typical father in this sense, with the "mothers" in development doing the job after conception. But the seed, the kindling, cannot be taken away from him.

AO was conceived from 1995–1997. The very first movements generated by Marius resulted in a game concept in 1995. The concept was never used, but the platform and technology were intriguing. After throwing the idea back and forth for some time, it was the base technology platform that started taking shape within our Research and Development department in winter 1996. The lead man back then was Martin Amor, who followed the game all the way to launch.

The focus the first year and a half was basically server technology. We needed a platform on which to run *any and all* games. So, *AO* did not start as an idea or story; all that was added later. The motivation for this was, of course, to have a totally different revenue model. The Internet could give us all that: a place to effectively market our games, a place to sell our games, a place to gain income from our games, and a place where people could gather around our games. It was a bypass of the whole normal revenue model, in which the creative people were standing on the lowest rung, begging for morsels.

The First Trimester—Development of the Bone Structure (The Technology)

It was quickly decided that the server technology would be UNIX-based. I do not believe Linux gained wind as the platform for the finished server until halfway through development. Although the servers were developed on that operating system, the engineers believed for a long time we had to use "real UNIX" on the live servers. The projections for "Intel"-based servers at the very beginning were 5–10 simultaneously playing customers per PC. We obviously needed other numbers to make money. The story of this first projected number of simultaneous players is a great joke with us these days.

One of the things I believe we accomplished well was to actually develop the core server technology ourselves. During the long development, many nay-sayers said the technology was never going to perform, that buying third-party tools would be much better, and that the 5–10 people per server was probably dead on.

Our early plans, which didn't end well, were the projections to make a universal online game engine. The idea was to develop an independent core engine, with many independent layers, that could be used for any online game. We wanted to use this engine not only in more RPG games, but also any type of game—from shooters to backgammon. As time passed, several "hacks" in between those engines (from the game code to the bottom layers) were made, and the layers now live more or less in symbiosis.

It is hard to say today if we should have scaled back ambitions and made the core engine smaller and more easily manageable. What I can say is that making these quick fix methods cost us more in development than if they had been better planned for. But then again, thinking reuse is critical, and it is very hard to find the optimum level.

Some things that did not work well from the very start were the game data development tools. From previous experience, we knew that getting the tools used to develop the game up and running as soon as possible was critical. (I am talking world designer tools, item tools, monster tools, and so on.) The first iteration of these game tools was almost totally useless, though. We shifted some personnel, made some changes, and the tools became usable. I guess there are many reasons for this, but the 8–12 months already spent left us with a bitter feeling.

Developing a Central Nervous System—A Brain

After the technology had been in development for some months, the game engine left the research and development phase and had a team assigned to it. After 12 months (we are now in 1998–99), the design was still completely incoherent; there was no direction, and many of the team members seemed to be working toward their own vision, not a central one.

Looking back at this, it is not hard to understand why the first months were botched. First of all, if Marius was the father, the womb into which he sowed his seed was a very hostile environment. The organization was not motivated; we did not want to make an MMP online game. The core development people of Funcom simply did not understand why players would think MMP online games would be fun (talk about people set in their ways). There were many, many feet-dragging exercises being performed throughout the organization.

"What did we learn from this," you ask? We learned that the game concept should be present as early as possible to be used as a sell-in. It is not always easy to sell only a business model and a piece of technology to an organization with other ideas in mind. When people saw the game and the possibilities to interact, battle, show off, socialize, and have fun *together*—they wanted to participate. Many seeds fell on stones, but when a seed found earth, it grew and blossomed with a speed not often seen before.

Sadly though, the above-mentioned half-heartedness seemed to have found its way all the way to the core of the team, in my personal opinion. Suddenly, after 12 months, the original producer of *AO* left. He had been starting his own company on the side, at least mentally, for some time.

Just to be precise, I believe the core technology team, headed by Martin, the lead programmer, was working steadily and well toward its goal. The lack of development was mostly on the "brain" side—not in the muscles or bone structure. The problems were design and concept, not technology.

This was when Tommy Strand, Tor Andre Wigmostad, and I were added to the project. This was a tough but very fruitful cooperation, I think. Tommy's genius comes from his understanding of technology and complete enthusiasm in trying to make it work in the most general way possible. Many of the core game systems in use were designed by him (and me) in that period. Tor was partly also working as a designer, but mostly producing and acting as project manager to track the tasks. I must add that the cooperation with the main game programmer was really good, and that many of the ideas bounced back were better looking than before this point.

Hands and Feet—The Item System

One of the things we really wanted to do was make a completely flexible item system—a system where object-oriented code and thinking almost magically made everything interact in a logical way (*cough*). Well, at least the end result was pretty good. The idea of an item system where you can attach any script on any event is still there at the core. That is why an item in *AO* today can pretty much do anything to the objects around it: animate, make sound, change the weather, change abilities on characters, move you around, and so on. The only thing it does not interact with in the way we wanted is the GUI.

This item system, I think, was a good investment of time, and its use has been constantly expanded on. Many of the items in the game, including nanos, implants, armor, weapons, utilities, doors, chests, and so on, are various types of similar items.

The Interpolation System

The *AO* design team was understaffed. The end result was that there was little time to create the content. We needed a dynamic way of creating a lot of content very quickly. The end result was the interpolation system. Basically, with this system, we can cluster as many "templates" (item instances) as we want, making them one item. The defining difference is their "level," or quality level, as it is called in the game. The system enables us to handcraft 2 items and put 200 into the game. We make one template at Level 1 and one at Level 200; then you can ask the system for an item anywhere in between those levels. It mixes those two, making a unique item for the level you request.

I think this is similar to the system actually seen in quite a few other games, just not yet in an MMORPG until *AO*. With the system, items scale with the characters. The system is also applied to monsters, chests—everything but nanotechnology items. We wanted the nanos to be unique, defining the profession, and I think Andrew Griffin did a great job here. He hand-assembled more than 4,000 nanos. (A nano is our equivalent of a magic spell.)

The good thing about the interpolation system is that it is very easy to make loads of content. The bad thing about it is that things feel similar—they *are* similar. If one chooses to go with a system like this, it is the drawback one has to live with. What we have learned from this is that in some ways, *quantity is quality* in an MMORPG—the more, the merrier. It is not *enough*, though. You need handcrafted, rare objects for the up-market players.

The Categorization System

One of the other things that I believe distinguishes *AO* from the other MMORPGs so far is its categorization system. We call it the "Categorytree." In this, we can group objects into meaningful categories. Every object can belong to many categories, and we can request random objects from any category; for example, the fictitious weapon "Brutalis-Shotgun" can be added to the shotgun category, which in turn belongs to the explosive weapons category, which in turn belongs to the distance weapon category, which belongs to items you may carry around, which belongs to man-made objects, and so on. This mimics the way people group objects in the real world, so it is quite easy to understand. The trick here is that you can, at any one level, request any object.

So you may say to the system: "Give me a shotgun, or give me a distance weapon." This makes the whole item system extremely versatile. Every object with a meaning in the whole game is found at least once in this system: missions, monsters, nanos, doors, traps, everything. Let me give a simple example. I make a monster. I decide I would like for this monster to drop some loot when it's killed. I can then easily decide the level of abstraction of its loot; it can be everything from *one specific* item to *every item* in the game. All the levels in between are possible. This ability to control the *level of randomization* at the item level is very important to *AO*.

Truth be told, it was a difficult system to get running. The first iteration of this data system was very unstable and crashed the servers all the time. I can still remember being shouted at by two red-faced programmers because their code depended on this data working, and it didn't.

Anyway, now it works fine, and it is really integral to the heart of our game system.

The Second Trimester: The Heartbeat of the Auto Content Generator System

This is something truly unique to the MMORPGs so far (though you can see this to some degree in *Diablo* and *Daggerfall*): the ability of the player to request content on-demand. Central to this for *AO* is the mission system. Here a player can use a terminal anyplace in the world and request a mission just for him/her. I think this was a very important selling point for many players wanting to migrate from other similar games. People were tired of waiting—camping as it is called—and downtime. I think my idea here was basically to enable people to have a single-player or limited-number-of-players experience in a multiplayer world. Today in *AO*, it is used all the time. People spend as much time in the auto content generator (ACG) areas as outside in the "static" world.

For example, let's say you ask for a mission, such as finding an item. The mission system then assembles a bunch of rooms, more or less like auto-assembling a puzzle. Next, these rooms are populated with monsters, chests, traps, and so on using the category system and interpolation system. The creation of these areas is done in a "hands-off" way, with designers simply pulling strings, setting down rules, and making building blocks. It is like setting the rules of DNA and letting evolution take its course.

I have no regrets about this system, save one. We invested too little resources in it. The major part of the system was made by only three people: a programmer, a world designer, and myself. Only toward the very end, when it was appearing to everyone how big it might become, did we add more people. The problem here was really convincing people that something made so hands-off would be fun. We had only three designers on the game at that time, and it was completely impossible for us to deliver "static" dungeons and play areas for everyone. I wish we had more people on this part, though; the data in the system is too repetitive, basically. The system itself can handle much, much more, and so it will! Just wait and see.

The Skin, Hair, and Eyes: The Client

Few things in *AO* have gone through as many steps of development as the client and control system. First, when we started development, we decided to go with a system of prerendered two-dimensional (2D) characters, such as those found in *Diablo* and *Ultima Online (UO)*. The point of view was supposed to be overhead isometric, and the control indirect (point, click, and run).

The first thing that became apparent was that we weren't happy with the quality of the models in the game. The graphic artists wanted real 3D, polygon characters. We stumbled about for some time on this issue.

One of the more funny things we investigated for the client was actually a totally weird technology called spheroids. We thought of, and used energy on investigating, having the characters rendered as a series of blobs stacked on top of each other. Happily, we only used four months to find out that a spheroid character was rendered slower than a polygon one. This was just at the time when 3D cards exploded onto the market. I'm glad they did—those spheroids sure looked ugly.

One of the things we wanted to do was make the game more social than previous MMORPGs—at least more social-*looking*. Luckily, Tommy really believed in motion capture and a great animation system. We invested in MOCAP equipment and he worked like a maniac creating the MOCAP studio. He did everything from working as a carpenter, building the stage, to setting up all the computers and equipment and actually starring as the actor in many moves. He is the male in the game. Every time I see a solitus, nano, or opifex male running around, it is him!

The vision was to give people the ability to express themselves with their bodies as well as with written text. The end resulting quality of animation is still some of the very best on the market today, well after *AO*'s launch. I especially remember "the emotes." Having worked at Funcom for nine years, those hours when we made that list of emotes were like a dream—what being a game designer was all about. We stayed late into the night, climbed all over the chairs and tables in the meeting room, ate pizza, and played out emotes. We wanted emotes that interacted with the world, emotes that changed with time and breed, emotes you would have to do *to*—and *with*—another character (by the way, we didn't enact everything). We wanted the whole package. The end result was pretty good and quite fun, if not quite as lofty as creative minds can become late at night.

We also ended up with a good animation system, with the ability to split upper and lower body, to interpolate animations, and to have animations react to impulses from the world. That is why you may see your character walk, fire a gun, and get hit at the same time.

The problem here was not the technology, but the game mechanics. Some animations are simply so much more important than others. We needed to abort some animations to display vital things. These became vital as the game feedback was linked to the animations.

In the beginning of development, a character would basically "simulate" a fight, while the real fight was running in the chat box. That was no good. We needed to link it more directly. So, when we got a message from the server—"You are hit"—we ran a get-hit animation. That also meant that we "delayed" the message on the client. The system waited for the "keyframe" in the animation to appear before reducing health and printing a "You got hit" message in the chat box. This led to a lot of problems. Mostly, players felt their characters died for no obvious reason. Often, this came as a result of the hit keyframe simply being "smoothed" away. I don't know how many times that piece of code was rewritten to change the priority of animation smoothing.

If you make a system where visuals get priority over gameplay, or become gameplay, you should have a clear, well-thought-through priority system. You have to display a bullet entering your chest, even though the player wants to display "combing her hair" animation.

The Last Trimester—Getting Ready to Be Born

AO moved into that last bit of the gestation period, addressing the final ontogenetic elements.

Senso-Motoric Development: The Control

The control of the game was indirect for a long time. The reason was that we felt people would perceive a direct control, with an indirect fighting system, to be a schism. We did not want direct fighting, as we did not think the technology could support it.

It took the launch of *EverQuest* (*EQ*) in 1999 to make us believe that direct control systems worked, even with indirect fighting. It wasn't fully changed until Beta 2, though. Many of the programmers were very much against it; their system was built around an indirect control. Still, today, you can see the split focus. The character creation is built for third-person indirect control. The ACG system, with its narrow hallways and tiny rooms, is built for first-person direct control. Even today, many people play in third-person when fighting and first-person when exploring. I guess a system that can cater to both is the best, even though adding it that late was more difficult.

Environment

One of the things we have really, really succeeded in doing is making a great environment. The planet Rubi-Ka is simply stunningly beautiful. Talented artists, talented art direction, talented world designers, and simply extremely talented environment programmers made the game life-like. Rubi-Ka simply takes your breath away!

I have to expand on the environment programming, though, as I think it is the 3D technology and rendering engine in itself that did the trick. It was made in-house and it makes the look completely different from anything else. Until Beta 2, the game looked very "average." You could only see some few hundred meters until the fog hit you. Then, Martin Amor, the lead programmer, changed the engine and opened the world to everyone. Now you can actually see the whole 4-kilometer-by-4-kilometer play field all the time (Lod'ed, of course). In a game where you let people pretend they are a character for hours, days, weeks, and months, there is *never*, *ever* enough eye-candy. If you love your environment, you might love spending time in the game.

The Development Potential of the DNA: Skills and Abilities—Your Phenotype

The skill and ability system of *AO* is different from most other MMORPGs. I wanted a system where a person decides for him/herself what a character should be like. This led to a system with around 90 or so skills, and hopefully where *no* character is the same.

This is still one of *AO*'s strongest points, what many players say they really enjoy: the possibility of having all skills available to everyone, although to a different degree. Another aspect is that I wanted people to be able to select how their character should be molded themselves, directly and through direct choice. I did not want a system like those found in many RPGs where what you *do* defines who you are. (If you find a stick and wave that around, you become good at blunt weapons, and so on.)

This system is somewhat inspired by the system found in the popular *Might and Magic* series by 3DO and pen-and-paper RPGs such as *RoleMaster*. Wed those two games, put their offspring on steroids, and voilá, you have *AO*'s skill system.

Now the downside: The problem with such a system is not in the balancing, as some people would think, at least not in the inter-profession balancing. It is in the presentation to the player. There simply is too much information for the newbie. It is so easy to make mistakes developing your character, and it is so easy to regret them. The skills and abilities almost *explode* in your face, their descriptions are too vague, and there are too many of them.

What could have been done was to make some skills dependent on others and dole them out with time and development. Some skills should be hidden from your profession at startup, and there should have been a tutorial. All this was in the plans but was sacrificed on the altar of launching quicker.

Another downside is that not all the skills are operational; a cutback should have been performed earlier. Also, some skills are underpowered.

The Quickening of Life: The Pace of the Game

So many things changed with *UO* and *EQ*. Not only did we all love those games, but we also saw flaws in our own game and room for different development. We learned a lot and the game changed a lot. This is something that we have seen happen time and time again. You develop a game, and then, as you are getting ready to go—boom— someone launches something else that makes you rethink. It's the purest sign of not being a technology leader, or creative driving force, in the game industry. It seems to me that so many ideas come from the "collective unconscious" of this industry, sort of popping into life at many places at the same time. I guess it also says a lot of people are catering to the existing technology. If you are the first, everyone else must strive to adapt.

You can tell that *AO* is a game with a much higher pace than some of the other MMORPGs. We did not want downtime to be the driving force, or *modus operandi*, of *AO*. We wanted a game where you could play alone (solo) and not wait for hours of that time. We didn't want a game where twitch control decided your fate.

If you could play solo, you should be able to see your effectiveness increase in a group. Thus, the team play in *AO* is defined by a really hectic pace—things happening quickly, including on lower levels. My experience was that this was the pace in high-level teams in other games with team play.

The downside to this was that some players felt a lack of control on lower levels. We were also afraid people didn't have enough time to socialize. Still, I feel it led people to be more open and friendly, wanting to group with you because they weren't forced to do so. Any profession was welcome; there was no pariah class. People keep telling me *AO* has one of the best core communities. I hope the pace of the game lends itself to that.

Anyway, downtime should not be forced on you.

The Preparations for Giving Life Meaning: The Story

One of the core things we wanted to do with *AO* was to give players meaning in the game. We didn't want to simply run the levelling treadmill. Thus, we came up with the story.

Ragnar Tørnquist and I stayed several days in his living room, talking story and basically building a universe. We called it the Funcom Universe, and it has the highpoints of the history of mankind from its awakening until the end of time. We wanted players to be enmeshed in this. We wanted a true fairy tale, where people chose sides and played out their dark or white destiny.

One of the things we found interesting with previous MMORPGs was the lack of story and setting. The interesting thing about it was that players often created their own, like the PKers versus the non-PKers in the early *UO* age.

When we discussed this with the players and with other "experts" (like one of the esteemed authors of this book), we were told that telling a story would be virtually impossible. There were many words, but the conclusion was that "You cannot direct players in a story; they will do what they like." It is not that I disagree with that; it is simply that we never tried directing anyone. It was more like making a great history, making a fantastic setting, and letting the wheel run its course downhill. Of course we would be there giving a little kick from time to time, left or right, but basically, the players would give it speed.

Sadly, though, the storytelling today has been reduced to "history," "setting," and "acts of God," happening only once in a while—not the tight cooperative communication we wanted. The reason for this was economical. We had to scale back and save money. The story with its lead characters, its "costly rendered" story episodes, with all its internal disbelievers, couldn't survive a cutback. I must say, if I could have, I would have continued with the story episodes. They gave *AO* something different, and the people working on them were/are really talented. The graphic artists, musicians, and storywriters worked day and night to achieve something *brand new*. I hope they gain cult status someday, if nothing else.

I still believe that the story and immersive setting are two of the reasons why people play *AO*. We offer a meaningful relationship with other people on the sociological and cultural levels. The *conflict* (Omni-Tek versus clans) is the driving force in this, and people have made the conflict their own. It seems to me that the players often identify with one side and stick to it.

I don't think the science-fiction (sci-fi) setting (which was decided by the very first producer, the one who left) was the best move, money-wise. If you look at the 3D engine and the fantastic environment, I am tempted to believe we would have scored better with a fantasy setting. Being the first, and so far only, sci-fi-based MMORPG game surely didn't make *AO* a dead-on hit. Most likely there are other, more important reasons for that.

Being a sci-fi game has affected the type of customer we have attracted, though. You will see crossover "guilds" from *Quake* and other first-person shooters. In that sense, we have made the MMORPG market grow with a different perspective than before. I think it is likely that the sci-fi setting, coupled with the conflict focus, have also attracted a bit more people focused on PvP than before. At least the percentage of people with PvP rating is higher than the number of PvP players on PvP servers in other games.

Anyway, summing up the story: It became a disappointment to many players, I think. Due to organizational struggles internally, lack of funds, and lack of tools, it has faded back to a setting with "acts of God." I still know it has more to say for the everyday life of the *AO* player than the story has had in most other MMORPGs so far, except *Asheron's Call (AC)*, which has done more and better than we ever did. I haven't totally given up on it, though.

The Birth: The Launch

This became our gravest mistake, if one can be said to have control over the time of birth. The child was premature. It had to be put in an incubator. We lost more players than we thought possible. I have spent countless hours thinking so much about the reason why it went so horribly, horribly wrong. What made us launch so early, and generally be so unprepared? I don't really know how honest I can be in aiding our competitors to avoid making the same mistakes, but it might be good for mental hygiene anyway. I must confess, it is still a touchy subject for many of us. Anyway, I will run quickly through the major mistakes made at launch. (These mistakes are listed in an arbitrary manner. Who knows which was the most important one?)

Mistake: Not Enough Testing in Realistic Environments

We had many thousands of Beta players—but not online at the same time—fighting monsters, trading items, running nanos, or playing in tightly packed areas. Basically, the tests we had pre-launch could in no way prepare us for what happened at launch. The servers crashed. The clients crashed. People lost characters and items. (Thankfully, we managed to stop people from losing their characters really quickly!)

What We Learned from This

I don't know how we could have possibly prepared better for launch, testing-wise, other than simply to have spent a lot more time on it. It is very hard to "simulate" the rush of several hundred new players every hour. We also learned that "simulating" players by using an auto-client wasn't enough, in our case. We could not predict player behavior enough. What we did do correctly is make the entrance areas "virtual." We had the ability to make "indexes" of all play areas—to make virtual instances, that is.

Mistake: Group Thinking, or the Bay of Pigs Revisited

What makes for interesting reading in Psych101 and history books about the US invasion of the Bay of Pigs still happens in 2001. This is the deal: We launched early because no one had the strength or will to resist the launch anymore, it seemed. Normally, there is a function within game developers/publishers where management and marketing push for a punctual release (according to plan, in other words) and product QA and development teams resist if the game is not ready to go on the shelves. This is a healthy process normally, because the development team wants to tweak and polish forever and management wants to make money yesterday. In this "conflict," you make the right decision most of the time. Not so with *AO*. People on the development team were too tired to resist the launch; there was fatigue felt to the bone.

In addition, almost 100% of the Funcom employees have shares/options. This is one of the greatest things about working for Funcom, and it still makes people feel strongly about their job and company—you know, the feeling of ownership and all that. We all knew that we didn't have enough money to continue development of *AO* past the summer without another round of investments. We all knew our shares would be watered down—again. We wanted *so* much to succeed.

It is not as if I am saying the launch day wasn't defined by management; it just made us all "on the same side." Our internal, normally *extremely good* and impartial Testing department became compromised as well, due to pressure and being tired to the bone. Group thinking, where any nay-sayers were seen as a collective evil, was making the company go into labor.

What We Learned from This

One needs to be aware of how fatigue is affecting group behavior. The next time there will be different, fresh people deciding if we are ready, not the people who will gain from it. Maybe we will enlist an outside consultant to aid in this process.

Mistake: Too Many Features/Not Enough Focus

We let the wishes of the players guide us. We tried to incorporate what they said they wanted (during Beta and before), and it slapped us in the face. A good piece of advice: Decide for yourself what you want to listen to/what you want to include. I will give an example.

One of the features people were *really* excited about before launch was player-made missions/quests. "Ooh, that is nice! Yes! I want to try it!" everyone said. We put it in. We launched it. The result? No one used it, except for the exploiters. (And man, was it great for them!) After trying to fix it for several patches, we simply disabled it. The button is still there in the GUI; it simply does nothing. No one complained because no one missed it. If only that time had been spent on something else....

Players have complained about several other features "promised" pre-launch, but not that one. I'll get back to that.

What We Learned from This

Don't try to please everyone. Although you have a community to cater to, you can *never, ever* please everyone; by pleasing some, you displease others. Stay true to your idea and focus on it. Cut early rather than late.

Mistake: Inadequate Customer Service

CS was completely understaffed. Also, the poor people there had terrible tools at launch. The result was several days turnaround per petition. The first thing we did post-launch was try to improve those tools and staff up.

What We Learned from This

Yes, you need CS. You need them more than you think. Also, it is wise to moderate official boards heavily. One "grief" community member does more damage than you can imagine.

Mistake: Lack of Focused Project Management

At launch, project management was done by too many people. The responsibility was divided and crumbled further at launch. Of the managers, one suffered almost a near burnout, one left for vacation for five weeks, and two left the project to do other stuff. The result was that the development team became too unfocused and stayed that way more or less until Thomas Howalt was assigned to the project in September 2001. (He worked on *Midgard* until that time.) In addition, the design department was reorganized to cater to people leaving or working less. This led to a loss of creative focus as well.

What We Learned from This

The launch is but the beginning. It is when you need people, fresh and eager, to focus on the onward development.

Mistake: Believing the Game Was a Normal PC Game Before Launch

Having worked on other games before, we followed our usual pattern. We worked like mad, night and day, up to launch. The result was a back-catalog of vacation to be incorporated into a busy post-launch schedule and *severely* tired people. This is not the way to launch an MMOG. The launch day should be seen as something happening in the "middle" of development, like the start of a marathon. It is not the end; it is the beginning. It is the birth, not the death. (This is why a post-mortem is rather misplaced, but never mind....) You need fresh, motivated people for a launch—not dead-tired burnouts ready for the beach.

What We Learned from This

Again, the launch is the beginning. If your organization has developed other games before, it might make our mistake. If this is your first game, you are almost bound to make our mistake; you simply will work too hard toward launch. Do not let your guard down!

Mistake: Totally Wrong System Requirements on the Box

They were wrong—horribly wrong. A lot of the players who had a terrible experience when trying out the game would have had a much better time if they were told their PCs were underpowered before buying the game. It worked more or less on the original system requirements, but only if you cranked the rendering options all the way down, and who does that?

The game still suffers from what the players refer to as "lag." Most of the time, people believe this is data from the servers being delayed or something like that. It is not. It is the client PC loading textures. On an AMD 1.4GHz with 512MB DDR RAM, 64MB Geforce3, and striped hard drives, there is no "lag" at all.

What We Learned from This

Try to delay marketing from printing the box, or make "stickers" to put on the boxes if you are unsure about how the game will perform until the very end. That is not too weird because a lot of optimization is done toward the end, when you see where the pressure of the game applies.

Mistake: Underestimating the Power of Pre-Launch Promises

Speaking with the media and fan sites covering MMORPGs is actually quite different from the ones covering non-online games. First, the player community is totally different. They track you, store your words, and try to hold you to the things you said. It feels very much like being "in office," I have realized. If two years before launch you admit to a journalist, "I am thinking about doing this or that," it is like President Bush saying, "I am thinking of attacking Iraq." You can bet the world will not forget him saying that. You have to have a different mindset to make, and communicate about, an online game. You have to weigh your words all the time. That was never easy to understand for an organization that has always had to *hype* what it wanted to sell!

What We Learned from This

You are a politician! Yep, you are. You are running for office, and there is no filter between you and the world. Stick to the party program! Don't enter into a "design session" with a reporter, even though you can make his/her eyes glow and make headlines.

Mistake: Overestimating the Community's Ability to Forgive and Forget

At the time of the launch we rationalized, "We have been players during the launch of other online games. It was terrible, but we still played on. So will our players!"

Of course, that was true of the previous generation of such games, but not the current generation. There were no alternatives back then. Players suffered, but forgave; the world was wonderful.

In June 2001, people who are used to the stability of a 2-year-old *EQ*, 1.5-year-old *AC*, or 3–4-year-old *UO* will not easily forgive having to go through birth pains again. People forgive childhood diseases the first time a new technology comes to market, but the second or third time around—no way!

If you, the esteemed reader, are planning to launch something similar to *AO*, you should have something you are 110% sure of! Otherwise, test until you are. The entry barrier in this market is becoming more and more terrible. It makes me kind of proud to think that a small company like Funcom can compete with the likes of EA, Sony, and Microsoft.

What We Learned from This

Things change, the world changes; what was true will not necessarily be so again. The consumer is not a forgiving fool; he carries spears and phazers. When there is monopoly, anything goes. When there is competition, nothing but the best will survive (or sometimes, the mediocre with the biggest marketing budget.

Mistake: Not Enough Unique Content

We should have had more designer content resources added to the game. Too much became too generic. It is like we offered people dinner at McDonalds, or simply the bread and butter of online life, every day. They quickly wanted more, and we should have had it there. Especially for the high-level players, special content is vital.

What We Learned from This

Handcraft *and* mass-produce. As a designer catering for a world, you need both. If you only handcraft, there will be "camping," waiting, and irritation. If you only mass-produce, there will be nothing to want, only grayness, drabness, and repetition. We luckily have both now, but it takes time!

Mistake: The Learning Curve

The learning curve is too steep. The GUI is great when you know it but bad when you start out. Likewise, it is difficult to learn the skill system. This is something that should have been fixed pre-launch, and when added to crashes, lag, and other problems, it simply became too big a hurdle to many players. You need a tutorial for these types of games. You need an easy learning curve. You are creating a world, not a game. People are not forgiving of you when they are left feeling stupid and not empowered—and other people are watching.

What We Learned from This

You need a tutorial. You need to make the game easy to get into. We knew it long before launch; we just thought launching early was more important. It wasn't.

Mistake: The Patcher

We had a big bug in this at launch, which was unforgivable. We launched with a game many couldn't start.

What We Learned from This

We learned nothing—we already knew this. There is no excuse.

What Went Well at Launch?

There *were* things that went well.

The Team

The team simply rose to the challenge. It became an even more extremely focused group of people during hardship. Most did not give up or leave. We tracked down and cracked so many bugs that the floor was green with bug juice. We also managed to do necessary adjustments to the game, although the capability to communicate these was not present at first.

The Core Technology

The technology actually held together; its ideas weathered the storm. I remember in our darkest hour, post-launch, that we felt we had to rip out the core technology, from the bottom up, and change it all. We didn't. It sustained; it still does. Looking at all the mistakes mentioned, you would think it was a miracle. It wasn't. The technology was sound.

The "Lastability" of the Role-Playing System

Once you get past the learning curve, *AO* has proved to be remarkably last-able. It has great depth, and it keeps growing and growing. Sometimes one can almost be tempted to believe that the width of the game is the depth of the game. Most other competitors put your character on a levelling treadmill, just like we do. In *AO*, you can at least control its direction as you want. It is not on boring, predictable tracks.

The Beauty of the 3D Environment

The 3D environment has stood the test of time, so far. We shall improve it to stay ahead.

Post-Launch: Infancy and Toddler Years

The learning continues post-launch.

Learning to Crawl, Walk, and Run: Running the Game

Funcom's ability to learn, adapt, and *rise* to the challenge has amazed me. We have grown a CS department and reorganized and changed the development team from having a long-term focus into having a short-term focus (patches). We have also adapted to cutbacks in the staff to cater to the loss of customers. Still, the pace only seems to increase.

I haven't really digested these last post-natal months to as great a degree as the pre-natal months. I guess others are better suited to talk about them. What I can say is that running a game is different from making a game. You have to have both long-term and short-term focus as you leave the womb. Every step matters, but you have to have a destination.

Learning to Speak: Communicating About Changes

I think this really took us by surprise—not so much that communication with the player is important, but to the *degree* it matters. Online games change post-launch; at least, that is what people partially pay for. The rule here is that the bigger the change, the more detailed the information. People want predictability!

I think we have also been flabbergasted by what might be seen as "nerfs," or changes that are seen as disadvantages to the players. Let me give you an example. After launch, I realized the cost of increasing *one* skill for *one* profession (class) was too high. I wanted to make it cheaper. "Nice!" I thought, "People are going to be so happy with the reduced cost!" In my mind, it was as if someone reduced my mortgage rate. I was thrilled—not so in the collective minds of the players, though. It was as if they had bought an expensive Mercedes and, when driving away from the place of purchase, saw in the rearview mirror the price on that same model being halved! They wanted their money back! The reduction in cost was seen as a "nerf," although I was quite sure people would love it.

Another interesting example would be when we increased the availability of an item in the game. All the people who had already gotten one, using much more time, were very pissed off; we had "nerfed" the uniqueness of that item.

I guess we have learned to become paranoid on behalf of the players. The players spend more time in *AO* than with almost any other leisure activity; it is almost no longer a game. It is life and competition and social classes and gender and culture and all those other things that belong to the real world. Above all else, it is time invested. Life is short. We have no time to waste!

Anyway, if *we* invest the time to explain to the players, "This is our problem; we would like to do this or this or this," they are normally very sensible. They dislike imbalance and cheating as much as we do. The players are intelligent, and it is their world—their future.

Well, I think this is it for now. The future and life of Rubi-Ka is alive and developing quickly. Writing a post-mortem on an online game in the middle of its life is silly, but at least it's a post-natal scriptum, or something. We have had our terminal disease, as Archbishop Tutu recommended in the quote at the beginning of this tract. I hope we take nothing for granted.

Chapter 15

Glory and Shame: Powerful Psychology in Multiplayer Online Games

by **Jonathan Baron**, Executive Producer for Microsoft's Xbox Online
(jonbaron@microsoft.com)

AUTHOR NOTE

An earlier version of this article appeared on the Internet about a year ago. We asked Jonathan if he'd like to take a look at rewriting it for this book and he graciously accepted the commission. Jonathan has been a fixture in the online game arena for over a decade, first with Kesmai, then EA, and now as the executive producer for Microsoft's Xbox Live online console gaming service. He has also been an aide to Barney Frank of the US Congress, is an accomplished aircraft pilot, and is such a great speaker that he is regularly asked to present at the Game Designer's Conference and Electronic Entertainment Exposition, the two most important trade conferences for computer game developers.

Jonathan reigns as the Philosopher King of persistent worlds (PWs) and sometimes as our conscience. In this article, he clearly lays out one of the fundamental issues of PW design and management: how to create interesting relationships with the players.

When you play a standalone computer game, you experience challenge, release, escape, frustration, and satisfaction, but you cannot experience glory. Glory can only take place with an audience. Similarly, no computer game can shame you, again because shame requires that other people be present. But it takes more than merely the existence of other people in your environment to create opportunities for glory and shame—you also need a relationship with those people, one of either knowledge or recognition. This is why server network games that involve dating, such as *Unreal*, offer no special embarrassment when you perish or when you prevail.

Having large numbers of simultaneous players in an environment that records and preserves player records and actions transforms player anonymity into pseudonymity; I want my alter-ego to be persistent and known because I care about the people I'm playing with, and I want them to care about me. The only entertainment medium that offers a true sense of belonging is online gaming, and it's a powerful lure. Online games build relationships among players through conflict. It is the managed conflict of the online game that accelerates the development of bonds among total strangers. These bonds are real because the way we react to stress is like a fingerprint: it demonstrates who we are at our core.

The problem is that games designed by developers who are unaware of the medium's strengths and underlying mechanics often unwittingly create emotionally charged possibilities of glory and shame in a game world. As long as the conflict is too strong and the emotions too extreme, online gaming will remain esoteric at best. It all springs from the same misguided notion: that online is just a feature. Quite the contrary; online is a medium apart from all others, that fortunately or unfortunately has been initially expressed in the milieu of computer gaming. This can be seen if you contrast the two as in Table 15.1.

Table 15.1 Contrasts: Single-Player Versus Multiplayer

Single-Player	Massively Multiplayer
Alternative to social activities	A social activity
Forget you're alone	By yourself but not alone
More powerful than you are	Product of who you are
Escape from the world	Another world
Scripted/directed by the game	Directed by the players
Plays to motive of an individual	Collection of players' motives
Mastering posed challenges is the point and the end	Mastering posed challenges is the beginning

The fortunate aspect of online entertainment's current alignment with computer gaming is that computer games are interactive. The unfortunate aspect is that computer gaming, like static media, such as motion pictures and television, feels the burden to deliver a story. The chief purpose of storytelling is to elicit emotion, which the players in a good online game will do on their own and feel more intimately because they are there. The virtual nature of game worlds be damned: The human heart cannot distinguish between emotions felt in a virtual setting from a physical one. So powerful are glory and shame that they have bound cultures together for centuries, motivated countless people to risk their lives, and driven countless others to end theirs. Thus, while this provides an emotional depth to true online gaming, it must be employed with thought and care, if employed at all.

Let's explore how glory and shame work in online gaming, note their consequences, and show how they influence the underlying community culture a game creates. Glory and shame also offer a clue to why multiplayer gaming has yet to achieve a prominent place among entertainment media.

Buzzword Snow

Industry buzzwords such as "massively multiplayer," "persistent universe," "investment in character," "game community," and the like only hint at their meaning. They cover the medium's landscape like soft snow, providing comfort to the ignorant and obfuscation to the keen. To a larger audience, games either make no sense or seem a strangely unnatural activity for people to engage in unless they're suffering severe deficiencies in their lives.

The fact is that most people see games played on a computer or console as pretty much the same thing: video games. Gaming, prior to computers, has always provided a low-risk way of interacting with people and getting to know them. Add an electronic device, and you've cleaved a chasm. There's more to it, of course. Regular folk, after all, don't go home each night with thoughts of slaughtering boss monsters or bombing Berlin.

A Unique Audience

Today's online gamers have fought past common misconceptions. Many of you may question just how real or powerful the audience influence is in multiplayer online gaming. Most online games today have no persistence or scale to them at all—they are but a series of evanescent encounters among total strangers on a variety of hosts scattered across the world, from which no record is written. Although the power of audience influence is present in these games, and many of the principles I will discuss apply to them, the focus of this paper is on what people refer to today as, for the lack of a better word, massively multiplayer (MMP) games. It is this segment of the online multiplayer medium that has the potential to attract a broad enough cross-section of people in the future to make it a major entertainment medium one day.

Certainly, many of you are thinking, however, that even the large-scale, PW multi-player games don't have an audience influence over players that comes remotely close to the effect of real-life, face-to-face people in the same room with you. People don't actually *see* one another. People don't actually *know* one another. Most don't live anywhere near one another. What force can any audience in the virtual world of cyberspace truly exert on people?

A Unique Medium

The power of this audience, as well as the reason it's unique, comes from the most important difference between multiplayer games and all other forms of entertainment: The audience is the medium. This is because the audience in multiplayer games is unlike an audience in any other form of entertainment: Participant and audience are one. As a player, you are, at once, participant and spectator, beholder and creator of the game environment. In this there are no analogies, nothing to compare, other than that experience that people who do not understand claim the online gamer is lacking: a life.

In short, fully realized, online gaming is a narrative told by the audience. Because the multiplayer game contains the force and influence that groups of people bring to real life, but does so in an imaginative setting that real life too often either lacks or dares not attempt, multiplayer gaming can have a social impact on people more powerful than real life can provide. Thus, the influence of the online game audience, without anyone physically being in the room with you when you play, can rival or exceed its real-life counterpart. While there are plenty of games that have no audiences, have no audience/player/entertainer boundaries, none has the ability to so consume and involve its participants, as everyone who has been involved with this medium for many years has seen, often much to their amazement.

But the medium is primitive. Unlike any other product offered for sale, MMP games are not welcoming—often quite the opposite. They require action and learning on your part before anyone will pay attention to you, and rarely is it obvious what a new player is supposed to do next. Thus, the first experience most new online gamers experience is humiliation and shame.

The Power of Shame

Shame is so powerful an emotion that entire societies have been held together by it. Many still are today, Japan being a splendid example. Echoes of shame's once prime importance in our society exist in a variety of figures of speech: "Shameless. Have you no shame? You should be ashamed of yourself." Japanese warriors, when shamed, would beg not just for death, but for the right to kill themselves in rather horrible ways. Although people no longer plead for the "privilege" of killing themselves and thereby mitigating their shame, every person reading this has wished, at one time or another, that the ground would mercifully swallow him or her up after an embarrassing situation. No matter the words we choose to describe it, no matter what we actually do in response to it, shame has the power to make us wish we were dead. There is no more powerful emotion.

Furthermore, shame is an emotion that most game developers today have no idea they've tapped. Lots of folks in the industry wonder why the market for multiplayer games has grown so slowly. Others bemoan the so-called lack of an economic model for them. People dwell on learning curves, barriers to entry, interface design, and compelling content. What they fail to understand is that the principle reason more people aren't playing hosted persistent online games tonight is due to shame—the experience of it, or the fear of it. Name me a single MMP online game that does not absolutely require that every new player undergo a period of embarrassment or humiliation.

Yes, learning any new game requires that you do badly before you can do better, but multiplayer has an audience—an audience, as noted previously, unique in all of entertainment—generally forcing you not just to do badly at first, but to do badly in front of people. Embarrassment, even on a very slight level, is completely unheard of in all other entertainment media, all of which are hell-bent to make you feel good about yourself, *now*.

The Problem with Glory

Okay, you know that shame is bad, but there are other emotions multiplayer gaming can tap that are quite positive—the opposite emotion of shame: glory. And shame can feed glory; the greater the shame, the greater the feeling of glory. What did Conan say when asked what's good in life?

But there are plenty of opportunities for glory, or at least opportunities to reward players and make them feel good about themselves, that don't require that other players be humiliated. What then is the problem with glory? Ask yourself this question: What is the problem with money? Stressing glory—even when it comes without shaming others—emphasizes achievement in the game developer's system over development of your belonging to the community of the game world. Although we may think we're after recognized achievement in a multiplayer game—and, the more competitive people would argue, in most life activities—the sustaining motive, the reason we keep coming back after we know what we're doing, is due to our development in the social fabric of the game's community. This distinction can be confusing, and I will try to clear it up some. I'll start with the most recognized forms of today's true online games, how they handle issues of achievement versus development, and by extension how gracefully they manage matters of glory and shame.

Pure Meritocracy: The Ultimate Glory Game

In the MMP realm, this sort of game is best represented by the multiplayer air combat simulation (sim). This can also apply to some degree to the first-person shooter, but I will restrict my comments to the air combat sim, as it has a long, established history.

These games demand skills that are rare in human beings—skills that you're expected to master to become a force in the community. Earning respect here is not like religion; you can't get there through devotion alone. If you can't think in terms of 3D geometry and interpolate multiple vectors in your head, then you'll never achieve star status here. It doesn't matter how many hours you play. There is no cumulative character scheme. You cannot earn extra hit points for your fighter aircraft. Put another way, achievement and development are very closely coupled.

Glory and shame here are unambiguous. The two major examples of this genre broadcast notice of your demise, when you perish, to everyone in the game world at that time. One goes so far as to broadcast the game names of both the victor and the vanquished. Not surprisingly, both games have an unspoken ethic that approves of, encourages in fact, attacks with words as well as war planes. Finally, both player communities prefer to resolve major disputes through duels. If they could issue dueling challenges by slapping each other with gloves, they would. Yes, most of the players of these games are guys.

That said, both have developed communities that have, over time, matured to include members that aren't hot-shot fighter pilots. This is, in part, due to the spiritual influence of the underlying subject matter of these games—aviation in an important and actual war that is still in living memory. The point is that the ultimate depth and eventual development of elders, as opposed to just killers, in these communities was not a direct product of the design of these games originally.

Is this genre successful? Although it was the very model of online gaming with graphics, rather than text, for nearly 15 years, the online air combat sim is fading away, and no wonder. Did it represent a worthy model of multiplayer game design? Yes, if you'd prefer a small but dedicated customer base. Ninety percent of the people who try these games don't hang around. Quite simply the glory and shame levels are so high—in particular the shame level for every new player, the pure humiliation each must endure—that there will only be a mass market for this sort of game when society as a whole gives over to the worship of sadomasochism.

Cumulative Character Games: The Devoted All Go to Heaven

Best represented by the fantasy role-playing (FRP) adventure genre, in these games you can get there through devotion alone. Nobody, regardless of native skill, intellect, reasoning ability, or reflexes, can be anything more than meat in these games until they've put in time acquiring attributes and qualities bestowed by the game. Being smart can help you become a force to be reckoned with faster, but you have to pay your dues.

Although at first these may seem purely achievement-oriented games, probably because you usually spend your first few hundred hours acquiring skills and game goods, they do evolve into development games. Players either acquire so much stuff that it loses its meaning and utility, or they carve out a niche for themselves, deciding, in effect, to leave the rat race behind them. In either case, players will eventually develop beyond, or in spite of, the reliance of these games on game-created goodies to drive their game mechanics. Although most examples of the genre are established in early medieval settings, online FRP design is dominated not by the pre-Christian mythology of swords and sorcery, but by pure, raw, unseasoned capitalism. You are who you are because of what you have, what you've acquired, and what you can afford to buy.

But, like the occasional over-wealthy soul, player communities move from achievement to development when they learn there's more to life than money, and you're not something special because you have more of it. Just like the meritocracy-based game, cumulative character games over the years develop rich and warm societies that value their members and bring out the best in them. And just like the meritocracy game, they do so for reasons that seldom have anything to do with the intended design of their creators.

Achievement Versus Development

That's enough abstract and semi-concrete examples. What, once and for all, is the difference between achievement and development in multiplayer game design, and what does any of this have to do with glory and shame? Achievement is all about meeting the challenges posed by game design. Development is your growth in the society of the game world. Achievement in a competitive environment where hundreds or thousands are striving for a sharply defined set of goals is glory for the winners, shame for the losers and also-rans.

Development comes not from your ability to achieve game goals, but rather from the ability of the game, intended or not, to reveal who you are. This is how people can come to believe they know—really know—people they've played an online game with. This is where the lasting bonds among online gamers come from. This is the reason why the emergence of online gaming as a major entertainment medium is inevitable. As game designers, however, it is our preoccupation with the achievement side of the games we make—and their side-effects of glory and shame that we, with little thought, unleash upon our customers—that retard this medium's emergence.

Summary: Development over Achievement

The day we become conscious of the power of our medium and of the power our design decisions have over it is the day when online gaming leaves its Keystone Cops, silent movie era. Here are a few suggestions that can help you get there:

➤ **Don't build a pyramid**—If your game mechanic can only be mastered by a rarified slice of humanity, then you will have the harsh, rough, chest-beating culture of the meritocracy game. It may evolve into something better, but no thanks to you. People tend to think that these games have the testosterone-poisoned cultures they do simply because they usually involve combat. This is simply not true. Look at *Tribes* and its ability to employ a variety of contributions from people in a combat setting. Imagine the culture it would create if it became an MMP offering. Instead of a pyramid, build a game structure like a collapsible camping cup—many interlocking layers, nearly equal in size, needing each other to work.

➤ **Shelter your young**—Perhaps the most powerful development tool the multiplayer game has is rites of passage, yet only rarely does this medium employ them. Don't tack on training to your game. Make raising your players part of the game. One major difference between shame in multiplayer games and in real life is that, in the former, it can happen inexplicably and without warning. This, more than any other single factor, drives promising new players away from multiplayer games—forever.

➤ **Don't be afraid of alienating the hard-core gamer**—Online gaming is a social activity; standalone gaming is not—it's just that simple. Thus, you can eliminate the solo player role entirely and be pleased that you've turned the lone wolves away. Just make sure you design your grouping schemes in a manner that feels natural to players and not forced on them. The tagline of one of the remarkable failures in the online medium was: "The Game That Plays You." People don't want to be played.

➤ **Devise a game design where achievement allows and encourages many different sorts of people to make themselves useful in many different ways**—Do that, without falling back to the database-driven, cumulative character scheme, and player and community development will follow. Do that and you'll conquer the world.

Chapter 16

Case Study: Online Game Lifecycles

by **Jessica Mulligan** and **Bridgette Patrovsky**

AUTHOR NOTE

The lifecycle of a successful massively multiplayer online role-playing game (MMORPG) is virtually unlimited. Good examples of this phenomenon are games still generating revenue over a decade after being released, including *MUD II* by MUSE, Ltd. (16 years), *Gemstone III* by Simutronics (14 years), and *Air Warrior* by Kesmai Corporation (14 years, until closed down by EA in 2001).

Examples of current popular MMORPGs with "legs" would be *EverQuest (EQ)* by Sony Online Entertainment (3+ years, released March 1999), *Ultima Online (UO)* by EA (over 5+ years, released September 1997), and *Asheron's Call (AC)* by Microsoft Gaming Zone (over 3+ years, released October 1999).

Of the four MMORPGs discussed in this article, the important point to note is that all four have been in a constant state of growth since release to the public. That means each has more subscribers each month and year than previously.

Achieving Mass Market Status

The Holy Grail for subscription games is to create similarly compelling games that can crack the mass-market niche, which contains the bulk of the potential customers with about 70% of the total market. Examples of mass-market brands as MMORPGS include *Star Trek* (rumored to be in development by Activision), *Harry Potter* (rumored to be in development at EA in 2000, but now rumored to be dropped from the development list), *Star Wars* (in development by Verant/Sony), *Barbie* (Mattel is rumored to be searching for a developer), and *Dungeons & Dragons* (*D&D*) (purchased from Hasbro by Infogrames).

The first one to three months of an MMORPG's lifecycle see a tremendous rush of customer subscriptions. This rush then levels out and stabilizes at a predictable rate, marked by growth spikes when a retail add-on pack is released to refresh the game. Figure 16.1 charts the growth line for three popular US PWs, showing the variation between the initial launches and subsequent growth periods.

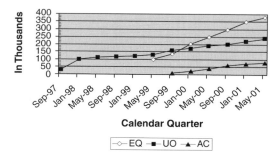

Figure 16.1   Subscription growth for three US MMORPGs.

Note that *EQ* was released initially in North America alone, and *EQ* is now available in Europe and Korea. Versions for China, Taiwan, and Japan are planned for the first quarter of 2003. The Asian market makes up approximately 30–40% of the world MMORPG market; if *EQ* were more available in that market today, the game's monthly subscriber base would likely be between 520,000 and 560,000. If Far East versions had been ready at launch in March 1999, at the end of the game's first year of life, it would have had between 325,000 and 350,000 monthly subscribers.

The Current Top Four MMOGs Worldwide as of December 2002

Important facts about the top four MMOGs are presented in the following sections.

Lineage: The Blood Pledge

Developer/Publisher: NCSoft in Korea

Type: Fantasy/Medieval

Style: Isolinear ("bird's-eye view")

Released: September 1998

Territory: Korea and Taiwan; opened in US in the fourth quarter of 2001

Subscribers: Four million registered subscribers at various price plans, with the bulk of revenue coming from PC gaming clubs in Korea, known as "PC baangs"

Total revenue from release to this date: Estimated at approximately $140 to 170 million USD. Current revenue flow is approximately $10 million in monthly revenues as of late 2002. Fiscal year 2000 sales were 58.2 billion won, or $44,838,212 US. Sales for 2001 were approximately $96 million USD (see www.ncsoft.co.kr/eng/ir/financial.asp for details). It is commonly believed in the industry that over 90% of NCSoft's revenues are derived from *Lineage*, due to statements by Jake Song, NCSoft's US representative. *Lineage* currently owns well over 40% of the Korean market.

COMMENTS:

Lineage is the current big success story in non-US MMP games. South Korea is probably the most "wired" nation in the world, not excluding the US. This game went from $6 million in revenue in 1999 to the current levels, mainly by cutting deals with Internet cafés in South Korea. Internet cafés are a huge industry in South Korea, with over 200,000 seatings in play at peak hours (think 200,000 simultaneous players). The Internet cafés pay NCSoft per seat for access; each café usually buys between 16 and 64 seats for *Lineage* play.

Notably, *Lineage* has seen far less success in US subscription rates, even with the venerable Lord British (Richard Garriott of *Ultima* fame) at the helm.

Figure 16.2 *Lineage: The Bloodpledge.*

EverQuest

Developer/Publisher: Verant Interactive/Sony Online Entertainment

Type: Fantasy/Medieval

Style: 3D, first-person

Released: March 1999

Territory: Mostly in English-speaking countries; accessible worldwide by any English-speaking player. Recently available in Korea via an agreement with NCSoft and in European countries via an agreement with UbiSoft. *EQ* expects to open in China, Taiwan, and Japan early in 2003.

Subscribers: 430,000 monthly subscribers at $12.95 each

Total revenue from release to this date: Estimated at approximately $100–130 million USD, including monthly subscriptions and retail sales of the boxed game. Retail sales figures are estimated at about 900,000 units, totaling about $27 million in revenue for Sony.

COMMENTS:

The most high-profile success in MMORPGs; this one gets quite a bit of press. This game sold about 30,000 units the first day of availability in 1999 and garnered almost 250,000 subscribers in the first year from launch. It passed the 400,000-subscriber mark 24 months after release.

EQ is now the "gold standard" for US MMP games.

Figure 16.3   *EverQuest.*

Ultima Online

Developer/Publisher: Origin Systems/EA

Type: Fantasy/Medieval

Style: Isolinear ("bird's-eye view")

Released: September 1997

Territory: Available worldwide in several languages, including English, Spanish, Korean, Chinese, German, French, and Japanese

Subscribers: 208,000 monthly subscribers at $9.95 each

Total revenue from release to this date: Estimated at approximately $120 million USD, including monthly subscriptions and retail sales of the boxed game

COMMENTS:

UO is widely considered the game that broke open the Internet for subscription gaming in 1997. For the first six months, *UO* was the fastest-selling product in parent corporation EA's history. The fact that it has fewer subscribers than *EQ*, even though it has been out 18 months longer than *EQ*, is due to the sheer complexity of the game and the technical and gameplay problems the game experienced from launch in 1997 until major changes were made in the game.

What is key to note is that, despite the complexity of the game, *UO* has grown steadily over the years until recently. It has had more subscribers every quarter than the last quarter until about June 2001; since then, the game has slowly been losing subscribers, but the rate of churn is low compared to the total subscriber base, which is about 5% annually. The recent release of the *Lord Blackthorne's Revenge* expansion pack has probably caused a temporary spike in subscription rates.

Figure 16.4   *Ultima Online.*

Dark Age of Camelot

Developer/Publisher: Mythic Entertainment/Vivendi Universal

Type: Fantasy/Medieval

Style: 3D, first-person

Released: October 2001

Territory: US and Canada; European launches in Germany and France expected in late 2002 and in Asia in early 2003

Subscribers: Approximately 250,000 monthly subscribers at $12.95 per month, as of December 2002

Total revenue from release to this date: Approximately $25 million, including monthly subscriptions and retail sales of the boxed game

COMMENTS:

Camelot is considered to have had the smoothest launch of any of the big MMORPGs; it premiered virtually without a hitch. It is also the current fastest-growing MMORPG, with 200,000 subscribers in the first six months post-launch and approximately 250,000 as of December, 2002. The European and Asian launches of the game will add another 100,000 subscribers to the growth. If Mythic can sustain its US growth gracefully, it is estimated that will have well over 350,000 subscribers by October 2003.

Figure 16.5   *Dark Age of Camelot.*

Chapter 17

Fighting Player Burnout in Massively Multiplayer Games

by **Damion Schubert**, Founder, Ninjaneering.com

(damion@ninjaneering.com)

> **AUTHOR NOTE**
> This is another article that was originally published online and which
> we asked the author to revisit. You can read Damion's biography
> Appendix B, "Bios of Interviewees"; he's "been there and done that."
> What he writes about here is crucial to the long-term survival of any
> persistent world (PW).

When creating a role-playing game, most design teams try to
aim toward providing 40 hours of gameplay. More expansive
visions, such as *Ultima Ascension* or *Baldur's Gate*, easily surpass that, offering 80, 120, or even 200 hours of gameplay,
depending on who you ask. The costs of providing this additional content are substantial—both games cost millions of
dollars and had schedules that surpassed two years—and in
the end, all but the most hard-core fans had a hard time
completing every quest and exploring every area in these
two games.

However, in the arena of massively multiplayer (MMP)
games, 200 hours can be one-*tenth* of the time that a player
spends online. Indeed, there have been numerous reports of
players who surpass the 200-hour mark in a month—every
month. And as a result, MMP designers feel compelled to
extend the playability of the game well beyond what is
healthy for either the game or the player.

KEY TOPICS

- The Exponential Curve
  of Death

- More Content?

- Play Less, Please

- Conclusion

The Exponential Curve of Death

The designer's first impulse is to create long-term play with extreme exponential character progression—one where it gets harder to advance as the game progresses. This is nothing new to gaming, but we MMP designers often take this to an absurd level, sometimes going so far as to double the number of experience points needed to advance to each level. Given that the actual work that a player has to do to gain experience hasn't changed much, this can get real old real fast.

Typically, when designing the curve, designers say something like, "It's so steep that I guarantee it will take 6 months to reach level 100!" Also typically, this is often initially compounded by extreme penalties for failure, such as steep death penalties that can undo hours or even days of work.

The problem then, of course, is that your game starts to feel a lot more like work than fun. The results of this are stark:

> ➤ **Players come to resent your game and your staff**—The tedium of doing the same action over and over again eventually wears on the players. It doesn't matter how fun that particular activity is either—once you've done it eight hours a day for a week to get to your next milestone, it's just not that thrilling anymore.

> ➤ **Hard-core gamers devour your game faster and demand more**—To your hard-core gamers, the whole concept of needing six months to get to your highest level is a joke—they figured out how to get there in three months with their first character, and can now do it in one month with their new characters.

> ➤ **Casual gamers feel they cannot compete**—Seeing another player display remarkable power can actually inspire you to try to reach that plateau yourself—unless, of course, you realize that it would take you six months to get halfway there. At that point, casual gamers and weekend warriors decide whether or not it's worth it to even try.

> ➤ **Your game narrows**—Because it takes so much time and effort to make a tiny gain, it begins to feel as if every moment of your life where you are not doing that activity is wasted time. As a result, other features of your game fall away. These features typically offer no reward or aren't very efficient ways of reaching that reward. The best example is when players say that they "can't role-play" in your

game space. You can role-play anywhere, even in a parking lot with a broken broom handle. What players are saying is that role-playing takes too much time away from the daily grind, which they feel compelled to do every moment online.

➤ **Bandwidth costs go through the roof**—Finally, this us the reason your bosses will care. Bandwidth is one of the largest costs of running an online game. If your gameplay is encouraging players to log on for eight hours at a time, you are reducing the amount of money you can spend on other things, including additional content, better support, or even development on other games.

The end result of this is *player fatigue*, a situation where the player is sick to death of the game but unwilling to leave. And why shouldn't they be sick of the game? After all, he or she has played the game 5 to 10 times as much as we would expect anyone to enjoy a single-player game. However, the connections the player has to other friends, and the blood, sweat, and tears that the player has devoted to building online characters at that point prevents him or her from leaving. Yes, you then have a whole bunch of paying subscribers, but are they happy? Are they having fun? Or have they become poisonous enemies of the state?

More Content?

When one thinks about how to expand the life of a game, the first thought on a designer's mind might be to identify ways to give the player more content for relatively little dollar.

The addition of more content (dungeons, quests, and so on) at runtime and/or the running of periodic in-game events is one commonly cited strategy for keeping players involved. While these are considered expected by the player base and can have many other benefits inside of the game space, additional content and quests often don't help the problem. First, players can devour in an hour content that takes a designer a month to create. There is simply no way to keep up. Second, content invariably has to be aimed at one portion of the player base. An example is creating a dungeon that only high-level players can enter. Putting in content like this can really exacerbate feelings of frustration and fatigue that other players (in this case, low-level players) might be having.

Random content generation is one interesting arena that has not been explored much, although the challenges in adding new content without oversight have some interesting ramifications for a persistent-state world. However, one can make a good argument that the random content (both the magic weapons as well as the dungeon layouts) has contributed mightily to the success of *Diablo*.

And, of course, the final course to consider is the possibility of allowing players to create and add content to the world. However, this has a number of challenges regarding quality control, hardware costs, and exploit-proofing that implementation of this in a full-scale MMP is unlikely in the near future.

Play Less, Please

When examining under these circumstances, one wonders if it is worthwhile to examine the problem from another angle. It becomes clear that the goal of designers may well be to design a game that hard-core players feel compelled to play *less*—admittedly a stance that most designers are unprepared to take.

Ultima Online (*UO*) was the first major MMP to recognize that and to experiment with changing the paradigm of player advancement dramatically. In *UO*, a player advances significantly faster during the first hour after he/she logs on. The results were starkly positive: Players would still log in daily, but they would spend only an hour advancing their character. During that time, they were guaranteed to see meaningful advancement of their character and were ensured a taste of success. After they had done their daily advancement, players would either log off, feeling good about their success, or they would engage in the more fun and less work-like aspects of the game's design: role-playing, socializing, and exploring the world, for example. Both of these possible outcomes are better than the days of the endless treadmill.

This is not to say that *UO*'s implementation of power hour didn't have problems:

> ➤ **It was introduced late**—Since power hour was introduced well after the launch of the game, players who had gotten their characters up in levels "the hard way" felt that power hour had made their hard work suddenly meaningless. Most of the player criticism of power hour centered on this point.

> ➤ **It discouraged party adventuring**—The clock for power hour kicks off the moment you enter the game. Given that it can take a significant amount of time to get to your friends to join a party and get that adventure rolling, most players would choose to adventure alone for power hour to maximize benefits.

> ➤ **It was unrealistic**—Fans of realism can be starkly offended that the game rules can change so arbitrarily for no apparent good reason, but the designer has to do ultimately what is best for the health of the game. At any rate, any good designer should realize that game fiction is the most flexible tool in the designer's toolbox, and should use the background story when possible to describe and rationalize the limitations of the game.

> ➤ **It reduced player attachment to their characters**—Because players had spent less time developing their characters, those characters theoretically would be less powerful "anchors" keeping the player in the game. One could argue, however, that casual players might have more attachment to their characters, as they could get them up to a higher level.

> ➤ **The parameters weren't quite right**—Some have argued that power hour still creates a gulf, only now between the player who can play daily and the weekend warrior. Others have argued that players can push their stats up too high during power hour, making it too easy to create a new character. Both are certainly arguable, and both points are also certainly tunable in a new system with the same principles.

> ➤ **It only affected stat advancement**—Power hour did not affect gold gain, and as a result, power-gamers would switch to this as a goal to endlessly acquire. However, some designers have actually argued that that is optimal, as you have then given casual gamers goals they can meet, while still providing hard-core gamers with a separate track that they can run on.

Despite these negatives, power hour was perceived to be a strong success among the team that was supporting *UO*, as it was extremely effective in empowering casual players and reducing the overall tedium of the game. This was despite a huge amount of skepticism about the feature among many designers at Origin (myself included) before the feature was implemented.

However, the lesson from power hour is simple: If there is a particular play pattern that you feel is ideal for your game, then don't just hope players don't act that way—enforce the behavior in code. If you don't want players to advance too quickly, cap them. If you don't want players to spend all day online macro-ing, then limit the effectiveness of such tactics. If you feel it's important to have control of these aspects of the game, then take control of them.

Conclusion

When players perform any game function for a significant length of time, the game ceases to be fun. The addictive nature of these online games is strong enough without forcing endless hours on the treadmill on the player. Quite the opposite; if you can reduce the number of hours that a player spends online, and increase the number of those hours that a player can spend having fun, socializing, role-playing, and exploring, then the good feelings that your player base will have toward your game and your service will increase dramatically.

Chapter 18

Post-Mortem: *Mythic's* Dark Age of Camelot

KEY TOPICS

- The Community
- The Beta Starts
- Server Backend
  Configuration
- The Business
  Arrangement
- Lessons Learned

by **Matt Firor**, Producer, Mythic Entertainment

AUTHOR NOTE

Anarchy Online (AO) was a poor launch that made a turnaround; *Dark Age of Camelot* is that other elusive beast in the industry of persistent worlds (PWs): the flat-out success from day one. *Dark Age of Camelot* had the smoothest launch of any PW in recent memory and has since seen unfettered growth. In the eight months from its launch in October 2001 until May 2002, the game acquired 200,000 subscribers. If Mythic can sustain that pace, it will have 300,000 subscribers by *Dark Age of Camelot's* first anniversary, taking the crown from *EverQuest (EQ)* and making it the fastest-growing PW in US history.

This success should really come as no surprise; Mythic has been around for over 18 years and has developed a number of PWs in that time. That's why we asked producer Matt Firor to write a post-mortem for this book, noting what went right and what went wrong. As you'll see, experience may be a key to a smooth launch and management, but there are shoals to navigate even so.

When *Dark Age of Camelot* hit the market on October 9, 2001, it was the culmination of about 18 months of development. About 25 developers worked on the game in that time, evenly divided among programmers, artists, and world developers.

The genesis of *Dark Age of Camelot* came about when we at Mythic saw the immense popularity of the new generation of online RPGs, such as *EQ*, *Ultima Online (UO)*, and *Asheron's Call (AC)*, and realized that we could do that type of game. In the past, we'd created many text-based MUDs as well as graphical action games. It made perfect sense to us to combine the two technologies and make a graphical MUD.

But which MUD to make graphical? We'd created many different types of RPGs over the years, from standard player versus monster games to games where players were actively encouraged to fight one another. At that time, the most recent online RPG developed by Mythic was *Darkness Falls: The Crusade*. This text-based MUD featured realm-based combat, where players chose to be one of three different teams. Each team (realm) was in conflict with one another and was in a state of constant warfare, with the goal being to steal the other realm's idols. We liked the dynamic that realm versus realm (RvR) combat gave the game because it gave a sense of purpose to PvP combat that was missing in other PvP-centric games. So, we decided to base our new graphical online RPG on three-team, realm-based RvR conflict.

This decision was not taken lightly; we had many discussions where we brainstormed about what players wanted to play. *EQ*, the most popular graphical online RPG to date, did not even really offer PvP combat in any meaningful sense. Many players touted that feeling of safety as one of the primary reasons why they played *EQ*, instead of other, more PvP-oriented games such as *UO*. We wanted our RvR combat to be compelling enough to attract players who wanted to play such a game, but we also didn't want to alienate potential players who were looking for a more sedate game style. Hence, we hit upon the plan of having safe zones where players could play the game solely against monsters—where they could group up with other online players in a cooperatively, friendly fashion and adventure together. Because the game would have three realms, we needed to have three different home areas—one for each realm. However, there would also be a frontier area that was RvR-oriented; players would make the choice of whether they wanted to fight other players or not by traveling (or not traveling) to the frontier areas.

Darkness Falls: The Crusade was developed around a good versus evil system where the three realms were Evil, Light, and Chaos. This was compelling enough for a game of its type, and we started designing the game and working on the game's graphical engine. Soon after development started, Mythic's president, Mark Jacobs, hit up on the idea of making the game based on the legends of King Arthur. Having a recognizable background to the game would go far toward making the game more appealing to players. He decided the game should be situated after the death of King Arthur, in the times not really covered by the legends, and that the game should be appropriately entitled "*Dark Age of Camelot.*" The only task left was to add the other two realms, and soon Viking Scandinavia (Midgard) and Celtic Ireland (Hibernia) were added to Arthurian England (Albion).

At the time, we were far ahead of the technological curve. We had already created 13 online games by that point—most of which built up on the code base of the previous games. In essence, we had been testing our technology—by having it in our older games—for five years by the time *Camelot*'s development started.

In general, Mythic's pre-*Camelot* games were separated into two distinct categories: text-based MUDs such as *Dragon's Gate* and *Darkness Falls: The Crusade*, and first- (and sometimes third-) person shooters like *Rolemaster: Magestorm*, *Aliens Online*, *Godzilla Online*, and *Spellbinder: the Nexus Conflict*. As designed, *Camelot* would fuse the two technologies together—use the graphical frontend from the shooters and the server backend from the MUDs.

The first versions of our shooters were software only; most were created before 3D-accelerated video cards became prevalent. However, our most recent—*Spellbinder*—was our first 3D-accelerated game. It was built using the Netimmerse 3D API from NDL, Inc. Because of this, we had a great head start on developing *Camelot*'s client; we had a stable base to start from, which already supported our messaging and art requirements.

Spellbinder's engine, while accelerated, still needed some major work in order to bring it up to the level that today's online gamer demands. First, we had to add the concept of "outdoors" to the engine—*Spellbinder*'s gameplay took place exclusively inside castles or caves. We also needed to add rolling, organic-looking terrain, which again did not exist in *Spellbinder*. Rob Denton, Mythic's primary programmer, made it his first task to upgrade the engine.

While Rob was hard at work on the client, Brian Axelson, the main programmer on *Darkness Falls: The Crusade*, was working on *Camelot*'s server, ensuring that the database, editor, and in-game tools from *Darkness Falls: The Crusade* would work when accessed from the new graphical client. Eventually, both would be done and would work exceptionally well. With some other code integrated from *Spellbinder* (lobby, login, player authentication), we were ready to start content development on the game.

I cannot overstate the importance of this fusion of existing technology on *Camelot's* timely and stable development. Basically all parts of the game's underlying systems had been tested for years by their inclusion in other Mythic games. All artists and programmers were familiar with the tools needed to create content and new features. Once new versions started rolling out for testing, they were stable, and we could test game balance and other features almost immediately without having to worry about stability.

We assigned co-lead artists Lance Robertson and CJ Grebb on the game. Lance was assigned management and technical art duties, and CJ was in charge of the game's look and feel. Lance and Rob worked out a scheme for creating player and monster models, animating them and putting armor/outfit textures on them. Their team then geared up to create figures and outfits, as well as other in-game models such as houses, trees, rocks, and the myriad of other landscape features that are in the game.

Soon after getting the initial versions of the game running, our lead world developer, Colin Hicks, started assembling a team that would place the art provided by the artists into the game. His team was responsible for quest development, terrain creation and object placement, and the general background/stories that defined the player's interaction with the game.

I was responsible for class and race creation, which was made interesting by the fact that we had three separate realms, each of which had separate races and classes. We didn't want to make the classes the same across all realms, so eventually I (with a lot of input and help from everyone on the team) came up with 32 different classes and 12 races across the three realms, none of which were exact copies.

The Community

Soon after *Camelot's* development started, we got serious about developing a fan base for the game. We enlisted the aid of the Vault Network, who provided us with some message board space and a moderator. This gave us an outlet to the Internet community—we could post ideas and updates on the game, as well as entice potential customers with screenshots.

The mood on the fan boards was initially quite dubious—no one had really ever heard of Mythic before, and few thought we could create *Camelot* at all. Many other online RPGs had been announced, and most never saw the light of day. The gaming community was frustrated by this and viewed any announcement of a new title with extreme skepticism.

However, after the game started Beta testing and word got out that the game was actually functional, the boards turned more and more into a place for players to express their hope that *Camelot* would turn out well and for them to give us their ideas and comments on the game design. Eventually we hired an Internet relations manager, Sanya Thomas, who was put in charge of managing the community and for keeping all of us developers appraised of what the community was thinking.

The Beta Starts

After about six months in development, it was time to start testing the game. We identified the fans we thought would make the best testers and invited them into *Camelot*'s first Beta test. The test would eventually have four stages and would run for almost a year; the first versions tested had only one realm and a limited number of classes, but as time went on, the game got more and more content.

The Beta test was very important to *Camelot*'s maturation; it allowed players to tell us what was going on in the game, how the different classes performed, and how the world was designed and set up. We made many changes and tweaks to all aspects of the game during the Beta period; most were made because of tester feedback.

Server Backend Configuration

From our experience with our other online games, we had a rough idea of how many servers we'd need and how much bandwidth would be required for *Camelot*. We standardized on Linux as our server operating system, as it was our standard server operating system for other games. Linux was rock-solid and we had lots of in-house expertise with it. Because Linux runs so well on Intel-based boxes, we shopped around and

settled on Pentium 4 dual-processor Dell boxes. We contacted several PC manufacturers, but Dell clearly rose above the others in terms of understanding what we were
trying to do, as well as providing a great price/service combination.

We had planned on using Oracle or Microsoft SQL Server as the character/account
database for *Camelot*. I had a lot of experience developing and maintaining Oracle
applications from my previous career in the IT industry, so I contacted Sales departments of both companies and solicited bids. Oracle came back with the ridiculous
price of about $975,000, while SQL Server, at $30,000, was more reasonable. It was
still far outside our price range. So, we instead settled on a hybrid of MySQL—a freeware Linux database—and an in-house-developed flat-file character database. This
solution cost us only the development time it took to create the databases; no licensing
fees were required. MySQL manages all account and customer service (CS) records,
and the flat file handles all character information. This combination has worked
essentially without a hitch since launch.

The Business Arrangement

Almost as soon as *Camelot* started to be developed, we began to try to interest other
companies in publishing it for us. The traditional relationship between developer and
publisher is that the developer handles all design and implementation of the game,
while the publisher handles business arrangements; distribution, advertising, marketing, and so on. Typically the publisher finances the game and then takes a cut of all
profits. For the first year that *Camelot* was in development, we simply could not
interest a company in publishing it, which left us in a financial bind; we couldn't
afford to develop *Camelot*.

We then turned to the only source of revenue available to us: We sold a minority share
of Mythic's stock to Abandon Entertainment, a New York-based entertainment company. With this sale of stock, we financed *Camelot*'s entire development, as well as
some of its marketing and advertising. It also paid for a booth at E3.

By the time E3 rolled around, we had two of the three realms done and were well on
our way to hashing out the RvR combat system. In fact, our primary focus at the show
was to demonstrate our RvR system. By that time—five months before release—it was
obvious that the game was going to be done on time and that it was good. Publisher

interest was heating up, but by that time, we didn't need one—we had the game financed and produced. What we needed was a distributor, so we used E3 to set up meetings with many large game companies interested in distributing *Camelot* for us.

One such company, Vivendi Universal, impressed us more than all the others, and we signed up with them to promote and distribute *Camelot*. Vivendi has a great system of regional sales; through their sales chain, *Camelot* has been distributed to just about any retail outlet that wants to sell it. Vivendi has been a stable, reliable, and overall a great partner for Mythic.

Lessons Learned

It wasn't all roses, of course, during the time that *Camelot* was being created. We ran into problems just like everyone else who makes an incredibly complex game like *Dark Age of Camelot*. Here's a sample:

➤ We launched without nearly enough in-game and support tools for our CS department to be able to do their jobs effectively. It took almost a month before we got them the tools they needed in order to answer questions, figure out who was having problems, be able to see logs, and a myriad of other small utilities. Not having tools of this type made players wait far too long for help.

➤ We had big plans for in-game cities that would be "alive" with NPCs and would serve as hubs for in-game commerce and player community building. Sadly, it took us far longer to create the cities than we estimated, so we had to launch with only one city per realm.

➤ Also lacking at launch were dungeons. We wanted many more dungeons than were included with the game at launch, a problem we are still attempting to overcome. Because cities and dungeons are basically large models that don't use the terrain system, we ran into many monster AI problems, as well as players getting "stuck" on geometries and even falling through the floors.

In general, *Camelot*'s development was a wonderful experience. Sure, we made some mistakes, but all in all, the game came out beautiful, stable, and most of all, fun to play.

Chapter 19

Managing Deviant Behavior in Online Worlds

By **Talin**

AUTHOR NOTE

Talin is one of those interesting, highly educated thinkers of the gaming industry with many years of experience in both solo and persistent world (PW) games. Talin left the industry for greener pastures, much to our detriment. He sees the problems and solutions to "grief" players more clearly than many of us.

This article has been around for some time, but the points Talin makes are still applicable today. Handing this article to a community management team will probably save them a ton of time, heartache, and grief.

This article attempts to outline a number of strategies for managing "deviant" or undesirable behavior in massively multiplayer (MMP) online worlds.

What is "deviant" behavior?

Webster's dictionary defines the word "deviant" as "straying from the norm"—in other words, behavior that is outside the envelope of what is considered customary.

Unusual or idiosyncratic behavior is not in itself harmful and can sometimes be of great value. (The "good Samaritan," as described in the Bible, was certainly a "deviant" by this definition.) However, when we think of a person who is a "deviant," we typically connote a more pejorative meaning: someone whose behavior is somehow perverted, twisted, corrupt, or destructive.

Such "deviant" behavior may not be rare or idiosyncratic at all! If the online environment is such that destructive and abusive acts are encouraged and rewarded, then such behavior all too quickly *becomes* the norm.

Thus, we can only speak of behavior being "deviant" in the context of an online world where there is a *code of conduct*, and in which the vast majority of players adhere to this code. In this case, "deviant" behavior is simply behavior that violates this code of conduct.

I think it's important to avoid pejorative language, and in particular, "moralistic" language when discussing undesirable behavior. The issues here can be both sensitive and emotionally charged. It's all too easy for us, as the creators and maintainers of the system, to feel "besieged" by a deluge of abuse and to think of our less tractable customers as "bad" people. But the line between desirable and undesirable behavior is fuzzy and often crossed inadvertently and innocently. What may be "bad" in our view may be perfectly legitimate in the value system of the customer. Many of the violators of our codes of conduct are not "scum" but merely overzealous.

That is not to say that we do not have the right to take punitive action to protect the integrity of our world. But in my view, such action should be taken dispassionately and without moral condemnation.

I believe that the best policy is to always treat our customers with a high degree of respect, even when they have gone "astray."

What Are Some Kinds of Undesirable Behavior?

For an online world, undesirable behavior is behavior that damages or inhibits the proper functioning of the technical infrastructure, the game balance, or the social fabric. The following sections contain some examples of undesirable behavior, but they are by no means complete (human inventiveness will always outstrip attempts to classify it).

Attacks Against Technical Infrastructure

There are at least three types of attacks against technical infrastructure:

> ➤ **Denial of service**—This could include crashing or locking up the servers, tying up the network bandwidth, corrupting the account database, or any other method of making the game unplayable for other players.

> ➤ **Unauthorized access**—This could include access to internal parts of the system, or it could mean that the abuser is able to enjoy unpaid-for services. The most common type of unauthorized access is the use of another player's account by obtaining that login and password (typically via email scam).

> ➤ **Disclosure of private or sensitive information**—This could include disclosure of credit card numbers, passwords, and other personal user data, or secure system data such as encryption keys and digital certificates.

Disruption of Game Balance

Game balance can be disrupted in a couple of ways:

> ➤ **Exploitation of design loopholes or bugs**—In an ideal world, the gameplay would be perfectly balanced, and no player could gain an unfair advantage over any other or be able to advance their goals more rapidly than the designer of the system had intended. However, in complex systems like these, it is often the case that the design overlooks some subtle interaction between features of the environment. Players will inevitably find these loopholes and exploit them.

> The situation is exacerbated by the fact that players have a strong incentive not to report the loopholes when they are discovered. This is part of the *paradox of challenge*—we like challenge, but we also want it to go away (by overcoming it). As game designers, it is our goal to create challenges, to "disempower people in interesting ways." It is the goal of players to re-empower themselves, perhaps in ways that we designers did not anticipate. (Part of the joy of building these systems is seeing the clever and unanticipated strategies that players come up with.) Thus, although players and designers are set in opposition, at a higher level, we are all on the same team, and the behavior of both sides should reflect this. But it is sometimes hard for players to keep this in mind.

➤ **Denial of access to game resources**—Many coveted game items (for example, special ingredients) can only be obtained at certain places or at certain times. Part of the "puzzle" of the game is figuring out where an item is available or completing a difficult journey to where the item is located. However, players who are powerful or adept at gameplay may monopolize the resource—not necessarily out of a desire to deny access to other players but out of a need to advance their own character's goals.

An example is the phenomena of "farming" seen in *EverQuest* (*EQ*). High-level players will enter a low-level dungeon, seeking some rare item that is obtained by killing and looting a particular type of monster. Often the item will only "drop" a small fraction of the time, so many monsters of a particular type need to be killed in order to obtain the item. When the high-level players enter the scene, however, they quickly dispatch all of the monsters in the region, leaving none for the lower level players who are also trying to obtain the same item. In addition, the high-level players may decide to "camp" the area, rapidly harvesting each new monster as it spawns. The result is an effective denial of the resource to any but the most powerful players.

Disruption of the Social Fabric

Disruption of the social fabric can be seen in several forms:

➤ **Harassment**—Harassment is a broad class of behavior, typically involving repeatedly directing unwanted attention, via speech or action, toward another player, despite clear signals from the other player that such attention is unacceptable. The line between what is harassment and what is legitimate gameplay is fuzzy, especially in an environment in which players are competing directly against one another.

➤ **Spamming**—Online games benefit from having a wealth of communication options, but many kinds of communication are unwanted. In particular, flooding a communication channel with unwanted messages negates the benefit of that channel and makes it harder for users to receive "legitimate" messages.

➤ **Begging**—One very popular form of annoyance is begging—asking random passersby for gifts of money, items, and so on. Just as in the real world, beggars often take steps to ensure that they appear much worse off than they actually are, even going so far as to create a brand-new character (which then gives the received items to their primary character).

It should be noted, however, that while begging is annoying and undesirable, it is not technically speaking an abuse. Begging can be appropriate in some situations, although it should always be discouraged.

➤ **Frauds and scams**—Various kinds of scams, particularly involving an exchange of material goods, are quite popular in game environments. Players may attempt to misrepresent the capabilities of an item, its rarity, or its monetary value. Players may attempt to substitute one item for another, in a classic "bait and switch" tactic. While most games provide for a two-phase commit transaction system for the exchange of goods, in which both players must agree before the exchange can take place, many kinds of exchanges (such as "heal me and I'll pay you 100 gold") are not directly fungible and cannot be handled within the scope of a single transaction.

➤ **Identity scams**—A particular type of scam is the attempt to pose as another player, especially if that player is well known and has a positive reputation. The perpetrator of the scam can then use the illicitly acquired reputation to gain advantages or favors from other players. Often the true character's reputation will suffer as a result of these actions.

Often this is done via ambiguities in the text font used for the display of character names—for example, in *EQ*, which uses a Helvetica-like font for the chat transcript, the number one, the lowercase "l," and the uppercase "I" all look identical.

➤ **Slander and libel**—There are a number of reasons why a player might want to damage the reputation of another. The player may be angry at some real or imagined slight; the player may have been done real harm; the player might be enjoying the thrill of a practical joke; or the player might simply be engaged in a primate dominance game of some sort, stroking his own ego by undermining others. A popular pastime among adolescent males (who are often insecure about their own developing sexuality) is to advertise, "So-and-so is gay!"

➤ **False charges of abuse**—One of the more difficult types of abuse to deal with is misuse of the system for reporting abuse. This is a special kind of libel, in which one player attempts to file a false charge of abuse or unacceptable behavior against another. This is a type of abuse in which automated collection of corroborating evidence can be helpful.

➤ **Inappropriate language**—In order to gain the widest possible customer base, we need to ensure that the "norm" of social behavior is one that would be approved of by the larger culture outside. Parents are unlikely to let their children play on a system that is reputed to teach them habits of which they disapprove. Unfortunately, online worlds allow a limited form of escape from those very parents, and may be perceived by those same children as a way of avoiding the parental restrictions.

➤ **Inflammatory language, especially racial or cultural slurs**—In a similar vein, there are certain topics or utterances that can trigger the feeling of a hostile environment. Many people have "hot buttons," that is, highly charged issues that habitually invoke strong feelings, especially feelings of anger. Others will not be able to enjoy the online experience in an environment in which they do not feel "safe." (It is unfortunate that a "least common denominator" approach to discourse of this type must be enforced—that is, limiting the discussion to language and topics that would be acceptable to nearly everyone. In particular, the intersection of the community standards of, say, San Francisco, California, and Charlotte, North Carolina is smaller than you might think.)

Note that attacks against the technical infrastructure are, for the most part, "out of game" activities—that is, the attack is conducted not within the game itself, but against the technical infrastructure (servers and network) that supports the game. This document is primarily concerned with "in-game" countermeasures—that is, remedies that occur at the design level, rather than at the infrastructure level. For this reason, technical attacks and countermeasures will not be discussed further in this document.

This document will also not attempt to address the issue of "out of game" email scams or other actions that are disruptive to the larger community outside of the context of the game itself.

All of the behavior types listed can be divided into three categories of severity:

➤ **Violations**—This category of behavior is always inappropriate and should always carry a negative consequence when detected. An example of this category is false charges of abuse.

➤ **Annoyances**—This category of behavior is usually inappropriate, but done in moderation is acceptable. An example of this category is begging. These kinds of behaviors should be handled via in-game punishments or incentives, unless the behavior is extreme.

➤ **Too much of a good thing**—There are some types of behavior that are actually positive, but if overused or used in the wrong context can be undesirable. This kind of behavior should also be handled at the design level by in-game punishments and rewards.

Why Undesirable Behavior Is a Complex Problem

If a particular behavior is undesirable, why not simply modify the program code to make that behavior impossible? The problem is that in many cases, undesirable behavior is very similar in outward form to permissible or even desirable behavior. Distinguishing between the two often requires a human value judgment. For example, a computer subroutine would have a hard time distinguishing between someone who was "stalking" another player, and someone who was merely following a player because he was lost and too shy to ask for help directly.

In addition, different people have different opinions about what is and is not desirable, and that may change with a given context.

Many kinds of undesirable behavior are easily identified by human perception and judgment. However, the supply of "trusted" humans is limited. Reports from untrusted humans (the vast majority) need to be accompanied by corroborating evidence; otherwise, the reporting facility itself can become a kind of systemic abuse.

Why Do People Engage in Abusive or Undesirable Behavior?

One of the most desirable things about being in an online world is the freedom it offers. Being in an imaginary world, one is freed from real-world consequence and real-world accountability. With any reduction in accountability, there is always a strong temptation to explore the limits of one's newfound freedom, in particular by pushing the boundaries of acceptable behavior.

This is exactly what toddlers do during the "terrible twos"; having discovered a new world and a new perception that other peoples' feelings and judgments are not the same as their own, they attempt to discover the boundaries of this world—much to the consternation of parents whose job it is to set those boundaries.

Establishing a Code of Conduct

A code of conduct has multiple functions:

> ➤ The primary purpose of the code of conduct is to inform the player population as to what kinds of behavior are considered permissible and to establish a social norm. Most players, if given a structure or set of boundaries, will willingly conform to them, especially if mild incentives are provided.

> ➤ A few individuals will, of course, rebel against the restrictions in the code of conduct. Thus, the second function of the code of conduct is to establish a basis for taking corrective action against these recalcitrant users. The goal is to have users that conform to the code, with a minimum use of force or penalties.

> ➤ Finally, a third function of the code is to assure parents or legal guardians that the environment we are creating is a wholesome one for their children. (This also applies to individuals who are considering joining for themselves but are not sure that they will feel safe within the environment.)

In a real online game there will, in fact, be two codes of conduct: an explicit, written code that is imposed by the designers of the system, and an implicit code that will emerge from the social interactions within the game itself. This second code is an important component of a rich and diverse play experience, possessing a homegrown feeling of authenticity that may be lacking in the first, explicit code. Thus, the growth of this implicit code of conduct should be watched and nurtured.

However, the code of conduct is more than just a set of rules. It is an integral part of the game's social discourse. In an MMORPG, most conversations tend to be "about" the goals of the game—leveling, getting better weapons, and so on. In an ideal situation, the codes of conduct, both formal and informal, are an important part of these conversations. By establishing goals, the designers of the game define an omnipresent context in which all actions, and in particular all conversations, take place.

A Mild Tangent

I like to visualize this as a "gradient" in the mathematical sense—that is, at any given moment in a multi-dimensional realm, you can always tell which direction is "up" and which is "down" by the gradient—sort of like standing on the slope of a hill in the fog; you always know which direction will take you higher. Thus, applying this metaphor to a game experience, it means that no matter what situation you find yourself in, you can always determine which actions will lead you nearer or farther from a specified goal, at least locally. And you can converse with those near you about the nearness of the goal and the direction to it, since you are in a shared context. We can talk about "unipolar" worlds, in which there exists a single overarching goal to which all other goals are subsidiary [such as leveling in *EQ*], versus "poly-polar" worlds, in which there are multiple orthogonal goals, another time.

Of course, in order for a code of conduct to be effective, it has to be enforced. Two steps for doing that are detection and corrective action.

Detection

Because the difference between desirable and undesirable behavior is often subtle, detecting when such behavior occurs is often a challenge. Typically, it's easy enough to see the final consequence of undesirable behavior (angry parents, lost customers); it's often much more difficult to establish the root cause.

More significantly, there will always come a point where someone needs to make a value judgment as to whether a particular act was acceptable or not within a particular context. This judgment may occur far in advance of the actual act (as, for example, prohibitions that are embedded in program code), or it may take place immediately after the event (as when someone reports a violation). It may in some cases even be made long after the fact, when someone notices a statistical pattern or analyzes a set of user complaints.

Fortunately, many of the more serious abuses tend to be consistent behavior patterns on the part of individuals. These behaviors tend to be a reflection of the underlying value system of the player, and that is not something that changes quickly. Bruce Schneier, security consultant and author of *Applied Cryptography*, once said this about online games: "It's not important to detect every cheat. It's important to detect every cheater." Thus, it is in many cases possible to get a history of significant actions and judgments associated with a particular individual, and use that information in making future judgments.

The two primary means of data collection will be:

➤ Reports by automated agents within the system

➤ Reports by witnesses within the game

Unfortunately, neither of these sources of information is reliable, but there is hope because they are unreliable in different ways and can be corroborated in order to gain a more accurate picture. In particular, witnesses can be biased or untrustworthy but are really good at interpreting what they see in terms of values. Automated agents are all too easily misled (mistaking legitimate behavior for impermissible behavior, for example) but are incapable of dissembling or shading the truth.

Verification

Simply detecting the presence of an undesirable behavior is often not sufficient to take corrective action, especially if the corrective action has a large potential negative impact or cost. A trust value needs to be assigned to the detection report and supporting or refuting evidence gathered.

For simple cases, where the cost of corrective action is low, the reports can be collected by an automated system and the corrective action taken automatically. An example is profanity filtering; there is no need to report to a human customer representative each time someone uses an impermissible word or phrase.

For more complex cases, especially where the players in question have a considerable stake, a trusted human may be required to intervene. It is likely that there will be several "tiers" of trust, where there will be a large outer layer of "slightly trusted" individuals and an inner core of "highly trusted" individuals.

For extremely sensitive cases, there may be a "commit/no-commit" protocol that requires multiple trusted representatives to be involved, so that no single individual (either inside or outside the company) can gain great advantage by manipulating the system.

When combining witness testimony with data gathered by automated agents, care must be taken to ensure that the proper context of the event is maintained. A sentence taken in isolation can easily be misinterpreted. The customer service (CS) user interface should be designed so that arbiters can easily access and comprehend the relevant details of an incident without wasting too much time searching through log files.

Corrective Action and Remedies

This section contains a number of ideas for corrective action.

Make It Impossible

The most obvious way to deal with undesirable behavior is to modify the game rules so that the behavior is simply impossible.

This strategy works well if the distinction between permissible and impermissible behavior is easily discriminated by an algorithm. Care should be taken, however, to understand the long-term side effects of a prohibition.

Disincentivization

If there is no way to prohibit the behavior outright, then it may be possible to make it either unprofitable or unenjoyable.

This can be done by associating a cost with the action (which would be low enough not to deter legitimate instances of the behavior), by removing the rewards gained, or by providing an alternate, easier way to achieve the same rewards.

This particular strategy only works, however, if the incentives are amenable to manipulation. In particular, games tend to have lots of overlapping incentive structures, and it is not always possible to remove an incentive without destroying the game.

Deterrence

This is the threat of punishment against players who engage in proscribed behavior. This "punishment" action can be taken against the account holder (such as "banning" or canceling the account), or it can be taken against the avatar (removal of game capabilities).

One special type of punishment that has been used in some MUDs is public humiliation—turning the character into a "toad," public floggings of the avatar, and so on. These types of "virtual body punishments" are only effective if the player has an emotional investment in his or her character. There is even a danger that players will seek out such extreme punishments for the thrill of causing a bizarre spectacle.

Social Ostracism

This technique attempts to deter violators by making their actions known to the community and encouraging them to shun the violators. This approach is quite limited, for several reasons. First, if the rule being violated is an unpopular one, the community might sympathize with the transgressor. Also, there is a possibility that the transgressor may actively seek notoriety. ("There's no such thing as bad publicity!") This type of strategy is most effective in enforcing the emergent, unwritten code of behavior, rather than the explicit and formal one.

Subjective State

One concept that has been used a number of times is the idea of "subjective state." In this strategy, it is impossible for players to monopolize resources or spoil another player's experience because each player has his or her own independent experience. A classic example is the idea of the "subjective dungeon"—when a party of adventurers enters a dungeon to explore, a personal copy of the dungeon is created just for them, so that no other players can affect or spoil the experience for them. A subtler example is the "subjective quest" system used in *Dark Age of Camelot*. In this system, a quest is given to a specific character, and only that character can gain the benefits of that particular quest (although other characters may have their own quests).

Subjective state is a great strategy; however, it has one drawback—it undermines the sense that the player is participating in a shared world. Competing with other players for resources, causing events to happen that affect the experience of other players, creating complex interactions between factions; all of these are part of the fun. Thus, the "subjective" state strategy needs to be used in moderation, balanced with a global "objective" state that all players can share.

Vigilantism

The idea behind this method is to give into the hands of the players themselves the ability to take corrective action against abusers—to create a kind of "checks and balances" so that the outlaws are deterred in their efforts by the actions of other players.

There are two forms of this: defensive and offensive. Defensive vigilantism allows players to assist other players in defending against undesirable behavior but does not allow players to take retribution against miscreants, which offensive vigilantism does.

The advantage of this technique is that it creates a whole new dimension to the game, which can be quite enjoyable. The disadvantage, however, is that the same powers that can be used against abusers can also be used against innocent players. (Remember that the reason for giving the players this power in the first place is that we can't always tell the difference.) In particular, the difference between a vigilante and an outlaw is often just a matter of how they select targets.

Vigilantism is most effective when there is an easy way to keep the vigilantes accountable.

Assimilation

If you can't beat 'em, join 'em! With assimilation, we attempt to turn a weakness into a strength by incorporating the undesirable behavior into the game itself. The primary challenge is channeling the behavior so that it occurs primarily in the times and places that are appropriate to the design. For example, we might notice that a number of players like to ambush and rob other players; we could then encourage those players to take up residence in New York Central Park and become muggers, perhaps by discretely letting it be known that the police presence in that area is especially thin, and that a mugger could make a good living there. In this way, we create a "place of danger" that is part of the game.

Encouraging Desirable Behavior

It is not enough to discourage undesirable behavior—we would also like to reward players for exceptionally desirable actions. Here are some examples of behaviors we would like to reward:

> ➤ Politeness and diplomacy

> ➤ Competence and knowledge

> ➤ Drama

> ➤ Heroism

> ➤ Role-playing

One interesting approach to creating an online community is the notion of a "web of trust," which is an automated system that tracks trust relationships between individuals (see `www.advogato.org` for a robust example). By allowing players and system administrators to assign a level of trust to their relationships (and allowing that trust to be repudiated as a deterrent to bad behavior), not only can abusive or trusted individuals be profiled and identified by the number and strength of such linkages, but also the system offers a holistic deterrent to abusive behavior. In other words, part of the game becomes "about" gaining trust. The social discourse of a game based on trust relationships would most likely revolve around ethics and trust.

Of course, this "web" would be part of the game and conceptualized in game terms. Mapping the concepts of the trust web onto the game milieu is a challenge for the designer.

Chapter 20

The Lighter Side of Meridian 59's *History*

by **Damion Schubert**, Former Designer of *M59*

AUTHOR NOTE

We wanted to include this history for a couple reasons. First and foremost, *Meridian 59 (M59)* was the first of the "modern era" persistent world (PW) games, and we thought it important that the industry learn a bit about its history. There are still "professionals" running around who think *Ultima Online (UO)* was the first PW ever done. Even *M59* wasn't the very first, but it did take Internet PWs to a whole new level.

Second, we tried to buy the game when we were with Engage. We were actually given first shot; Archetype called us before it called 3DO. We knew this was the engine that would let us get one of our *Dungeons & Dragons (D&D)* games online fast. We will always be fiercely angry that the person responsible for calling back Archetype from our parent company (Interplay) made it a low priority, even though we had decided to make an initial offer. By the time that person got around to it, 3DO had already made an offer for the entire company. Another opportunity missed....

And last of all, we wanted to include this article because it is simultaneously funny and instructive. You can learn a lot about online gaming just by reading it.

This is the lighter, more amusing side of *M59*'s history. One might read this and assume that we were troubled, or screwed up, or clueless. I suppose, to some degree, that this is true, but for the most part, this was the golden age of MMP games; everyone was feeling their way through the dark and trying to figure out every aspect of the business, from technology to design to management to marketing to CS and QA. Answers that seem obvious now were still waiting to be discovered. I do know that the team that worked on *M59* was, while I was there, the most passionate and hardworking team that I knew of.

Prologue

M59 benefited mostly from being in the right place at the right time. It had most of its network code done, in order to be a Bulletin Board System (BBS) door game, at the same time that the ability to use the Internet escaped the college campuses and entered the homes of thousands of Americans. As a result, we were able to get to market very, very quickly. Perhaps too quickly, as we never achieved nearly the success that *UO* recognized.

Possibly the most interesting thing about reading this timeline is that many of the odd problems, scenarios, and conflicts that are now thought of as being unique to *UO* and *EverQuest* (*EQ*) have been around for a very long time. Now that I've worked with former members of Simutronics (*Dragon Realms, Gemstone*) and Kesmai (*Legends of Kesmai, Air Warrior*), I know that these problems are somewhat endemic to the industry. Perhaps realizing this, we can think of better global solutions instead of band-aids.

Getting *M59* to ship and supporting it selflessly for two years in the role of lead designer is probably the greatest and most satisfying achievement of my life. It also gave me the majority of the knowledge, experience, and maturity that I brought to take on leadership of Origin's *Ultima* project. And while I may not agree with every decision that management ever made (a common enough event in any industry and company), I do feel enormously thankful to the 3DO company for taking the risk to buy a fledgling company and invest so much into making it happen.

As for the game, I do not lament *Meridian*'s death but praise its life. *Meridian* had a great ride for something that started in a garage and had the muscle of EA, Sony, and Microsoft waiting to crush it like a grape.

The Timeline

➤ Zaphod and Zandramas write the core of the game systems at home. They form a company with a pair of brothers (one calls himself *Meridian*) to build a graphical MUD.

➤ A friend and former player on a MUD I helped to run, Raph Koster, turns down a job at Archetype to go do something at Origin and recommends me to *Meridian-the-designer*. I send him 20 pages of ideas, most of which I now recognize as complete and total crack. I get the job.

➤ Archetype is a virtual company. I have never met any of these people before, in person. I have only interviewed with one person over the telephone. Everything is surreal and dreamy. I live in total terror that maybe this is all a joke and I will be on the curb come rent time. Miraculously, a paycheck actually appears in my mailbox at the beginning of the month.

➤ I spend many, many, many hours downloading the latest builds of the game over a 14.4 modem. I discover the hard, grueling, stay-up-all-night way that the *Meridian* editor will only compile rooms that have walls at 90-degree angles. Our lead programmer's response is, "Hmmm, that's odd."

➤ I convince the team to hire my brother, Mocker. He proves to be a much better world-builder than I am.

➤ The company starts arguing about the name of the game. One member of the team passionately believes that the game should be called *TOS*, short for *The Other Side*. Attempting to placate him, I say, "Don't like the name for the game, but hey, wouldn't that make a great city name?" The city of Tos would be our first city, and always our most popular one.

➤ We settle on the name "*Meridian*" for the game that we are working on, based primarily on two reasons: (1) we're sick of arguing about it, and (2) everything else we came up with was already taken or trademarked.

➤ The name "*Meridian*" turns out to be trademarked—it is the name of a printer driver somewhere. Rather than fight that battle, we change the name to "*Meridian 59*," figuring we'd write some background story that would explain what "59" meant later.

➤ *M59* hits Alpha. It can hold a scant 35 people. It has seven rooms, two spells, no skills, three monsters (all giant insects), one quest, and no form of PK control whatsoever. The newbie spawn point is a sea of bodies. The game is so full that we have to (randomly and without warning) kick people off the server to debug our own game.

➤ Trying to get investors into the game, we want to show off all of our 1337 art. The problem is, all of our customers are playing men, and our women look much better. I somehow get volunteered to have a female moniker in-game. Mostly through laziness, I never bother to change it. Oddly enough (and thankfully), never as an immortal was I hit on, except by women.

➤ In a time when we are desperately trying to impress investors, the original *NeverWinter Nights* (*NWN*) closes down. Without warning, we are flooded with MMPRPG-starved fans, and they all want every single *NWN* feature.

➤ One of my co-designers chooses a bad time to bug me. I haven't slept in 36 hours, and I'm acting as the combination QA/CS department for our new Alpha, frantically taking calls and bug reports from the fans when the designer sends me a completely random, out-of-the-blue idea. I send him an extremely angry, confrontational /tell laced with profanity, press ENTER—and then realize I have sent a /shout, not a /tell. The entire game goes silent. I quickly log off and get some sleep.

➤ Working remotely, we realize we haven't heard from one of our contract artists in about a month, much less gotten any art from him. Given that he lives in Arizona, there is no way to check up on him. He later returns, mentioning mostly that he needed a "break."

➤ Broke, we hire a guy to build levels for free, some guy named Q. He turns out to be worth a hundred times that much—well, more, anyway.

➤ Running on fumes, we convince 3DO to buy us. They may still hate us for that. My salary was tripled overnight—and I was still grossly underpaid.

➤ I meet my co-workers in person for the first time. We are all a lot less intimidating in person.

➤ 3DO doesn't have art resources to spare, so we hire an outside art house to replace some of our art for us. For some reason, this house seemed to be under the impression that we were a *Sierra*-like game. As a result, a small segment of our art looked like it belonged in a Hanna Barbara cartoon.

➤ In what may be the single worst ad in gaming history, we tell *PCGamer* readers that *M59* is "the single most fun thing you can do with hundreds of other people without wearing anything made of latex."

➤ One of our new guardians chooses the very original name "Gandalf." When told by his co-workers that they were all going to start a tradition of having names that start with "Z," he sullenly changes his name to "Zgandalf."

➤ Setting a time-honored precedent for the genre, we ship off our gold master to duplication while still fixing server-side bugs.

➤ 3DO ships *M59* on September 27, 1996. Our marketing guy tells us that he spent lots of marketing cash to get the product on the endcaps of every CompUSA in the country. We pile into Q's Mustang to go and see our product on the shelves for the first time. It is not on the endcap. It is hidden behind a pole.

➤ At launch, we have something like 20 different monster models, a full third of which are giant insects of some form.

➤ Within one day of being live, *Meridian* has its first virtual prostitute, making that *Meridian's* oldest profession.

➤ I smite my first player, an annoying person named "Sexy" who emoted "wraps her legs around you" and similar phrases as I was attempting to tell her (in front of an audience) that she needed to stop killing newbies and doing odd things with their corpses.

➤ We ban a guild for duping, as we finally catch on that the 10 bucks a jerk gives you is *not* worth as much as the 10 bucks a peaceful player gives you. The guild en masse writes to *PCGamer.com*, which promptly reports of our vindictive, evil CS department on the front page. Our policy on not commenting on account cancellation prevents us from responding.

➤ Our first major hack program goes into existence. I forget the name of it (*Meridian Extreme?*). Neatest feature—someone discovered that there was no room check on shopkeepers, so you could sell your loot to the shopkeeper from anywhere in the room.

➤ www.3dosucks.com goes live. Just as good cannot exist without evil and *UO* cannot exist without Lum; we feel our existence is justified. It's far better than if they didn't care enough to hate us.

➤ *Meridian Extreme* is improved. Its interface is now much, much better than that of the game.

➤ Perhaps trying to compete with ourselves for worst ad ever for a computer game, we tell readers, "The next time someone tells you to get a life, tell them you've already got one. A virtual one. *M59.*"

➤ *Meridian* wins GameCenter's award for RPG of the Year, beating out *Daggerfall.*

➤ In a round of layoffs, I am forced to lay off my own brother. We rehire him a month later.

➤ Starting another fine tradition of MMPRPGs, in a desperate attempt at self-defense, someone releases a version of *Meridian Extreme* that will log in your character, suicide your character, and log out. Our guardians actually take great pleasure at fielding calls from cheaters begging to have their accounts reinstated.

➤ The program *EZ Macro* convinces me that I hate use-based systems.

➤ We perform our first major "nerf." *M59* has a political system that gives bonuses to you based on what faction you are in and how powerful it is. The duke is too powerful, and so we (accidentally) overcompensate by making the princess too powerful. However, the term "nerf" has not been popularized by *UO* and *EQ* yet, so instead I get an angry email complaining that we "castrated the duke." I often wonder what the mail would have read if we had nerfed the princess.

➤ We ship the *Vale of Sorrows* expansion pack, after a long discussion with marketing about whether or not that is an appropriate name for a product released two weeks after major layoffs. Our new producer, a guy named Rich Vogel, defends the development team's choice in names and wins.

➤ A dupe bug renders money useless overnight. In an interesting economic development, the players almost immediately fall upon dark angel feathers (DAFs) as a replacement currency until things return to normal. DAFs are valuable because they are rarely dropped yet stackable items that are required to cast player-killing spells. PKers have an interest in getting them, and non-PKers have an interest in keeping them out of PKers' hands.

➤ We change the palette of all the art in the game. The only art excluded is some of the very old textures used for the forests way back in Beta. These rooms still exist, and the textures that were formerly green are now orange, red, and yellow.

Mischievous guides enjoy teleporting players to these old zones and telling them that it was a new area we were working on that was half-done, the land of the burning trees. We never successfully combat these rumors.

➤ One of our guardians parts ways with the company, muscled out for giving favors to his favorite customers. He is so popular that dozens of people write messages on boards that cover hot tech stock tips saying that 3DO is going down because it can't keep its best CS people. Our stock actually dips that day.

➤ The infamous GuideWozzle episode: A player volunteer guide goes crazy. He goes to the ghost room and uses a bug to spawn several ghosts (by far the hardest monsters in the game). He then marches down the who list, teleporting people in the room one at a time. They have enough time to say "WTF" before being cut down like weeds to a weed-whacker. I teleport into a room full of hundreds of corpses. I ban GuideWozzle. The last two people teleported into the room (who were saved by my intervention) immediately begin looting the corpses of all the other players.

➤ Starting a time-honored tradition in MMPRPGs, a guardian is banned for fraternizing with the counselors.

➤ Not to be outdone by 3dosucks, a new web site goes live, detailing how Q will give personal favors in the game for oral gratification. This is accompanied by doctored images of his in-game character. The entire team is quite amused, except for Q.

➤ In another round of layoffs, I am forced to lay off my own brother. We rehire him two months later.

➤ We release *Revelations*, the second expansion for *M59*. It is a sizeable tropical island that is hard to get to and full of sentient yet primitive races; it sets a precedent for the genre.

➤ Setting a time-honored precedent for the genre, the advertising for the *Revelations* product has a scantily clad female that literally has nothing to do with the game. Given our previous advertising, we are delighted by this.

➤ The stupidest thing the design team ever did: In order to get to the island, you needed to cast "dispel illusion" to open an illusionary wall and enter the caves that led to the island of Ko'catan. Unfortunately, the only place to get the reagents for dispel illusion at launch was on the island. We quickly add a quest that teleports users to a new room that contains a new monster (hued version of an old monster) that drops the reagents as loot. The fans wildly applaud the brilliance and convoluted nature of the first opening of the passage to Ko'catan—except for a couple of players who said, "Funny, I tried doing exactly that quest yesterday, and nothing happened."

➤ The entirety of server 109 gets bored and raids server 108. They don't player-kill. Instead, they all choose names starting with clone, as in "clone1," "clone2," "clone3," "clone4," and so on. They all use the same character model and they only speak in binary. One person, the master, does all the talking for the group. Server 108 freaks the hell out. They blame us. We try to explain that we aren't that smart.

➤ In an admirable example of the community defending itself, a player on server 108 starts a new character, calls it "clone16," and joins the game. Immediately, the other clones include him in the clone's in-game chat channel and start talking normally, saying things like, "Ha ha ha! I can't believe they R so freakd!" He quietly listens. The next day, he posts a log on the message board complete with a listing of which clone is which 109 player and which clone guy is cheating on which clone woman with which other clone woman.

➤ I drop a rare artifact on the ground by accident. A nearby thief snags the item and runs off with it. When I found out what happened, I delete his arm. The team is stunned that this is even possible.

➤ In a cunning grasp of the economics of the Internet (and over the development team's strong objections), the pricing model of *M59* is changed from $10 a month to $2.49 a day but never more than $10 a week or $30 a month. This effectively tripled the price of the service, with the added benefit that it confused the people it didn't insult. Hundreds of accounts are cancelled. Tragically, the move proved to be profitable in the short term because two-thirds of the population did not cancel their accounts. However, the damage to the community was very, very deep, and *Meridian* never fully recovered.

➤ I leave the *Meridian* design team to work on 3DO's new project, *Might and Magic Online*.

➤ *UO* goes live. Surprisingly, few people leave, partially because the gameplay is so different, but largely also due to the fact that most people who were going to leave already did so in the price change defection.

➤ 3DO cancels *Might and Magic Online*, citing the "failure" of *UO*. (Note: Origin kept its numbers close to its vest for quite some time.)

➤ The *Renaissance* update is released. I had little to do with this update, other than helping with initial designs. It introduced the hunters and the necromancers. The necromancers got neat buffs but had to feed their hunger by player-killing. The hunters got neat buffs but had to kill necromancers. Players promptly proceeded to power-game the system (using mules for necromancer fuel, thus allowing them to get the buffs without cost). They then complained that we never added cool PvP scenarios for elder players.

➤ I do a summary of all the magazine and web reviews that *UO* and *M59* got. *M59* almost always had the better review.

➤ I quit my job to take a position of greater responsibility at Origin. Before I quit, I implemented what is in my opinion the coolest Easter egg ever—a room full of statues that pay tribute to the original design and support staff of *M59*.

➤ At my new place of employment, a key member of the *UO* design team tells me that they were, at the time, "terrified" of *Meridian's* impending launch.

➤ I log into the *EQ* chat rooms with my *M59* name while waiting for the servers to open for phase 4 Beta. Humorously, enough people recognize me and start chatting *Meridian* old times that the volunteer in the room has trouble answering *EQ* questions.

➤ The necromancers had a safety valve built in. They had an Achilles' heel—the lich queen—who, if killed, would kill all the necromancers and therefore reset the scenario (removing the buffs). Since the necromancers and the hunters were conspiring to power-game the buffs, this never happened. Finally, one player got bored. He killed the lich, with one stroke killing 50+ necromancers. It was possibly the single most impressive player-killing action in MUD history. Fifty death messages in a row, interspersed with occasional "LOLs" and "WTFs," makes for highly amusing reading. It had been so long since the lich had died that the necromancers actually argued that the lich killer was a grief player.

➤ Noted *Meridian* fanatic and self-admitted troublemaker convinces her company, World Fusion, to begin work on an MMP game called *Atriarch*.

➤ A player, Ixit, achieves immortality in my mind by performing a feat of spectacular power-gaming—something that I thought was mathematically impossible—becoming a master in every spell and skill school in the game. (Most players are masters of only three instead of seven.) When he tells me how he did it (a process of meticulous ping-ponging of skills in the use-based system that literally took hours a day for months), I say to myself, "Wow, yeah, I guess that would work."

➤ *EQ* goes live. Given that the gameplay is similar but much, much deeper, it devastates the *Meridian* community. The diehards cling to the notion that *EQ* sux and *M59* will rule forever, but numbers dwindle quickly.

➤ While strolling through *EQ* with my *Meridian* name, someone gives me free healing, SoW, and buffs because "Your chat system didn't suck like this one does."

➤ *Meridian* enters the new millennium with no 3D graphics card support and no hope of ever getting it.

➤ *M59* is #91 in GameSpot UK's most important games of the millennium.

➤ A noted player, Dementia, is banned from *M59*. He attempts to get someone in trouble by doctoring the logs of a chat session and sending them to a GM. Little does he know that the other player was that GM's mortal character.

➤ I log into *Meridian* for the first time in a year. "Oh my dear God," I think to myself, "we never put mouselook in this stupid game."

➤ A key member of the *AC* design team tells me that he was "terrified" of the speed that we could make *Meridian* happen.

➤ Horizon's core members, Dave Allen and James Jones, mention in passing that they were both *M59* addicts, and that it came up frequently during their design sessions.

➤ A general amnesty is declared for all players banned from *M59*. The exceptions are "those banned for credit card fraud, those banned for racist and sexist activities, and Dementia."

➤ A key member of the *EQ* design team tells me that he was "very worried" about competing against *Meridian*.

➤ I tell a former member of the *Underlight* team that the *M59* team was "terrified" about their impending launch.

➤ 3DO announces that *Meridian* will be brought down on August 31, 2000.

➤ Rob Ellis and Brian Green, two former 3DO employees and workers on *Meridian 59*, cut a deal with 3DO in 2002 to revive the game under a new company, Near Death Studios (`http://www.neardeathstudios.com/NDS-Team.shtml`).

Part V

Appendices and Glossary

Appendix A

Executive Considerations Checklist

1. Type of Game

   a. Classic ☐

   b. Hybrid ☐

   c. Persistent World ☐

2. Style

   a. 3D First-/Third-Person ☐

   b. Isolinear, Top-Down ☐

   c. Other: _____ ☐

3. Primary Mode

   a. Real-Time Strategy ☐

   b. First-Person Shooter ☐

   c. Virtual World ☐

   d. Card/Board Game ☐

4. Genre

   a. Fantasy ☐

   b. Science-Fiction ☐

   c. Other: _____ ☐

5. Primary Market

    a. Mass ☐

    b. Moderate or Casual ☐

    c. Hard-Core ☐

6. Competitive Analysis

    a. Current Competitors ☐

    b. Competitors in Development or Testing ☐

7. Development Timeline

    a. Design ☐

    b. Development ☐

    c. Alpha Testing ☐

    d. Beta Testing ☐

    e. Anticipated Launch Date ☐

8. Cost of Entry

    a. Property Licensing and Royalty Costs ☐

    b. Development Budget ☐

    c. Marketing Budget ☐

    d. Launch Budget ☐

    e. Bandwidth Needs ☐

        i. How Many Bits/Bytes per User/Minute? ☐

        ii. Cost per MB of Access ☐

    f. Annual Maintenance Budget ☐

g. Live Team Costs ☐

h. Hardware and Bandwidth Costs ☐

i. Total Estimated Cost, Development
Through First Year Post-launch ☐

9. Revenue Projections

a. Estimated Retail Sales ☐

b. Expansion Pack Sales ☐

c. Subscription Fees ☐

10. Risk/Reward Analysis

a. Development and Launch Costs Versus
Customer Market Niche of the Product ☐

b. Team Experience Versus
Nearest Competition ☐

c. Licensed Versus Original Product ☐

d. Expected Return on Investment ☐

i. Amortization Time of Development
and Launch Costs ☐

ii. Profit Margin, Years 1–5 ☐

11. Permission to Proceed

a. Perform the Preliminary Design:
Go or No-Go ☐

b. Design Document Review:
Go (Continue to Final Design) or No-Go
(Cancel the Project) ☐

Bios of Interviewees

Jeffrey Anderson

Company: Turbine Entertainment Software

Current title: President and CEO

Favorite game that you've worked on: *Asheron's Call: Dark Majesty*

Current favorite game to play: *Asheron's Call*

Favorite game of all time: *Warcraft*

Prior to joining Turbine, Mr. Anderson was the executive in charge of production for Origin Systems Inc. (a subsidiary of EA). At Origin, Mr. Anderson managed the *Ultima Online (UO)* franchise, where he was directly responsible for expanding its online business. In particular, he produced EA's first-ever MMP expansion pack and focused on building the next generation of 3D online worlds. Prior to that, Mr. Anderson was executive director for the Consumer Products division of Viacom, Inc. In that role, he directly managed Paramount Pictures' worldwide interactive licensing, merchandising, and business development. Before Viacom, he was vice president of operations at Mission Studios Corporation, a game developer. Mr. Anderson also practiced law at the firm of Holleb & Coff in Chicago, Illinois, where he concentrated in both intellectual property and corporate litigation. He graduated summa cum laude from the University of Illinois (B.A., 1989) and served on the Law Review at the University of Chicago Law School (J.D., 1992).

Richard A. Garriott

Company: NCSoft

Current title: Producer

Current project: *Tabula Rasa* (working title)

Favorite game that you've worked on: *Ultima*

Current favorite game to play: *Diablo II*

Favorite game of all time: *MYST*

Mr. Garriott was the creator of the *Ultima* series; he was also a co-founder of Origin Systems. Here's his own take on things:

"I published my first game, *Akalabeth* (the *Ultima* prequel), in 1980 and then began work on the *Ultima* series. My brother Robert and I founded Origin in 1983 with some friends and family. Through the end of the century, my teams and I created *Ultimas 1–9*, *UO*, three *Worlds of Ultima* games, a handful of mission disks, and a few other spin-off games. At my new company, NCSoft, we now operate the world's number-one online game with more than four million subscribers, and we hope to create grand new worlds for players to explore and adventure within!"

Gaute Godager

Company: Funcom

Current title: Game Director

Current project: *Anarchy Online*

Favorite game that you've worked on: *Anarchy Online*

Current favorite game(s) to play: *Medal of Honor, Allied Assault* (Too hard for me!)

Favorite game(s) of all time: *Lords of Midnight, Elite,* and *EverQuest*

In Mr. Godager's own words:

"I was born July 23, 1970. I had an uneventful and happy childhood close to Oslo, Norway. I started playing and programming on my brother's C64 in 1982, the same year I read *Lord of the Rings*. My fate was sealed.

"Fast forward to 1989: I was dead-bored studying law at the University of Oslo. I started doing my own computer role-playing game on the Amiga called *Destinies*. (I made the graphics and music and designed and programmed it myself. It was total crap, except for the design.) I thought I was almost finished when the Amiga died in 1992. Frustrated, I started studying psychology and founded Funcom with four others in the spring of 1993.

"I've had the following titles/positions at Funcom during the years:

➤ System Programmer, Producer *Håkon the Viking* (Namco US, canned 1993)

➤ Head of Design Department, Producer *Pocahontas* (Disney 1993–1994)

➤ Creative Director, Vice President Product Development, Chairman of the Board

➤ Funcom Oslo Board (these last three titles were my foray into management from 1994–1997)

➤ Designer *Molekult*, 1997

➤ Designer *AO* 1996/7–2001

➤ Game Director *AO* 2001 (I'm a real Funcom potato; I can be mashed into anything!)

"During the last few years (1996–2002), I've also almost completed (eh, minus a class or two) my education as a clinical psychologist. Previously, I've dabbled in politics and have worked as a 'reporter/editor' on two pro-bono magazines.

"I was married September 2001, and my wife is expecting our first child in July 2002. I love playing pen-and-paper role-playing games, twiddling with my computer, watching movies, reading books, and eating Indian food."

Scott Hawkins

Company: Sega of America and Sneaky Rabbit Studios

Current title: Consultant/Executive Producer for Sega and Co-Founder and Vice President of Production at Sneaky Rabbit Studios

Current project: *SEGA Swirl 2* and several unannounced projects

Favorite game that you've worked on: *SEGA Swirl DC* or *Quake III Arena DC*

Current favorite game to play: *Super Monkey Ball* for GameCube

Favorite game of all time: *Doom II*

In Mr. Hawkins' own words:

"While getting my degree in computer science at the University of California at Santa Barbara, I quickly became addicted to network games like *Doom, Descent, Doom II,* and any other game that would work over our homemade 10 Base-T Ethernet network. After getting my degree (and having worked at Panasonic for two years as a research programmer), I followed my dreams and got my foot in the door at Sega through the Test department. After getting an opportunity to show I could program by writing a program to make it easier to burn EEPROMs for Genesis, Pico, Game

Gear, and 32X, several doors opened up for me. I took an opportunity as an assistant producer in Sega's new PC group. My passion and dedication showed (and paid off) as I got to work on over 50 PC and console titles in five and a half years, including games like *Sonic* and *Knuckles Collection*, *Virtua Fighter PC, Quake III Arena* for Dreamcast, *SEGA Smash Pack* (PC and Dreamcast versions), and *SEGA Swirl*.

"Although we had already been working on networkable games for a while on our Sega PC titles, networkable games on consoles were an unexplored territory. Since Sega was on the cutting edge of networkable console games, I was able to help contribute to several of the first online console games in history. *SEGA Swirl*—which started out as a PC puzzle game that I programmed on my laptop—became the first modem-playable Dreamcast game in the US. Another one of my projects, *Quake III Arena* for Dreamcast, is the world's first broadband-capable console game.

"After five and a half years at Sega, I took an opportunity to help co-found some new development studios, including CodeFire in December 2000 and Sneaky Rabbit Studios in January 2002. During my time at both of these companies, we have been continuing to push online console games to a new level."

Thomas Howalt

Company: Funcom Oslo AS

Current title: Project Manager

Current project: *Anarchy Online*

Favorite game(s) that you've worked on: *Anarchy Online, Skipper & Skeeto 6, and The Mystery of the Talking Sundial*

Current favorite game(s) to play: *Anarchy Online, SimGolf, Medal of Honor, RTCW, Civ3, Commandos 2, Fifa 2002, Capitalism 2, The Sims*

Favorite game(s) of all time: *Pong, Elite, Duke Nukem3d, Zelda64, Donkey Kong64, Deus Ex, Thief 2, System Shock 1&2, Ultima Underworld 1&2, SimCity*

A native of Europe, Mr. Howalt comes to gaming after a long and successful career in the theater as both an actor and a director. Using the organizational skills he learned managing theater groups, he began producing children's games in the late 1990s and moved to Funcom in 2001 as a project manager. Some of the highlights of his career include the following:

➤ Background in theatre: directing, acting, writing, designing sets, and producing. More than 40 professional productions as director

➤ General manager for three years of a public music, theatre, and cultural center in Copenhagen

➤ Worked with CD-ROM games for children and families for three years (producing, designing, writing, voice-directing, and so on)

➤ Began working on *Midgard* for Funcom in April 2001 as project manager

➤ Project manager on *AO* since late September 2001

When Mr. Howalt isn't working, he spends time with his wife and two children, plays computer games, cooks, reads, writes, takes time with friends, sees theatre and movies, and travels. He also plays and listens to music, fixes his old apartment, wall-climbs, bicycles, swims, and hikes.

Daniel "Savant" Manachi

(Savant@themis-group.com)

Company: The Themis Group

Current title: Community Relations Specialist

Current project: *Jumpgate*

Favorite game that you've worked on: *Ultimate Baseball Online*

Current favorite game to play: *Etherlords*

Favorite game of all time: *Gemstone III*

Mr. Manachi has over a decade of experience in gaming. Most recently, he was the producer and project manager of the soon-to-be released MMP games *Fallen Age*, *Battlesaurs*, and *Ultimate Baseball Online (UBO)* for Netamin Communications Corp. Formerly a senior writer/columnist for the popular online gaming commentary web site "Lum, The Mad," Mr. Manachi also served as the community relations manager for Netamin's games, providing players with an honest and widely appreciated voice. Prior to his work with Netamin, Mr. Manachi was a product manager of *Camelot Adventures* and a designer on the game *Unwritten Legends*, both multiplayer online games. He was also a volunteer sentinel for *AC*. Currently, Daniel is with The Themis Group, an MMOG consulting and full-service solution company, working on *AO* and *Jumpgate*.

Kathy Schoback

Company: Sega of America

Current title: Director of External Development and Publishing

Current project: Secret!

Current favorite game to play: *Rez PS2* (Sega)

Favorite game of all time: *Pitfall* for Atari 2600

Ms. Schoback got her industry start as a trainer in Sega's call center during the "good old days" of Genesis. She then suffered in sales during the "bad old days" of Saturn, and after a refreshing stint working on the Game Designer's Conference, returned to Sega for more punishment in third-party relations for Dreamcast. As Sega's director of external development and publishing, Ms. Schoback thoroughly enjoys overseeing first-party console relations, outbound property licensing, product acquisitions, and not worrying about hardware sales.

Damion Schubert

Company: Ninjaneering

Current title: Creative Director/CEO

Current project: *Hollyworld*

Favorite game that you've worked on: *Meridian 59*

Current favorite game to play: *Civilization 3*

Favorite game of all time: *Civilization*

Mr. Schubert has been working with MUDs for more than 10 years, and he has been working professionally in the MMP game space for six years. At 3DO, he was the lead designer of *M59* when it shipped, and he also shipped three expansions to *M59*. He served an almost unmentionably short role on the *UO* live team before being named lead designer of *UO2*. Upon cancellation of that project, Damion forged his own studio, called Ninjaneering, where he is currently employed. He is reportedly up to no good.

Jack D. Smith

Company: PeopleSpace Inc.

Current title: President

Current project: *Retro Trivia Tournament*

Favorite game that you've worked on: *Mutant Pigs on Ice*

Current favorite game to play: *PipeDreams*

Favorite game of all time: *MYST*

Mr. Smith has been a trailblazer in online entertainment for over two decades. He is founder and president of PeopleSpace Inc., a leader in helping companies build and retain online communities. PeopleSpace's client list reads like a corporate who's who, including companies like Sesame Street, Playboy, Fox Sports, Microsoft, NBC, EA, AOL, and TV Guide. Mr. Smith has been involved in the online industry since its infancy, or at least since its toddler years. At General Electric, he was a key employee with GEnie, their online service (and at one time a primary force in the online industry). Many of the business models and systems now used by industry leader AOL were developed at GEnie.

In the early 1980s, Mr. Smith was one of the first to recognize the marketing and promotional potential of the online environment. As the proprietor of Writer's Ink, a digital writers' community, Smith worked with well-known writers like Tom Clancy, Michael Crichton, Clive Barker, Lawrence Block, and Anne McCaffrey, making them available to thousands of fans online. Writer's Ink included online poetry slams, a screenwriter's school, and numerous workshops.

Mr. Smith has been involved in the development of online games and has worked with industry leaders like EA, Kesmai, and Simutronics. Before *UO*, *AC*, and *EQ*, there were *Gemstone*, *Island of Kesmai*, and *Stellar Warrior*. He worked in the realm of these MMP games from 1984–1996.

Mr. Smith has consulted for AOL, Microsoft, Delphi, and other online services on issues of community and digital marketing. He was one of the early proponents of using online games and entertainment as user acquisition and retention tools. PeopleSpace was chosen by Sesame Street to develop a special game to help them celebrate their 30th anniversary and by NBC to help them when they needed games and activities for their Summer Olympics site.

The PeopleSpace offices are located in a 19th Century haunted house in Charlottesville, VA. Mr. Smith can usually be found there either designing online activities for one of his clients or playing games.

Gordon Walton

Company: Maxis

Current title: Vice President, Executive Producer

Current project: *The Sims Online*

Favorite game that you've worked on: *Ultima Online*

Current favorite game to play: *Ultima Online*

Favorite game of all time: *Ultima Online*

Mr. Walton has been authoring games and managing game development since 1977. He has a bachelor of science from Texas A & M in computer science. He has personally developed over two dozen games and managed the development of hundreds more.

Mr. Walton has spoken at every Game Developers Conference since it began, on topics ranging from game design to programming to business. He has had his own development company (twice), been development manager for Three-Sixty Pacific and Konami America, vice president of development for GameTek, senior vice president and general manager of Kesmai Studios, vice president online services for Origin Systems managing *UO,* and is currently vice president and executive producer of *The Sims Online* at Maxis. He is personally committed to building the medium of MMP games to surpass the reach and impact of standalone computer games.

The Bartle Quotient Survey Questions and Some Results

AUTHOR NOTE

These are the questions from the Bartle Quotient web survey of MUD and online game players. The players use these 30 questions to rate their preferences and motivations in online gameplay. The results are then collated into overall totals. See `www.andreasen.org/bartle/` for full details on the survey.

Also please note that this is not a scientific survey, and the results should not be taken as gospel, but as a good indication of the overall goals and motivations of online persistent world (PW) game players.

The Bartle Test

Keep in mind that the questions below should be answered in the context of how you play your character on MUDs.

1. **What's more important in a MUD to you?**

    ☐ The number of people
    ☐ The number of areas to explore

2. **What's more important to you?**

    ☐ The quality of role-playing in a MUD
    ☐ The uniqueness of the features and game mechanics

3. **When playing a video game, is it more fun to:**

    ☐ Have the highest score on the list?
    ☐ Beat your best friend one-on-one?

4. **Which do you enjoy more in MUD quests?**

    ☐ Getting involved in the storyline
    ☐ Getting the rewards at the end

5. **Are you more comfortable as a player on a MUD:**

    ☐ Talking with friends in a tavern?
    ☐ Out hunting orcs by yourself for experience?

6. **Would you rather:**

    ☐ Defeat an enemy?
    ☐ Explore a new area?

7. **On a MUD, a new area opens up. Which do you look forward to more?**

    ☐ Being the first to get the new equipment from the area
    ☐ Exploring the new area and finding out its history

8. **What's worse?**

    ☐ To be without friends
    ☐ To be without power

9. **Which would you enjoy more as a MUD player?**

    ☐ Running your own tavern
    ☐ Making your own maps of the world and then selling them

10. **Someone has PKed you. Do you want to:**

    ☐ Find out why and try to convince that person not to do it again?
    ☐ Plot your revenge?

11. **Would you rather:**

    ☐ Know where to find things?
    ☐ Know how to get things?

12. **On a MUD, would you rather be known for:**

    ☐ Knowledge?
    ☐ Power?

13. **Would you rather win:**

    ☐ A trivia contest?
    ☐ An arena battle?

14. **Which would you rather be noticed for on a MUD?**

    ☐ Your personality
    ☐ Your equipment

15. **Would you rather:**

    ☐ Convince your enemies to work for you, not against you?
    ☐ Vanquish your enemies?

16. **You're a player on a MUD about to go into an unknown dungeon. You have your choice of adding one more person to your party. Do you bring:**

    ☐ A bard who's a good friend of yours and who's great at entertaining you and your friends?
    ☐ A wizard to identify the items that you find there?

17. **On a MUD, would you rather be known as:**

    ☐ Someone who can run from any two points in the world, and really knows his/her way around?
    ☐ The person with the best, most unique equipment in the game?

18. **On a MUD, would you rather:**

    ☐ Be the most feared person in the game?
    ☐ Have a sword twice as powerful as any other in the game?

19. **On a MUD, would you rather join a clan of:**

    ☐ Assassins?
    ☐ Scholars?

20. **You meet a new player. Do you think of him/her as:**

    ☐ Potential prey?
    ☐ Someone who can appreciate your knowledge of the game?

21. **Would you rather:**

    ☐ Show someone the sharp blade of your axe?
    ☐ Hear what someone has to say?

22. **Would you rather have:**

    ☐ A spell to damage other players?
    ☐ A spell that increases the rate at which you gain experience points?

23. **You are being chased by a monster on a MUD.**
    Do you:

    ☐ Ask a friend for help in killing it?
    ☐ Hide somewhere you know the monster won't follow?

24. **Would you rather be:**

    ☐ Wealthy?
    ☐ Popular?

25. **Which would you enjoy more?**

    ☐ Getting accepted by a clan
    ☐ Winning a duel with another player

26. **Would you rather receive as a quest reward:**

    ☐ Experience points?
    ☐ A wand with three charges of a spell that lets you control other players against their will (become a charm person)?

27. **Which is more enjoyable to you?**

    ☐ Killing a big monster
    ☐ Bragging about it to your friends

28. On a MUD, would you be more prone to brag about:

 ☐ How many other players you've killed?
 ☐ Your equipment?

29. Do you tend to:

 ☐ Have items no one else does?
 ☐ Know things no one else does?

30. Would you rather:

 ☐ Become a hero faster than your friends?
 ☐ Know more secrets than your friends?

Bartle Survey Results for Five Leading Games

The tables in this appendix are the Bartle Quotient Survey results for five of the top for-pay PWs. The results were captured on March 4, 2002 at 2:28 p.m. EST.

EverQuest

There are 3,568 people who have selected *EverQuest* as one of the MUDs they're playing.

The popularity of the combinations is shown in Table C.1.

Table C.1   *EQ* Player Survey Results

Overall Totals	Combination Play	Combinations of Three
1. E 34% (1232)	1. ES 17% (621)	1. SEA 12% (439)
2. A 25% (927)	2. SE 16% (579)	2. ESA 12% (431)
3. S 24% (869)	3. EA 13% (482)	3. EAS 10% (380)
4. K 15% (540)	4. AS 10% (381)	4. ASE 6% (243)
	5. AE 8% (301)	5. AES 6% (226)
	6. KA 7% (265)	6. ESK 5% (190)
	7. AK 6% (245)	7. KAE 4% (145)
	8. SA 4% (164)	8. SEK 3% (140)
	9. KE 4% (150)	9. ASK 3% (138)
	10. EK 3% (129)	10. AKS 3% (131)
	11. SK 3% (126)	11. KAS 3% (120)
	12. KS 3% (125)	12. AKE 3% (114)

Ultima Online

There are 1,861 people who have selected *Ultima Online* as one of the MUDs they're playing.

The popularity of the combinations is shown in Table C.2.

Table C.2 *UO* Player Survey Results

Overall Totals	Combination Play	Combinations of Three
1. E 31% (585)	1. SE 15% (287)	1. SEA 11% (215)
2. K 26% (488)	2. ES 14% (276)	2. ESA 10% (197)
3. S 23% (440)	3. KA 14% (265)	3. EAS 8% (158)
4. A 18% (348)	4. EA 12% (224)	4. KAE 8% (154)
	5. AE 6% (130)	5. KAS 5% (111)
	6. AS 6% (129)	6. ASE 4% (89)
	7. KE 6% (122)	7. AES 4% (81)
	8. KS 5% (101)	8. KEA 4% (80)
	9. AK 4% (89)	9. ESK 4% (79)
	10. SK 4% (86)	10. SEK 3% (72)
	11. EK 4% (85)	11. EAK 3% (66)
	12. SA 3% (67)	12. KSE 3% (58)

Asheron's Call

There are 1,065 people who have selected *Asheron's Call* as one of the MUDs they're playing.

The popularity of the combinations is shown in Table C.3.

Table C.3 *AC* Player Survey Results

Overall Totals	Combination Play	Combinations of Three
1. E 36% (389)	1. ES 18% (192)	1. ESA 12% (135)
2. A 27% (294)	2. EA 14% (155)	2. EAS 10% (115)
3. S 18% (202)	3. SE 12% (135)	3. SEA 9% (100)
4. K 16% (180)	4. AS 10% (112)	4. ASE 7% (82)
	5. KA 9% (104)	5. KAE 5% (60)
	6. AE 8% (95)	6. AES 5% (58)
	7. AK 8% (87)	7. ESK 5% (57)
	8. KE 4% (44)	8. AKE 4% (47)
	9. EK 3% (42)	9. KAS 4% (44)
	10. SA 3% (38)	10. EAK 3% (40)
	11. KS 3% (32)	11. AKS 3% (40)
	12. SK 2% (29)	12. AEK 3% (37)

Dark Age of Camelot

There are 998 people who have selected *Dark Age of Camelot* as one of the MUDs they're playing.

The popularity of the combinations is shown in Table C.4.

Table C.4   *Dark Age of Camelot* Player Survey Results

Overall Totals	Combination Play	Combinations of Three
1. E 32% (328)	1. ES 14% (144)	1. SEA 9% (91)
2. K 25% (251)	2. KA 13% (133)	2. ESA 8% (86)
3. A 21% (210)	3. EA 12% (128)	3. EAS 8% (84)
4. S 20% (209)	4. SE 12% (126)	4. KAE 8% (81)
	5. AS 8% (87)	5. ESK 5% (58)
	6. KE 6% (68)	6. ASE 5% (53)
	7. AK 6% (66)	7. KAS 5% (52)
	8. AE 5% (57)	8. EAK 4% (44)
	9. EK 5% (56)	9. AKS 3% (36)
	10. KS 5% (50)	10. SEK 3% (35)
	11. SK 4% (44)	11. KSE 3% (34)
	12. SA 3% (39)	12. KES 3% (34)

Anarchy Online

There are 811 people who have selected *Anarchy Online* as one of the MUDs they're playing.

The popularity of the combinations is shown in Table C.5.

Table C.5   *AO* Player Survey Results

Overall Totals	Combination Play	Combinations of Three
1. E 34% (281)	1. ES 16% (136)	1. SEA 12% (104)
2. S 24% (197)	2. SE 16% (135)	2. ESA 10% (88)
3. A 24% (195)	3. EA 13% (111)	3. EAS 10% (84)
4. K 17% (138)	4. AS 9% (74)	4. ESK 5% (48)
	5. KA 8% (71)	5. AES 5% (44)
	6. AK 8% (67)	6. KAE 5% (41)
	7. AE 6% (54)	7. ASE 4% (38)
	8. KE 4% (40)	8. ASK 4% (36)
	9. EK 4% (34)	9. AKS 4% (35)
	10. SA 4% (33)	10. AKE 3% (32)
	11. SK 3% (29)	11. SEK 3% (31)
	12. KS 3% (27)	12. KAS 3% (30)

Appendix D

Hearts, Clubs, Diamonds, Spades: Players Who Suit MUDs

by **Richard Bartle** (`richard@mud.co.uk`)[1], MUSE Ltd, Colchester, Essex, United Kingdom

2002 Introduction to the Article by Dr. Bartle

People ought to think about virtual world design.

Well, yes, of course—isn't that obvious? You can't simply sit right down and program, as with regular computer games; to do the job properly, you need a 600-page design document that took a team of people four months to write. How are the designers going to produce one of those if they don't think about it?

Well, by thinking about virtual worlds as if they were computer games. They are not. They are places. Furthermore, they are places inhabited by real, live people.

Traditional computer game design concentrates primarily on technical and gameplay issues; rarely are the people who are going to play the game taken into account. Yes, there are exceptions: Some games aim at a particular demographic (other than the default—computer game designers); some games are tailored to change the gaming experience the more expert a player becomes. Basically, though, the aim is to persuade people to buy the game. What happens after they've bought it isn't really important.

---

1. This paper is an April 1996 extension of an earlier article, "Who Plays MUDs" (Bartle, 1990a). As a result of this, and of the fact that I am not a trained psychologist, do not expect a conventionally rigorous approach to the subject matter.

With virtual worlds, it's not so simple. Different types of people will play the game; indeed, for a game to be healthy and keep on growing, a mix of playing styles is essential. They are ongoing products. They are only virtual WORLDS because of interactions between disparate players. If everyone is there for the same experience, it's not a world; it's a game or a chat-line or something else.

Programmers make the environment; people make it a world.

Nowadays, designers of virtual worlds routinely look at the kinds of players they expect (or hope) to attract and what those players will do. Will they spend most of their time battling monsters? Perhaps they'll manufacture goods and form trade networks to sell them? Maybe they simply like exploring, experiencing the sheer wonder of the world, seeking for it to amaze them at every turn? Or could they devote their time to politics, implementing changes that will tangibly affect all other players? So many people, so much variety!

It wasn't always this way.

When I wrote "Hearts, Clubs, Diamonds, Spades," few designers of virtual worlds gave any thought to how the people who inhabited them would act; those that did chose not to articulate their thoughts in public. As I saw more and more virtual worlds appearing and continual bickering between the proponents of "social" and "game-like" MUDs, it occurred to me that much of what was wrong was that many people lacked a basic understanding of why things in their favorite kind of virtual world were the way that they were. Design was by evolution: Take a working model, change it in some way, and see if the new model is better. The changes weren't entirely blind—the designers had reasons for making them—but, crucially, the effects of earlier designers' decisions were in general a mystery. Why do most virtual worlds organize players by levels, classes, races, and skills? Because the virtual world their designers cut their teeth on did!

My purpose in writing "Hearts, Clubs, Diamonds, Spades" was to make people *think* about virtual world design. I felt (and still feel) that the observations I was making were essentially sound, but it wouldn't have bothered me if they had been disproved within months; the central point of my article wasn't "this is how people in virtual worlds interact," but "think how people in virtual worlds interact!"

When I wrote it, almost all virtual worlds were text-based MUDs. There were, and remain, several thousand of these in existence, some of which have been running for years. (And by "years," I mean more than 15—how many regular computer games last that long?)

Today, however, we also have the large-scale graphical MUDs that Jessica and Bridgette have described in detail elsewhere in this book, which are variously known as "massively multiplayer online role-playing games (MMORPGs)," "persistent worlds (PWs)," and (as I've been calling them here) "virtual worlds." Do the points I raised in my mid-1990s article still hold true?

In essence, yes, they do.

The dynamics do change when there are several thousand people in a virtual world instead of several hundred at most. In particular, players who like to pick on other players can cluster in sufficient numbers that they can hunt in packs, which makes it harder for them to be controlled by guru-types who know all the answers but are individualistic. However, the basic relationships are still true: If you have a virtual world with far more socializers than achievers or far more achievers than socializers, you'd better have a host of newbies constantly adding to the pool or you're going to end up with a lump of die-hards and no one else.

Would I change any of the article were I to rewrite it today? Yes, I'd change the designation "killer" to be something else—"busybody" or "bully," perhaps—anything but "killer!" I've had more grief from that choice of word than everything else in the article combined! If only the temptation to map these players to the suit of clubs hadn't been so seductive....

Am I surprised that my article is still regarded as the first point of entry for anyone wanting to take a serious look at virtual world design? Well yes, actually I am; not because I believe that what I wrote is untrue, but because when I wrote it I assumed that by now some more apposite model would have superseded it. I remain convinced that this must happen (because research in the field can't remain stuck in 1995 forever!); however, for the moment it does seem to be holding up well.

This isn't to say that there aren't those who regard it as having been discredited. I've engaged in many debates on Usenet and web-based forums where people have criticized it heavily. The attacks are typically of two kinds: "This article promotes player-killing" and "You can't make these changes to the virtual world I use." The former is incorrect, in that the article merely predicts what will happen if you have no, some, or too much player-on-player activity. The latter is incorrect in theory (all games can be changed if you are prepared to make the effort), but correct in practice (generally, you can't afford to make the effort!).

But ultimately, whether the article is "right" or "wrong" isn't the point. The point is to set you thinking. Look on it as a spark to light the fire of your own imagination and understanding.

And, as always, have fun!

Dr. Richard A. Bartle
Colchester, Essex, UK
March 17, 2002

Abstract

Four approaches to playing MUDs are identified and described. These approaches may arise from the inter-relationship of two dimensions of playing style: action vs. interaction, and world-oriented vs. player-oriented. An account of the dynamics of player populations is given in terms of these dimensions, with particular attention to how to promote balance or equilibrium. This analysis also offers an explanation for the labeling of MUDs as being either "social" or "game-like."

Preface

Most MUDs can trace their lineage directly back to Trubshaw's 1978 game (Bartle, 1990b; Burka, 1995) and, perhaps because of this heritage, the vast majority are regarded as "games" by their "players." For the convenience of its readers, this paper continues to view MUDs in this tradition; however, it should be noted that MUDs can be of considerable value in non-game (i.e., "serious") applications (Bruckman, 1994a;

Kort, 1991; Bruckman & Resnick, 1993; Curtis & Nichols, 1993; Evard, 1993; Fanderclai, 1995; Riner & Clodius, 1995; Moock, 1996). Indeed, the thrust of this paper emphasizes those factors which should be borne in mind when attempting to create a stable MUD in general, whatever the application; it is only the terminology which is that of "fun" MUDs, not the subject matter. In any case, even those MUDs that are built, from the ground up, to be absolutely straight are still treated by users as if they were games in some respects, e.g., by choosing whimsical names rather than using their real ones (Roush, 1993).

It is worthwhile considering for a moment whether MUDs (as they are generally played) really are games, or whether they're something else. People have many recreational activities available to them, and perhaps MUDs fit some other category better. Looking up the word "game" in a dictionary of synonyms (Urdang and Manser, 1980) elicits three related nouns: "pastime," "sport," and "entertainment" (a fourth, "amusement," is the general class of which the others are all examples). So it might be useful to ask "Are MUDs":

➤ Games? Like chess, tennis, *AD&D*?

➤ Pastimes? Like reading, gardening, cooking?

➤ Sports? Like huntin', shootin', fishin'?

➤ Entertainments? Like nightclubs, TV, concerts?

Or are they a combination of all four? Perhaps individual players even see the *same* MUD differently from each other.

These questions will be returned to at the end of this paper, along with some proposed answers.

A Simple Taxonomy

This work grew out of a long, heated discussion that ran from November 1989 to May 1990 between the wizzes (i.e., highly experienced players of rank wizard or witch) on one particular commercial MUD in the UK (Bartle, 1985). The debate was sparked by the question "What do people want out of a MUD?" It comprised several hundred bulletin-board postings, some of considerable length, typically concerning what the players liked, what they didn't like, why they played, and changes they would like to see to "improve" the game. Some 15 individuals took a major part, with perhaps another 15 adding their comments from time to time; this comprised almost the entire set of active wizzes during that period. Although at times the debate became quite intense, never did it lapse into the flaming that typically ends most open-ended, multi-speaker, online discussions.

The fact that the people contributing to this argument were the most advanced players in a MUD that allowed player-killing might, on the face of it, be taken as evidence that they would probably prefer more "game-like" aspects over "social" ones. However, this was not the case: The MUD in question had players of all types in it, even at the wiz level. (Later in this paper, an analysis is given as to how such a MUD can come to be.)

When the participants had finally run out of new things to say, it became time for me (as senior administrator) to summarize. Abstracting the various points that had been raised, a pattern emerged; people habitually found the same kinds of thing about the game "fun," but there were several (four, in fact) sub-groupings into which opinion divided. Most players leaned at least a little to all four, but each tended to have some particular overall preference. The summary was generally well-received by those who had participated in the debate.

Note that although this MUD was one in which player-killing was allowed, the taxonomy that is about to be described does (as will be explained later) apply equally to "social" MUDs. The advice concerning changes which can be made to affect the player make-up of a MUD is, however, less useful to social MUDs, or to ones with a heavy role-playing component. Also, the original discussion concerned only non-administrative aspects of MUDding; people who might play MUDs to learn object-oriented programming, for example, are therefore not addressed by this paper.

The four things that people typically enjoyed personally about MUDs were:

➤ Achievement within the game context.

Players give themselves game-related goals and vigorously set out to achieve them. This usually means accumulating and disposing of large quantities of high-value treasure or cutting a swathe through hordes of mobiles (i.e., monsters built into the virtual world).

➤ Exploration of the game.

Players try to find out as much as they can about the virtual world. Although initially this means mapping its topology (i.e., exploring the MUD's breadth), later it advances to experimentation with its physics (i.e., exploring the MUD's depth).

➤ Socializing with others.

Players use the game's communicative facilities and apply the role-playing that these engender as a context in which to converse (and otherwise interact) with their fellow players.

➤ Imposition upon others.

Players use the tools provided by the game to cause distress to (or, in rare circumstances, to help) other players. Where permitted, this usually involves acquiring some weapon and applying it enthusiastically to the persona of another player in the game world.

So, labeling the four player types abstracted, we get: achievers, explorers, socializers, and killers. An easy way to remember these is to consider suits in a conventional pack of cards: achievers are Diamonds (they're always seeking treasure); explorers are Spades (they dig around for information); socializers are Hearts (they empathize with other players); killers are Clubs (they hit people with them).

Naturally, these areas cross over, and players will often drift between all four, depending on their mood or current playing style. However, my experience having observed players in the light of this research suggests that many (if not most) players do have a primary style and will only switch to other styles as a (deliberate or subconscious) means to advance their main interest.

Looking at each player type in more detail, then, we could say the following:

➤ Achievers regard points-gathering and rising in levels as their main goals, and all is ultimately subservient to this. Exploration is necessary only to find new sources of treasure or improved ways of wringing points from it. Socializing is a relaxing method of discovering what other players know about the business of accumulating points, that their knowledge can be applied to the task of gaining riches. Killing is only necessary to eliminate rivals or people who get in the way or to gain vast amounts of points (if points are awarded for killing other players).

Achievers say things like:

> "I'm busy."

> "Sure, I'll help you. What do I get?"

> "So how do YOU kill the dragon, then?"

> "Only 4211 points to go!"

➤ Explorers delight in having the game expose its internal machinations to them. They try progressively esoteric actions in wild, out-of-the-way places, looking for interesting features (i.e., bugs) and figuring out how things work. Scoring points may be necessary to enter some next phase of exploration, but it's tedious, and anyone with half a brain can do it. Killing is quicker, and might be a constructive exercise in its own right, but it causes too much hassle in the long run if the deceased return to seek retribution. Socializing can be informative as a source of new ideas to try out, but most of what people say is irrelevant or old hat. The real fun comes only from discovery and making the most complete set of maps in existence.

Explorers say things like:

> "Hmm..."

> "You mean you *don't know* the shortest route from <obscure room 1> to <obscure room 2>?"

> "I haven't tried that one; what's it do?"

> "Why is it that if you carry the uranium you get radiation sickness, and if you put it in a bag you still get it, but if you put it in a bag and drop it then wait 20 seconds and pick it up again, you don't?"

➤ Socializers are interested in people and what they have to say. The game is merely a backdrop, a common ground where things happen to players. Inter-player relationships are important: empathizing with people, sympathizing, joking, entertaining, listening, even merely observing people play can be rewarding—seeing them grow as individuals, maturing over time. Some exploration may be necessary so as to understand what everyone else is talking about, and points-scoring could be required to gain access to neat communicative spells available only to higher levels (as well as to obtain a certain status in the community). Killing, however, is something only ever to be excused if it's a futile, impulsive act of revenge, perpetrated upon someone who has caused intolerable pain to a dear friend. The only ultimately fulfilling thing is not how to rise levels or kill hapless drips; it's getting to *know* people, to understand them, and to form beautiful, lasting relationships.

Socializers say things like:

> "Hi!"

> "Yeah, well, I'm having trouble with my boyfriend."

> "What happened? I missed it; I was talking."

> "Really? Oh no! Gee, that's terrible! Are you sure? Awful, just awful!"

➤ Killers get their kicks from imposing themselves on others. This may be "nice," i.e., busybody do-gooding, but few people practice such an approach because the rewards (a warm, cozy inner glow, apparently) aren't very substantial. Much more commonly, people attack other players with a view to killing off their personae (hence the name for this style of play). The more massive the distress caused, the greater the killer's joy at having caused it. Normal points-scoring is usually required so as to become powerful enough to begin causing havoc in earnest, and exploration of a kind is necessary to discover new and ingenious ways to kill people. Even socializing is sometimes worthwhile beyond taunting a recent victim, for example, in finding out someone's playing habits or discussing tactics with fellow killers. They're all just means to an end, though; only in the knowledge that a real person, somewhere, is very upset by what you've just done, yet can themselves do nothing about it, is there any true adrenaline-shooting, juicy fun.

Killers says things like:

> "Ha!"

> "Coward!"

> "Die!"

> "Die! Die! Die!"

(Killers are people of few words.)

How many players typically fall within each area depends on the MUD. If, however, too many gravitate to one particular style, the effect can be to cause players of other persuasions to leave, which, in turn, may feed back and reduce the numbers in the first category. For example, too many killers will drive away the achievers who form their main prey; this in turn will mean that killers will stop playing, as they'll have no worthwhile victims (players considered by killers to be explorers generally don't care about death, and players considered to be socializers are too easy to pose much of a challenge). These direct relationships are discussed in more detail toward the end of this paper.

For the most part, though, the inter-relationships between the various playing styles are more subtle. A sharp reduction in the number of explorers for whatever reason could mean a gradual reduction in achievers, who get bored if they're not occasionally told of different hoops they can jump through for points; this could affect the number of socializers (the fewer players there are, the less there is to talk about), and it would certainly lower the killer population (due to a general lack of suitable victims).

Making sure that a game doesn't veer off in the wrong direction and lose players can be difficult; administrators need to maintain a balanced relationship between the different types of player, so as to guarantee their MUD's "feel." Note that I am not advocating any particular form of equilibrium; it is up to the game administrators themselves to decide what atmosphere they want their MUD to have, and thus define the point at which it is "balanced" (although the effort required to maintain this desired state could be substantial). Later, this paper considers means by which a MUD can be pushed in different directions, either to restore an earlier balance between the player types, to define a new target set of relationships between the player types, or to cause the inter-play between the player types to break down entirely. However, first a means is required of formally linking the four principal playing styles into aspects of a unified whole; this helps account for different degrees of adherence to particular styles, and aids visualization of what "altering the balance" of a MUD might actually *mean*.

Interest Graph

Consider the abstract graph shown in Figure D.1.

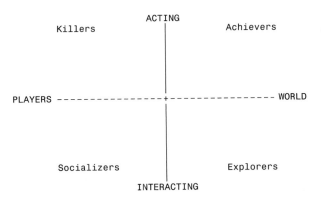

Figure D.1   Interest graph.

The axes of the graph represent the source of players' interest in a MUD. The X-axis goes from an emphasis on players (left) to an emphasis on the environment (right); the Y-axis goes from acting with (bottom) to acting on (top). The four extreme corners of the graph show the four typical playing preferences associated with each quadrant. To see how the graph works, it is appropriate to consider each of the four styles in detail:

➤ Achievers are interested in doing things to the game, i.e., in ACTING on the WORLD. It's the fact that the game environment is a fully-fledged world in which they can immerse themselves that they find compelling; its being shared with other people merely adds a little authenticity and perhaps a competitive element. The point of playing is to master the game and make it do what you want it to do; there's nothing intrinsically worthwhile in rooting out irrelevant details that will never be of use or in idling away your life with gossip.

Achievers are proud of their formal status in the game's built-in level hierarchy and of how short a time they took to reach it.

➤ Explorers are interested in having the game surprise them, i.e., in INTERACTING with the WORLD. It's the sense of wonder that the virtual world imbues that they crave for; other players add depth to the game, but they aren't essential components of it, except perhaps as sources of new areas to visit. Scoring points all the time is a worthless occupation because it defies the very open-endedness that makes a world live and breathe. Most accomplished explorers could easily rack up sufficient points to reach the top, but such one-dimensional behavior is the sign of a limited intellect.

Explorers are proud of their knowledge of the game's finer points, especially if new players treat them as founts of all knowledge.

➤ Socializers are interested in INTERACTING with other PLAYERS. This usually means talking, but it can extend to more exotic behavior. Finding out about people and getting to know them is far more worthy than treating them as fodder to be bossed around. The game world is just a setting; it's the characters that make it so compelling.

Socializers are proud of their friendships, their contacts, and their influence.

➤ Killers are interested in doing things to people, i.e., in ACTING on other PLAYERS. Normally, this is not with the consent of these "other players" (even if, objectively, the interference in their play might appear "helpful"), but killers don't care; they wish only to demonstrate their superiority over fellow humans, preferably in a world that serves to legitimize actions that could mean imprisonment in real life. Accumulated knowledge is useless unless it can be applied; even when it is applied, there's no fun unless it can affect a real person instead of an emotionless, computerized entity.

Killers are proud of their reputation and of their oft-practiced fighting skills.

The "interest graph" is a representational structure that can chart what players find of interest in a MUD. The axes can be assigned a relative scale reflecting the ratio of an individual's interest between the two extremes that it admits. Thus, for example, someone who thinks that the people who are in the world are maybe twice as important as the world itself would lie on a vertical line intersecting the X-axis at a point 1/6 of the distance from the origin to the left edge; if they had little interest in bending the game to their will, preferring their actions to have some give and take, then they would also lie on a horizontal line at the bottom of the Y-axis. The intersection of the two lines would put them in the socializer quadrant, with leanings to explorer.

It is, of course, possible to analyze the behavior of individual players quantitatively by processing transcripts of their games. Unfortunately, this is very difficult to do except for very limited domains (e.g., forms of communication [Cherny, 1995a; Cherny, 1995b]). An alternative approach might simply be to ask the players what they themselves like about a particular MUD; even a short questionnaire, completed anonymously, can give a fair indication of what players find enjoyable (Emert, 1993). Such information can then be used to determine the make-up of the MUD's player base, so that in times of falling player numbers the current composition could be compared against some earlier ideal, and remedial action taken to redress the imbalance. This "ideal" configuration would, however, be specific to that particular MUD, and its precise form is therefore not addressed here. Instead, the more general issue of how to alter the balance between player types is considered, along with the gross effects that can be expected to follow from having done so.

Changing the Player Type Balance

A stable MUD is one in which the four principal styles of player are in equilibrium. This doesn't imply that there are the same number of players exhibiting each style; rather, it means that over time, the proportion of players for each style remains roughly constant, so that the balance between the various types remains the same. Other factors *are* important, to do with the rate at which new players arrive and overall player numbers, but their consideration is not within the brief of this paper; the interaction between players of different types *is* within its brief, however, and is discussed in some detail later.

The actual point of balance (i.e., whereabouts in the interest graph the center of gravity of the individual players' points lie) can vary quite enormously; it is up to individual administrators to determine where they want it to lie and to make any programming or design changes necessary to ensure that this is where it actually does. What kind of strategies, though, can be employed to achieve this task?

In order to answer this question, consider the interest graph. If it is regarded as a plane in equilibrium, it can be tilted in a number of ways to favor different areas. Usually, this will be at the expense of some other (opposite) area, but not necessarily. Although tilting can in theory occur along any line in the plane, it makes sense (at least initially) to look at what happens when the tilt lines coincide with the X and Y axes of the graph.

What follows, then, is a brief examination of means by which a MUD can be adjusted so as to favor the various extremes of the interest graph, and what would happen if each approach were taken to the limit.

Players

Putting the emphasis on players rather than the game is easy—you just provide the system with lots of communication commands and precious little else. The more the scales are tipped toward players, though, the less of a MUD you have and the more of a Citizen's Band (CB) radio-style chat-line. Beyond a certain point, the game can't provide a context for communication, and it ceases to be a viable virtual world; it's just a communications channel for the real world. At this stage, when all sense of elsewhere presence is lost, you no longer have a MUD.

World

Tilting the game toward the world rather than its inhabitants is also easy: You simply make it so big and awkward to traverse that no one ever meets anyone in it. Alternatively, you can ensure that if they do meet up, then there are very few ways in which they can interact. Although this can result in some nice simulations, there's a loss of motivation implicit within it; anyone can rack up points given time, but there's not the same sense of achievement as when it's done under pressure from competing players. And what use is creating beautifully crafted areas anyway, if you can't show them to people? Perhaps if computer-run personae had more AI, a MUD could go further in this direction (Mauldin, 1994), but it couldn't (yet) go all the way (as authors of single-player games have found [Caspian-Kaufman, 1995]). Sometimes, you just *do* want to tell people real-world things—you have a new baby, or a new job, or your cat has died. If there's no one to tell or no way to tell them, you don't have a MUD.

Interacting

Putting the emphasis on interaction rather than action can also go a long way. Restricting the freedom of players to choose different courses of action is the mechanism for implementing it, so they can only follow a narrow or predetermined development path. Essentially, it's MUD-as-theatre; you sit there being entertained, but not actually participating much. You may *feel* like you're in a world, but it's one in which you're paralyzed. If the bias is only slight, it can make a MUD more "nannyish," which newcomers seem to enjoy, but pushing it all the way turns it into a radio set. Knowledge may be intrinsically interesting (i.e., trivia), but it's meaningless unless it can be applied. If players can't play, it's not a MUD.

Acting

If the graph is redrawn to favor doing-to over doing-with, the game quickly becomes boring. Tasks are executed repeatedly, by rote. There's always monotony, never anything new, or, if there *is* something new, it's of the "man vs. random number generator" variety. People do need to be able to put into practice what they've learned, but they also need to be able to learn it in the first place! Unless the one leads to the other, it's only a matter of time before patience is exhausted and the players give up. Without depth, you have no MUD.

From the above list of ways to tilt the interest graph, a set of stratagems can be composed to help MUD administrators shift the focus of their games in whatever particular direction they choose. Some of these stratagems are simply a question of management; if you don't tell people what communication commands there are, for example, people will be less likely to use them all. Although such approaches are good for small shifts in the way a MUD is played, the more powerful and absolute method is to consider *programming* changes (programming being the "nature" of a MUD, and administration being the "nurture").

Here, then, are the programming changes that administrators might wish to consider in order to shape their MUD:

- ➤ Ways to emphasize PLAYERS over WORLD include:
  - ➤ Add more communication facilities
  - ➤ Add more player-on-player commands (e.g., transitive ones like TICKLE or CONGRATULATE, or commands to form and maintain closed groups of personae)
  - ➤ Make communication facilities easy and intuitive
  - ➤ Decrease the size of the world
  - ➤ Increase the connectivity between rooms
  - ➤ Maximize the number of simultaneous players
  - ➤ Restrict building privileges to a select few
  - ➤ Cut down on the number of mobiles

➤ Ways to emphasize WORLD over PLAYERS include:

  ➤ Have only basic communication facilities

  ➤ Have few ways that players can do things to other players

  ➤ Make building facilities easy and intuitive

  ➤ Maximize the size of the world (i.e., add *breadth*)

  ➤ Use only "rational" room connections in most cases

  ➤ Grant building privileges to many

  ➤ Have lots of mobiles

➤ Ways to emphasize INTERACTING over ACTING:

  ➤ Make help facilities produce vague information

  ➤ Produce cryptic hints when players appear stuck

  ➤ Maximize the effects of commands (i.e., add *depth*)

  ➤ Lower the rewards for achievement

  ➤ Have only a shallow level/class system

  ➤ Produce amusing responses for amusing commands

  ➤ Edit all room descriptions for consistent atmosphere

  ➤ Limit the number of commands available in any one area

  ➤ Have lots of small puzzles that can be solved easily

  ➤ Allow builders to add completely new commands

➤ Ways to emphasize ACTING over INTERACTING:

  ➤ Provide a game manual

  ➤ Include auto-map facilities

  ➤ Include auto-log facilities

  ➤ Raise the rewards for achievement

  ➤ Have an extensive level/class system

➤ Make commands be applicable wherever they might reasonably
have meaning

➤ Have large puzzles that take over an hour to complete

➤ Have many commands relating to fights

➤ Only allow building by top-quality builders

These strategies can be combined to encourage or discourage different styles of play. To appeal to achievers, for example, one approach might be to introduce an extensive level/class system (so as to provide plenty of opportunity to reward investment of time) and to maximize the size of the world (so there is more for them to achieve). Note that the "feel" of a MUD is derived from the position on the interest graph of the MUD's players, from which a "center of gravity" can be approximated. It is, therefore, sometimes possible to make two changes simultaneously that have "opposite" effects, altering how some individuals experience the MUD but not changing how the MUD feels overall. For example, adding large puzzles (to emphasize ACTING) and adding small puzzles (to emphasize INTERACTING) would encourage both pro-ACTING and pro-INTERACTING players, thereby keeping the MUD's center of gravity in the same place while tending to increase total player numbers. In general, though, these stratagems should not be used as a means to attract new players; stratagems should only be selected from one set per axis.

The effects of the presence (or lack of it) of other types of players are also very important and can be used as a different way to control relative population sizes. The easiest (but, sadly, most tedious) way to discuss the interactions that pertain between the various player types is to enumerate the possible combinations and consider them independently; this is the approach adopted by this paper.

First, however, it is pertinent to discuss the ways that players generally categorize MUDs today.

The Social Versus Game-Like Debate

Following the introduction of *TinyMUD* (Aspnes, 1989), in which combat wasn't even implemented, players now tend to categorize individual MUDs as either "social" or "game-like" (Carton, 1995). In terms of the preceding discussion, "social" means that the games are heavily weighted to the area below the X-axis, but whether "game-like" means the games are weighted heavily above the X-axis or merely balanced on it is a moot point. Players of social MUDs might suggest that "game-like" means a definite bias on and above the X-axis, because from their perspective, any explicit element of competitiveness is "too much." Some (but not most) players of game-like MUDs could disagree, pointing out that their MUDs enjoy rich social interactions between the players despite the fact that combat is allowed.

So strongly is this distinction felt, particularly among social MUDders, that many of their newer participants don't regard themselves as playing "MUDs" at all, insisting that this term refers only to combat-oriented games, with which they don't wish to be associated. The rule of thumb applied is server type, so, for example, LPMud => game-like, MOO => social; this is despite the fact that each of these systems is of sufficient power and flexibility that it could probably be used to implement an interpreter for the other one!

Consequently, there are general Internet-related books with chapter titles like "Interactive Multiuser Realities: MUDs, MOOs, MUCKs and MUSHes" (Poirier, 1994) and "MUDs, MUSHes, and Other Role-Playing Games" (Eddy, 1994). This fertile ground is where the term "MU*" (Norrish, 1995) originates—as an attempt to fill the void left by assigning the word "MUD" to game-like (or "player-killing") MUDs; its deliberate use can therefore reasonably be described as a political act (Bruckman, 1992).

This attitude misses the point, however. Although social MUDs may be a major branch on the MUD family tree, they are, nevertheless, still on it, and are therefore still MUDs. If another overarching term is used, then it will only be a matter of time before some-one writes a combat-oriented server called "KillerMU*" or whatever, and causes the wound to reopen. Denial of history is not, in general, a wise thing to do.

Besides, social MUDs do have their killers (i.e., people who fall into that area of the interest graph). Simply because explicit combat is prohibited, there is nevertheless plenty of opportunity to cause distress in other ways. To list a few: virtual rape

(Dibbell, 1993; Reid, 1994); general sexual harassment (Rosenberg, 1992); deliberate fracturing of the community (Whitlock, 1994a); and vexatious litigancy (Whitlock, 1994b). Indeed, proper management of a MUD insists that contingency plans and procedures are already in place such that antisocial behavior can be dealt with promptly when it occurs (Bruckman, 1994b).

Social MUDs do have their achievers, too: people who regard building as a competitive act and can vie to have the "best" rooms in the MUD (Clodius, 1994) or who seek to acquire a large quota for creating ever-more objects (Farmer, Morningstar, and Crockford, 1994). The fact that a MUD might not itself reward such behavior should, of course, naturally foster a community of players who are primarily interested in talking and listening, but there nevertheless *will* still be killers and achievers around—in the same way that there will be socializers and explorers in even the most bloodthirsty of MUDs.

Researchers have tended to use a more precise distinction than the players, in terms of a MUD's similarity to (single-user) adventure games. Amy Bruckman's observation that:

> *There are two basic types [of MUD]: those which are like adventure games, and those which are not.*
>
> *(Bruckman, 1992)*

is the most succinct and unarguable expression of this dichotomy. However, in his influential paper on MUDs, Pavel Curtis states:

> *Three major factors distinguish a MUD from an adventure-style computer game, though:*
>
> ➤ *A MUD is not goal-oriented; it has no beginning or end, no "score," and no notion of "winning" or "success."*
>
> *In short, even though users of MUDs are commonly called players, a MUD isn't really a game at all.*
>
> ➤ *A MUD is extensible from within; a user can add new objects to the database such as rooms, exits, "things," and notes.*
>
> ➤ *A MUD generally has more than one user connected at a time.*

All of the connected users are browsing and manipulating the same database and can encounter the new objects created by others. The multiple users on a MUD can communicate with each other in real time.

(Curtis, 1992)

This definition explicitly rules out MUDs as adventure games—indeed, it claims that they are not games at all. This is perhaps too tight a definition, since the very first MUD was most definitely programmed to be a game. (I know, because I programmed it to be one!) The second point, which states that MUDs must involve building, is also untrue of many MUDs; in particular, commercial MUDs often aim for a high level of narrative consistency (which isn't conducive to letting players add things unchecked), and, if they have a graphical front-end, it is also inconvenient if new objects appear that generate no images. However, the fact that Curtis comes down on the side of "social" MUDs to bear the name "MUD" at least recognizes that these programs *are* MUDs, which is more than many "MU*" advocates are prepared to admit.

This issue of "social or game-like" will be returned to presently, with an explanation of exactly *why* players of certain MUDs that are dubbed "game-like" might find a binary distinction counter-intuitive.

Player Interactions

What follows is a brief explanation of how players predominantly of one type view those other players whom they perceive to be predominantly of one type. Warning: These notes concern *stereotypical* players and are not to be assumed to be true of any individual player who might otherwise exhibit the common traits of one or more of the player classes.

The effects of increasing and decreasing the various populations is also discussed, but this does *not* take into account physical limitations on the amount of players involved. Thus, for example, if the number of socializers is stated to have "no effect" on the number of achievers, that disregards the fact that there may be an absolute maximum number of players that the MUD can comfortably hold, and the socializers may be taking up slots that achievers could otherwise have filled. Also, the knock-on effects of other interactions are not discussed at this stage; a game with fewer socializers means the killers will seek out more achievers, for example, so there is a secondary effect of having fewer achievers even though there is no primary effect. This propagation of influences is, however, examined in detail afterwards, when the first-level dynamics have been laid bare.

Achievers Versus Achievers

Achievers regard other achievers as competition to be beaten (although this is typically friendly in nature, rather than cut-throat). Respect is given to those other achievers who obviously are extraordinarily good, but typically achievers will cite bad luck or lack of time as reasons for not being as far advanced in the game as their contemporaries.

That said, achievers do often cooperate with one another, usually to perform some difficult collective goal, and from these shared experiences can grow deep, enduring friendships that may surpass in intensity those commonly found among individuals in other groups. This is perhaps analogous to the difference between the bond that soldiers under fire share and the bond that friends in a bar share.

Achievers do not need the presence of any other type of player in order to be encouraged to join a MUD; they would be quite happy if the game were empty but for them, assuming it remained a challenge (although some do feel a need to describe their exploits to anyone who will listen). Because of this, a MUD can't have too many achievers, physical limitations excepted.

Achievers Versus Explorers

Achievers tend to regard explorers as losers—people who have had to resort to tinkering with the game mechanics because they can't cut it as a player. Exceptionally good explorers may be elevated to the level of eccentric, in much the same way that certain individuals come to be regarded as gurus by users of large computer installations; what they do is pointless, but they're useful to have around when you need to know something obscure, fast. They can be irritating, and they rarely tell the whole truth (perhaps because they don't know it?), but they do have a place in the world.

The overall number of explorers has only a marginal effect on the population of achievers. In essence, more explorers will mean that fewer of the really powerful objects will be around for the achievers to use, the explorers having used their arcane skills to obtain them first so as to use them in their diabolical experiments. This can cause achievers to become frustrated and leave. More importantly, perhaps, the number of explorers affects the *rate of advancement* of achievers because it determines whether or not they have to work out all those tiresome puzzles themselves. Thus, more explorers will lead to a quicker rise through the ranks for achievers, which will tend to encourage them (if not overdone).

Achievers Versus Socializers

Achievers merely tolerate socializers. Although they are good sources of general hearsay on the comings and goings of competitors, they're nevertheless pretty much a waste of space as far as achievers are concerned. Typically, achievers will regard socializers with a mixture of contempt, disdain, irritation, and pity, and will speak to them in either a sharp or patronizing manner. Occasionally, flame wars between different cliques of socializers and achievers may break out, and these can be among the worst to stop. The achievers don't want to lose the argument, and the socializers don't want to stop talking!

Changing the number of socializers in a MUD has no effect on the number of achievers.

Achievers Versus Killers

Achievers don't particularly like killers. They realize that killers as a concept are necessary in order to make achievement meaningful and worthwhile (there being no way to "lose" the game if any fool can "win" just by plodding slowly unchallenged). However, they don't personally like being attacked unless it's obvious from the outset that they'll win. They also object to being interrupted in the middle of some grand scheme to accumulate points, and they don't like having to arm themselves against surprise attacks every time they start to play. Achievers will, occasionally, resort to killing tactics themselves, in order to cause trouble for a rival or to reap whatever rewards the game itself offers for success; however, the risks are usually too high for them to pursue such options very often.

Increasing the number of killers will reduce the number of achievers; reducing the killer population will increase the achiever population. Note, however, that those general MUDs that nevertheless allow player-killing tend to do so in the belief that in small measure it is good for the game; it promotes camaraderie, excitement, and intensity of experience (and it's the only method that players will accept to ensure that complete idiots don't plod inexorably through the ranks to acquire a degree of power which they aren't really qualified to wield). As a consequence, reducing the number of killers *too* much will be perceived as cheapening the game, making high achievement commonplace, and it will put off those achievers who are alarmed at the way any fool can "do well" just by playing poorly for long enough.

Explorers Versus Achievers

Explorers look on achievers as nascent explorers, who haven't yet figured out that there's more to life than pursuing meaningless goals. They are, therefore, willing to furnish them with information, although, like all experts, they will rarely tell the full story when they can legitimately give cryptic clues instead. Apart from the fact that they sometimes get in the way and won't usually hand over objects that are needed for experiments, achievers can live alongside explorers without much friction.

Explorers' numbers aren't affected by the presence of achievers.

Explorers Versus Explorers

Explorers hold good explorers in great respect but are merciless to bad ones. One of the worst things a fellow explorer can do is to give out incorrect information, believing it to be true. Other than that, explorers thrive on telling one another their latest discoveries and generally get along very well. Outwardly, they will usually claim to have the skill necessary to follow the achievement path to glory but have other reasons for not doing so (e.g., time, tedium, or having proven themselves already with a different persona). There are often suspicions, though, that explorers are too theoretical in most cases and wouldn't be able to put their ideas into practice on a day-to-day basis if they were to recast themselves in the achiever or killer mold.

Explorers enjoy the company of other explorers, and they will play more often if they have people around them to whom they can relate. Unfortunately, not many people have the type of personality that finds single-minded exploring a riveting subject, so numbers are notoriously difficult to increase. If you have explorers in a game, hold on to them!

Explorers Versus Socializers

Explorers consider socializers to be people whom they can impress, but who are otherwise pretty well unimportant. Unless they can appreciate the explorer's talents, they're not really worth spending time with. There *are* some explorers who treat conversation as their specialist explorer subject, but these are very rare indeed; most will be polite and attentive, but they'll find some diversion if the conversation isn't MUD-related or if their fellow interlocutor is clearly way below them in the game-understanding stakes.

The explorer population is not directly affected by the size of the socializer population.

Explorers Versus Killers

Explorers often have a grudging respect for killers, but they do find their behavior wearisome. It's just *so* annoying to be close to finishing setting up something when a killer comes along and attacks you. On the other hand, many killers do know their trade well and are quite prepared to discuss the finer details of it with explorers. Sometimes, an explorer may try attacking other players as an exercise, and they can be extremely effective at it. Explorers who are particularly riled by a killer may even decide to "do something about it" themselves. If they make such a decision, then it can be seriously bad news for the killer concerned; being jumped and trashed by a low-level (in terms of game rank) explorer can have a devastating effect on a killer's reputation and turn them into a laughingstock overnight. Explorers do not, however, tend to have the venom or malice that true killers possess, nor will they continue the practice to the extent that they acquire a reputation of their own for killing.

The effect of killers on the explorer population is fairly muted because most explorers don't particularly care if they get killed (or at least they profess not). However, if it happens too often, then they will become disgruntled and play less frequently.

Socializers Versus Achievers

Socializers like achievers because they provide the running soap opera about which the socializers can converse. Without such a framework, there is no uniting cause to bring socializers together (at least not initially). Note that socializers don't particularly enjoy talking *to* achievers (not unless they can get them to open up, which is very difficult); they do, however, enjoy talking *about* them. A cynic might suggest that the relationship between socializers and achievers is similar to that between women and men.

Increasing the achiever/socializer ratio has only a subtle effect; socializers may come to feel that the MUD is "all about" scoring points and killing mobiles, and some of them may therefore leave before matters "get worse." Decreasing it has little effect unless the number of active achievers drops to near zero, in which case new socializers might find it difficult to break into established conversational groups, and thus decide to take their play elsewhere.

> **NOTE**
> Although earlier it was stated that this paper does not address people who play MUDs for meta-reasons, e.g., to learn how to program, I believe that their empirical behavior with regard to the actions of other players is sufficiently similar to that of socializers for the two groups to be safely bundled together when considering population dynamics.

Socializers Versus Explorers

Socializers generally consider explorers to be sad characters who are desperately in need of a life. Both groups like to talk, but rarely about the same things, and if they do get together, it's usually because the explorer wants to sound erudite and the socializer has nothing better to do at the time.

The number of explorers in a MUD has no effect on the number of socializers.

Socializers Versus Socializers

A case of positive feedback: Socializers can talk to one another on any subject for hours on end and come back later for more. The key factor is whether there is an open topic of conversation. In a game-like environment, the MUD itself provides the context for discussion, whether it be the goings-on of other players or the feeble attempts of a socializer to try playing it; in a non-game environment, some other subject is usually required to structure conversations, either within the software of the MUD itself (e.g., building) or without it (e.g., "This is a support MUD for the victims of cancer"). Note that this kind of subject-setting is only required as a form of ice-breaker; once socializers have acquired friends, they'll invariably find other things that they can talk about.

The more socializers there are in a game, the more new ones will be attracted to it.

Socializers Versus Killers

This is perhaps the most fractious relationship between player group types. The hatred that some socializers bear for killers admits no bounds. Partly, this is the killers' own fault: They go out of their way to rid MUDs of namby-pamby socializers who wouldn't know a weapon if one came up and hit them (an activity that killers are only too happy to demonstrate), and they will generally hassle socializers at every opportunity simply because it's so easy to get them annoyed. However, the main reason that socializers tend to despise killers is that they have completely antisocial motives, whereas socializers have (or like to think they have) a much more friendly and helpful attitude to life. The fact that many socializers take attacks on their personae personally only compounds their distaste for killers.

It could be argued that killers do have a positive role to play from the point of view of socializers. There are generally two defenses made for their existence: 1) without killers, socializers would have little to talk about; 2) without evil as a contrast, there is no good. The former is patently untrue, as socializers will happily talk about anything and everything; it may be that it helps provide a catalyst for long conversations, but only if it isn't an everyday occurrence. The second argument is more difficult to defend against (being roughly equivalent to the reason why God allows the devil to exist); however, it presupposes that those who attack other players are the only example of nasty people in a MUD. In fact, there is plenty of opportunity for players of all persuasions to behave obnoxiously to one another; killers merely do it more openly, and (if allowed) in the context of the game world.

Increasing the number of killers will decrease the number of socializers by a much greater degree. Decreasing the number of killers will likewise greatly encourage (or, rather, fail to discourage) socializers to play the MUD.

Killers Versus Achievers

Killers regard achievers as their natural prey. Achievers are good fighters (because they've learned the necessary skills against mobiles), but they're not quite as good as killers, who are more specialized. This gives the "thrill of the chase" that many killers enjoy; an achiever may actually be able to escape, but will usually succumb at some stage, assuming they don't see sense and quit first. Achievers also dislike being attacked, which makes the experience of attacking them all the more fun; furthermore, it is unlikely that they will stop playing after being set back by a killer, and thus they can be "fed upon" again, later. The main disadvantage of pursuing achievers, however, is that an achiever can get so incensed at being attacked that they decide to take revenge. A killer may thus innocently enter a game only to find a heavily armed achiever lying in wait, which rather puts the boot on the other foot.

Note that there is a certain sub-class of killers, generally run by wiz-level players, who have a more ethical point to their actions. In particular, their aim is to "test" players for their "suitability" to advance to the higher levels themselves. In general, such personae should not be regarded as falling into the killer category, although in some instances the ethical aspect is merely an excuse to indulge in killing sprees without fear of sanction. Rather, these killers tend to be run by people in either the achievement category (protecting their own investment) or the explorer category (trying to teach their victims how to defend themselves against *real* killers).

Increasing the number of achievers will, over time, increase the number of killers in a typically Malthusian fashion.

Killers Versus Explorers

Killers tend to leave explorers alone. Not only can explorers be formidable fighters (with many obscure, unexpected tactics at their disposal), but they often don't fret about being attacked—a fact that is very frustrating for killers. Sometimes, particularly annoying explorers will simply ignore a killer's attack and make no attempt whatsoever to defend against it; this is the ultimate in cruelty to killers. For more long-term effects, though, a killer's being beaten by an explorer has more impact on the game: the killer will feel shame, their reputation will suffer, and the explorer will pass on survival tactics to everyone else. In general, then, killers will steer well clear of even half-decent explorers, except when they have emptied a game of everyone else and are so desperate for a fix that even an explorer looks tempting.

Increasing the number of explorers will slightly decrease the number of killers.

Killers Versus Socializers

Killers regard socializers with undisguised glee. It's not that socializers are in any way a challenge, as usually they will be pushovers in combat; rather, socializers feel a dreadful hurt when attacked (especially if it results in the loss of their persona), and it is this that killers enjoy about it. Besides, killers tend to like to have a bad reputation, and if there's one way to get people to talk about you, it's to attack a prominent socializer.

Increasing the number of socializers will increase the number of killers, although, of course, the number of socializers wouldn't remain increased for very long if that happened.

Killers Versus Killers

Killers try not to cross the paths of other killers, except in pre-organized challenge matches. Part of the psychology of killers seems to be that they wish to be viewed as somehow superior to other players; being killed by a killer in open play would undermine their reputation, and therefore they avoid risking it (compare "Killers Versus Explorers"). This means that nascent or wannabe killers are often put off their chosen particular career path because they themselves are attacked by more experienced killers and soundly thrashed. For this reason, it can take a very long time to increase the killer population in a MUD, even if all the conditions are right for them to thrive; killer numbers rise grindingly slowly, unless competent killers are imported from another MUD to swell the numbers artificially.

Killers will occasionally work in teams, but only as a short-term exercise; they will usually revert to stalking their victims solo in the next session they play.

There are two cases where killers might be attacked by players who, superficially, look like other killers. One of these is the "killer killer," usually run by wiz-level players, which has been discussed earlier. The other is in the true hack-and-slash type of MUD, where the whole aim of the game is to kill other personae, and no one particularly minds being killed because they weren't expecting to last very long anyway. This type of play does not appeal to "real" killers because it doesn't cause people emotional distress when their personae are deleted. (Indeed, socializers prefer it more than killers do.) However, it's better than nothing.

The only effect that killers have on other killers is in reducing the number of potential victims available. This, in theory, should keep the number of killers down; however, in practice, killers will simply attack less attractive victims instead. It takes a very drastic reduction in the number of players before established killers will decide to stop playing a MUD and move elsewhere, by which time it is usually too late to save the MUD concerned.

Dynamics

From the discussion in the previous section, it is possible to summarize the interactions between player types.

To increase the number of achievers:

➤ Reduce the number of killers, but not by too much.

➤ If killer numbers are high, increase the number of explorers.

To decrease the number of achievers:

➤ Increase the number of killers.

➤ If killer numbers are low, reduce the number of explorers.

To increase the number of explorers:

➤ Increase the number of explorers.

To decrease the number of explorers:

➤ Massively increase the number of killers.

To increase the number of socializers:

➤ Slightly decrease the number of killers.

➤ Increase the number of socializers.

To decrease the number of socializers:

- ➤ Slightly increase the number of killers.

- ➤ Massively increase the number of achievers.

- ➤ Massively decrease the number of achievers.

- ➤ Decrease the number of socializers.

To increase the number of killers:

- ➤ Increase the number of achievers.

- ➤ Massively decrease the number of explorers.

- ➤ Increase the number of socializers.

To decrease the number of killers:

- ➤ Decrease the number of achievers.

- ➤ Massively increase the number of explorers.

- ➤ Decrease the number of socializers.

What are the dynamics of this model? In other words, if players of each type were to trickle into a system, how would it affect the overall make-up of the player population?

Figure D.2 illustrates the flow of influence. Each arrow shows a relationship, from the blunt end to the pointed end.

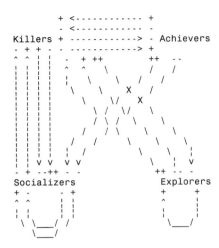

Figure D.2 Flows of influence in player interactions.

Ends are marked with a plus or minus to show an increase or decrease, respectively; the symbols are doubled up to indicate a massive increase or decrease. For example, the line shown in Figure D.3 means that increasing the number of killers will decrease the number of achievers.

```
Killers + ------------> - Achievers
```

Figure D.3 Example relationship.

From this, it can be seen that the numbers of killers and achievers are basically an equilibrium; increasing the number of achievers will increase the number of killers, which will in turn dampen down the increase in the number of achievers and thereby reduce the number of excess killers.

The explorer population is almost inert; only huge numbers of killers will reduce it. It should be noted, however, that massively increasing the number of explorers is the *only* way to reduce the number of killers without also reducing the player numbers in other groups. Because increasing the number of explorers in a MUD generally encourages others to join (and non-explorers to experiment with exploration), this gives a positive feedback that will eventually reduce the killer population (although recall the earlier point concerning how few people are, by nature, explorers).

The most volatile group of people is that of the socializers. Not only is it highly sensitive to the number of killers, but it has both positive and negative feedback on itself, which amplifies any changes. An increase in the number of socializers will lead to yet more socializers, but it will also increase the number of killers; this, in turn, will reduce the number of socializers drastically, which will feed back into a yet greater reduction. It is possible for new socializers to arrive in large enough quantities for a downward spiral in numbers not to be inevitable, but it is unlikely that such a system could remain viable over a long period of time.

This analysis of the dynamics of the relationships between players leads naturally to a consideration of what configurations could be considered stable. There are four:

> ► Killers and achievers in equilibrium. If the number of killers gets too high, then the achievers will be driven off, which will cause the number of killers to fall also (through lack of victims). If there aren't enough killers, then achievers feel the MUD isn't a sufficient challenge (there being no way to "lose" in it), and they will gradually leave. New killers could appear, attracted by the glut of potential prey; however, this happens so slowly that its impact is less than that of the disaffection among achievers. Socializers who venture out of whatever safe rooms are available eventually fall prey to killers and leave the game. Those who stay find that there aren't many interesting (to them) people around with whom to talk, and they too drift off. Explorers potter around, but are not a sufficient presence to affect the number of killers.

> ► A MUD dominated by socializers. Software changes to the MUD are made that prevent (or at least seriously discourage) killers from practicing their craft on socializers; incoming socializers are encouraged by those already there, and a chain reaction starts. There are still achievers and explorers, but they are swamped by the sheer volume of socializers. The number of socializers is limited only by external factors, or the presence of killers masquerading as socializers. If the population of socializers drops below a certain critical level, then the chain reaction reverses and almost all the players will leave; however, only events outside the MUD would cause that to happen once the critical mass had been reached.

> ► A MUD where all groups have a similar influence (although not necessarily similar numbers). By nurturing explorers using software means (i.e., giving the game great depth or "mystique," or encouraging non-explorers to dabble for a while by

regularly adding new areas and features), the overall population of explorers will gradually rise, and the killer population will be held in check by them. The killers who remain do exert an influence on the number of socializers, sufficient to stop them from going into fast-breeder mode, but insufficient to initiate an exodus. Achievers are set upon by killers often enough to feel that their achievements in the game have meaning. This is perhaps the most balanced form of MUD since players can change their position on the interest graph far more freely; achievers can become explorers, explorers can become socializers, socializers can become achievers—all without sacrificing stability. However, actually attaining that stability in the first place is very difficult indeed; it requires not only a level of game design beyond what most MUDs can draw on, but time and player management skills that aren't usually available to MUD administrators. Furthermore, the administrators need to recognize that they are aiming for a player mix of this kind in advance, because the chances of its occurring accidentally are slim.

➤ A MUD with no players. The killers have killed/frightened off everyone else and left to find some other MUD in which to ply their trade. Alternatively, a MUD structured expressly for socializers never managed to acquire a critical mass of them.

Other types could conceivably exist, but they are very rare if they do. The dynamics model is, however, imprecise; it takes no account of outside factors that may influence player types or the relationships between them. It is thus possible that some of the more regimented MUDs (e.g., role-playing MUDs, educational MUDs, group therapy MUDs) have an external dynamic (e.g., random interest in a subject, instructions from a teacher/trainer, tolerance of others as a means to advance the self) that adds to their cohesion, and that this could make an otherwise flaky configuration hold together. So other stable MUD forms may, therefore, still be out there.

It might be argued that "role-playing" MUDs form a separate category, on a par with "game-like" and "social" MUDs. However, I personally favor the view that role-playing is merely a strong framework within which the four types of player still operate: some people will role-play to increase their power over the game (achievers); others will do so to explore the wonder of the game world (explorers); others will do so because they enjoy interacting and co-operating within the context that the role-playing environment offers (socializers); others will do it because it gives them a legitimate excuse to hurt other players (killers). I have not, however, undertaken a study of role-playing MUDs, and it could well be that there is a configuration of player types peculiar to many of them that would be unstable were it not for the order imposed by enforcing role-play. It certainly seems likely that robust role-playing rules could make it easier for a MUD to achieve Type 3 stability.

At this point, we return to the social/game-like MUD debate.

Ignoring the fourth (null) case from the above, it is now much easier to see why there is a schism. Left to market forces, a MUD will either gravitate toward Type 1 ("game-like") or Type 2 ("social"), depending on its administrator's line on player-killing (more precisely: how much being "killed" annoys socializers). However, the existence of Type 3 MUDs, albeit in smaller numbers because of the difficulty of reaching the steady state, does show that it is possible to have both socializers and achievers co-existing in significant numbers in the same MUD.

It's very easy to label a MUD as either "hack-and-slash" or "slack-and-hash," depending on whether or not player-killing is allowed. However, using player-killing as the only defining factor in any distinction is an over-generalization, as it groups together Type 1 and Type 3 MUDs. These two types of MUD should *not* be considered as identical forms; the socializing that occurs in a Type 3 MUD simply isn't possible in a Type 1, and as a result, the sense of community in Type 3s is very strong. It is no accident that Type 3 MUDs are the ones preferred commercially because they can hold onto their players for far longer than the other two forms. A Type 1 MUD is only viable commercially if there is a sufficiently large well of potential players to draw upon because of the much greater churn rate these games have. Type 2 MUDs have a similarly high turnover; indeed, when *TinyMUD* first arrived on the scene, it was almost slash-and-burn, with games lasting around six months on university computers before a combination of management break-down (brought on by player boredom) and resource hogging would force them to close down—with no other MUDs permitted on the site for perhaps years afterward.

This explains why some MUDs perceived by socializers to be "game-like" can actually be warm, friendly places, while others are nasty and vicious; the former are Type 3, and the latter are Type 1. Players who enter the Type 3s, expecting them to be Type 1s, may be pleasantly surprised (Bruckman, 1993). However, it should be noted that this initial warm behavior is sometimes the approach used by administrators to ensure a new player's further participation in their particular MUD, and that, once hooked, a player may find that attitudes undergo a subtle change (Epperson, 1995).

As mentioned earlier, this paper is not intended to promote any one particular style of MUD. Whether administrators aim for Type 1, 2, or 3 is up to them—they're all MUDs, and they address different needs. However, the fact that they *are* all MUDs and not "MU*s" (or any other abbreviation-of-the-day) really should be emphasized.

To summarize: "Game-like" MUDs are the ones in which the killer-achiever equilibrium has been reached, i.e., Type 1; "social" MUDs are the ones in which the pure social stability point has been reached, i.e., Type 2, and this is the basis upon which they differ. There is a Type 3 "all-round" (my term) MUD, which exhibits both social and game-like traits; however, such MUDs are scarce because the conditions necessary to reach the stable point are difficult or time-consuming to arrange.

Overbalancing a Mud

Earlier, the effect of taking each axis on the interest graph to its extremes was used to give an indication of what would happen if a MUD was pushed so far that it lost its MUDness. It was noted, though, that along the axes was not the only way a MUD could be tilted.

What would happen if, in an effort to appeal to certain types of player, a MUD was overcompensated in their favor?

Tilting a MUD toward achievers would make it obsessed with gameplay. Players would spend their time looking for tactics to improve their position, and the presence of other players would become unnecessary. The result would be effectively a single-player adventure game (SUD?).

Tilting toward explorers would add depth and interest but remove much of the activity. Spectacle would dominate over action, and again there would be no need for other players. The result of this is basically an online book.

Tilting toward socializers removes all gameplay and centers on communication. Eventually, all sense of the virtual world is lost, and a chat-line or IRC-style CB program results.

Tilting toward killers is more difficult because this type of player is parasitic on the other three types. The emphasis on causing grief has to be sacrificed in favor of the thrill of the chase and bolstered by the use of quick thinking and skill to overcome adversity in clever (but violent) ways. In other words, this becomes an arcade ("shoot 'em up") type of game.

It's a question of balance: If something is added to a MUD to tilt the graph one way, other mechanisms will need to be in place to counterbalance it (preferably automatically). Otherwise, what results is a SUD, book, chat-line, or arcade game. It's the *combination* that makes MUDs unique—and special. It *is* legitimate to say that anything that goes too far in any direction is not a MUD; it is *not* legitimate to say that something that doesn't go far enough in any direction is not a MUD. So long as a system is a (text-based) multi-user virtual world, that's enough.

Summary

To answer the questions posed in the preface, "Are MUDs?":

➤ Games? Like chess, tennis, *D&D*?
   Yes—to achievers.

➤ Pastimes? Like reading, gardening, cooking?
   Yes—to explorers.

➤ Sports? Like huntin', shooting', fishin'?
   Yes—to killers.

➤ Entertainments? Like nightclubs, TV, concerts?
   Yes—to socializers.

References

Aspnes, J. (1989). TinyMUD [C] (`http://ftp.tcp.com/ftp/pub/mud/TinyMUD/tinymud-pc.1.0.tar.gz`).

Bartle, R. A. (1985). *MUD2 [MUDDLE]*. MUSE Ltd, Colchester, Essex, UK.

Bartle, R. A. (1990a). "Who Plays MUAs?." *Comms Plus!* October/November 1990, pp. 18–19.

Bartle, R. A. (1990b). *Interactive Multi-Player Computer Games.* MUSE Ltd, Colchester, Essex, UK (`ftp://ftp.lambda.moo.mud.org/pub/MOO/papers/mudreport.txt`).

Bruckman, A. S. (1992). "Identity Workshop: Emergent Social and Psychological Phenomena in Text-Based Virtual Reality." MIT Media Laboratory, Cambridge, Massachusetts (`ftp://media.mit.edu/pub/asb/papers/identity-workshop.ps`).

Bruckman, A. S. (1993). "Gender Swapping on the Internet." Proc. INET-93 (`ftp://media.mit.edu/pub/asb/papers/gender-swapping.txt`).

Bruckman, A. S. and Resnick, M. (1993). "Virtual Professional Community: Results from the MediaMOO Project." MIT Media Laboratory, Cambridge, Massachusetts (`ftp://media.mit.edu/pub/asb/papers/convergence.txt`).

Bruckman, A. S. (1994a). "Workshop: 'Serious' Uses of MUDs?" Proc. DIAC-94 (`ftp://media.mit.edu/pub/asb/papers/serious-diac94.txt`).

Bruckman, A. S. (1994b). "Approaches to Managing Deviant Behavior in Virtual Communities." MIT Media Laboratory, Cambridge, Massachusetts (`ftp://media.mit.edu/pub/asb/deviance-chi94.txt`).

Burka, L. P. (1995). "The MUDline" (`www.ccs.neu.edu/home/lpb/mudline.html`).

Carton, S. (1995). *Internet Virtual Worlds Quick Tour: MUDs, MOOs and MUSHes: Interactive games, Conferences and Forums.* Ventana Press, Chapel Hill, North Carolina.

Caspian-Kaufman, J. (1995). *Sid Meier's CivNET: Instruction Manual.* Microprose, Hunt Valley, Maryland.

Cherny, L. (1995a). "The Modal Complexity of Speech Events in a Social MUD." *Electronic Journal of Communication.* Summer 1995 (`ftp://bhasha.stanford.edu/pub/cherny/ejc.txt`).

Cherny, L. (1995b). "The Situated Behavior of MUD Back Channels." Dept. Linguistics, Stanford University, California (`ftp://bhasha.stanford.edu/pub/cherny/aaai.ps`).

Clodius, J. A. (1994). "Concepts of Space in a Virtual Community" (`http://tinylondon.ucsd.edu/~jen/space.html`).

Curtis, P. (1992). "Mudding: Social Phenomena in Text-Based Virtual Realities." Proc. DIAC-92 (`ftp://ftp.lambda.moo.mud.org/pub/MOO/papers/DIAC92.txt`).

Curtis, P. and Nichols, D. A. (1993). "MUDs Grow Up: Social Virtual Reality in the Real World." Xerox PARC, Palo Alto, California (`ftp://ftp.lambda.moo.mud.org/pub/ MOO/papers/MUDsGrowUp.txt`).

Dibbell, J. (1993). "A Rape in Cyberspace." *The Village Voice*. December 21, 1993 (`ftp://ftp.lambda.moo.mud.org/pub/MOO/papers/VillageVoice.txt`).

Emert, H. G. (1993). "'X' Marks the Spot." East Stroudsburg University, Pennsylvania (`www-f.rrz.uni-koeln.de/themen/cmc/text/emert.n01.txt`).

Eddy, A. (1994). *Internet After Hours*. Prima, Rocklin, California.

Epperson, H. L. (1995). "Patterns of Social Behavior in Computer-Mediated Communications." Dept. Sociology, Rice University, Houston, Texas (`www.eff.org/pub/Net_culture/Misc_net_culture/ web_social_behaviour.paper`).

Evard, R. (1993). "Collaborative Networked Communication: MUDs as System Tools." Proc. LISA-93 (`www.ccs.neu.edu/home/remy/documents/cncmast.html`).

Fanderclai, T. F. (1995). "MUDs in Education: New Environments, New Pedagogies." *Computer-Mediated Communication Magazine*, 2(1), 8.

Farmer, F. R., Morningstar, C., and Crockford, D. (1994). "From Habitat to Global Cyberspace." Proc. CompCon-94, IEEE (`www.communities.com/paper/hab2cybr.html`).

Kort, B. (1991). "The MUSE as an Educational Medium." BBN Labs, Cambridge, Massachusetts (`ftp://musenet.bbn.com/pub/micromuse`).

Mauldin, M. L. (1994). "Chatterbots, TinyMUDs and the Turing Test: Entering the Loebner Prize Competition." Proc. AAAI-94 (http://fuzine.mt.cs.cmu.edu/mlm/aaai94.html).

Moock, C. (1996). "Virtual Campus at the University of Waterloo" (http://arts.uwaterloo.ca:80/~camoock/virtual_classroom.htm).

Norrish, J. (1995). "MU*s" (www.vuw.ac.nz/~jamie/mud/mud.html).

Poirier, J. R. (1994). *Interactive Multiuser Realities: MUDs, MOOs, MUCKs, and MUSHes. The Internet Unleashed.* SAMS Publishing, Indianapolis, Indiana, pp. 1192–1227.

Reid, E. (1994). "Cultural Formations in Text-Based Virtual Realities." Dept. English, University of Melbourne, Australia (ftp://ftp.lambda.moo.mud.org/pub/MOO/papers/CulturalFormations.txt).

Riner, R. D. and Clodius, J. A. (1995). "Simulating Future Histories: The NAU Solar System Simulation and Mars Settlement." *Anthropology & Education Quarterly*, 26(1), pp. 95–104 (http://tinylondon.ucsd.edu/~jen/solsys.html).

Rosenberg, M. S. (1992). "Virtual Reality: Reflections of Life, Dreams and Technology, An Ethnography of a Computer Society" (ftp://ftp.lambda.moo.mud.org/pub/MOO/papers/ethnography.txt).

Roush, W. (1993). "The Virtual STS Center on MediaMOO: Issues and Challenges as Non-Technical Users Enter Social Virtual Spaces." MIT Media Laboratory, Cambridge, Massachusetts (ftp://media.mit.edu/pub/MediaMOO/Papers/STS-Centre).

Urdang, L. and Manser, M. (1980). *The Pan Dictionary of Synonyms and Antonyms.* Pan Reference, London, UK.

Whitlock, T. D. (1994a). "F*** Art, Let's Kill!: Towards a Post Modern Community" (gopher://actlab.rtf.utexas.edu/00/art_and_tech/rtf_papers/pmc.terrorism).

Whitlock, T. D. (1994b). "Technological Hierarchy in MOO: Reflections on Power in Cyberspace" (www.actlab.utexas.edu/~smack/papers/TechHier.txt).

Appendix E

Online World Timeline

AUTHOR NOTE

Back in 1999, after 13 years of working with online games and 2 years of writing a rant column, "Biting the Hand (BTH)," I finally got fed up with the gaming press treating online games like a latecomer to the interactive market. The final straw was an article by a major computer game magazine that contained the line: "It looks like online games might not be just a flash in the pan after all."

That one made me go ballistic because online games have actually been around longer than PC games. (Remember the "big iron" of mainframes and shared computing?) You'd never have known it from the gaming press in 1999, however, which tends not to care about anything that doesn't bring in advertising money. Until Sony Online started advertising *EverQuest (EQ)* regularly in the pages of the magazines in 1999 and Microsoft finally launched *Asheron's Call (AC)* late that same year, online gaming remained opaque to them.

So I used BTH as the platform for a series of three columns entitled "Happy 30th Birthday, Online Games." I figured no one would care; it was a personal imperative and I didn't expect to get much mail about the series. I just wanted to set the record straight and not give the press an excuse not to know anymore.

Boy, was I ever wrong. The mail response flowed in. When the columns first appeared in October and November of 1999, Raph Koster, then a co-worker at Origin Systems, grabbed them off the Internet and distributed them to a mailing list of MUD developers, where they excited some comment. I had no idea people involved in online gaming were starved for some sense of history about what we do. Of the over 100 BTH columns I've written since 1997, those three columns are the most reprinted of the bunch. Not a month goes by that I don't get a request for a reprint.

Not long afterwards, Raph wrote up his own timeline, this time on the broader subject of online worlds. It is far more extensive and comprehensive than my online game timeline, going back to 1937 and the pre-genesis of the technology industry, and Raph updates it regularly. There is some fascinating stuff in there. It is well worth the time to read the whole thing.

Raph has graciously given us permission to reprint some of the timeline here, starting with 1969. For reasons of space, quite a few of the side and contributory comments for some years have been edited out. Besides, you should really read the whole thing, including some of the comments and history from contributors. The whole of it is shot through with references to important or influential events and works published in those years, with comments from some of the people responsible for them—utterly and completely compelling stuff.

This edited version is just to give a fairly complete timeline of major events from 1969 on. For the full monty, head over to Raph's personal web site at `www.legendmud.org/raph/gaming/ mudtimeline.html`.

You'll be glad you did.

—**Jessica Mulligan**

1969

➤ Rick Blomme writes two-player *Spacewar* on PLATO. It works on the remote network, so it is now true network gaming.

➤ ARPANet is founded. (The Cyberpunk Timeline puts the date at August of 1968.)

➤ UNIX is written.

➤ CompuServe is founded by John Goltz.

1970

➤ Dave Arneson starts the first "role-playing game" campaign, called *Blackmoor*. (Arneson himself is not sure whether this occurred in 1970 or 1971.)

1971

➤ Ted Nelson works with various guys individually. (1971–1972: Ted invents/ discovers first "Model T" enfilade; redesigns *Xanadu* around it.)

1972

➤ PLATO reaches capacity at 1,000 users.

➤ *Hunt the Wumpus* is developed by Gregory Yob on a time-sharing system at the University of Massachusetts in Dartmouth. This is not an adventure game (it's a text-only maze game), but a precursor (Hans Persson, Adventureland timeline).

➤ Atari is founded by Nolan Bushnell.

➤ The second edition of the *Chainmail* miniatures war-gaming rules are published, including a "fantasy supplement." This ruleset will go on to inspire *Dungeons & Dragons (D&D)*.

1973

➤ *Airfight*, a.k.a. *Dogfight* (flight sim), on PLATO.

"In Dogfight, *two players tried to shoot down each other's 'airplane'—a tiny spot on the screen—and avoid being shot down. You could control the position of your own airplane using the various keys on the keyboard. (This, of course, was 10 years before joysticks and computer mice became common.) Unfortunately, the person with the fastest connection to the main computer in Illinois usually won that game."* —**Guy Consolmagno**, SJ

"PLATO also had Airfight, *a 3D real-time flight simulator with 3D views of horizon and airport and enemy (icon only). One of the authors was Brand Fortner. These authors went on to found the company that became Microsoft* Flight Simulator. *I think 1973 is the right year for the existence of* Airfight—*it was EARLIER than* Empire. *I think it's very important to realize that Microsoft* Flight Simulator *came from PLATO, from the guys who wrote* Airfight. *I cannot remember the name of the company they founded, but it was really successful for a few years before Microsoft bought it in the mid-1980s."* —**Don Gillies**

➤ Talk-O-Matic, a proto-IRC with handles and chat rooms, is on PLATO at this point (it may have existed earlier).

"One of the more popular activities was 'Talk-O-Matic.' Five people at a time could write messages and read each other's messages on the same screen. Today, Internet chat rooms work on the same principle. One of the remarkable new features of this page was that you could log in with an invented name and pretend you were anyone you wanted— any name, any age, any gender. One favorite trick was to log in using the name of someone else already logged into the page, simply to confuse everyone else."
—**Guy Consolmagno,** SJ

➤ The "Hacking Into Computer Systems: A Beginner's Guide" doc reports PLATO gets hacked with the starship *Enterprise* attacking people on *Airfight* (who were expecting airplanes!).

➤ *D&D* is first sold by Arneson and Gary Gygax as typewritten rulesets.

1974

➤ The original *D&D* set is published, though it had been well-distributed prior to this.

➤ Somewhere in here, *Mines of Moria* (it had 248 mazes, according to *Antic* magazine in 1984) on PLATO.

➤ *Empire*: multiplayer space empire game on PLATO supporting 32 players.

"Empire was a MIND-BLOWING game. It had three million contact hours before 1980. Think about it. PLATO only had 1,000 terminals. So, there were only something like 9M contact hours in a PLATO-year." —**Don Gillies**

➤ *D&D* (*Avatar*) existed by now, according to Steve Gray, who was 11 at the time and writing code for PLATO. *D&D* was apparently the command-line name, and *Avatar* the game name. Dr. Cat says that *Wizardry* (*"one of the first PC RPGs"* —JMM) was directly based on *Avatar*, down to the spell names.

"D&D, by Flint and Dirk Pellett, predates Avatar. So does Orthanc, by Paul Resch, Larry Kemp, and myself, and done about the same time. Both have overhead 3x3 views. Orthanc allowed players to meet and talk in the dungeon, but otherwise was a single-player game. This is 1973." —**Eric Hagstrom**

➤ According to Peter Zelchenko, the original authors of *D&D* were Gary Whisenhunt and Ray Wood; Flint and Dirk Pellet were subsequent authors.

➤ Notes files created on PLATO, the first bulletin-board systems (BBSes), almost exactly like today's Usenet. Also, around now Xerox visits PLATO and they trade ideas, according to Doug Jones.

"Actually, the first version of PLATO Notes opened in August 1973. Personal Notes (email) came along about a year later in 1974. Group Notes, the new version of PLATO Notes that allowed anyone to create a Notes file, came out in January 1976." —**David Woolley**

➤ Somewhere in here, *DECWAR* was created. It was *Star Trek*-based also—perhaps a relationship to the *Empire* game on PLATO?

"That was called DECWAR. Yes, it ran on VAX/VMS. We used to play it on a PDP-10. It used shared memory to communicate, not files, which was one of the ways the sys admins could detect it. We generally played 5+ players per side. It had a lot of intelligent multiplayer design considerations." —**S. Patrick Gallaty**

➤ The first first-person shooter? Dave Lebling and Greg Thompson write a multiplayer first-person maze for the Imlac PDS-1, with PDP-10 as a server. It supported up to eight players, chat, and bots.

➤ *Star Trader* is written by Dave Kaufman.

"People's Computer Company (PCC), a company that is still around today and who brought us Dr. Dobb's Journal *among other things, publishes Volume 2, Number 3 of its newsletter in January. In this publication is BASIC source code for* Star Trader *by Dave Kaufman. This game outlined the general details of a sector-based game with ports and a player moving between sectors trading three basic products (fuel, organics, and equipment) to earn credits."* —**John Pritchett's** *History of Tradewars 2002*

1975

➤ A paper is published on "Teaching Mathematics with Games" on PLATO. This is the only formal reference I can find to PLATO and games. PLATO eventually banned games.

➤ Bridge on PLATO.

"I was the main author of the bridge game (called Contract). Martin Wolff wrote the bidding logic, and I did pretty much everything else. Karen Walker says 'PLATO's primitive bidding was random after the first round of the auction, and its defense and declarer play defied logic …' Well, it was indeed a pretty pathetic player, I have to admit. However, the bidding was deterministic, not random. It may have *seemed* random, though…" —**David Woolley**

➤ John Taylor *(co-founder of Kesmai Corporation – JMM)* reports that he was writing and playing multiplayer games at the University of Virginia in this year.

➤ John Brunner's *Shockwave Rider* is published.

1976

➤ Will Crowther creates the first version of *ADVENT* in FORTRAN on a PDP-1 while working for Bolt, Beranek, and Newman (BBN) in Boston.

➤ Don Woods put *ADVENT* on the PDP-10. This is the version everyone knows.

➤ Apple Computer is founded.

➤ Control Data Corporation (CDC) buys the PLATO network.

1977

➤ PLATO is up to PLATO V by now.

➤ Lebling and Blank start work on *Zork* on the PDP-10, inspired by *ADVENT*. They form a startup with some friends, called Infocom.

"The original Zork, started in 1977, was written by me, Marc Blank (note spelling), Tim Anderson, and Bruce Daniels. Infocom wasn't founded until 1979. One source for Zork is that I was in the game D&D group, which was mostly BBN people, that Wil Crowther was in. Not at the same time, though; I think I actually replaced him when we dropped out. Zork was 'derived' from ADVENT in that we played ADVENT, liked it, wished it were better, and tried to do a 'better' one. There was no code borrowed, or anything like that, and we didn't meet either Crowther or Woods until much later." —**Dave Lebling**

➤ A new version of *D&D* with simplified rules, later to be called *Basic Dungeons & Dragons* (*BD&D*), is published. It contains the first known use of the term "role-playing game."

➤ The *Advanced Dungeons & Dragons Monster Manual* is published.

➤ Kelton Flinn works on "the text-based amoeboid-like ancestor" to *Air Warrior*, called *AIR*, between 1977 and 1979.

"If Air Warrior *was a primate swinging in the trees,* AIR *was the text-based amoeba crawling on the ocean floor. But it was quasi-real-time, multiplayer, and attempted to render 3D on the terminal using ASCII graphics. It was an acquired taste."* —**Kelton Flinn**

1978

➤ Roy Trubshaw begins *MUD1* development. In the fall, he and Richard Bartle complete the first version, which runs on a PDP-10. The name, "multi-user dungeon," refers to a variant of *ADVENT* known as *DUNGEON*.

➤ Alan Klietz writes *Sceptre of Goth*, also a MUD system. These two developments were completely independent. Lauren Burka puts this date at 1979. *Sceptre of Goth* was also known as *Empire* for a while, but is not generally referred to that way because of the numerous other games with the same name.

➤ *AD&D Player Handbook* is published.

➤ Interestingly, according to Lauren Burka, early MUD developers never played the game. Richard Bartle clarifies: "In my case, that's only true because *AD&D* wasn't out yet; I had played *D&D* quite a bit in 1976–1978. The only real impact it made on *MUD1* was the "levels" system, though, which I thought was a neat way to give players short-to-medium-term goals. Roy Trubshaw knew about *D&D* and may have tried it once or twice, but I don't think he ever dived in deeply; he certainly never designed his own dungeons."

➤ Walter Bright's version of *Empire* makes it to the DEC-10.

➤ Somewhere in here, *Oubliette* on PLATO.

"Oubliette, the first group-oriented dungeon on PLATO, was the model the early Wizardry series ripped off, and also predates Avatar. Spells were cast by typing their names (i.e., alito, fieminamor), and you had to type them as fast as possible to beat the monster. 1977?" —**Eric Hagstrom**

1979

➤ *Zork* released as a standalone game by Infocom.

➤ The *Advanced Dungeons & Dragons Dungeon Master's Guide* is published.

➤ *S*, the multiplayer space combat and colonization game by Kelton Flinn and John Taylor, is coded over the summer at the University of Virginia.

"S was written in BASIC and supported eight users on the HP-2000." —**Kelton Flinn**

1980

➤ *Basic Dungeons & Dragons* and *Expert Dungeons & Dragons* are published.

"This publication marks a split between D&D and AD&D, as TSR modifies the rules of BD&D to be less like AD&D. The split was made for legal reasons—David Arneson, the co-creator of D&D, had left TSR and sued for royalties from D&D. TSR maintained that AD&D was a different game, and they therefore should not have to pay royalties to Arneson on it or its products. Maintaining this, however, required that they not replace D&D with AD&D, as had been their original intent. For this reason, TSR continued to produce both D&D and AD&D, and to change the two game lines to be different from each other, into the early 1990s." —**Travis S. Casey**

➤ *Empire* introduces annual tournaments.

➤ Final version of *MUD1* completed by Richard Bartle. Essex goes on the ARPANet, resulting in Internet MUDs!

➤ Steve Jackson releases *Advanced Melee* and *Advanced Wizard*, along with *In The Labyrinth*. The changes made from previous versions make the games into a role-playing system.

➤ *Drygulch* exists on PLATO by now.

"Another PLATO game existing at that time (around 1980) was Panzerkrieg. *You and an opponent would carry out extended campaigns against each other in a WWII simulation. Another was* Wolfpack *(German, American, and British multiplayer subs vs. destroyers)."*
—**Mike Lindeland**

➤ Kelton Flinn and John Taylor write *Dungeons of Kesmai*. It used ASCII graphics.

"The summer of 1980, we wrote the game that became Dungeons of Kesmai, *which supported six users on a souped-up Z-80."* —**Kelton Flinn**

"They didn't know about MUD at the time. No. The fantasy Lineage *started with the single-player fantasy game written for the HP-2000 in BASIC during 1979–1980, basically extending a maze combat program I wrote earlier in 1979, to see if I could capture some of the essence of D&D. That game was rewritten in UCSD Pascal for the Z-80 running CPM, and as I mentioned, at that point became a six-user multiplayer.* Dungeons *was the cut-down single-player version of that game, still Pascal because CompuServe had a compiler. There was a TRS-80 Model 1 BASIC version in there also. At that time, I hadn't even heard of* Adventure *yet. Of course, by the time we were doing the* Island *late in 1980, I had seen* Adventure *and* Zork, *but we were heading off in our own direction by that time, a lot more action-oriented and very little puzzle-solving."* —**Kelton Flinn**

1981

➤ Atari starts trying to put PLATO on eight bits, but negotiations break down.

➤ *Island of Kesmai* is written by Kelton Flinn and John Taylor.

*"Island of Kesmai *was written in 1980 and 1981, the goal being to soak up every bit of performance in the CS department's new VAX. We succeeded."* —**Kelton Flinn**

➤ William Gibson publishes *Johnny Mnemonic* in Omni.

➤ Vernor Vinge publishes *True Names*.

1982

➤ Kesmai is founded by Kelton Flinn and John Taylor.

"In November 1981, John saw an ad for CompuServe, namely a MegaWars ad ('If you had written this, you'd be making $30,000 a month in royalties!' I think the ad said. Bill [Louden] was actually trolling for new games!) That kinda got our interest, so we sent a copy of the Island of Kesmai manual to Bill Louden and also to The Source. Even though the game already ran on the Prime computers that The Source used, they never responded intelligibly. Louden, on the other hand, was interested. We tried to bring the original UNIX version of Island of Kesmai up on CompuServe's DEC 20s, and chewed up $100,000 of CPU time (at the-then commercial rate) in three days. We got it working, but as Bill said, the lights dimmed in Columbus when it was running. So we headed back to Charlottesville to retrench. The first step was porting the old Z-80 code, that became Dungeons of Kesmai, which was cut back to single-player (probably the only time in history a multiplayer game was made into a single-player game!)." **—Kelton Flinn**

➤ Teletel is created.

"Minitel was the outgrowth of a French government telecom project in the early 1980s called the 'Teletel' network. This went live in 1982. It wasn't until early 1984 that the Minitel service—'phone- top boxes' in many French telephone customers' homes, etc.—went live." **—Josh Kirkpatrick**

1983

➤ *MegaWars I* launches on CompuServe. (According to S. Patrick Gallaty, the design of *MegaWars I* was based on that of *DECWAR*.)

➤ The film *War Games* is released.

1984

➤ The first commercial version of *MUD1* opens on Compunet in the UK.

➤ *Island of Kesmai* launches ($12 an hour!).

➤ AUSI, a predecessor company to Mythic Entertainment, forms and launches *Aradath* for $40 a month.

➤ Atari finally puts PLATO on eight bits. It has a $5/hour connect fee.

➤ Minitel goes live. A detailed history can be found at:
`http://appli1.oecd.org/olis/1997doc.nsf/a0c602508a90ce00412566`
`9e003b5adf/a8093b855bd4ea32802566ad0056749d/$FILE/10E87215.ENG.`

➤ Sometime prior to 1984, John Sherrick writes *Tradewars* (*TW*). It's similar to *Star Trader*, written in BASIC, and is for BBSes.

"It's not known whether or not Sherrick was inspired by Star Trader, *but I suspect this to be the case since they were both written in BASIC. Sherrick's TW is developed in BASIC until December 1989, when it is ported to C. I believe that Sherrick's earliest work was freeware, without any restrictions. It is because of this public-domain code, and the* Star Trader *code, that so many TW variations have been and continue to be written. At some point, Sherrick closed his code, releasing it under the new name of TW II. His version continues to be developed by John Morris, I am told."*
—**John Pritchett**, TW *history*

"Another BBS door game. This is such an influential game, at least to me. This was a multiplayer turn-based space-trading game with a bit of combat thrown in. You couldn't actually play this at the same time as another player. You had X amount of moves per day. When your moves ran out, somebody else got a turn. Yes, it was persistent as your merchant and fleet were left in the game for other players to destroy or destroy them if they found you." —**Jon Lambert**

➤ *Neuromancer* is published, and the word "cyberspace" is coined.

1985

➤ *Island of Kesmai* is released on CompuServe.

"My memory says that Island of Kesmai *went live on CompuServe on December 15, 1985, after a very long internal test. The price was actually $6 an hour for 300 baud, $12 for 1200 baud. Serious players paid the bucks."* —**Kelton Flinn**

➤ *Stellar Warrior* (rewrite of *MegaWars*) launches on GEnie.

"On the same day (as the launch of Island of Kesmai*), we rolled out* Stellar Warrior *on GEnie ($5 an hour for 1200 baud, raised a year or so later to $6).* Stellar Warrior *was a cut-down and simplified version of* MegaWars III *(not* MegaWars*), ported to FORTRAN."*
—Kelton Flinn

➤ GEnie launches at $6 an hour.

"For example: On GEnie during 1991, our average MMOG customer spent $156 per month, the equivalent of 32 hours at $3 per hour to play. However, the hard-core players averaged three times that and accounted for nearly 70% of the total revenue. The top 0.5% had truly astronomical bills, well over $1,000 per month." **—Jessica Mulligan**

➤ QuantumLink, predecessor to AOL, launches in November.

➤ *Habitat* is developed by Randy Farmer and Chip Morningstar at Lucasfilm, as a product for QuantumLink. The client runs on a C64.

➤ Richard Bartle starts work on *MUD2*.

➤ Peter Langston creates *PSL Empire*, apparently as a single-player game. This is not to be confused with the other game termed *Empire* that ran on PLATO and which was *Star Trek*-based.

"Also Rabbitjack's Casino *was the first graphic multiplayer online game from QuantumLink for the C-64 (1985 or 1986, maybe?), and was later ported to the PC for AOL."* **—Dr. Cat**

"This was developed by Rob Fulop's company (name forgotten) and Ernest Adams was involved." **—Jessica Mulligan**

"The (name forgotten), Rob Fulop's company (for Rabbitjack's Casino*), was Advanced Program Technology. I worked on the sound player code for this project back in 1985. :) 1985–1986 sounds about right for when the game was launched. Rob Fulop was earlier the author of many Atari 2600 games, including* Demon Attack *and* Night Driver*."*
—Dan Peri

1986

➤ *xtrek*, the predecessor to *Netrek*, is released.

➤ Jessica Mulligan does first play-by-email game on commercial online server: *Rim Worlds War*.

➤ *Air Warrior* hits pre-Alpha.

➤ *MUD2* launches in the UK as a pay-for-play service.

➤ *UCSD Empire*, by Dave Pare, made *Langston's Empire* a multiplayer game.

➤ *MTrek* is first run.

"MTrek (Multi-Trek) was up and running at University of California at Santa Cruz from 1986 through the early 1990s—at least through 1993. Mainly through the good graces of then-sys admin Tim Garlick, who designated ucscb.ucsc.edu as a 'social and games' system and thereby created an entire community. There was an author-endorsed variant called S&MTrek (supposedly standing for Sean and Madonna Trek*) hosted by Jon Luini (IUMA founder) at gorn.com, back when Jon worked for SCO."* —**Jame Scholl**

➤ Macromind (later Macromedia) releases Dave Lebling's game *MazeWars*, based on the 1974 game *Maze*.

"Macromind's version was based on the one for the Xerox Alto written by Jim Guyton (who heard about it from a friend who had been at MIT) in the late 1970s. Macromind's version used the Appletalk network. It and the Alto version had a HUD of the maze (which we always refused to put in—cheating!). There was no mouselook in any of these versions, if my memory is correct: it was all keystrokes." —**Dave Lebling**

➤ *Air Warrior* is released on GEnie.

"Air Warrior debuted on GEnie in February 1986, Jessica has that one right. The initial client was on the Macintosh; the Amiga and Atari ST versions came along later that year, and the IBM PC the next. One thing that was unique about Air Warrior *was that we supported Macintosh, Amiga, Atari ST, and IBM PC all in the same game, flying against each other. In 1988, we rolled out* Air Warrior *on the FM-TOWNS for Fujitsu. It was available in Japan for several years, but the price was too high due to telecom charges, so it never reached the level of popularity it had on GEnie."* —**Kelton Flinn**

1987

➤ Simutronics is founded; *Gemstone* goes Alpha late in the year.

➤ *MUD1* is launched as *British Legends* on CompuServe.

➤ *AberMUD* is released by Alan Cox.

1988

➤ *Gemstone* launches as *Gemstone II* on GEnie.

➤ IRC is invented.

"If you're going to mention IRC, you might mention the invention dates of CompuServe CB, GEnie's chat, and the first chat on French Minitel (which was in the dawning days of Minitel and led to some users dropping off with multi-thousand-dollar phone bills). No, I don't know these dates." —**Dr. Cat**

➤ Mark Baldwin does a GUI version of *Bright's Empire* for the PC.

➤ QuantumLink launches AppleLink, soon to be AOL. Turns down *Aradath* and *Galaxy II* (by AUSI, later Mythic – JMM), though.

➤ Rich Skrenta at Northwestern University (NU) releases *Monster*, a multiplayer adventure game written in Pascal that supported online creation.

"I wrote Monster *in about three months, during NU's 'winter quarter.' I was totally obsessed with coding it. Project obsession was normal with me (really boosts the productivity :-), but* Monster Madness*, as I called it then, really got out of hand. I was spending all night in the comp center, leaving at 7 a.m., skipping classes, skipping everything. (My 10,000-line VMS Pascal wonder would compile faster when no one was around, which encouraged the nocturnal work.) I went on spring break, and when I got back, I forced myself to not continue working on* Monster*. I was afraid I'd fail out of school if I did. I left it alone until November of that year, when I started sending it out on the Bitnet."* —**Rich Skrenta** (from Lauren Burka's MUDLine)

➤ *Club Caribe*, a derivative of *Habitat*, is released on QuantumLink.

1989

➤ *TinyMUD* is released by Jim Aspnes. It ran on UNIX and was written in C. It was originally conceived as a front-end to IRC.

➤ *Galaxy I* launches on GEnie.

➤ *A-Maze-ing*, a 3D online shooter, launches on GEnie.

"A-Maze-ing was authored by Greg Corson and ran on the Macintosh only. Greg's an old friend of mine from South Bend, who taught me how to write a DDA line-drawing routine to do faster graphics back in 1981 or so. He started doing multiplayer online stuff in the 1970s at Purdue and is another PLATO guy from way back. He was later the lead engineer at Virtual World Entertainment (who made the Battletech centers with the sit-down cockpits linked together in groups of eight), worked at NEC coordinating the 3D chip stuff with Sega for the Dreamcast, and is now at Sony in San Francisco." —**Dr. Cat**

➤ Lars Penjske creates *LPMud* and opens *Genesis*.

"Having fun playing TinyMUD and AberMUD, Lars Penjske decides to write a server to combine the extensibility of TinyMUD with the adventures of AberMUD. Out of this inspiration, he designed LPC as a special MUD language to make extending the game simple. Lars says, '...I didn't think I would be able to design a good adventure. By allowing wizards coding rights, I thought others could help me with this.' The first running code was developed in a week on Unix System V using IPC, not BSD sockets. Early object-oriented features only existed accidentally by way of the nature of MUDs manipulating objects. As Lars learned C++, he gradually extended those features. The result is that the whole LPMud was developed from a small prototype, gradually extended with features." — **George Reese's** *LPMud Timeline*

➤ Simutronics launches *Orb Wars* on GEnie. Darrin Hyrup was the lead programmer on it. Later that year, Hyrup leaves Simutronics for AUSI.

"It was a tactical multiplayer mage vs. mage combat game, top-down, with a windowed interface similar to the old Island of Kesmai." —**Darrin Hyrup**

➤ *Legends of the Red Dragon* is written by Seth Robinson in TurboPascal.

"This was a multiplayer hack-n-slash adventure game that scaled up to eight to ten users. It ran as a BBS door game. It accomplished this on DOS through some kludgy software interrupt time-slicing. Anyway, I recall it had both PvP and PvCritter action. This game was wildly popular from its inception until the decline of BBSs. I remember redialing and waiting for hours to get into a slot on the BBSes that ran it." —**Jon A. Lambert**

1990

➤ *TinyMUD* shuts down.

➤ *TeenyMUD* is created as a disk-based alternative to the *TinyMUD* codebase. It was written by Andrew Molitor and Marcus Ranum.

"It didn't do much other than crash a lot, but it was the first TinyMUD *clone that kept its database on disk instead of memory (or in swap, as was more likely)."* —**Jason Downs**

➤ *Diplomacy* launches on GEnie, done by AUSI and Eric Raymond (yes, the open source guru).

➤ *Federation II* launches on GEnie.

➤ Negotiations for *Ultima Online (UO)* begin with Origin, Kesmai, and GEnie. Nothing comes of them, however.

➤ *100 Years War* launches on Genie.

➤ *Gemstone II* converted into chat space called *ImagiNation*.

➤ *TinyMUCK* is written by Stephen White—over a weekend, he claims. Later that year, he releases MOO, which stands for "MUD, object-oriented."

➤ Pavel Curtis does substantial modifications to White's MOO code, creating *LambdaMOO. LambdaMOO* opens, hosted at Xerox PARC, where it promptly becomes a major influence in the development of social issues in virtual spaces.

➤ *Islandia* opens using *TinyMUD* code.

➤ *TinyTIM* opens.

➤ *TinyMUSH* is written.

➤ *FurryMUCK* opens. It features avatars that are anthropomorphic animals.

➤ Fujitsu launches a Japanese version of *Habitat* that works on FMTowns at first and other platforms later.

➤ DIKU MUDs are released.

➤ The MUD client *tinyFugue* is available now in version 1.4 Beta.

➤ *Shattered World*, the first Australian LPMud, opens.

"This MUD is the source of a private-distribution LPMud server used by a handful of spin-off MUDs in the US." —**George Reese**

➤ The pay-for-play text MUD *Avalon* opens in the UK.

➤ AUSI's *Dragon's Gate* launches on GEnie, written by Mark Jacobs and Darrin Hyrup. According to Jessica Mulligan's *History of Online Games*, published on Happy Puppy and in Imaginary Realities, it's a revised and expanded version of *Aradath*. However, Hyrup says, "It was a new creation, inspired by *Aradath*, but bearing little physical resemblance to it. We actually did do an *Aradath* remake a few years later, but the project never surfaced."

Jessica adds, "Darrin's correct. What Mark Jacobs and I agreed to was *Aradath* for GEnie, but he and Darrin really went to town and gave us a far more interesting game. It cost an extra six months of development, which really irritated me at the time, but turned out to be worth the wait."

"We had one Dragon's Gate *player who spent $2,000 per month every month for over a year (at the time, GEnie's access fees during the period 7 a.m. to 7 p.m. were close to $20 per hour, and this guy would play during that time)."* —**Jessica Mulligan**

➤ *BatMUD* opens.

➤ *TW 2002* is licensed to High Velocity Software to port it to MajorBBS. This changed the game, which was already multiplayer and persistent, to also be interactive, since MajorBBS supported far more concurrent users.

➤ The apparent first reference to the word "avatar" in print, using the definition commonly accepted today, of a representation of a user in a virtual environment. The appearance is in Benedikt's *Cyberspace*, in multiple papers. The word apparently originated on *Habitat*. Many claim Neal Stephenson's *Snow Crash* as the coinage for the term, including Stephenson himself in some editions.

"The usage of 'avatar' to mean 'the graphical representation of yourself in a shared digital world' was first used in 1984–1988 in a product that was then called Lucasfilm's Habitat. *Chip Morningstar coined the usage. I was with him at the time. Yes, it was derived from the Hindi usage. This significantly predates any other similar usage that I am aware of. (In 1988, the product changed names to* Club Caribe, *and the documentation changed the term for this concept, but by then some in the alt.cyberspace/VRML community had picked up the term. Neal Stephenson says that he had thought that the term was original with him, but when I contacted him at the time, he graciously put a corrected afterword in the paperback version of* Snow Crash.*)*

"It is important to note that the term 'avatar' was used in another game around later in that period (Ultima IV) *and the concept of an 'avatar' was in several works of fiction prior to the development of* Habitat, *including Vernor Vinge's* True Names *and John Brunner's* Shockwave Rider.*"* —**Randy Farmer**

1991

➤ BSX MUDs are developed by Bram Stolk.

➤ *LambdaMOO* opens officially—however, there have already been several hundred regular players. That same year, it acquires tools such as site tracking, blacklists, and review boards for user building.

➤ PernMUSH is founded.

➤ Howard Rheingold's *Virtual Reality* is published.

➤ *Multiplayer Battletech* is designed by Kelton Flinn as an attempt to appeal to exactly the opposite market as *Air Warrior* (e.g., a more community-oriented market).

➤ Electric Communities is founded by Farmer, Morningstar, and Douglas Crockford. They handle the WorldsAway contract as well as begin design work on a secure distributed "cyberspace operating system."

➤ At the suggestion of Walter Feurzig of BBN, *MicroMush* changes its name to *MicroMuse*. It develops into the first educational outreach MUD, focusing on grades K–12.

➤ The Sierra Network (TSN) launches.

"Sierra Network was first Beta-tested in a 16-color EGA version as Constant Companion in 1990 or 1991 (I think 1990). The idea was that senior citizens would love to use this to play board and card games with each other. Ken Williams sent Richard Garriott a Beta copy and said he'd like to get UO on there." —**Dr. Cat**

"TSN, often overlooked for its contribution to online gaming, started in 1991. Version 2.0 (v2) was released in October/November of 1992. Included in v2 was The Shadow of Yserbius, Red Baron, *and* Leisure Suit Larry Vegas *(gambling, cyber-ing, etc.), along with the v1 games of bridge, chess, checkers, etc. I once played bridge with Bill Gates, as he is an avid bridge player and had an account on TSN."* —**Brian Thomson**

➤ Stormfront Studios' *NWN* launches on AOL. It was based on the Gold Box SSI *AD&D* games, and was programmed by Cathryn Mataga.

➤ *Discworld* opens. It is an LPMud based on the Terry Pratchett novels.

1992

➤ *LambdaMOO* takes a new direction—an attempt to have a democratic, player-run government within a MUD.

➤ MPGNet; founded, launches *Kingdom of Drakkar* (top view, graphical).

➤ Simutronics launches *Cyberstrike* (graphical).

➤ QuantumLink renames itself AOL.

➤ *Valhalla*, an LPMud, supports itself by charging money.

"Though the MUD was given permission to charge players by Lars, this move was still controversial among the LPMud community who believed that Lars no longer had the right to give such permission given the amount of code which had been donated to LPMud from various sources." —**George Reese**

➤ First instances of interMUD networks created using LP.

"LPC sockets are added to the MudOS driver. This allows TMI to create a very rough TCP interMUD network. This protocol is later replaced first by the CDlib UDP protocols, and later by InterMUD 3." —**George Reese**

➤ *Legends of Future Past* opens to the public.

➤ Neal Stephenson publishes *Snow Crash*.

➤ The film *Lawnmower Man* is released.

1993

➤ Mosaic makes the Internet graphical.

➤ *Doom* comes out in December.

➤ The *Discworld* MUDlib is released.

"The choice of MUDlibs for MudOS helps add to the driver's growing popularity. At this time, the Discworld *MUDlib contains the most advanced command parser and user interface available in a MUDlib."* —**George Reese**

➤ *Worlds of Carnage* closes. It will reopen later in the year, but several players and admins leave, never to return, including Damion Schubert, Rick Delashmit, and the Kosters.

➤ CDC sells PLATO to The Roach Organization. CDC stays in computer-aided instruction, but calls their clone of PLATO Cybis. CERL at University of Illinois started NovaNET to replace it, but that was then transferred to University Communications, Inc.

➤ On *LambdaMOO*, Mr. Bungle is toaded. This leads to Julian Dibbell's article "A Rape in Cyberspace" in the *Village Voice*, which catapults MUDs into the lime-light. This also leads to the formation of a petition system on *LambdaMOO*, which is a voting mechanism for players with votes being binding on the MUD admins.

➤ TSN first expands, then is purchased by AT&T and becomes the ImagiNation Network.

"In 1993, TSN expanded and then collapsed—well was eaten by AT&T. When they expanded, they added on to The Shadow of Yserbius *with* Fates of Twinion. *Both games were written by Joe Yberra, who last I heard was at Ensemble. After AT&T ate TSN, it became The ImagiNation Network. Ken Williams was moving toward the realm anyway. The bandwidth of running TSN was killing it. I believe the backbone was Sprint-net. Sierra leased the lines and subscribers could buy blocks of hours per month or unlimited hours for about $120 a month. This is what killed it. Ken had no idea how the hard-core gamers would eat his bandwidth."* —**Brian Thomson**

1994

➤ *Dragonspires* is opened by ex-Originite Dr. Cat.

➤ News Corp buys Kesmai.

➤ AT&T buys INN. They subsequently lose their shirt.

➤ *LegendMUD* opens with *Carnage* refugees (both Kosters and Delashmit, as well as others); first classless MUD? Uses a reverse-engineered and improved scripting language based on *Worlds of Carnage's.*

➤ Fujitsu's Cultural Technologies division reintroduces *Habitat* in the US as *WorldsAway.* It is later shipped in Japan as Fujitsu *Habitat II.*

➤ Worlds Inc, founded in Seattle, launches *WorldsChat.*

➤ *Avalon* opens as a pay-for-play MUD on the Internet after four years as a dial-up MUD in the UK. Is this the first commercial MUD on the Internet?

➤ Nexon, based in Korea, begins work on *Kingdom of the Winds*, a graphical tile-based MUD.

➤ Total Entertainment Network (TEN) gets going.

"TEN went into national Beta testing in 1994, before Jack Heistand, Kleiner Perkins, or Outland (it was just Planet Optigon then) were on the scene. It had a multiplayer version of SimCity, *chess, checkers, chat spaces, multiple interface themes, game-partner matching, editorial, and the ability to play games like* Descent *with two players via the service. There were just about 12 people in the company. Outland and Kleiner Perkins joined in 1995. Jack Heistand joined in 1996."* —**Daniel Goldman**

"Jack Heistand was formerly of EA Sports. Funding came from Vinod Khosla of Kleiner Perkins, who merged Outland *with* Optigon *and pumped in $10 million."* —**Jessica Mulligan**

➤ A company called Cyberspace, Inc. gets going. This will eventually be Turbine (*developers of* AC – JMM).

"Founders were Jeremy Gaffney (CEO), Jonathan Monserrat (President/Treasurer), Kevin Langevin (Secretary), and Timothy Miller. None of the rest of the founders are still in the games biz; they all left Turbine before I did (in January 1998)." —**Jeremy Gaffney**

1995

➤ Id starts testing *Quake*, which is going to be their real effort at making online multiplayer games. It becomes an instant phenomenon, redefining online gaming and virtual reality in the process.

➤ *Gemstone III* goes live on AOL.

➤ Archetype Interactive begins *Meridian 59 (M59)*, with Mike Sellers as a designer and the Kirmse brothers, Chris and Andrew, as programmers. Mike offers Raph Koster a job, but he declines because of a job offer from Origin. He recommends Damion Schubert for the job instead. *Archetype* and *Meridian* are later acquired by 3DO, where Rich Vogel acts as producer for a time.

➤ *Air Warrior* goes live on AOL.

➤ LIMA MUDlib offers infocom-style parsing.

➤ Rick Delashmit, hired by Origin for *UO*, joined Starr Long and Ken Demarest. Demarest shortly thereafter leaves for Titanic, a startup. Later that year, Origin also hires the Kosters as designers.

➤ *AlphaWorld* launches, also by Ron Britvich. It's a successor product to *WorldsChat*, but not the same engine. It supports a whole 12 avatar appearances.

➤ Electric Communities officially incorporates and gets venture capital. Their product is a major revision of *Habitat*, called both *Habitat* and *Microcosm*. It features a secure distributed architecture. It is later shelved as being ahead of its time, according to Farmer.

➤ Time Warner Interactive launches Jim Bumgartner's *The Palace*.

➤ Jake Song of Nexon leaves Nexon to join Inet, and branches TK server to create *Lineage*. He joined NCSoft later in 1997.

➤ *Illusia*, a graphical MUD with static backdrop scenes, opens to the public.

➤ *TeenyMUD 2.0* is released.

➤ The TV show *VR5* appears on US television. In this show, a researcher has found a way to enter virtual reality, and through it enter other peoples' minds. The show is cancelled after one season.

1996

➤ *LambdaMOO* takes another new direction—the admins take back over.

➤ *M59* opens.

"Until M59 *launched in 1996 and* UO *launched in September of 1997 with flat monthly rates, billing for commercial MMOGs was mainly on a per minute/hourly basis (with a brief period of free access to AOL's games from December 1996 to about July 1997). Thus, the number of total subscribers was less important than how long you kept your hard-core players (the top 10%) in-game."* —**Jessica Mulligan**

➤ *The Realm* enters Beta.

➤ *AD&D: Dark Sun Online* enters Beta.

➤ *AmigaMUD*, a graphical free MUD system, is released.

➤ AOL takes on *Dragon's Gate*. At this point, AUSI has morphed into Interworld Productions.

➤ *Quake* is released.

➤ Origin demos *UO* at E3.

➤ Engage is announced at E3. Its first Beta opens in December, on AOL, with a multiplayer version of *Castles II*.

➤ AOL buys INN.

- Sherry Turkle publishes *Life on the Screen*.

- John Smedley at Sony's 989 Studios hires Brad McQuaid and Steve Clover to begin development on *EQ*.

- Cyberspace, Inc. learns that the name is taken, and changes to Second Nature Interactive. Someday, they'll make it to being called Turbine!

- Nexon launches *Kingdom of the Winds*.

- *Splatterball*, by Interworld Productions, is released on Engage. Shortly after, Interworld becomes Mythic Entertainment.

- The *Journal of MUD Research* launches. In the first issue is an article by Richard Bartle, "Hearts, Clubs, Diamonds, Spades: Players Who Suit MUDs."

- TEN officially launches in September.

- MPlayer launches in early November.

- *The Eternal City* (TEC) goes into Beta. *TEC* focuses on providing the most immersive role-playing environment to date, as well a sense of space and a rich environment. The founders of *TEC* (Scott Martins, Ichiro Lambe, and Charles Passmore) were originally staff at *Legends of Future Past*.

1997

- *Diablo* launches, from Blizzard. Though not a true MUD, it is immensely popular and brings awareness of graphical multiplayer RPGs to the masses.

- *UO* launches commercially and breaks 100,000 users very quickly. Rich Vogel joins Origin before launch.

- Janet Murray's *Hamlet on the Holodeck* is published.

- Second Nature Interactive discovers that its name is taken and renames itself Turbine Entertainment Software.

- A development deal is signed for *AC*, to be developed by Turbine. Jeremy Gaffney is among those involved, though he later leaves before it ships. Toby Ragaini is principal designer.

- NCSoft launches *Lineage*.

➤ *NWN* on AOL was shut down on July 19, 1997, when AOL made the official switch to WorldPlay (formerly INN) for the Games Channel.

➤ Mythic releases *Darkness Falls*, a commercial text MUD.

➤ In September, UOX, the first *UO* server emulator, manages two simultaneous connections with UOX3. By 2000, there would be several hundred *UO* server emulators running.

1998

➤ *UO* is sued in a class-action lawsuit. The suit is later settled out of court. Oddly, one of the plaintiffs is an ex-player of *LegendMUD*.

➤ Verant's *EQ* opens in Beta.

➤ *Rubies of Eventide* opens.

➤ Lyra's *Underlight* launches doing a role-play-enforced graphical game on MPlayer.

➤ Electric Communities acquires *The Palace* from Time Warner. It also holds a closed Beta of *ECHabitats/Microcosm*.

➤ Titanic releases *NetStorm*, an online-only strategy title. The company folds later that year.

➤ Delashmit and others (including Todd McKimmey, formerly of *LegendMUD* and *UO*) form Wombat Games. One of the first contracts is to help get Sega's MMP action-strategy game *10six* off the ground.

➤ Julian Dibbell's *My Tiny Life* is published. The first chapter is "A Rape in Cyberspace."

➤ Sierra announces *Middle Earth*, an MMP based on *Lord of the Rings*. Steve Nichols, creator of *The Realm*, leads the team with Janus Anderson, also of *The Realm*, and Daniel James of *Avalon*.

➤ Mike Sellers plays a role in bringing *TEC* to The Big Network, where it becomes one of the first (if not the first) commercial text-based RPGs to be supported by banner ads, using a Java client.

➤ John Pritchett creates the *TW* game server, which makes *TW* into a TCP/IP game playable over the Internet. He also founds EIS.

1999

➤ *EQ* opens and quickly becomes the second huge success in the newly dubbed MMORPG genre.

➤ Nine months later, *AC* releases on the Microsoft Gaming Zone.

➤ VR-1's *UltraCorps (UC)* closes on The Zone.

➤ TEN ditches hard-core and persistent world (PW) gaming to become pogo.com.

➤ *DWANGO* dies in the US.

➤ EA buys Kesmai (and PlayNation). This is part and parcel of a deal to become the exclusive games channel provider for AOL.

➤ MPGNet bought from founder and owner, Jim Hettinger, by Interactive Magic. They combined I-Magic Online and MPGNet and eventually renamed it IEN.

➤ Verant's *Sovereign* announced. It looks to borrow design elements heavily from *Empire*.

➤ Simutronics announces a graphical version of their game, to be called *Hero's Journey*.

➤ Bioware announces a new *NWN*, to be a distributed MUD server, at GenCon in August.

➤ Electric Communities mothballs *Microcosm*.

➤ Nexon develops distributed game servers for *Kingdom of the Winds*. They subsequently peak with 12,263 simultaneous users in a single world using this technology.

➤ Mythic releases *Darkness Falls: The Crusade*, also a text-based game.

➤ *UO2* announced with Starr Long, Damion Schubert, and Jeremy Gaffney. Jack Heistand becomes general manager of Origin. The game is later renamed *Ultima Worlds Online: Origin*.

➤ Sierra restarts development on *Middle Earth Online* and abandons *The Realm*. Codemasters picks up *The Realm* and Nichols joins them.

➤ *Legends of Future Past* closes on December 31.

➤ *Project Entropia* is announced. The novel twist is that real-world currency will be freely convertible to game currency, and vice versa.

➤ On December 2, CompuServe stops running *MUD1* after 13 years of operation.

"We were given a whole zero day's notice." —**Dr. Richard Bartle**

➤ The film *The Matrix* is released.

➤ The film *eXistenZ* is released.

2000

➤ LucasArts and Verant announce a *Star Wars* online project.

➤ Sony Online Entertainment acquires Verant.

➤ Squaresoft announces *Final Fantasy Online*. Other major console series also announce later that year, including *Phantasy Star*.

➤ Sony announces that PlayStation 2 will have a broadband solution by 2001.

➤ Mythic Entertainment announces *Dark Age of Camelot*, a large-scale graphical MUD using some design elements from their *Darkness Falls* games. Both Hyrup and Jacobs are involved.

➤ Richard Garriott leaves Origin.

➤ Koster, Vogel, and others leave Origin. It is revealed late in the year that Rich Vogel is producer and Raph Koster is creative director on *Star Wars Galaxies*. Other team members include Chris Mayer (former lead programmer for *UO Live*) and Anthony Castoro (former lead designer for *UO Live*). All except Castoro had been on a cancelled unannounced project, *Privateer Online*, at Origin, and departed for Verant in the wake of the cancellation.

➤ Wombat Games, composed of Delashmit, McKimmey, and Jason Spangler (former lead programmer on *UO: Second Age*), among others, announces *Dark Zion*, a graphical MUD with a fully player-modifiable environment, no built-in currencies, and a number of other experimental features.

➤ Funcom's *Anarchy Online (AO)* is a hit at both E3 and ECTS.

➤ In May, EA announces the shutdown of most of the Kesmai games, including *Legends of Kesmai* and *Air Warrior Classic*.

➤ Also in May, Erwin Andreasen holds the 16K MUD competition (`www.andreasen. org/16k.shtml`). The 18 scratch-written MUD entries are later released to the public.

➤ In late August, Wombat Games closes, after failing to acquire a publisher.

➤ On August 31, 3DO ceases operation of *M59*. The game continues to run in Germany.

➤ It is announced that Toby Ragaini has left Turbine and is now working on LithTech's unannounced MMP title.

➤ Several games try to break MMP graphical online games out of the RPG mold:

  ➤ *World War II Online* is announced. It is envisioned as a tiered military sim where players give each other orders. Members of the team formerly worked on *Warbirds*.

  ➤ Also publicly displayed is *StarPeace*, a management and city-building MMP game (think *SimCity* in space).

  ➤ The already-open *Mankind* is a large-scale economics and trading sim.

➤ A group of ex-volunteers from *UO* file a lawsuit demanding back-pay for their volunteer activities.

➤ *British Legends*, a.k.a. *MUD1*, returns when Viktor Toth, administrator of *MUD2*, completes a port of the original game to a new server codebase.

➤ Verant announces *Planetside*, an MMP first-person shooter. The principal technologist on the team is John Ratcliff, former lead programmer on Simutronics' *Hero's Journey*, which appears to have gone dormant.

➤ A small-scale online game, *SiSSYFiGHT 2000*, makes all the players into female high-school students and casts the PvP dynamic as being about peer pressure, putdowns, and cliques.

➤ In October, EIS transfers trademark rights of *Trade Wars 2002* to Realm Interactive, a startup in Arizona. They begin work on *Trade Wars: Dark Millenium*, to be a graphical Massively Multi-Play Online Real-Time Strategy (MMORTS) game.

2001

- *Phantasy Star Online* releases for Dreamcast and is extremely well-received. But Dreamcast is discontinued shortly thereafter.

- Communities.com folds. Says a former executive, "It was a dot-com company with dot-com problems." Randy Farmer says, "I wasn't done!"

- *Fallen Age* is announced. Its producer is a former writer for the MMP editorial site "The Rantings of Lum, The Mad." The game is later cancelled due to creative differences between the US-based and Korea-based portions of the team.

- *EQ* bans the sale of in-game items on auction sites, and eBay and Yahoo agree to remove the items from their listings. In response, a group of *EQ* players threatens to sue over their rights to sell in-game items on Internet auction sites.

- Nexon continues to produce online games, announcing *Elemental Saga*.

- Westwood, a division of EA, announces *Earth and Beyond* with a cover article in major gaming magazines. It is an MMP Real-Time Strategy/Role-playing Game set in space. Janus Anderson is the lead designer.

- Will Wright starts to talk publicly about *The Sims Online*.

- *Lineage* goes commercial in the US in May. It acquires only a few thousand users in the US.

- EA publicly tests and launches *Majestic*, a conspiracy theory online game that contacts players via instant messaging, faxes, and email. A key force behind the game is Neil Young, who was general manager of Origin during the early days of *UO*'s live service.

- EA purchases pogo.com.

- Gamespy.com purchases MPlayer.

- The never-announced *Dungeons & Dragons Online* is cancelled.

- Steven Spielberg's film *A.I.* makes use of a game extremely similar to *Majestic* as a form of virtual marketing.

- *Ultima Worlds Online: Origin*, a.k.a. *UO2*, is cancelled. There's a "wake" for the game where design documents are burned in a huge pile.

"At the wake, I crack a joke to Richard saying that maybe his next company should be called 'destination or something.' I can only assume I was not the only one to make the joke!" —**Raph Koster**

➤ Richard Garriott, Starr Long, Kirk Black, Jeremy Gaffney, Carly Staehlin, and many others from *UO* and the cancelled *Ultima Worlds Online: Origin* form a new company entitled Destination Games. Shortly after, the company is acquired by NCSoft of Korea, makers of *Lineage*, and Jake Song moves to Austin to begin work with the aforementioned on a new project called *Tabula Rasa*.

➤ *Dark Age of Camelot* starts public testing.

➤ There is legal trouble surrounding the development of a new version of *Middle Earth Online* as developer MM3D sues Sierra.

➤ *Mudpie*, an MMP world based on *MYST*, begins to be discussed by Cyan.

➤ *Seducity* is live—it's an online world about sex, and it offers nudity and sexual animations in a 2D environment.

➤ *World War II Online* launches and has a very rough time of it.

➤ *AO* also has a rocky launch.

➤ Funcom announces *Midgard*. It is intended to be an RPG with a heavy focus on community-building.

➤ EA begins testing Multiplayer Battletech 3025.

➤ The nonviolent crafting and socialization world *A Tale in the Desert* begins public testing.

➤ *Jumpgate*, an online space and trading sim, is published by 3DO.

➤ Numerous former writers from commentary web sites join the staffs of various online games; among them: *Jumpgate*, *Dark Age of Camelot* (where Lum, The Mad—the person—went), and *Shadowbane*.

➤ Blizzard announces *World of Warcraft*, an MMPRPG.

➤ Codemasters announces *Dragon Empires*. Steve Nichols is involved at first, but later departs.

➤ *Dark Age of Camelot* launches to glowing reviews and quickly outpaces *AC* to become the third most popular American online world.

➤ EA stops development of *Multiplayer Battletech 3025* and kills *Air Warrior III*.

➤ *Fighting Legends*, which is perhaps best termed as a party-based tactical online world where you manage a group of units, launches.

2002

➤ 3DO drops *Jumpgate*; the makers, NetDevil, decide to run it on their own.

➤ Brian Green and Rob Ellis purchase *M59* from 3DO and revive it.

➤ The Imagineering group within Disney publicly tests *Toontown*, a Disney animation themed online world that sticks close to the "groups of players kill critters" paradigm, but changed around for a young child audience. It's notable for not letting people communicate directly in-game, to satisfy the US government's Children's Online Privacy Protection Act rules.

➤ *Majestic* is shuttered by EA, having failed to garner enough subscribers or retain them. The episodes of the game are released all together on one CD to the retail market.

➤ Funcom's *Midgard* is put on hold so they can concentrate on *AO*.

➤ Mythic is sued by Blacksnow Interactive (BSI), a small firm that makes its money by gathering in-game items to sell to other players. BSI alleges that Mythic is damaging their business by preventing the sale of in-game items via online auction sites.

Sources

Raph Koster

Lauren Burka's MUDLine

Amy Bruckman

Mike Sellers

Dr. Cat

Damion Schubert

Randy Farmer

Jessica Mulligan

Richard Bartle

XYZZYNews

"Hacking Into Computer Systems"

"The Dot Eaters"

University of Illinois

...and a host of others. Please check Raph's full timeline at
`www.legendmud.org/raph/gaming/mudtimeline.html`.

Appendix F

Glossary

A

achiever
One of the four recognized Bartle player types, these players seek to build their character's skills, abilities, attributes, and possessions as high as they will go, as fast as they can. See also **power-gamer**.

admin
Slang form of administrator. The common name for those who run PWs. Also known as wizards, gods, or operators.

Alpha
Alpha is the period during an online game's development cycle when it first becomes functional or playable. Note that this is different from the traditional software development engineer's definition of Alpha. During Alpha, the game is tested by the developer's internal QA department. Alpha is followed by **Beta**.

anti (or anti-PK)
A vigilante-style player who exclusively attacks players who engage in **PK**. Contrast with a **carebear**.

attribute(s)
Usually used in reference to a role-playing game character's vital statistics, such as strength and intelligence. Attributes can be raised or lowered, depending on the actions of the player.

avatar
An image worn by a player to represent him/herself within the world. Also known as a persona or character.

B

balance

A state in a PW in which the chance of success at certain tasks within the game (for example, **PvP** or **leveling**) are deemed to be fairly distributed across **characters** of different **class**, **skill**, **inventory**, and/or **level**.

Bartle types

A system developed by Dr. Richard Bartle, the creator of the first **MUD**, to categorize online gamers based on two axes "players–world" and "action–interaction." The four recognized Bartle types are **achiever**, **explorer**, **killer**, and **socializer**.

Beta

Beta is the period following **Alpha** when an online game first becomes tested by third-party gamers, or "Beta testers." A closed Beta is by invitation only, while an open Beta is a test that anyone can join. Beta is only nominally related to being feature-complete, as most online games over-promise on their features and end up launching without features planned in the design. Beta is nowadays frequently seen as a marketing effort to build hype as much as it is part of the QA process.

Beta tester

A player who participates in a closed or open **Beta**.

big four

The four leading MMP online games in the US, namely *EverQuest*, *Ultima Online*, *Dark Age of Camelot*, and *Asheron's Call*.

binding

Choosing at which location a character will respawn following death in combat.

buff

To use a magic spell, device, skill, or other means to temporarily improve a player/character; for example, "I used my strength spell to buff John's character."

bugs

Unintentional errors or flaws in a game. Opinions vary sharply as to whether the unintended consequences of a properly executed design decision count as a bug or a feature.

C

camping

The act of waiting around the respawning point of powerful or rare items or monsters in a PW in an attempt to monopolize their acquisition, use, and/or distribution.

carebear

A derogatory term often used by PKs to describe those who play online games that don't allow PvP combat.

character

A player's persona within an online game, used to interact with other players and the game environment. Usually has a number of **attributes** and **skills** that grow or decline over time and use, and may collect **inventory** possessions.

chat

Text-based communication with other players in an online game. Because socialization is such an important aspect of online games, most online games since *UO* have included powerful global chat features.

cheat

To use a **bug**, **exploit**, or **hack** for one's personal gain.

churn rate

The rate at which players cancel their subscriptions to a game. Usually expressed as a percentage, such as "a 0.5% daily churn rate."

class

An overall profession or archetype that defines a **character**'s role in a PW. Class usually affects the **skills** and **items** a character can use. Popularized by the classic dice version of TSR's *Dungeons & Dragons* back in the 1970s and carried over to online gaming by designers.

client

The software program that runs on the players' machines. A "free client" is one that is distributed at no cost to the players, usually via the Internet, while a "retail client" must be purchased in stores.

client/server
Currently, the standard model for PW games. It describes the process whereby many individual remote clients connect to a host server.

community
A game's community consists of its developers plus its current, past, and potential subscribers. A commonly heard mantra within online gaming is that "Players come for the game, but stay for the community."

community relations
Also called online community relations, or OCR. Refers to the support given to the players outside of the normal play of the game. Normally web-based and can include use of web page news postings, message boards, chat programs for live help, and download sections for information and software applications pertaining to the game.

content
The substance of an online game, including things such as **dungeons**, **items**, **quests**, and **mobs**. Content is frequently contrasted with game mechanics, or "features." Content can be **dynamic** or **static**.

cowboy programming
Describes the act of a programmer or designer making a change in a live online game without prior notification to the development team or players. This is a holdover from the MUD implementer (imp) mentality, in which MUD programmers felt free to change the game at any time because it was a free service.

crunch mode
Any phase of development when people work day and night to catch up on a milestone that has slipped or to complete a project on time.

D

dewdspeak
A form of jargon used by online gamers in which ASCII characters are substituted for the alphabet. For example, E is often replaced with 3, A with 4, and S with $. Also sometimes called "l33tsp34k" (elite speak).

devs
Slang term for online game developers.

downtime
1. A period of time spent in a PW in which a player cannot engage in **leveling** or any other desired activity due to the need for his/her character to rest, shop, re-equip, and the like. Downtime is usually used for chatting; thus, a certain amount of downtime leads to more socialization.

2. Any period during which the game **servers** are unavailable.

dungeon
An area or region in a PW that **spawns mobs** and **items**, and is usually visited for the purposes of **leveling**. Dungeons can be **static** or **dynamic**.

dynamic
1. Content that allows for permanent or semi-permanent changes to the game world based on player actions.

2. Content that is generated "on-the-fly" based on the state of the game world at the time it is created. Frequently used with reference to **dungeons** or **quests**.

E

elder player
A veteran gamer whose continued participation in the game is usually based on community involvement or **PvP**, rather than **leveling**, **loot**, or other similar game mechanics.

emote
Using short text combinations or character movements to denote an emotion. For example, in a text **MUD**, the characters ":)" are used to denote happiness or amusement. In a 3D first-person game such as *AC* or *AO*, emotes can be programmed in as **macro**-ed body movements, such as waving, sitting, smiling, and so on.

event
1. An activity or encounter run by an interest and events GM (IGM) or player that offers a level of interaction and participation beyond that usually offered by the game's mechanics.

2. A one-time, pre-scripted occurrence within a PW that impacts the story or game world.

experience points
A point value that is accumulated by gameplay activity such as **leveling** and is used as a measure of a character's power. Popularized by the classic dice version of TSR's *Advanced Dungeons & Dragons* back in the 1970s and carried over to online gaming by designers.

exploit
To use a **bug** or loophole in the game for one's personal gain. Whether or not to punish players for exploits based on loopholes in the game design (rather than game code) is somewhat controversial. Also used as a noun, as in: "He used an exploit to cheat."

explorer
One of the four recognized Bartle player types. Describes a player who loves to map out a world, find hidden artifacts, and just generally tool about the countryside, developing information and passing it on to others.

F

frag
To kill a character in an online game. Also expressed as "rip." Derived from the term that came into popularity in the US Army during the Vietnam War era, when "fragging" an unpopular officer or other soldier meant to roll a fragmentation grenade into that person's tent.

G

gamemaster (GM)
A person with special administrative game powers assigned to assist players in the game by solving problems. Normally assigned or associated with the CS department.

grief player or griefer
A player who derives his/her enjoyment not from playing the game, but from performing actions that detract from the enjoyment of the game by other players. See also **ninja loot**, **PK**, **kill steal**, **spamming**, and **train**.

grouping
To join with other players in an online game for non-social purposes such as **leveling** or **PvP**. Also sometimes called teaming.

guild
Long-term associations of online gamers. Guilds are often formal, game-specific organizations supported by the game's mechanics, but the term also extends to informal associations of players across games. Also known as clans, allegiances, squadrons, and so on.

H

hack
A program that modifies the client or the datastream to the client in such a way as to give the user a gameplay advantage. Famous hacks include winHACK and ShowEQ. See also **cheat** and exploit.

handle
A nickname or callsign used by a player and/or developer of online games. Players may assign their **characters** unique names, but they often adopt a distinct handle that sticks with them across several games.

hard-core
A term oriented toward serious or dedicated gamers, as compared to casual game players.

hit points

A point value that represents a player's, NPC's, or monster's ability to withstand damage from the weapons of others before the character "dies" in the game. Popularized by the classic dice version of TSR's *Advanced Dungeons & Dragons* back in the 1970s and carried over to online gaming by designers.

hunt

To kill **mobs**, usually for the purposes of **leveling**.

hybrid

Also known as a retail hybrid. Describes a game intended to be sold at retail with both solo-play and Internet multiplayer capabilities.

I

immersion

The ability of a game to "immerse" a player in the interface and gameplay. The Holy Grail of online gaming is to completely immerse a player in the gameplay to the point that he/she loses track of time and, in some cases, reality during the game session.

interest and events gamemaster (IGM)

A person with special game administrative powers assigned to create and manage special events, scenarios, storylines, quests, adventures, and the like. Normally assigned or closely associated with the live team, and sometimes with CS.

inventory

Depending on context, refers to both the portable **item** storage that a character carries and items stored in chests or housing that the player owns.

item

A piece of equipment in an online game that has an effect on gameplay. Items that are found as treasure are known as **loot**.

K

kill steal
To manipulate an activity in-game, usually the killing of **mobs**, in such a way as to unfairly take the credit or reward (usually **experience points** or **loot**) for the activity.

killer
Also known as a player-killer. One of the four recognized Bartle player types, these online game players enjoy the challenge of PvP conflict over player versus environment (PvE) conflict.

L

l33t
Dewdspeak for "elite." Often used ironically or derogatorily.

lag
Slang term for latency.

latency
The amount of time it takes for a packet to transmit from a PC to the server and back again. Usually compounded by the distributed nature of the Internet, which causes some latency at each router or server that a piece of data must "hop" through to arrive at its destination.

launch
To release an online game. The equivalent of "ship" for a retail game.

level
A rank or rating of a character's power. Popularized by the classic dice version of TSR's *Advanced Dungeons & Dragons* back in the 1970s and carried over to online gaming by designers.

leveling
Activity in-game devoted to increasing a character's experience, level, and/or skills. Leveling usually consists of killing **mobs**.

live team

The people assigned to maintain an online game after it has launched. This includes the developers (programmers, artists, server code specialists, designers, and so on), community relations, player relations and support, technical support, and billing and account management.

loot

Treasure received as a reward from **mobs**, **quests**, and so on.

M

macro

One or more tasks or commands assigned to a "hot key" or interface button. Activating the hot key or clicking on the button activates the macro. Most often refers to player-configurable macros.

MMOG

Acronym for massively multiplayer online game, loosely defined as a persistent or virtual world game that permits at least 128 simultaneous players to interact with each other and the game world.

MMORPG/MMPRPG

Acronym for massively multiplayer online role-playing game. The "role-playing" in the title refers to the use of game mechanics such as **hit points** or **leveling**, which were derived from pen-and-paper role-playing games. MMOGs, which are not MMORPGs, tend to be simulations such as *World War 2 Online*.

mob

Slang Term for **mobile**.

mobile

1. An autonomous creature within an online game world. Most often used to refer to NPCs and environment creatures such as monsters.

2. European word for mobile phone, such as, "I'll ring you on your mobile later."

MUD
Acronym for multi-user dungeon, coined by Richard Bartle and Roy Trubshaw to describe what is now considered the first true online game, built by them at the University of Essex in Colchester, England in 1979. The term "MUD" has since spawned a variety of other acronyms such as MOO, MUCK, and MUSH, but the term is also occasionally used to describe the whole field of PW gaming.

multiplayer game
A game that allows two or more people to play the same game in the same game session or period. May be turn-based or real-time, and can include styles such as games-by-email and trivia games in which thousands may be answering the same questions, but are not interacting on a personal level.

N

nerf
To change an existing game mechanic, player-usable item, NPC, monster ability or carried item, or character attribute or skill in a way that is detrimental to the affected player(s). Contrast with **buff** and **proxy nerf**.

newbie
Slang term for a player new to a particular game or online gaming as a whole. Originally used in a derogatory manner, but now broadly applicable. Variants include noob and n00b.

ninja loot
Taking **loot** that was earned by another player, by speed, guile, or a **cheat**.

NPC
Acronym for non-player character, a creature that inhabits an online game and performs some function, such as a shop-keeper, but is not under the direct control of a player. Derived from *Dungeons & Dragons* in the 1970s.

O

online game
Any game playable via a modem and/or remote network connection, including modem-to-modem and Internet network connections, but specifically excluding LAN-only game sessions.

owned
Slang for defeated.

P

patch
The process used by online games to add features, content, and/or fix bugs via a downloading mechanism. Sometimes called a content update.

peer-to-peer
A method of network gaming where there is no dedicated server, as with PW games. Most often used by hybrids, one home PC being used in the game session is chosen as the host and resolves game issues for the other players.

persistence
See also the elements of persistence in **persistent world**. Persistent elements may be modified over time during gameplay (in which case, they are also **dynamic**), but the then-current state of the persistent element reacts consistently to all current observers. For example, if a player demolishes a house, other players in the immediate area also see a demolished house. Players who pass by the house later on will also see a demolished house.

persistent world (PW)
Also called a persistent-state world. A game in which several elements retained on remote servers and the current state are the same to all observing players. Examples may include geographic terrain such as mountains, lakes, caves, and rivers; player/character attributes and skills; player object inventory items such as clothing, armor, and weapons; terrain objects such as buildings and trees; and NPCs. PWs are also called **MMOGs**.

player base
The total number of subscribers and/or registered users of a game. Sometimes also used to describe the total subscribership of all online games.

player/character (PC)
The avatar or persona that a player creates and uses for gameplay in an online game.

player relations
1. Department of CS responsible for any issues arising after the game client has successfully begun operating.

2. The art or science of promoting a favorable relationship with the subscribers of an online game, encompassing both customer support and community relations.

PK or PKilling
Slang for player-killing, the act of killing or being killed by another player/character in an online game. A "PKer" is a player who engages in PKilling. PK usually has a negative connotation and is associated with **grief players** when it is nonconsensual. Engaging in PK on a consensual basis is usually called **PvP**. See also **Anti**.

power leveling
Leveling in such a way as to earn the maximum reward (usually **experience points**) in a given amount of time.

power-gamer
A player whose goal is to have the most powerful **character** the game permits. See also **achiever**.

premium server
A **server** or "shard" in an MMOG that is only accessible to subscribers who agree to pay an extra fee in exchange for improved levels of CS, better **events**, faster **leveling**, or other benefits.

proxy nerf
When one group of players is **buffed** and a second group is not, the second group is said to be "proxy nerfed." See also **nerf**.

PvP
Acronym for player versus player. Describes any conflict performed by players against each other, within the context and mechanics of the game (usually combat). A "PvPer" is a player who engages in PvP.

Q

quest
An act to be performed by a player for another player or NPC that will give him/her a specified reward upon completion. Also known as a mission. Quests can be **static** or **dynamic**.

R

release
To **launch** an online game. Also, the period following launch.

resolve time
The length of time it takes for a subscriber contacting customer support to have his/her problem satisfactorily resolved.

response time
The length of time it takes for a subscriber contacting customer support to receive a live response.

retention rate
The rate at which players retain their subscriptions to a game. Usually expressed as a percentage, for instance, "a 55% retention rate after six months." See **churn rate**.

role-player

A player who attempts to consistently adopt an "in-character" persona while playing in an online game. In the following example, Player 2 is role-playing; Player 1 is not:

> Player 1: "Hey bitch, gimme buffs!"

> Player 2: "Sirrah! Dost thou address a lady thus?"

roxor

Dewdspeak for "rocks," via r0x0r. Slang for great or awesome.

S

server

1. The physical computer or virtual connection that hosts players using clients to connect to an online game.

2. Sometimes used to describe a cluster of two or more physical computers that, in toto, make up one world iteration of an online game. Sometimes called a dimension, shard, or world. In PWs, this actually refers to a number of server computers linked together to form the hardware infrastructure on which the game operates, generally in a contiguous fashion. Most PWs have two or more servers, each representing a distinct but nearly identical iteration of the game. For example, the *AC* game world named Leafcull is composed of several server computers that make up one game server.

server cluster or server set

See **server** (2).

skill

1. Character skill: Most commonly, a role-playing game character's area of knowledge, such as swordsmanship or riding. Skills can be raised or lowered depending on the actions of the player. Usually used in conjunction with **attributes**, **class**, and **level**.

2. Player skill: Sometimes, a simulation game player's hand-eye coordination or other personal trait.

SKU
Acronym for stock-keeping unit, which is a number associated with a product for inventory purposes. In the game world, this abbreviation is used to describe both the general physical box to be shipped to retail ("What's the distribution status of the SKU?") and in conjunction with total numbers ("How many SKUs have we sold to date?").

socializer
One of the four recognized Bartle player types, socializers tend to spend more time gathering in groups and micro-communities such as guilds and teams for activities. The primary purpose of the game for them is making friends and indulging in game politics and diplomacy.

spamming
The art of repeating the same action over and over, until it harms everyone in the vicinity. Most often used to refer to players who repeat the same message over and over again, as quickly as possible, to make it impossible for other players in the local vicinity to carry on a conversation.

spawn
To create one or more creatures or objects with an online game. This usually happens via automatic processes coded into the game, but the term also refers to a GM or other super-user manually creating creatures or objects.

spawn point
Where creatures or objects are created. When spawning is done via an automatic process, it usually occurs at set points throughout the game world.

static
The opposite of **dynamic**:

1. Content that cannot be permanently or semi-permanently changed by player actions.

2. Content that is pre-generated rather than created on-the-fly. Frequently used with reference to **dungeons** or **quests**.

story

The fictional plot of an online game. A story may be implemented in-game via **events** or other **content**, or out-of-game via fiction, movies, and other media.

sunset

To cease operating an active MMOG.

T

TCP

A networking term that stands for Transmission Control Protocol, a method for sending packets to and from computers that is very reliable and incorporates data checks to ensure that data packets get to their destinations in the order they were sent. Developed by Internet pioneers, TCP made the Internet possible.

third-party utility

A program that indirectly helps a player in an MMOG by making information more accessible, reducing time spent calculating, or other similar functions. Popular utilities include *SplitPea* and *UOAssist*. Utilities are closely related to, but distinct from, **hacks** in that utilities do not directly affect gameplay and thus are generally permitted by the developers.

trade skill

A type of **skill** in a PW that allows players to create **items** from various ingredients. Sometimes also referred to as a craft skill.

train

1. A group of **mobs** all pursuing a character.

2. The act of leading a train onto another character so that he/she is attacked by the mobs in the train. This is a form of **griefing**.

treadmill

Derogatory term used to describe the process of **leveling**.

trial account

An account for an MMOG that gives free access to the game for a limited period of time, generally 10 days for a free client and 30 days for a retail client.

troll

A member of an online game community who makes comments solely for the purpose of getting a reaction.

twink

To help a new or low-level character become more powerful by assisting him/her in **leveling**, giving him/her **loot**, or other actions. A character that has been "twinked" is known as a "twinkie."

U

uber

Slang for powerful or, more derogatorily, overpowered.

UDP

A networking term that stands for User Datagram Protocol, a method of sending data packets that is much faster than TCP. Because the data checks have been removed, considered a less reliable method than TCP. Most PWs and many hybrids use UDP instead of TCP to help alleviate latency.

Z

zone

1. An area of land in a PW distinguished from other areas around it by some form of either hard stop (such as loading the new zone) or indicator (such as a zone name displaying). A PW without a hard stop between zones is said to be "seamless."

2. As a verb, the process of transitioning from one zone to another, generally accompanied by a lengthy wait as new zone information is downloaded ("Latency sucks today; it took me almost five minutes to zone.")

Index

V O I C E S   T H A T   M A T T E R

VISIT OUR WEB SITE

W W W . N E W R I D E R S . C O M

On our web site, you'll find information about our other books, authors, tables of contents, and book errata. You will also find information about book registration and how to purchase our books, both domestically and internationally.

EMAIL US

Contact us at: **nrfeedback@newriders.com**

- If you have comments or questions about this book
- To report errors that you have found in this book
- If you have a book proposal to submit or are interested in writing for New Riders
- If you are an expert in a computer topic or technology and are interested in being a technical editor who reviews manuscripts for technical accuracy

Contact us at: **nreducation@newriders.com**

- If you are an instructor from an educational institution who wants to preview New Riders books for classroom use. Email should include your name, title, school, department, address, phone number, office days/hours, text in use, and enrollment, along with your request for desk/examination copies and/or additional information.

Contact us at: **nrmedia@newriders.com**

- If you are a member of the media who is interested in reviewing copies of New Riders books. Send your name, mailing address, and email address, along with the name of the publication or web site you work for.

BULK PURCHASES/CORPORATE SALES

The publisher offers discounts on this book when ordered in quantity for bulk purchases and special sales. For sales within the U.S., please contact: Corporate and Government Sales (800) 382-3419 or **corpsales@pearsontechgroup.com**. Outside of the U.S., please contact: International Sales (317) 581-3793 or **international@pearsontechgroup.com**.

WRITE TO US

New Riders Publishing
201 W. 103rd St.
Indianapolis, IN 46290-1097

CALL/FAX US

Toll-free (800) 571-5840
If outside U.S. (317) 581-3500
Ask for New Riders
FAX: (317) 581-4663

New Riders

Maximize Your Impact

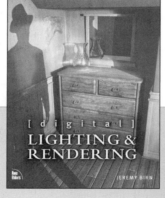

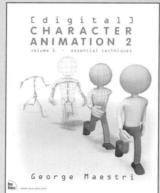